Java™ Thread Programming

Paul Hyde

SAMS

A Division of Macmillan Computer Publishing
201 West 103rd St., Indianapolis, Indiana, 46290

Java™ Thread Programming

Copyright ©1999 by Sams Publishing

International Standard Book Number: 0-672-31585-8

Library of Congress Catalog Card Number: 99-62245

Printed in the United States of America

First Printing: August 1999

01   00   99   4   3   2   1

Trademarks

EXECUTIVE EDITOR
Tim Ryan

ACQUISITIONS EDITOR
Steve Anglin

DEVELOPMENT EDITORS
Tiffany Taylor
Jon Steever

MANAGING EDITOR
Jodi Jensen

SENIOR EDITOR
Susan Ross Moore

COPY EDITORS
Margaret Berson
Kate Talbot

INDEXER
Rebecca Hornyak

PROOFREADERS
Mona Brown
Jill Mazurczyk

TECHNICAL EDITORS
Alexandre Calsavara
Mike Forsythe

TEAM COORDINATOR
Karen Opal

SOFTWARE DEVELOPMENT SPECIALIST
Michael Hunter

INTERIOR DESIGN
Anne Jones

COVER DESIGN
Anne Jones

COPY WRITER
Eric Borgert

LAYOUT TECHNICIANS
Stacey DeRome
Ayanna Lacey
Heather Miller

Contents at a Glance

Contents

About the Author

Paul Hyde graduated from Lehigh University with a Bachelor of Science degree in Electrical Engineering, and began his career at AT&T developing software. There he gained knowledge and experience working with many languages and tools, including C, PowerBuilder, Informix RDBMS, Sybase RDBMS, HTML/CGI, and Java. During this time he acquired a Master of Science degree in Computer Science from Stevens Institute of Technology. Shortly thereafter, while still employed at AT&T, he began teaching night classes in Sybase at the Chubb Institute in New Jersey. In April 1996, Paul started working with Java and realized the great potential it had. Later that year he left AT&T, moved to Minnesota, and founded Programix Incorporated. Programix is a software consulting company specializing in providing Java solutions. Paul is a Sun Certified Java Programmer for the 1.0, 1.1, and 1.2 releases.

In his spare time, Paul develops and teaches introductory and advanced Java courses in the Minneapolis area. He enjoys skiing and relaxing on the beach, and stays in shape for these activities by working out, mostly running. In fact, he even completed the 1998 Grandma's Marathon in Duluth, Minnesota. You can reach Paul at `phyde@programix-inc.com`.

Dedication

To my parents, Carol Hyde and the late Richard Hyde, for their
incredible support and encouragement throughout my life.

Acknowledgments

I would like to thank the many people who have helped to bring this book to fruition.

All the people at Macmillan Publishing have been a great help. In particular, I'd like to thank Steve Anglin, the Acquisitions Editor at Macmillan, for taking my idea and forming it into a practical project. He championed the concept within Macmillan and got the whole process started. This is my first book, and Steve has been a great guide for me throughout the process. His continual attention and encouragement helped keep me going.

Tiffany Taylor, the Development Editor at Macmillan, helped me to find my voice and style. She also made sure that what I thought made sense actually made sense! Her guidance has been invaluable throughout the writing of this book.

Thanks to Tim Ryan, the Executive Editor for approving and overseeing the whole project. Thanks to Jon Steever, Development Editor, for providing early feedback and good advice at several key times during the production. Thanks to Susan Moore, the Project Editor, for overseeing the editing and author review phase. Thanks to Kate Talbot and Margaret Berson, Copy Editors, for their attention to detail. Thanks to Alexandre Calsavara, the Technical Editor, for all the great suggestions on how to improve the book.

I would also like to thank my colleague, Jeff Whiteside, for taking his personal time to read the early chapters in their raw form. Jeff provided excellent advice and suggestions for improving the book.

Last, but certainly not least, I would like to thank my fiancé Deb Kostreba for her incredible support throughout this challenging project. Because she helped to streamline my life, I was able to concentrate on writing. At those times when I began to feel overwhelmed, Deb was there to provide encouragement.

Paul Hyde
Minneapolis, Minnesota
June 1999

Tell Us What You Think!

As the reader of this book, *you* are our most important critic and commentator. We value your opinion and want to know what we're doing right, what we could do better, what areas you'd like to see us publish in, and any other words of wisdom you're willing to pass our way.

As an executive editor for Sams Publishing, I welcome your comments. You can fax, email, or write me directly to let me know what you did or didn't like about this book—as well as what we can do to make our books stronger.

When you write, please be sure to include this book's title and author as well as your name and phone or fax number. I will carefully review your comments and share them with the author and editors who worked on the book.

Fax: 317-581-4770

Email: java@mcp.com

Mail: Tim Ryan
Executive Editor
Sams Publishing
201 West 103rd Street
Indianapolis, IN 46290 USA

Introduction

Structure of This Book

This book is for those of you who have started working with Java and have realized that you want to develop multithreaded applications and applets. I don't assume that you know anything about thread programming, so the book starts off with simple, straightforward examples. From there, the chapters become more advanced and comprehensively cover all aspects of thread programming in Java. The second part of the book is dedicated to demonstrating various advanced techniques that can be used in the real world. Chapters 1 through 10 can be read in order because each chapter builds upon the concepts in the preceding one. You can hop around the techniques in Chapters 11 through 18, reading them in just about any order. Some of the techniques are so valuable that they are used in demonstrating other techniques, so you can read up on each technique as you come across it.

I developed the example code used in this book using the *Java 2 SDK, Standard Edition, version 1.2* (also known as *JDK 1.2*) from Sun Microsystems. I used this development kit on an Intel Pentium 166MHz machine running Microsoft Windows 95. In this book, some of the statements in the code listings appear in bold-face type simply for emphasis. These source code files are available for download from www.samspublishing.com. When you reach that page, click the Product Support link. On the next page, enter this book's ISBN number (0672315858) to access the page containing the code.

The following is an overview of what is covered in each of the chapters.

Chapter 1—"Introduction to Threads"

Chapter 1 is an introduction to multithreaded programming and how threads are used in Java. I show you why threads are needed and how they can improve an application's performance.

Chapter 2—"A Simple Two-Thread Example"

In Chapter 2, you get to see the most basic example of a multithreaded application. In the application, two threads are running at the same time and print their own messages. I show you the fundamental steps necessary to spawn a new thread.

Chapter 3—"Creating and Starting a Thread"

Chapter 3 begins to explore the API for the class Thread. You'll see how to get a handle on the currently executing thread, how threads are named, how to check to see if a thread is still alive, and how to put a thread to sleep for while.

Chapter 4—"Implementing Runnable Versus Extending Thread"

In Chapter 4, I show you that there is a second way to get a thread to run within an object by using the interface Runnable. This is an especially important feature that works around the lack of multiple inheritance in Java.

Chapter 5—"Gracefully Stopping Threads"

Chapter 5 shows you how to get threads to stop running. I show you graceful and safe alternatives to the methods that have been deprecated as of JDK 1.2.

Chapter 6—"Thread Prioritization"

In Chapter 6, I show you how to assign relative priorities to the threads running in the Java Virtual Machine and the effects that priorities have on thread scheduling.

Chapter 7—"Concurrent Access to Objects and Variables"

When more than one thread is running, care must be taken to ensure that the threads interact safely with one another. Chapter 7 shows you how to take steps to prevent race conditions that can corrupt data. I show you the proper use of synchronized and volatile. I also show you how to use the classes in the Collections API in a thread-safe manner.

Chapter 8—"Inter-thread Communication"

When you have multiple threads safely interacting with shared data, you need a way for one thread to signal another that data has been changed. Chapter 8 shows you how to use wait(), notify(), and notifyAll() to send signals among the threads in an application. Also, I discuss the use of join(), pipes, and ThreadLocal variables.

Chapter 9—"Threads and Swing"

Chapter 9 shows you how to use multiple threads in an application with a graphical user interface. The Swing toolkit is not inherently multithread-safe, and in this chapter, I show you the steps that must be taken to safely work with it.

Chapter 10—"Thread Groups"

Chapter 10 explores the ThreadGroup API and ways that you can assign threads to groups.

Chapter 11—"Self-Running Objects"

Chapter 11 kicks off the technique section by showing you how to create classes that automatically start an internal thread running during construction. This frees a user of a class from having to know that an object has a thread running within it.

Chapter 12—"Exception Callback"

In Chapter 12, I show you how to find out that another thread has thrown an exception.

Chapter 13—"Thread Pooling"

Chapter 13 shows how threads can be pooled for shared use in executing short-running blocks of code. I show you how to write a simple Web page server that uses thread pooling to service client requests for pages.

Chapter 14—"Waiting For the Full Timeout"

As you'll discover reading Chapter 8, it is not always easy to determine if a thread was notified by another thread or simply timed out waiting to be notified. Chapter 14 shows a technique that can be used to be sure that a thread waits for the full timeout value.

Chapter 15—"Breaking Out of a Blocked I/O State"

Most of the I/O operations in Java block until the data is written or read. Unfortunately, blocked I/O methods do not respond to interrupts. Chapter 15 shows you some techniques for dealing with this issue.

Chapter 16—"The SureStop Utility"

In Chapter 16, I show you a class that can help ensure that a thread eventually dies.

Chapter 17—"The BooleanLock Utility"

Chapter 17 shows you a technique for encapsulating the wait/notify mechanism into a compact, multithread-safe class that can be reused in many places in a multithreaded application.

Chapter 18—"First-In-First-Out (FIFO) Queue"

In Chapter 18, I show you how to build a FIFO queue that is safe to use in a multithreaded environment. In particular, I show you how to create a FIFO queue for holding object references and how to create one for holding bytes.

Appendixes: "The Thread API" and "The ThreadGroup API"

At the end of the book, there is an appendix explaining the API for the Thread class and another appendix for the ThreadGroup class.

Conventions Used in This Book

This book uses different typefaces to differentiate between code and regular English, and also to help you identify important concepts.

Text that you type and text that should appear on your screen is presented in monospace type.

```
It will look like this to mimic the way text looks on your screen.
```

Placeholders for variables and expressions appear in *monospace italic* font. You should replace the placeholder with the specific value it represents.

This arrow (➡) at the beginning of a line of code means that a single line of code is too long to fit on the printed page. Continue typing all characters after the ➡ as though they were part of the preceding line.

> **NOTE**
>
> A Note presents interesting pieces of information related to the surrounding discussion.

> **TIP**
>
> A Tip offers advice or teaches an easier way to do something.

> **CAUTION**
>
> A Warning advises you about potential problems and helps you steer clear of disaster.

Threads

IN THIS PART

Introduction to Threads

IN THIS CHAPTER

Isn't it nice to be able to read and scroll the text of a Web page while the graphics continue to load? How about having a document in a word processor print in the background while you open another document for editing? Perhaps you've enjoyed writing a response to an email message while another incoming message with a large file attached is quietly downloaded simultaneously? Threads make all this convenient functionality possible by allowing a multithreaded program to do more than one task at a time. This book helps you learn the skills and techniques necessary to incorporate that kind of useful functionality into your Java programs.

What Is a Thread?

When a modern operating system wants to start running a program, it creates a new process. A *process* is a program that is currently executing. Every process has at least one thread running within it. Sometimes threads are referred to as *lightweight processes*. A *thread* is a path of code execution through a program, and each thread has its own local variables, program counter (pointer to the current instruction being executed), and lifetime. Most modern operating systems allow more than one thread to be running concurrently within a process. When the Java Virtual Machine (JavaVM, or just VM) is started by the operating system, a new process is created. Within that process, many threads can be *spawned* (created).

Normally, you would think of Java code execution starting with the main() method and proceeding in a path through the program until all the statements in main() are completed. This is an example of a single thread. This "main" thread is spawned by the JavaVM, which begins execution with the main() method, executes all the statements in main(), and *dies* when the main() method completes.

A second thread is always running in the JavaVM: the garbage collection thread. It cleans up discarded objects and reclaims their memory. Therefore, even a simple Java program that only prints Hello World to System.out is running in a multithreaded environment: The two threads are the main thread and the garbage collection thread.

When a Java program includes a graphical user interface (GUI), the JavaVM automatically starts even more threads. One of these threads is in charge of delivering GUI events to methods in the program; another is responsible for painting the GUI window.

For example, imagine that a GUI-based program's main thread is performing a complex and long-running calculation and that while this is going on, the user clicks a Stop Calculation button. The GUI event thread would then invoke the event handling code written for this button, allowing the calculation thread to be terminated. If only one thread was present, both of these could not be done simultaneously, and interruption would be difficult.

Why Use Multiple Threads?

In many situations, having more than one thread running in a program is beneficial. Here's a more in-depth look at why this can be good.

Better Interaction with the User

If only one thread was available, a program would be able to do only one thing at a time. In the word processor example, how nice it was to be able to open a second document while the first document was being formatted and queued to the printer. In some older word processors, when the user printed a document, he or she had to wait while the document was prepared for printing and sent to the printer. More modern word processors exploit multiple threads to do these two things at the same time. In a one-processor system, this is actually simulated by the operating system rapidly switching back and forth between two tasks, allowing for better user interaction.

From the perspective of a microprocessor, even the fastest typist takes a tremendous amount of time between keystrokes. In these large gaps of time, the processor can be utilized for other tasks. If one thread is always waiting to give a quick response to a user's actions, such as clicking the mouse or pressing a key, while other threads are off doing other work, the user will perceive better response from the system.

Simulation of Simultaneous Activities

Threads in Java appear to run concurrently, even when only one physical processor exists. The processor runs each thread for a short time and switches among the threads to simulate simultaneous execution. This makes it seem as if each thread has its own processor, creating a virtual multiple processor system. By exploiting this feature, you can make it appear as if multiple tasks are occurring simultaneously when, in fact, each is running for only a brief time before the context is switched to the next thread.

Exploitation of Multiple Processors

In some machines, several real microprocessors are present. If the underlying operating system and the implementation of the JavaVM exploit the use of more than one processor, multithreaded Java programs can achieve true simultaneous thread execution. A Java program would not have to be modified because it already uses threads as if they were running on different processors simultaneously. It would just be able to run even faster.

Do Other Things While Waiting for Slow I/O Operations

Input and Output (I/O) operations to and from a hard disk or especially across a network are relatively slow when compared to the speed of code execution in the processor. As a result, read/write operations may block for quite a while, waiting to complete.

In the java.io package, the class InputStream has a method, read(), that blocks until a byte is read from the stream or until an IOException is thrown. The thread that executes this method cannot do anything else while awaiting the arrival of another byte on the stream. If multiple threads have been created, the other threads can perform other activities while the one thread is blocked, waiting for input.

For example, say that you have a Java applet that collects data in various TextField components (see Figure 1.1).

FIGURE 1.1
The screen layout of the slow network transmission example.

Figure 1.2 shows an abstract pseudo-code model of how two threads can be used to provide better user interaction. The first thread is the GUI event thread, and it spends most of its time blocked in the waitForNextEvent() method. The second thread is the worker thread, and it is initially blocked, waiting for a signal to go to work in the waitUntilSignalled() method. After the fields are populated, the user clicks on a Transmit Data button. The GUI event thread unblocks and then enters the deliverEventToListener() method. That method invokes the actionPerformed() method, which signals the worker thread, and immediately returns to the waitForNextEvent() method. The worker thread unblocks, leaves the waitUntilSignaled() method, and enters the gatherDataAndTransmit() method. The worker thread gathers the data, transmits it, and blocks it while waiting to read a confirmation message from the server. After reading the confirmation, the worker thread returns to the waitUntilSignalled() method.

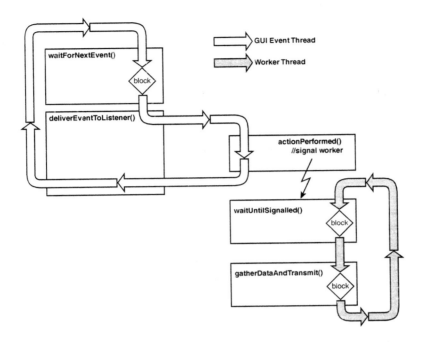

FIGURE 1.2

The partitioning of the work between two threads.

By dividing the work between two threads, the GUI event-handling thread is free to handle other user-generated events. In particular, you might want another button, labeled Cancel Request, that would signal the worker thread to cancel the interaction with the server. If you had not used a worker thread to perform the interaction with the server, but simply had the GUI event thread do the work, the interruption activity triggered by the Cancel Request button would not be possible.

Simplify Object Modeling

Object-oriented analysis of a system before it is built can lead to a design requiring some of the objects to have a thread running within them. This kind of object can be thought of as *active*, as opposed to *passive*. A passive object changes its internal state only when one of its methods is invoked. An active object may change its internal state autonomously.

As an example, consider building a digital clock graphical component that displays the current system time in hours and minutes. Every 60 seconds, the minutes (and possibly the hours) displayed on this component will have to change. The simplest design is to have a thread running inside the clock component and dedicated to updating the digits when necessary. Otherwise, an external thread would have to continually check whether it is time to update a digit, in addition to performing its other duties. What if that external thread had to read data from an InputStream, and it was blocked, waiting for a byte for longer than a minute? Here, exploiting the benefits of multithreaded programming simplifies the solution.

When Multiple Threads Might Not Be Good

It's not always a good idea to add more threads to the design of a program. Threads are not free; they carry some resource overhead.

Each Thread object that is instantiated uses memory resources. In addition to the memory used by the object itself, each thread has two execution call stacks allocated for it by the JavaVM. One stack is used to keep track of Java method calls and local variables. The other stack is used to keep track of native code (typically, C code) calls.

Each thread also requires processor resources. Overhead is inherent in the scheduling of threads by the operating system. When one thread's execution is suspended and swapped off the processor, and another thread is swapped onto the processor and its execution is resumed, this is called a *context switch*. CPU cycles are required to do the work of context switching and can become significant if numerous threads are running.

There is also work involved in starting, stopping, and destroying a Thread object. This cost must be considered when threads are used for brief background tasks. For example, consider the design of an email program that checks for new mail every 5 minutes. Rather than create a new thread to check for mail each time, it would be more efficient to have the same thread keep running and sleep for 5 minutes between each query.

When adding additional threads to the design of a system, these costs should be considered.

Java's Built-in Thread Support

One of the great things about Java is that it has built-in support for writing multithreaded programs. Java's designers knew the value of multithreaded programming and wisely decided to include support for threads directly in the core of Java. Chapter 7, "Concurrent Access to Objects and Variables," explores how in the Java language, the synchronized keyword is used to lock objects and classes to control concurrent access to data. The classes Thread and ThreadGroup are right in the core API in the java.lang package. The superclass of all classes in Java, Object, has inter-thread communication support built in through the wait() and `notify()` methods (see Chapter 8, "Inter-thread Communication"). Even if an underlying operating system does not support the concept of threads, a well-written JavaVM could simulate a multithreaded environment. In Java, thread support was not an afterthought, but included by design from the beginning.

Easy to Start, Tough to Master

It's relatively easy to get started with multithreaded programming in Java. By building automatic garbage collection into Java, the error-prone work of knowing exactly when the memory for an object can be freed is simplified for developers. Similarly, because threads are an integral part of Java, tasks such as acquiring and releasing a lock on an object are simplified (especially releasing a lock when an unanticipated runtime exception occurs).

Although a Java developer can incorporate multiple threads into his or her program with relative ease, mastering the use of multiple threads and communication among them takes time and knowledge. This book introduces the basics of multithreaded programming and then moves on to more advanced topics and techniques to help your mastery of Java threads.

A Simple Two-Thread Example

IN THIS CHAPTER

This chapter shows just how simple it is to get a new thread up and running in a tiny Java application. The first thread is the "main" thread that is always spawned by the Java Virtual Machine (JavaVM) and starts an application. This main thread then spawns the second thread. Each of these threads will print its messages to the console to demonstrate that they both appear to be running simultaneously.

The steps to spawn a new thread in this chapter's example are

- Extend the `java.lang.Thread` class.
- Override the `run()` method in this subclass of `Thread`.
- Create an instance of this new class.
- Invoke the `start()` method on the instance.

Extending the java.lang.Thread Class

An instance of the `java.lang.Thread` class is associated with each thread running in the JavaVM. These `Thread` objects serve as the interface for interacting with the underlying operating system thread. Through the methods in this class, threads can be started, stopped, interrupted, named, prioritized, and queried regarding their current state.

> **NOTE**
>
> There are two ways to create a new class that can have a thread running within it. One way is to extend the `Thread` class. The other is to extend *any* class and implement the `Runnable` interface. For the sake of illustration, extending `Thread` is the simplest approach and is initially used in this book. Implementing the `Runnable` interface tends to work much better in the real world; this technique is introduced in Chapter 4, "Implementing Runnable Versus Extending Thread."

In this example, the first step towards spawning a new thread is to extend the `java.lang.Thread` class:

```
public class TwoThread extends Thread {
    // ...
}
```

The subclass `TwoThread` IS-A `Thread` and consequently inherited the `protected` and `public` members from its superclass. `TwoThread` can be started, stopped, interrupted, named, prioritized, and queried regarding its current state, in addition to all the other behaviors added to the extended class. Figure 2.1 shows the class diagram for `TwoThread`.

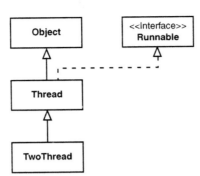

FIGURE 2.1
The class diagram for TwoThread.

NOTE

In this book, the notation used for class relationships is closely based on the Unified Modeling Language (UML). Figure 2.2 shows an example of relationships.

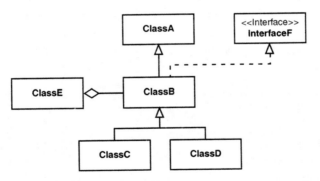

FIGURE 2.2
A sample class diagram showing generic relationships.

Different terms are used in this book to describe interclass relationships. All the following phrases are true about the relationships depicted in Figure 2.2:

- ClassA is the superclass of ClassB.

continues

- ClassB is a subclass of ClassA.
- ClassB extends ClassA.
- ClassB IS-A ClassA.
- ClassB implements InterfaceF.
- ClassB IS-A InterfaceF.
- ClassB is the superclass of ClassC and ClassD.
- ClassC is a subclass of both ClassB and ClassA.
- ClassC IS-A ClassB, ClassC IS-A ClassA, and ClassC IS-A InterfaceF.
- ClassE contains (at least one reference to) ClassB.
- ClassE HAS-A ClassB reference within it.

Overriding the run() Method

After extending Thread, the next step is to override the run() method because the run() method of Thread does nothing:

```
public void run() { }
```

When a new thread is started, the entry point into the program is the run() method. The first statement in run() will be the first statement executed by the new thread. Every statement that the thread will execute is included in the run() method or is in other methods invoked directly or indirectly by run(). The new thread is considered to be *alive* from just before run() is called until just after run() returns, at which time the thread *dies*. After a thread has died, it cannot be restarted.

In this chapter's example, run() is overridden with code to loop for 10 iterations and print the message New thread each time through:

```
public void run() {
    for ( int i = 0; i < 10; i++ ) {
        System.out.println("New thread");
    }
}
```

After the for loop completes, the thread returns from the run() method and quietly dies.

Spawning a New Thread

New threads are spawned from threads that are already running. First, a new Thread instance must be constructed. In this example, a new TwoThread object will work just fine because TwoThread IS-A Thread:

```
TwoThread tt = new TwoThread();
```

The next step is to kick off the execution of the thread by invoking the start() method on the TwoThread object (start() is inherited from Thread):

```
tt.start();
```

A call to start() returns right away and does not wait for the other thread to begin execution. In start(), the parent thread asynchronously signals through the JavaVM that the other thread should be started as soon as it's convenient for the thread scheduler. At some unpredictable time in the very near future, the other thread will come alive and invoke the run() method of the Thread object (or in this case, the overridden run() method implemented in TwoThread). Meanwhile, the original thread is free to continue executing the statements that follow the start() call.

The two threads run concurrently and independently. On a multi-processor machine, these two threads may actually be running *at the very same instant*, each on its own processor. This true simultaneity would also have to be supported in the port of the JavaVM for that platform in order to exploit multiple processors.

A more likely case is that only a single processor is present. The JavaVM and the operating system work together to schedule each thread for short, interleaved bursts of processor usage. Each thread takes a turn running while the other threads are frozen, waiting for their next turn on the processor. This context switching among threads generally occurs very quickly and gives the illusion of truly simultaneous execution.

CAUTION

A newly created thread may start executing (enter the run() method) at any time after start() is invoked. This means that the original thread might be swapped out before any statement that follows start() is executed.

If the original thread is executing this code

```
stmt1();
tt.start();
stmt2();
```

continues

and the new thread has a run() method such as this

```
public void run() {
    stmtA();
    stmtB();
}
```

the order of actual statement execution *in the processor* might be stmt1(), tt.start(), stmt2(), stmtA(), and stmtB(). Alternatively, it might be stmt1(), tt.start(), stmtA(), stmtB(), and stmt2(). Perhaps, it might be one of the other permutations!

Important to note is that although the order in which each thread will execute its own statements is known and straightforward, the order in which the statements will actually be run on the processor is indeterminate, and no particular order should be counted on for program correctness.

Putting It All Together

Combining the preceding code and adding a second 10-iteration loop for the main thread to run produces the complete code for TwoThread.java, shown in Listing 2.1.

LISTING 2.1   TwoThread.java—The Complete Code for the TwoThread Example

```
 1: public class TwoThread extends Thread {
 2:     public void run() {
 3:         for ( int i = 0; i < 10; i++ ) {
 4:             System.out.println("New thread");
 5:         }
 6:     }
 7:
 8:     public static void main(String[] args) {
 9:         TwoThread tt = new TwoThread();
10:         tt.start();
11:
12:         for ( int i = 0; i < 10; i++ ) {
13:             System.out.println("Main thread");
14:         }
15:     }
16: }
```

First, note that the new class TwoThread directly extends Thread, so it IS-A Thread and takes on all the capabilities of its superclass.

Application execution begins with the main thread, which is spawned by the JavaVM for all applications at startup, entering the `main()` method (line 8). It proceeds to create a new `TwoThread` instance (line 9). Next, it spawns a new thread of execution by invoking the `start()` method (line 10). This new thread will begin its execution by invoking the `run()` method (line 2) of `TwoThread`.

At this point, two threads are ready to run, and the thread scheduler runs each thread for short periods, alternating between them. If this switching back and forth is fast enough, they appear to be running simultaneously.

After the main thread spawns the new thread, the main thread proceeds into its loop (lines 12–14) and prints `Main thread` to the console 10 times. When it is done with the loop, it falls through and returns from `main()`. The main thread dies when it returns from `main()`.

At approximately the same time, the new thread enters the `run()` method (line 2), proceeds into its loop (lines 3–5), and prints `New thread` to the console 10 times. When it is done with the loop, it falls through and returns from `run()`. The new thread dies when it returns from `run()`.

When both threads have completed their work and died, the JavaVM shuts down and the application is done.

Listing 2.2 shows *possible* output from running this application (your output might differ). During this run of the application, the messages from the two threads happened to be perfectly interleaved, starting with the message from the main thread. There is no guarantee that this output would be the same if the application was run again. Thread scheduling is nondeterministic and depends on many factors, including what else is currently running in the operating system. The thread scheduler makes what seem to be random decisions about how long each thread should be allowed to run between context switches. The only thing that can be counted on from running this application is that each message will print exactly 10 times, regardless of the order of the messages.

LISTING 2.2   Possible Output from a Run of TwoThread.java

```
Main thread
New thread
Main thread
New thread
Main thread
New thread
Main thread
```

continues

LISTING 2.2 Continued

```
New thread
Main thread
New thread
Main thread
New thread
Main thread
New thread
Main thread
New thread
Main thread
New thread
Main thread
New thread
```

Summary

This chapter explores how to create a new thread by performing these tasks:

- Subclassing Thread
- Overriding the run() method of Thread to specify the statements to be executed by the new thread
- Creating a new instance of this subclass of Thread
- Spawning a new thread by invoking start() on this instance

That's all there is to getting a second thread up and running in Java! The following chapters explore the complexities of threads and the coordination of the intercommunication that usually must occur among them.

Creating and Starting a Thread

CHAPTER

3

IN THIS CHAPTER

This chapter explores more of the `Thread` API, including getting a handle on the currently executing thread, thread naming, some of the different constructors, and putting a thread to sleep for awhile. You will use these features to enhance the `TwoThread` example from Chapter 2, "A Simple Two-Thread Example."

Using Thread.currentThread()

At times, it's useful to know which of the threads currently running in the Java Virtual Machine (JavaVM) is executing a segment of code. In multithreaded programming, more than one thread may enter a method and execute the statements within it.

In the `TwoThread` example from Chapter 2, two threads execute the code in the `println()` method of the `PrintStream` object referred to by the `System.out` reference:

```
System.out.println("Main thread");
System.out.println("New thread");
```

This one `PrintStream` object is set up by the JavaVM during initialization for use by any class at any time in a Java program through the `System.out` reference. Any running thread can invoke the `println()` method. In this case, the `println()` method does not care which thread invoked it; it simply takes the `String` passed in and prints it.

In the `Thread` API, you can use the `static` method

```
public static native Thread currentThread()
```

to determine which thread is executing a segment of code. You can use this information to take different actions within the code segment.

> **NOTE**
>
> Many of the methods in `Thread` are listed with some of the following modifiers: `native`, `final`, `static`, and `synchronized`. As a quick review, `native` methods are implemented in non-Java code (typically C or C++ in the JDK). Methods declared to be `final` may not be overridden in a subclass. When a method is `static`, it does not pertain to a particular instance of the class, but operates at the class level. The `synchronized` modifier guarantees that no more than one thread is allowed to execute the statements inside a method at one time. Later in this book, the `synchronized` modifier is explained in detail.

As an example, look at a new version of `TwoThread` in Listing 3.1. This example is a bit ridiculous for real-world applications, but serves to illustrate a use of `Thread.currentThread()`.

LISTING 3.1   TwoThread.java—A Version of TwoThread That Uses currentThread()

```
 1: public class TwoThread extends Thread {
 2:     private Thread creatorThread;
 3:
 4:     public TwoThread() {
 5:         // make a note of the thread that constructed me!
 6:         creatorThread = Thread.currentThread();
 7:     }
 8:
 9:     public void run() {
10:         for ( int i = 0; i < 10; i++ ) {
11:             printMsg();
12:         }
13:     }
14:
15:     public void printMsg() {
16:         // get a reference to the thread running this
17:         Thread t = Thread.currentThread();
18:
19:         if ( t == creatorThread ) {
20:             System.out.println("Creator thread");
21:         } else if ( t == this ) {
22:             System.out.println("New thread");
23:         } else {
24:             System.out.println("Mystery thread —unexpected!");
25:         }
26:     }
27:
28:     public static void main(String[] args) {
29:         TwoThread tt = new TwoThread();
30:         tt.start();
31:
32:         for ( int i = 0; i < 10; i++ ) {
33:             tt.printMsg();
34:         }
35:     }
36: }
```

3

CREATING AND
STARTING A
THREAD

In this version, the System.out.println() statements have been removed from the loops and replaced by a call to the new printMsg() method (lines 11 and 33). This method does not take a String as a parameter, but instead determines which message to print, based on the thread that invokes it.

In the constructor (line 6), `Thread.currentThread()` is used to gain a reference to the `Thread` object for the thread that executed the new `TwoThread()`; statement.

This `Thread` reference is stored in the member variable `creatorThread` for later use.

To determine which message to print, `printMsg()` first gets a reference to the `Thread` that invoked it, by using the `static` method `Thread.currentThread()` (line 17). Next, it tests whether this reference `t` matches the `creatorThread` reference stored by the constructor. If so, it prints `Creator thread` (lines 19 and 20). If the reference doesn't match, `printMsg()` then checks whether `t` matches `this`. `TwoThread` IS-A `Thread` because it directly subclasses `Thread`. The `this` reference refers to the `Thread` object constructed on line 29 by the `main` thread. If the current thread equals `this`, `New thread` is printed (lines 21 and 22). Otherwise, another thread that was not accounted for invoked this method, and the message `Mystery thread --unex-pected!` is printed (lines 23 and 24). In this example, the `Mystery thread --unexpected!` message will never be printed because only two threads will run this code and they have both been accounted for.

Listing 3.2 presents possible output from running `TwoThread`. Remember that the exact order of the messages printed, as well as how long each thread will run between context switches, depends on the thread scheduler. Therefore, your output might differ somewhat.

LISTING 3.2 Possible Output from TwoThread Using currentThread()

```
Creator thread
New thread
Creator thread
New thread
Creator thread
New thread
Creator thread
New thread
Creator thread
New thread
Creator thread
New thread
Creator thread
New thread
Creator thread
New thread
Creator thread
New thread
Creator thread
New thread
Creator thread
New thread
```

Naming a Thread: getName() and setName()

Every Thread has a name associated with it. If a name is not explicitly supplied, a default one is generated during construction. By name, you can differentiate between the various threads running in the JavaVM.

Using getName()

In the Thread API, the method

```
public final String getName()
```

is used to retrieve the current name. Listing 3.3 shows a new class, TwoThreadGetName, that uses the getName() method to differentiate between two running threads.

LISTING 3.3   TwoThreadGetName.java—Using getName()

```
 1: public class TwoThreadGetName extends Thread {
 2:     public void run() {
 3:         for ( int i = 0; i < 10; i++ ) {
 4:             printMsg();
 5:         }
 6:     }
 7:
 8:     public void printMsg() {
 9:         // get a reference to the thread running this
10:         Thread t = Thread.currentThread();
11:         String name = t.getName();
12:         System.out.println("name=" + name);
13:     }
14:
15:     public static void main(String[] args) {
16:         TwoThreadGetName tt = new TwoThreadGetName();
17:         tt.start();
18:
19:         for ( int i = 0; i < 10; i++ ) {
20:             tt.printMsg();
21:         }
22:     }
23: }
```

All printing occurs in printMsg() when it is invoked from the loop in run() (lines 3–5) and from the loop in main() (lines 19–21). First, in printMsg(), a reference to the currently executing Thread is obtained using Thread.currentThread() (line 10). Next, the name of this particular Thread is retrieved through getName() (line 11). Finally, the name is printed (line 12).

Listing 3.4 shows possible output from running `TwoThreadGetName`. Different output can (and usually does) occur each time this is run. For this particular run, note that the messages alternate between threads at first. However, about midway, three `Thread-0` messages are printed consecutively without any messages from the other thread. At the end, the `Thread-0` thread has died, and the `main` thread is able to catch up and print the backlogged messages.

This is a perfect example of the nondeterministic behavior of multithreaded programs—a critical issue for skilled Java developers to be aware of. In later chapters, you will learn techniques for ensuring the *correctness* of multithreaded programs—regardless of the order in which the threads happen to be scheduled to run.

LISTING 3.4   Possible Output from TwoThreadGetName

```
name=main
name=Thread-0
name=main
name=Thread-0
name=main
name=Thread-0
name=main
name=Thread-0
name=main
name=Thread-0
name=Thread-0
name=Thread-0
name=main
name=Thread-0
name=Thread-0
name=main
name=Thread-0
name=main
name=main
name=main
```

In addition to a thread named `main`, the JavaVM starts up other threads automatically. Table 3.1 lists the names of these threads on each of the three released Java platforms. Each row presents the various names of the same thread.

TABLE 3.1   Threads Started by the JavaVM

JDK 1.2	JDK 1.1	JDK 1.0
`main`	`main`	`main`
`Finalizer`	`Finalizer thread`	`Finalizer thread`
`Reference Handler`	(none)	(none)
`Signal dispatcher`	(none)	(none)
`AWT-Windows`	`AWT-Windows`	`AWT-Win32`
`AWT-EventQueue-0`	`AWT-EventQueue-0`	`AWT-Callback-Win32`
`SunToolkit.PostEventQueue-0`	(none)	(none)
`Screen Updater`	`Screen Updater`	`Screen Updater`

Note that the `Reference Handler`, `Signal dispatcher`, and `SunToolkit.PostEventQueue-0` threads are new to JDK 1.2. The threads named `main` and `Finalizer` (`Reference Handler` and `Signal dispatcher` for JDK 1.2) are started automatically for every application. The remaining threads are also started by the JavaVM when the application contains any graphical components from AWT or Swing. Therefore, in a JDK 1.2 application with a graphical user interface (GUI), eight threads are automatically started by the JavaVM.

As mentioned previously, the `main` thread is responsible for starting application execution by invoking the `main()` method. This is the thread from which most other developer-defined threads are spawned by application code. The `Finalizer` thread is used by the JavaVM to execute the `finalize()` method of objects just before they are garbage collected. The `AWT-EventQueue-0` thread is more commonly known as the *event* thread and invokes event-handling methods such as `actionPerformed()`, `keyPressed()`, `mouseClicked()`, and `windowClosing()`.

Using setName()

In the preceding example, the names associated with threads are their default names. You can explicitly specify the name of a `Thread` object by using the `setName()` method:

```
public final void setName(String newName)
```

The name of a thread is typically set before the thread is started, but setting the name of a thread already running is also permitted. Two `Thread` objects are permitted to have the same name, but you should avoid this for clarity. The `main` thread started by the JavaVM can also have its name changed, but this is also discouraged.

> ### TIP
>
> Although Java requires none of the following, it's good practice to follow these conventions when naming threads:
>
> - Invoke setName() on the Thread before start(), and do not rename the Thread after it is started.
> - Give each thread a brief, meaningful name when possible.
> - Give each thread a unique name.
> - Do not change the names of JavaVM threads, such as main.

Listing 3.5 shows a new class, TwoThreadSetName, that uses the setName() method to override the default thread name.

LISTING 3.5   TwoThreadSetName.java—Using setName()

```
 1: public class TwoThreadSetName extends Thread {
 2:     public void run() {
 3:         for ( int i = 0; i < 10; i++ ) {
 4:             printMsg();
 5:         }
 6:     }
 7:
 8:     public void printMsg() {
 9:         // get a reference to the thread running this
10:         Thread t = Thread.currentThread();
11:         String name = t.getName();
12:         System.out.println("name=" + name);
13:     }
14:
15:     public static void main(String[] args) {
16:         TwoThreadSetName tt = new TwoThreadSetName();
17:         tt.setName("my worker thread");
18:         tt.start();
19:
20:         for ( int i = 0; i < 10; i++ ) {
21:             tt.printMsg();
22:         }
23:     }
24: }
```

The only difference between TwoThreadSetName and TwoThreadGetName is the addition of the statement to set the name of the new thread to my worker thread (line 17) before the thread is started. The name of the main thread remains untouched. Listing 3.6 shows possible output; your output might differ because of nondeterministic thread scheduling.

LISTING 3.6   Possible Output from TwoThreadSetName

```
name=main
name=my worker thread
name=main
name=my worker thread
name=my worker thread
name=main
name=my worker thread
name=main
name=my worker thread
name=main
name=my worker thread
name=main
name=my worker thread
name=main
name=my worker thread
name=my worker thread
name=main
name=my worker thread
name=main
name=main
```

Thread Constructors

The central constructor in Thread is

```
public Thread(ThreadGroup group, Runnable target, String name)
```

The parameter name allows you to specify the name of the thread at construction time, rather than set it later using setName().

The parameter target refers to an object of type Runnable. This object's run() method will be invoked by the new thread instead of the run() method of Thread. Unlike a thread's name, if you're going to specify the target, you must do so at the time of construction. Chapter 4 explores in detail the issues involved in making a decision to use Runnable instead of extending Thread.

The parameter group lets you specify the ThreadGroup to which the new Thread will belong. Figure 3.1 shows the relationships among Threads and ThreadGroups.

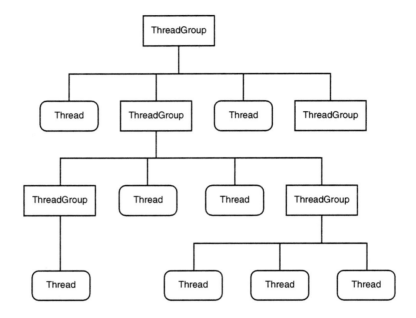

FIGURE 3.1

A sample hierarchy of ThreadGroups and Threads.

An analogy can be drawn between the file system concept of directories and files and the ThreadGroup/Thread relationship. In a file system, a directory can contain files and other directories. These other directories, in turn, can contain other files and directories. Every file is in exactly one directory, which may itself be in another directory. Every directory except the one "root" or "base" directory is in another directory.

In Java, a ThreadGroup (much like a directory) can contain Threads and other ThreadGroups. These other ThreadGroups can, in turn, contain other Threads and ThreadGroups. Every Thread (much like a file) is a member of a ThreadGroup, which may itself be a member of another ThreadGroup.

If a ThreadGroup is not specified at the time of a Thread's construction, the ThreadGroup is inherited from the Thread that constructed it. Chapter 10, "Thread Groups," discusses ThreadGroups in more detail.

The Thread constructor used so far has been as follows:

```
public Thread()
```

By default, the ThreadGroup is that of the Thread that constructs it. No external Runnable is specified, so the Thread's own run() method is called. Because no name is specified, the name of the Thread will be automatically generated as something such as Thread-0.

The other constructors of Thread come somewhere in between the zero-argument constructor and the three-argument constructor. They specify some parameters of the three-argument constructor, and the nonspecified parameters take on their default values.

Enlivening a Thread: start() and isAlive()

The start() method signals the thread scheduler that this new thread is ready to go and should have its run() method invoked at the scheduler's earliest convenience. Because of the nondeterministic nature of multithreaded programming, one cannot be sure just when the thread will begin execution, but only that it should begin soon.

The API for start() is

```
public native synchronized void start()
            throws IllegalThreadStateException
```

If the Thread has already been started, an IllegalThreadStateException will be thrown. When the start() method of a Thread is invoked, the new thread is considered to come alive. The thread remains alive until the run() method returns or until the thread is abruptly *stopped* by the stop() method (which is a deprecated method, as of JDK 1.2!).

The method

```
public final native boolean isAlive()
```

can be used on Thread to test whether a thread has been started and is still running. Listing 3.7 shows an example of how isAlive() can be used.

LISTING 3.7   TwoThreadAlive.java—Using isAlive()

```
 1: public class TwoThreadAlive extends Thread {
 2:     public void run() {
 3:         for ( int i = 0; i < 10; i++ ) {
 4:             printMsg();
 5:         }
 6:     }
 7:
 8:     public void printMsg() {
 9:         // get a reference to the thread running this
10:         Thread t = Thread.currentThread();
```

continues

LISTING 3.7   Continued

```
11:           String name = t.getName();
12:           System.out.println("name=" + name);
13:       }
14:
15:       public static void main(String[] args) {
16:           TwoThreadAlive tt = new TwoThreadAlive();
17:           tt.setName("my worker thread");
18:
19:           System.out.println("before start(), tt.isAlive()=" +
                     [ccc]tt.isAlive());
20:           tt.start();
21:           System.out.println("just after start(), tt.isAlive()=" +
                     [ccc]tt.isAlive());
22:
23:           for ( int i = 0; i < 10; i++ ) {
24:               tt.printMsg();
25:           }
26:
27:           System.out.println(
28:               "at the end of main(), tt.isAlive()=" + tt.isAlive());
29:       }
30: }
```

The code on line 19 checks whether the new `Thread` object is alive. This will always be false because the thread has not yet been started. Immediately after the thread is started, another check is done (line 20). At this point, the new `Thread` object will always be alive. At the end of `main()`, one last check is done (lines 27 and 28). Sometimes, the `Thread` object will still be alive, and other times it will have already died, depending on the exact thread scheduling that occurs.

Listing 3.8 presents output from a particular run of `TwoThreadAlive`. Nearly every time this is run, it gives slightly different output. In this case, note that three messages are printed from the `worker` thread before the `main` thread has a chance to execute the `isAlive()` check right after `start()`. The `worker` thread keeps its lead and finishes its work—and is therefore no longer alive—well before the `main` is done, so the check at the end shows that the `worker` thread is no longer alive.

LISTING 3.8   Possible Output from TwoThreadAlive

```
before start(), tt.isAlive()=false
name=my worker thread
name=my worker thread
name=my worker thread
```

```
just after start(), tt.isAlive()=true
name=my worker thread
name=main
name=my worker thread
name=main
name=my worker thread
name=main
name=my worker thread
name=main
name=my worker thread
name=my worker thread
name=main
name=my worker thread
name=main
name=main
name=main
name=main
name=main
at the end of main(), tt.isAlive()=false
```

Using Thread.sleep()

As beneficial as it is for threads to go about doing their work as fast as possible, sometimes it would be useful if a thread could take a break and go to *sleep* for a while. In a clock application, it might be the case that the thread in charge of updating the displayed time should pause for 60 seconds at a time between the changing of the minutes displayed. A *busy loop* such as

```
long startTime = System.currentTimeMillis();
long stopTime = startTime + 60000;

while ( System.currentTimeMillis() < stopTime ) {
    // do nothing, but loop back
}
```

takes up a lot of processor cycles. Instead, it would be better to use the following static method on Thread

```
public static native void sleep(long msToSleep)
            throws InterruptedException
```

to wait for 60 seconds, like this:

```
try {
    Thread.sleep(60000);
} catch ( InterruptedException x ) {
    // ignore the exception
}
```

Sleeping is a much better option than using a busy loop. A sleeping thread does not use any processor cycles because its execution is suspended for the specified duration.

The sleep() method is static and puts only the currently executing thread—the one that would be returned by Thread.currentThread()—to sleep. It is not possible for a thread to put any other thread to sleep.

The try/catch construct is necessary because while a thread is sleeping, it might be *interrupted* by another thread. One thread might want to interrupt another to let it know that it should take some sort of action. Later chapters further explore the use of interrupts. Here, it suffices to say that a sleeping thread *might* be interrupted and will throw an InterruptedException if this occurs.

Listing 3.9 shows how sleep() can be used to slow down the action and how two threads may be inside the same method of one object at the same time.

LISTING 3.9 TwoThreadSleep.java—Using sleep()

```
 1: public class TwoThreadSleep extends Thread {
 2:     public void run() {
 3:         loop();
 4:     }
 5:
 6:     public void loop() {
 7:         // get a reference to the thread running this
 8:         Thread t = Thread.currentThread();
 9:         String name = t.getName();
10:
11:         System.out.println("just entered loop() - " + name);
12:
13:         for ( int i = 0; i < 10; i++ ) {
14:             try {
15:                 Thread.sleep(200);
16:             } catch ( InterruptedException x ) {
17:                 // ignore
18:             }
19:
20:             System.out.println("name=" + name);
21:         }
22:
23:         System.out.println("about to leave loop() - " + name);
24:     }
25:
26:     public static void main(String[] args) {
27:         TwoThreadSleep tt = new TwoThreadSleep();
```

```
28:            tt.setName("my worker thread");
29:            tt.start();
30:
31:            // pause for a bit
32:            try {
33:                Thread.sleep(700);
34:            } catch ( InterruptedException x ) {
35:                // ignore
36:            }
37:
38:            tt.loop();
39:        }
40: }
```

The method `loop()` is used by both `run()` (line 3) and by `main()` (line 38) to print out all the messages. In `main()`, `sleep()` is used to delay the `main` thread's entry into the `loop()` method (lines 32–36). On lines 14–18, `sleep()` is also used to slow down the iterations through the `for` loop. Listing 3.10 shows sample output from a particular run.

LISTING 3.10 Sample Output from TwoThreadSleep

```
just entered loop() - my worker thread
name=my worker thread
name=my worker thread
just entered loop() - main
name=my worker thread
name=main
name=my worker thread
name=main
name=my worker thread
name=main
name=my worker thread
name=main
name=my worker thread
name=main
name=my worker thread
name=main
name=my worker thread
name=main
name=my worker thread
about to leave loop() - my worker thread
name=main
name=main
name=main
about to leave loop() - main
```

In examining the output, you notice that *both* threads are inside the `loop()` method *at the same time*. Yet, each thread has its own copy of the local variable `name` to print its proper identification. Local variables work well with multiple threads, but accessing and modifying member variables (the state of an object) with multiple threads is tricky business. You will learn more about this in Chapter 7, "Concurrent Access to Objects and Variables."

Summary

This chapter begins to explore some of the API for `Thread`:

- `Thread.currentThread()`
- `getName()`
- `setName()`
- `Thread(ThreadGroup, Runnable, String)`
- `Thread()`
- `start()`
- `isAlive()`
- `Thread.sleep()`

The next chapters explain more of the API.

Implementing Runnable Versus Extending Thread

CHAPTER

4

IN THIS CHAPTER

Until now, extending the class Thread has been the only way to define a new class that can have a thread running within it. This chapter shows that the Runnable interface provides a second, and more often used, mechanism for defining a new class that can have a thread running within it.

Visual Timer Graphical Component

Imagine that what you need is a timer graphical component that continually displays the time elapsed since it was started. To build this custom component, at a bare minimum, you must extend Component. Because this example uses Swing, you will instead extend JComponent (which indirectly extends Component). Figure 4.1 shows the initial class hierarchy for the new customized component, SecondCounter.

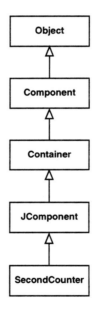

FIGURE 4.1

The initial class hierarchy for SecondCounter.

SecondCounter IS-A Component, so it can be added to any Container, just like the other Components. This SecondCounter has to keep track of the amount of time that has passed since it was started and update itself every 0.1 seconds to visually reflect the time that has elapsed.

Listing 4.1 shows the source code for a first cut at defining this class. This version definitely has serious problems, but it illustrates the necessity of another approach. To keep the evolving versions of SecondCounter straight, slightly different classnames are used for each version. In this case, the class name is SecondCounterLockup.

LISTING 4.1   SecondCounterLockup.java—The First Attempt at the Timer

```
1: import java.awt.*;
2: import javax.swing.*;
3: import java.text.*;
4:
5: public class SecondCounterLockup extends JComponent {
6:     private boolean keepRunning;
7:     private Font paintFont;
8:     private String timeMsg;
9:     private int arcLen;
10:
11:     public SecondCounterLockup() {
12:         paintFont = new Font("SansSerif", Font.BOLD, 14);
13:         timeMsg = "never started";
14:         arcLen = 0;
15:     }
16:
17:     public void runClock() {
18:         System.out.println("thread running runClock() is " +
19:                 Thread.currentThread().getName());
20:
21:         DecimalFormat fmt = new DecimalFormat("0.000");
22:         long normalSleepTime = 100;
23:
24:         int counter = 0;
25:         keepRunning = true;
26:
27:         while ( keepRunning ) {
28:             try {
29:                 Thread.sleep(normalSleepTime);
30:             } catch ( InterruptedException x ) {
31:                 // ignore
32:             }
33:
34:             counter++;
35:             double counterSecs = counter / 10.0;
36:
37:             timeMsg = fmt.format(counterSecs);
38:
39:             arcLen = ( ( ( int ) counterSecs ) % 60 ) * 360 / 60;
40:             repaint();
41:         }
```

continues

LISTING 4.1 Continued

```
42:       }
43:
44:       public void stopClock() {
45:           keepRunning = false;
46:       }
47:
48:       public void paint(Graphics g) {
49:           System.out.println("thread that invoked paint() is " +
50:                   Thread.currentThread().getName());
51:
52:           g.setColor(Color.black);
53:           g.setFont(paintFont);
54:           g.drawString(timeMsg, 0, 15);
55:
56:           g.fillOval(0, 20, 100, 100);   // black border
57:
58:           g.setColor(Color.white);
59:           g.fillOval(3, 23, 94, 94);   // white for unused portion
60:
61:           g.setColor(Color.blue);   // blue for used portion
62:           g.fillArc(2, 22, 96, 96, 90, -arcLen);
63:       }
64: }
```

This component draws itself with a text message and a circular dial. Initially, the text message is "never started" (line 13), and the dial is totally white (arcLen = 0, line 14). After the timer is started, the text message indicates the total elapsed time in fractional seconds. The dial sweeps out a blue-filled arc in a clockwise direction that completes 360 degrees every 60 seconds. The dial portion is very similar to the second hand on an analog watch or clock.

The paint() method (lines 48–63) handles the drawing of the component based on the current values of timeMsg and arcLen. In addition, on lines 49 and 50, paint() reveals the name of the thread that invoked it.

The runClock() method is called when the timer should begin counting (line 17), and it also shares the name of the thread that invoked it (lines 18 and 19). On line 21, the format for the textual display of the seconds elapsed is defined to show fractional seconds down to the millisecond (ms). The normalSleepTime is defined as 100ms, which is the 0.1-second interval between updates that was desired. The number of iterations is held in counter (line 24). Initially, keepRunning is set to true to indicate that the timer should continue to run (line 25). The remainder of the method is a while loop (lines 27–41). In this loop, a quick nap is taken for 1/10 second (lines 28–32). Then, `counter` is incremented to indicate that another 0.1 seconds has passed (line 34). This count is converted to seconds: `counterSecs` (line 35). On line 37, the number of seconds is formatted into a `String` for display in the `paint()` method. The arc length in degrees is calculated for use in the `paint()` method (line 39). Finally, `repaint()` is called to let the JavaVM know that it should schedule a call to `paint()` as soon as it can.

The method `stopClock()` (lines 44–46) is invoked to signal that the timer should stop running. It sets `keepRunning` to `false` so that the next time the `while` expression in `runClock()` is evaluated, it will stop looping.

To use this customized component in a `JFrame` with other components, another class is defined: `SecondCounterLockupMain`, shown in Listing 4.2.

LISTING 4.2   SecondCounterLockupMain.java—The Class Used to Demonstrate
SecondCounterLockup

```
 1: import java.awt.*;
 2: import java.awt.event.*;
 3: import javax.swing.*;
 4: import javax.swing.border.*;
 5:
 6: public class SecondCounterLockupMain extends JPanel {
 7:     private SecondCounterLockup sc;
 8:     private JButton startB;
 9:     private JButton stopB;
10:
11:     public SecondCounterLockupMain() {
12:         sc = new SecondCounterLockup();
13:         startB = new JButton("Start");
14:         stopB = new JButton("Stop");
15:
16:         stopB.setEnabled(false);  // begin with this disabled
17:
18:         startB.addActionListener(new ActionListener() {
19:             public void actionPerformed(ActionEvent e) {
20:                 // disable to stop more "start" requests
21:                 startB.setEnabled(false);
22:
23:                 // Run the counter. Watch out, trouble here!
24:                 sc.runClock();
25:
26:                 stopB.setEnabled(true);
27:                 stopB.requestFocus();
```

continues

LISTING 4.2   Continued

```
28:                  }
29:              });
30:
31:          stopB.addActionListener(new ActionListener() {
32:                  public void actionPerformed(ActionEvent e) {
33:                      stopB.setEnabled(false);
34:                      sc.stopClock();
35:                      startB.setEnabled(true);
36:                      startB.requestFocus();
37:                  }
38:              });
39:
40:          JPanel innerButtonP = new JPanel();
41:          innerButtonP.setLayout(new GridLayout(0, 1, 0, 3));
42:          innerButtonP.add(startB);
43:          innerButtonP.add(stopB);
44:
45:          JPanel buttonP = new JPanel();
46:          buttonP.setLayout(new BorderLayout());
47:          buttonP.add(innerButtonP, BorderLayout.NORTH);
48:
49:          this.setLayout(new BorderLayout(10, 10));
50:          this.setBorder(new EmptyBorder(20, 20, 20, 20));
51:          this.add(buttonP, BorderLayout.WEST);
52:          this.add(sc, BorderLayout.CENTER);
53:      }
54:
55:      public static void main(String[] args) {
56:          SecondCounterLockupMain scm =
➥                  new SecondCounterLockupMain();
57:
58:          JFrame f = new JFrame("Second Counter Lockup");
59:          f.setContentPane(scm);
60:          f.setSize(320, 200);
61:          f.setVisible(true);
62:          f.addWindowListener(new WindowAdapter() {
63:                  public void windowClosing(WindowEvent e) {
64:                      System.exit(0);
65:                  }
66:              });
67:      }
68: }
```

In the constructor, a new SecondCounterLockup is created and put into a JPanel with Start and Stop buttons (lines 12–14 and 40–52). In main(), this JPanel subclass, named SecondCounterLockupMain, is put into a JFrame and displayed (lines 55–67). Initially, the Stop button is disabled because the timer is not running (line 16).

When the Start button is pressed, the actionPerformed() method is invoked (lines 19–28) on the anonymous inner subclass of ActionListener (line 18). In there, the Start button is first disabled (line 21) to prevent any further pressing until the timer is stopped. Next, the runClock() method on the SecondCounterLockup object is invoked (line 24). Watch out, here's where the trouble starts! In fact, in this example, none of the other code is ever executed.

CAUTION

As the name suggests, running SecondCounterLockupMain will not work as intended and locks up the JavaVM. This is harmless and should not stop you from trying the example. When the Start button is pressed, nothing else happens in the application. The Stop button is never enabled. The window exit/close control is ineffective, even though code was written (lines 62–66) to handle this event.

The only way to stop the application is to kill the JavaVM (by going back to the console window and pressing Ctrl+C, or Delete, or whatever mechanism is used on your platform to kill/interrupt/break/terminate a runaway process).

Figure 4.2 shows how this application looks right after startup:

```
java SecondCounterLockupMain
```

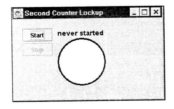

FIGURE 4.2
Just after starting SecondCounterLockupMain.

Figure 4.3 shows how it looks after the Start button is pressed (and how it looks until it is killed!). Although the clock variables are being updated internally, the external view never has a chance to be painted. The paint() method is called only one time, when the frame is first drawn, and never displays the changes requested by the repaint() call.

FIGURE 4.3
After clicking the Start button.

A clue to the problem can be found in the output on the console:

```
thread that invoked paint() is AWT-EventQueue-0
thread running runClock() is AWT-EventQueue-0
```

This shows that the AWT-EventQueue-0 thread is used for both painting and invoking the event handling methods. When the Start button is pressed, the AWT-EventQueue-0 thread invokes the actionPerformed() method (line 19, SecondCounterLockupMain.java). This method in turn invokes runClock(), which continues to loop until keepRunning is set to false. The only way this can be set to false is by the pressing the Stop button. Because the AWT-EventQueue-0 thread is busy in this loop, it never has a chance to invoke the paint() method again, and the display is frozen. No other event can be processed (including the window close event) until the actionPerformed() method returns. But this will never happen! The application is all locked up, spinning in the while loop!

Although this is only an example, this is a very real type of problem. Rather than do any major work in the event handling thread, you should use another thread as the worker and allow the event handling thread to return to the business of handling events.

TIP

GUI event handling code should be relatively brief to allow the event handling thread to return from the handler and prepare to handle the next event. If longer tasks must be performed, the bulk of the work should be passed off to another thread for processing. This helps keep the user interface lively and responsive.

Extending Thread and JComponent?

Using the event handling thread to run the timer proved to be an impossible idea. Another thread has to be used to run the timer. Based on what has been explored in earlier chapters, it would be nice if SecondCounter could inherit from both JComponent *and* Thread, as illustrated in Figure 4.4.

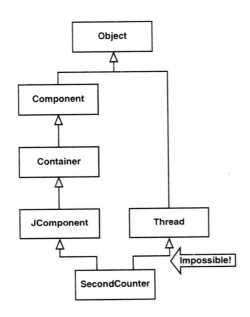

FIGURE 4.4

Inheriting from both JComponent and Thread—impossible in Java!

Because multiple inheritance is not permitted in Java, this approach won't work. It is most important that SecondCounter IS-A Component so that it can be added to a Container, like JPanel. How can it also allow a thread to run within it?

Interface java.lang.Runnable

Rather than inherit from Thread, a class can implement the interface java.lang.Runnable to allow a thread to be run within it. Runnable specifies that only one method be implemented:

```
public void run()
```

This is the same method signature that run() has in Thread. In fact, Thread also implements Runnable! Note that run() does not take any parameters, does not return anything, and does not declare that it throws any exceptions.

The Runnable interface can be used to get around the lack of multiple inheritance. Figure 4.5 shows SecondCounter extending JComponent and implementing Runnable. SecondCounter IS-A Component and can be added to containers. SecondCounter also IS-A Runnable and can have a new thread begin execution with its run() method.

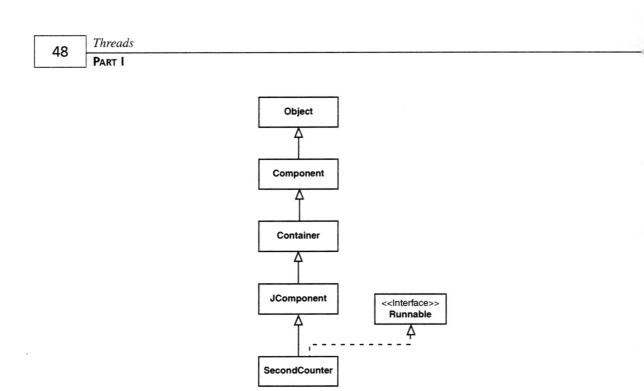

FIGURE 4.5

Getting around the multiple inheritance problem with Runnable.

Passing a Runnable Object to a Thread's Constructor

The Thread class has four constructors that take a Runnable object as a parameter:

```
public Thread(Runnable target)
public Thread(Runnable target, String name)
public Thread(ThreadGroup group, Runnable target)
public Thread(ThreadGroup group, Runnable target, String name)
```

Any instance of a class that implements the Runnable interface may be passed as the target to one of these constructors. When the Thread instance's start() method is invoked, start() will start the new thread in the run() method of target rather than in Thread's run() method. The Runnable to be used may be specified only at the time of a Thread's construction; the Thread holds a reference to it in a private member variable.

Because SecondCounter now implements Runnable, a new Thread instance should be created with a SecondCounter instance for a target, like this:

```
SecondCounter sc = new SecondCounter();
Thread t = new Thread(sc);
t.start();
```

When t.start() is executed, the newly spawned thread will begin execution by invoking the run() method of SecondCounter. Figure 4.6 presents the resulting object diagram. Note that Thread HAS-A reference to a Runnable (which in this case is more specifically a SecondCounter).

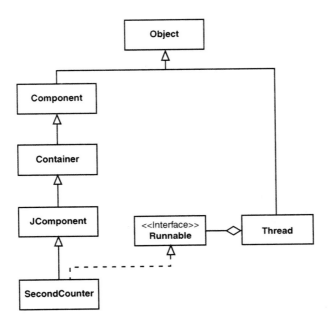

FIGURE 4.6
The object diagram for a Runnable SecondCounter passed as a target to a Thread constructor.

> **TIP**
>
> Implementing the Runnable interface, rather than extending Thread, is generally a better choice, even if the class only inherits from Object. This allows you to develop and use general techniques with classes that implement the Runnable interface, without any concern for which particular class this Runnable *extended*.

Modifying SecondCounter to Use Runnable

Listing 4.3 shows a new version of the timer component that now implements the Runnable interface. The bold text is used to indicate the most notable changes.

LISTING 4.3   SecondCounterRunnable.java—Implementing the Runnable Interface

```
1: import java.awt.*;
2: import javax.swing.*;
3: import java.text.*;
4:
5: public class SecondCounterRunnable
                       ➥extends JComponent implements Runnable {
6:     private volatile boolean keepRunning;
7:     private Font paintFont;
8:     private volatile String timeMsg;
9:     private volatile int arcLen;
10:
11:     public SecondCounterRunnable() {
12:         paintFont = new Font("SansSerif", Font.BOLD, 14);
13:         timeMsg = "never started";
14:         arcLen = 0;
15:     }
16:
17:     public void run() {
18:         runClock();
19:     }
20:
21:     public void runClock() {
22:         DecimalFormat fmt = new DecimalFormat("0.000");
23:         long normalSleepTime = 100;
24:
25:         int counter = 0;
26:         keepRunning = true;
27:
28:         while ( keepRunning ) {
29:             try {
30:                 Thread.sleep(normalSleepTime);
31:             } catch ( InterruptedException x ) {
32:                 // ignore
33:             }
34:
35:             counter++;
36:             double counterSecs = counter / 10.0;
37:
38:             timeMsg = fmt.format(counterSecs);
39:
40:             arcLen = ( ( ( int ) counterSecs ) % 60 ) * 360 / 60;
41:             repaint();
42:         }
43:     }
44:
45:     public void stopClock() {
```

```
46:            keepRunning = false;
47:        }
48:
49:        public void paint(Graphics g) {
50:            g.setColor(Color.black);
51:            g.setFont(paintFont);
52:            g.drawString(timeMsg, 0, 15);
53:
54:            g.fillOval(0, 20, 100, 100);   // black border
55:
56:            g.setColor(Color.white);
57:            g.fillOval(3, 23, 94, 94);   // white for unused portion
58:
59:            g.setColor(Color.blue);   // blue for used portion
60:            g.fillArc(2, 22, 96, 96, 90, -arcLen);
61:        }
62: }
```

Line 5 shows how the new class SecondCounterRunnable is simultaneously both a JComponent and a Runnable:

```
5: public class SecondCounterRunnable
              ➡extends JComponent implements Runnable {
```

This allows it to be added to GUI containers and to have a thread of its own running within it. The requirements of the Runnable interface are met by the run() method (lines 17–19). When the new thread enters run(), it simply invokes the runClock() method where the work of continually updating the component is done. This new thread continues to loop (lines 28–42) every 0.1 seconds until the member variable keepRunning is set to false. This member variable is set to false when another thread (probably the event handling thread) invokes the stopClock() method (lines 45–47).

NOTE

On lines 6, 8, and 9 of Listing 4.3, the modifier volatile is included for some of the member variables. By indicating that a member variable is volatile, you inform the JavaVM that its value might be changed by one thread while being used by another. In this case, one thread is checking keepRunning, and another thread will change its value to false some time after the timer is started. Under certain circumstances, if the variable was not marked as volatile, the while loop would not see the new value and would run the timer forever. This is an important detail often overlooked (even by experienced developers) and is discussed in detail in Chapter 7, "Concurrent Access to Objects and Variables."

Listing 4.4 shows the code for `SecondCounterRunnableMain` to work with `SecondCounterRunnable`.

LISTING 4.4   SecondCounterRunnableMain.java—Supporting Code to Use SecondCounterRunnable

```
 1: import java.awt.*;
 2: import java.awt.event.*;
 3: import javax.swing.*;
 4: import javax.swing.border.*;
 5:
 6: public class SecondCounterRunnableMain extends JPanel {
 7:     private SecondCounterRunnable sc;
 8:     private JButton startB;
 9:     private JButton stopB;
10:
11:     public SecondCounterRunnableMain() {
12:         sc = new SecondCounterRunnable();
13:         startB = new JButton("Start");
14:         stopB = new JButton("Stop");
15:
16:         stopB.setEnabled(false);  // begin with this disabled
17:
18:         startB.addActionListener(new ActionListener() {
19:                 public void actionPerformed(ActionEvent e) {
20:                     // disable to stop more "start" requests
21:                     startB.setEnabled(false);
22:
23:                     // thread to run the counter
24:                     Thread counterThread =
                                    ➥new Thread(sc, "SecondCounter");
25:                     counterThread.start();
26:
27:                     stopB.setEnabled(true);
28:                     stopB.requestFocus();
29:                 }
30:             });
31:
32:         stopB.addActionListener(new ActionListener() {
33:                 public void actionPerformed(ActionEvent e) {
34:                     stopB.setEnabled(false);
35:                     sc.stopClock();
36:                     startB.setEnabled(true);
37:                     startB.requestFocus();
38:                 }
39:             });
40:
41:         JPanel innerButtonP = new JPanel();
```

```
42:         innerButtonP.setLayout(new GridLayout(0, 1, 0, 3));
43:         innerButtonP.add(startB);
44:         innerButtonP.add(stopB);
45:
46:         JPanel buttonP = new JPanel();
47:         buttonP.setLayout(new BorderLayout());
48:         buttonP.add(innerButtonP, BorderLayout.NORTH);
49:
50:         this.setLayout(new BorderLayout(10, 10));
51:         this.setBorder(new EmptyBorder(20, 20, 20, 20));
52:         this.add(buttonP, BorderLayout.WEST);
53:         this.add(sc, BorderLayout.CENTER);
54:     }
55:
56:     public static void main(String[] args) {
57:         SecondCounterRunnableMain scm =
                        ➥new SecondCounterRunnableMain();
58:
59:         JFrame f = new JFrame("Second Counter Runnable");
60:         f.setContentPane(scm);
61:         f.setSize(320, 200);
62:         f.setVisible(true);
63:         f.addWindowListener(new WindowAdapter() {
64:             public void windowClosing(WindowEvent e) {
65:                 System.exit(0);
66:             }
67:         });
68:     }
69: }
```

Aside from the classname changes from `SecondCounterLockup` to `SecondCounterRunnable`, the main difference from the preceding example is what goes on when the Start button is pressed. Just after startup, the application looks the same as before (refer to Figure 4.2), except for the minor detail of the text in the title bar. After the Start button is pressed, the new application looks similar to Figure 4.7.

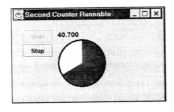

FIGURE 4.7

Approximately 40 seconds after the Start button is pressed while running SecondCounterRunnableMain.

When the Start button is pressed, the `actionPerformed()` method is invoked (lines 19–29) on the anonymous inner subclass of `ActionListener` (line 18). This method is invoked by the JavaVM's event handling thread. In there, the Start button is first disabled (line 21) to prevent any further pressing until the timer is stopped. Next, rather than directly call `runClock()` and tie up the event handling thread, a new `Thread` is instantiated using this constructor:

```
public Thread(Runnable target, String name)
```

A new `Thread` is created passing the reference to the `SecondCounterRunnable` component as the `Runnable target` for the `Thread` object to use (line 24). On this same line, a name for the thread is also passed in: `SecondCounter`. A new thread is spawned by invoking `start()` on this new `Thread` object (line 25). This new thread begins its execution asynchronously. The event handling thread proceeds to enable the Stop button (line 27) and requests that it have the focus (line 28). The event handling thread then returns from `actionPerformed()` and continues on with the business of handling other events as they come up.

Meanwhile, the new thread that was spawned enters the `run()` method of `SecondCounterRunnable` and calls `runClock()`. This newly spawned thread continues to be alive until it finds that `keepRunning` has been set to `false`, at which time it returns from `runClock()`, returns from `run()`, and dies.

When the Stop button is pressed, the other `actionPerformed()` method is invoked (lines 33–38) on the anonymous inner subclass of `ActionListener` (line 32). All event handling methods, including this one, are invoked by the JavaVM's event handling thread. In there, the Stop button is first disabled (line 34) to prevent any further pressing until the timer is restarted. Next, the `stopClock()` method is invoked on the `SecondCounterRunnable` object. In there, the `keepRunning` flag is set to `false` to signal the `while` loop to terminate. The event handling thread returns from `stopClock()` and proceeds to enable the Start button and give it the focus (lines 36 and 37). The event handling thread then returns from `actionPerformed()` and returns to the JavaVM's event queue to wait for new events to occur.

If the Stop button is pressed after approximately 1 minute and 15 seconds have elapsed, the application looks like Figure 4.8.

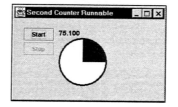

FIGURE 4.8

Stop was pressed after the timer ran for approximately 75 seconds.

Checking the Accuracy of SecondCounter

During every iteration of the while loop of SecondCounterRunnable, a 100ms sleep is used to achieve the 1/10-second delay between each increment of the counter. What about the time it takes to execute the other statements in the loop? Does this cause the timer to be inaccurate? Probably, but is it significantly inaccurate? To find out, the modified class SecondCounterInaccurate, shown in Listing 4.5, keeps checking the system's real-time clock to find out whether the timer is drifting into inaccuracy by any measurable amount.

LISTING 4.5   SecondCounterInaccurate.java—Checking the Timer's Accuracy

```
 1: import java.awt.*;
 2: import javax.swing.*;
 3: import java.text.*;
 4:
 5: public class SecondCounterInaccurate
                     ➥extends JComponent implements Runnable {
 6:     private volatile boolean keepRunning;
 7:     private Font paintFont;
 8:     private volatile String timeMsg;
 9:     private volatile int arcLen;
10:
11:     public SecondCounterInaccurate() {
12:         paintFont = new Font("SansSerif", Font.BOLD, 14);
13:         timeMsg = "never started";
14:         arcLen = 0;
15:     }
16:
17:     public void run() {
18:         runClock();
19:     }
20:
21:     public void runClock() {
22:         DecimalFormat fmt = new DecimalFormat("0.000");
23:         long normalSleepTime = 100;
24:
25:         int counter = 0;
26:         long startTime = System.currentTimeMillis();
27:         keepRunning = true;
28:
29:         while ( keepRunning ) {
30:             try {
```

continues

LISTING 4.5   Continued

```
31:                    Thread.sleep(normalSleepTime);
32:                } catch ( InterruptedException x ) {
33:                    // ignore
34:                }
35:
36:                counter++;
37:                double counterSecs = counter / 10.0;
38:                double elapsedSecs =
39:                    ( System.currentTimeMillis() -
                                          ➥startTime ) / 1000.0;
40:
41:                double diffSecs = counterSecs - elapsedSecs;
42:
43:                timeMsg = fmt.format(counterSecs) + " - " +
44:                        fmt.format(elapsedSecs) + " = " +
45:                        fmt.format(diffSecs);
46:
47:                arcLen = ( ( ( int ) counterSecs ) % 60 ) * 360 / 60;
48:                repaint();
49:            }
50:    }
51:
52:    public void stopClock() {
53:        keepRunning = false;
54:    }
55:
56:    public void paint(Graphics g) {
57:        g.setColor(Color.black);
58:        g.setFont(paintFont);
59:        g.drawString(timeMsg, 0, 15);
60:
61:        g.fillOval(0, 20, 100, 100);   // black border
62:
63:        g.setColor(Color.white);
64:        g.fillOval(3, 23, 94, 94);   // white for unused portion
65:
66:        g.setColor(Color.blue);   // blue for used portion
67:        g.fillArc(2, 22, 96, 96, 90, -arcLen);
68:    }
69: }
```

SecondCounterInacurrate is much the same as SecondCounterRunnable, with just a few
additions to the runClock() method to measure the real time that has elapsed. In runClock(),
before entering the while loop, the current system clock time in milliseconds is captured into a

local variable, startTime (line 26). Each time through the loop, the elapsed time in seconds is calculated based on the system clock and stored into the local variable elapsedSecs (lines 38 and 39). The discrepancy in fractional seconds between the real-time system clock and the iteration count is calculated and stored in the local variable diffSecs (line 41). The text message to be drawn in paint() is expanded to include the formatted elapsedSecs and diffSecs values (lines 43–45).

Listing 4.6 shows the code for SecondCounterInaccurateMain. The only differences between this code and the code for SecondCounterRunnableMain are the changes from using SecondCounterRunnable to SecondCounterInaccurate (lines 6, 7, 11, 12, 57, and 59).

LISTING 4.6   SecondCounterInaccurateMain.java—Code to Use SecondCounterInaccurate

```
 1: import java.awt.*;
 2: import java.awt.event.*;
 3: import javax.swing.*;
 4: import javax.swing.border.*;
 5:
 6: public class SecondCounterInaccurateMain extends JPanel {
 7:     private SecondCounterInaccurate sc;
 8:     private JButton startB;
 9:     private JButton stopB;
10:
11:     public SecondCounterInaccurateMain() {
12:         sc = new SecondCounterInaccurate();
13:         startB = new JButton("Start");
14:         stopB = new JButton("Stop");
15:
16:         stopB.setEnabled(false);   // begin with this disabled
17:
18:         startB.addActionListener(new ActionListener() {
19:             public void actionPerformed(ActionEvent e) {
20:                 // disable to stop more "start" requests
21:                 startB.setEnabled(false);
22:
23:                 // thread to run the counter
24:                 Thread counterThread =
                            ➥new Thread(sc, "SecondCounter");
25:                 counterThread.start();
26:
27:                 stopB.setEnabled(true);
```

continues

LISTING 4.6 Continued

```
28:                              stopB.requestFocus();
29:                  }
30:              });
31:
32:          stopB.addActionListener(new ActionListener() {
33:                  public void actionPerformed(ActionEvent e) {
34:                      stopB.setEnabled(false);
35:                      sc.stopClock();
36:                      startB.setEnabled(true);
37:                      startB.requestFocus();
38:                  }
39:              });
40:
41:          JPanel innerButtonP = new JPanel();
42:          innerButtonP.setLayout(new GridLayout(0, 1, 0, 3));
43:          innerButtonP.add(startB);
44:          innerButtonP.add(stopB);
45:
46:          JPanel buttonP = new JPanel();
47:          buttonP.setLayout(new BorderLayout());
48:          buttonP.add(innerButtonP, BorderLayout.NORTH);
49:
50:          this.setLayout(new BorderLayout(10, 10));
51:          this.setBorder(new EmptyBorder(20, 20, 20, 20));
52:          this.add(buttonP, BorderLayout.WEST);
53:          this.add(sc, BorderLayout.CENTER);
54:      }
55:
56:      public static void main(String[] args) {
57:          SecondCounterInaccurateMain scm =
                      ➥new SecondCounterInaccurateMain();
58:
59:          JFrame f = new JFrame("Second Counter Inaccurate");
60:          f.setContentPane(scm);
61:          f.setSize(320, 200);
62:          f.setVisible(true);
63:          f.addWindowListener(new WindowAdapter() {
64:                  public void windowClosing(WindowEvent e) {
65:                      System.exit(0);
66:                  }
67:              });
68:      }
69: }
```

Figure 4.9 presents three snapshots of `SecondCounterInaccurateMain` running. The first shows that after approximately a minute, the counter is off by 430ms. The second shows that after approximately 2 minutes, the counter is off by almost 1 second. The third shows that after approximately 3 minutes, the gap increased to 1.380 seconds.

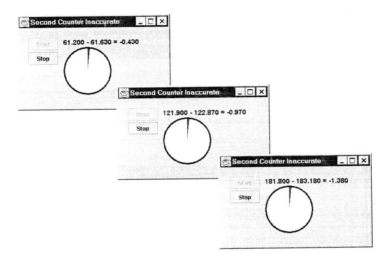

FIGURE 4.9
The timer shows that it falls a bit more behind each minute.

Improving the Accuracy of SecondCounter

Although not many statements exist in the `while` loop, it has been shown that over time, they cause the loop to run significantly more slowly than desired. To improve the accuracy, the sleep time should be varied based on the current system clock time. The final version of `SecondCounter` is simply called `SecondCounter`; its code appears in Listing 4.7.

LISTING 4.7   SecondCounter.java—The Most Accurate Timer

```
1: import java.awt.*;
2: import javax.swing.*;
3: import java.text.*;
4:
5: public class SecondCounter
                ➥extends JComponent implements Runnable {
```

continues

LISTING 4.7 Continued

```
6:      private volatile boolean keepRunning;
7:      private Font paintFont;
8:      private volatile String timeMsg;
9:      private volatile int arcLen;
10:
11:     public SecondCounter() {
12:         paintFont = new Font("SansSerif", Font.BOLD, 14);
13:         timeMsg = "never started";
14:         arcLen = 0;
15:     }
16:
17:     public void run() {
18:         runClock();
19:     }
20:
21:     public void runClock() {
22:         DecimalFormat fmt = new DecimalFormat("0.000");
23:         long normalSleepTime = 100;
24:         long nextSleepTime = normalSleepTime;
25:
26:         int counter = 0;
27:         long startTime = System.currentTimeMillis();
28:         keepRunning = true;
29:
30:         while ( keepRunning ) {
31:             try {
32:                 Thread.sleep(nextSleepTime);
33:             } catch ( InterruptedException x ) {
34:                 // ignore
35:             }
36:
37:             counter++;
38:             double counterSecs = counter / 10.0;
39:             double elapsedSecs =
40:                 ( System.currentTimeMillis() -
                                           ➥ startTime ) / 1000.0;
41:
42:             double diffSecs = counterSecs - elapsedSecs;
43:
44:             nextSleepTime = normalSleepTime +
45:                 ( ( long ) ( diffSecs * 1000.0 ) );
46:
```

```
47:              if ( nextSleepTime < 0 ) {
48:                  nextSleepTime = 0;
49:              }
50:
51:              timeMsg = fmt.format(counterSecs) + " - " +
52:                      fmt.format(elapsedSecs) + " = " +
53:                      fmt.format(diffSecs);
54:
55:              arcLen = ( ( ( int ) counterSecs ) % 60 ) * 360 / 60;
56:              repaint();
57:          }
58:      }
59:
60:      public void stopClock() {
61:          keepRunning = false;
62:      }
63:
64:      public void paint(Graphics g) {
65:          g.setColor(Color.black);
66:          g.setFont(paintFont);
67:          g.drawString(timeMsg, 0, 15);
68:
69:          g.fillOval(0, 20, 100, 100);   // black border
70:
71:          g.setColor(Color.white);
72:          g.fillOval(3, 23, 94, 94);   // white for unused portion
73:
74:          g.setColor(Color.blue);   // blue for used portion
75:          g.fillArc(2, 22, 96, 96, 90, -arcLen);
76:      }
77: }
```

A new local variable named nextSleepTime is used to vary the number of milliseconds to sleep each time through the loop (lines 24 and 32). The nextSleepTime value is recalculated based on the difference between the counter seconds and the system clock seconds (lines 42–45). If this value happens to be less than zero, zero is used instead because it's impossible to sleep for a negative amount of time (lines 47–49).

Listing 4.8 shows the code for SecondCounterMain. The only differences between this code and the code for SecondCounterInaccurateMain are the changes from using SecondCounterInaccurate to SecondCounter (lines 6, 7, 11, 12, 57, and 59).

LISTING 4.8   SecondCounterMain.java—The Supporting Code for SecondCounter

```
 1: import java.awt.*;
 2: import java.awt.event.*;
 3: import javax.swing.*;
 4: import javax.swing.border.*;
 5:
 6: public class SecondCounterMain extends JPanel {
 7:     private SecondCounter sc;
 8:     private JButton startB;
 9:     private JButton stopB;
10:
11:     public SecondCounterMain() {
12:         sc = new SecondCounter();
13:         startB = new JButton("Start");
14:         stopB = new JButton("Stop");
15:
16:         stopB.setEnabled(false);  // begin with this disabled
17:
18:         startB.addActionListener(new ActionListener() {
19:                 public void actionPerformed(ActionEvent e) {
20:                     // disable to stop more "start" requests
21:                     startB.setEnabled(false);
22:
23:                     // thread to run the counter
24:                     Thread counterThread =
                                ➥new Thread(sc, "SecondCounter");
25:                     counterThread.start();
26:
27:                     stopB.setEnabled(true);
28:                     stopB.requestFocus();
29:                 }
30:             });
31:
32:         stopB.addActionListener(new ActionListener() {
33:                 public void actionPerformed(ActionEvent e) {
34:                     stopB.setEnabled(false);
35:                     sc.stopClock();
36:                     startB.setEnabled(true);
37:                     startB.requestFocus();
```

```
38:                    }
39:                });

40:
41:            JPanel innerButtonP = new JPanel();
42:            innerButtonP.setLayout(new GridLayout(0, 1, 0, 3));
43:            innerButtonP.add(startB);
44:            innerButtonP.add(stopB);

45:
46:            JPanel buttonP = new JPanel();
47:            buttonP.setLayout(new BorderLayout());
48:            buttonP.add(innerButtonP, BorderLayout.NORTH);

49:
50:            this.setLayout(new BorderLayout(10, 10));
51:            this.setBorder(new EmptyBorder(20, 20, 20, 20));
52:            this.add(buttonP, BorderLayout.WEST);
53:            this.add(sc, BorderLayout.CENTER);
54:        }

55:
56:    public static void main(String[] args) {
57:        SecondCounterMain scm = new SecondCounterMain();

58:
59:        JFrame f = new JFrame("Second Counter");
60:        f.setContentPane(scm);
61:        f.setSize(320, 200);
62:        f.setVisible(true);
63:        f.addWindowListener(new WindowAdapter() {
64:            public void windowClosing(WindowEvent e) {
65:                System.exit(0);
66:            }
67:        });
68:    }
69: }
```

Figure 4.10 presents three snapshots of the SecondCounterMain application running. The first shows that after approximately a minute, the counter and the actual time are perfectly synchronized. The next snapshot shows that after approximately 2 minutes, the counter is just 40ms ahead. After approximately 3 minutes, the counter time and the actual time are perfectly synchronized again. With this implementation, the SecondCounter continually corrects itself to the system clock, regardless of how quickly or slowly the other code in the loop executes.

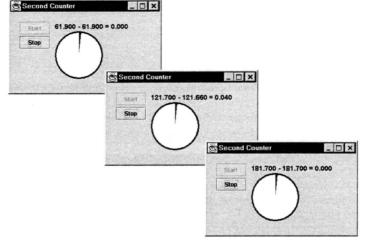

FIGURE 4.10
The timer now stays very close to the accurate time.

Summary

This chapter shows that extending `Thread` is not always an option and that a second way to allow a thread to run within a class is to have it implement `Runnable`. In fact, in most cases, implementing `Runnable` is preferable to extending `Thread`.

Here are a few other lessons learned:

- Do not use the event handling thread to perform long-running tasks; it should be allowed to return to the business of handling events relatively quickly. For the long tasks, use a worker thread. This is critical if a Stop or Cancel Request button exists and could be pressed before the original task completes.

- Proper use of the `volatile` keyword is not trivial and is necessary in many cases to guarantee desired code execution behavior when two or more threads access the same member variable. Chapter 7 explains `volatile` in detail.

- The amount of time it takes to execute even a few statements is not predictable. This time can become significant if the statements are executed over and over in a loop. When accuracy is important, you should check the system clock to see how much real time actually elapsed and then make adjustments accordingly.

Gracefully Stopping Threads

CHAPTER

5

IN THIS CHAPTER

In all the examples presented so far in this book, new threads stop running when they die a natural death by returning from the run() method. At times, a thread may be busy doing some involved task for a while (maybe indefinitely) or perhaps may be sleeping for a long time. Sometimes it is necessary to pause or terminate a thread that is executing a lengthy operation whose duration could not be predetermined because of external dependencies like waiting on I/O or for a signal (notification) from another thread. This chapter explores mechanisms used to suspend, resume, and permanently stop a thread's execution. This is an area where several methods presented in JDK 1.0 and 1.1 have been deprecated in JDK 1.2. I'll offer alternative techniques to virtually eliminate the necessity to use the deprecated methods.

Interrupting a Thread: interrupt()

While one thread is running, another thread can interrupt it by invoking its corresponding Thread object's interrupt() method:

```
public void interrupt()
```

This method simply sets a flag in the destination thread indicating that it has been interrupted and returns right away. It is possible that a SecurityException will be thrown by interrupt(), indicating that the thread requesting the interrupt does not have permission to interrupt the other thread. The security check is done by invoking the checkAccess() method on Thread, which in turn checks whether a SecurityManager has been installed, and if so, invokes its checkAccess(Thread) method. An in-depth exploration of security in Java is beyond the scope of this book, but you should note that some methods of Thread and ThreadGroup could throw SecurityExceptions.

CAUTION

SecurityException is a subclass of RuntimeException, so try/catch blocks are not *required* for any of the methods of Thread or ThreadGroup that might throw it. By default, an application does not have a SecurityManager defined (using JDK 1.0, 1.1, or 1.2 from Sun Microsystems). An applet, on the other hand, *might* have a SecurityManager present.

In general, provisions are not made throughout the code to catch this type of exception, but a general precheck may be done early in the application or applet code. To check whether a SecurityManager is present, use the static method System.getSecurityManager(). If it returns null, a SecurityManager is not installed. If it is *not* null, caution must be used when invoking methods that might throw a SecurityException.

Interrupting a Sleeping Thread

Listing 5.1 shows how you can use interrupt()to disturb a sleeping thread and cause it to throw an InterruptedException.

LISTING 5.1   SleepInterrupt.java—Interrupting a Sleeping Thread

```
 1: public class SleepInterrupt extends Object implements Runnable {
 2:     public void run() {
 3:         try {
 4:             System.out.println(
 5:                     "in run() - about to sleep for 20 seconds");
 6:             Thread.sleep(20000);
 7:             System.out.println("in run() - woke up");
 8:         } catch ( InterruptedException x ) {
 9:             System.out.println(
10:                     "in run() - interrupted while sleeping");
11:             return;
12:         }
13:
14:         System.out.println("in run() - doing stuff after nap");
15:         System.out.println("in run() - leaving normally");
16:     }
17:
18:
19:     public static void main(String[] args) {
20:         SleepInterrupt si = new SleepInterrupt();
21:         Thread t = new Thread(si);
22:         t.start();
23:
24:         // Be sure that the new thread gets a chance to
25:         // run for a while.
26:         try { Thread.sleep(2000); }
27:         catch ( InterruptedException x ) { }
28:
29:         System.out.println(
30:                 "in main() - interrupting other thread");
31:         t.interrupt();
32:         System.out.println("in main() - leaving");
33:     }
34: }
```

When `SleepInterrupt` is run, the following output occurs:

```
in run() - about to sleep for 20 seconds
in main() - interrupting other thread
in main() - leaving
in run() - interrupted while sleeping
```

Note that because of indeterminate thread scheduling, the last two lines might be swapped, but the first two will definitely appear in their current order.

After starting a second thread (line 22), the `main` thread proceeds to sleep for two seconds (line 26) to allow the new thread time to get up and running. The new thread prints its `about to sleep` message (lines 4–5) and proceeds to sleep for 20 seconds (line 6). About two seconds later, the `main` thread signals an interrupt to the new thread (line 31), prints its `leaving` message (line 32), and dies. Because it is interrupted, the new thread's 20-second nap is abruptly stopped, with about 18 seconds remaining, and `sleep()` throws an `InterruptedException` (line 6). Execution jumps ahead to the `catch` block (line 8). The new thread prints its `interrupted` message (lines 9–10), returns right away from `run()` (line 11), and dies.

Pending Interrupts

The `SleepInterrupt` example shows that the implementation of the `sleep()` method is kind enough to stop sleeping and throw an `InterruptedException` if it detects that the sleeping thread is interrupted. Additionally, if an interrupt is *pending* before the `sleep()` method is called, it immediately throws an `InterruptedException`. This is demonstrated in `PendingInterrupt`, shown in Listing 5.2.

LISTING 5.2   PendingInterrupt.java—An Interrupt Can Occur Before It Is Checked For

```
 1: public class PendingInterrupt extends Object {
 2:     public static void main(String[] args) {
 3:         if ( args.length > 0 ) {
 4:             Thread.currentThread().interrupt();
 5:         }
 6:
 7:         long startTime = System.currentTimeMillis();
 8:         try {
 9:             Thread.sleep(2000);
10:             System.out.println("was NOT interrupted");
11:         } catch ( InterruptedException x ) {
12:             System.out.println("was interrupted");
13:         }
14:
```

```
15:          System.out.println(
16:               "elapsedTime=" + ( System.currentTimeMillis() -
                          ⮕ startTime ));
17:     }
18: }
```

If `PendingInterrupt` is run without any command-line arguments, as follows,

```
java PendingInterrupt
```

it produces output much like this:

```
was NOT interrupted
elapsedTime=2080
```

In this mode, it simply sleeps for the specified two seconds and prints out the message that it was not interrupted. Alternatively, if `PendingInterrupt` is run *with* any command-line arguments, as follows,

```
java PendingInterrupt yes
```

it would instead produce output much like this:

```
was interrupted
elapsedTime=110
```

In this mode, the `main` thread interrupts itself (line 4). This does not have any effect other than setting an interrupted flag (which is internal to `Thread`) to `true`. Although interrupted, the `main` thread keeps running. The `main` thread proceeds to make note of the current real-time clock (line 7) and enters the `try` block (line 8). As soon as the `sleep()` is invoked (line 9), it notices that there is a pending interrupt and immediately throws an `InterruptedException`. Execution jumps to the `catch` block (line 11) and prints the message that the thread was interrupted. Finally, the elapsed time is calculated and printed.

Using isInterrupted()

You can check the interrupted status of any thread by invoking the `isInterrupted()` method on the `Thread` object:

```
public boolean isInterrupted()
```

This does not alter the status, but simply returns `true` if the thread has been interrupted and its interrupted flag has not yet been cleared. Listing 5.3 shows an example of how you can use `isInterrupted()`.

LISTING 5.3   InterruptCheck.java—Using isInterrupted()

```
 1: public class InterruptCheck extends Object {
 2:     public static void main(String[] args) {
 3:         Thread t = Thread.currentThread();
 4:         System.out.println("Point A: t.isInterrupted()=" +
                                    ➡ t.isInterrupted());
 5:         t.interrupt();
 6:         System.out.println("Point B: t.isInterrupted()=" +
                                    ➡ t.isInterrupted());
 7:         System.out.println("Point C: t.isInterrupted()=" +
                                    ➡ t.isInterrupted());
 8:
 9:         try {
10:             Thread.sleep(2000);
11:             System.out.println("was NOT interrupted");
12:         } catch ( InterruptedException x ) {
13:             System.out.println("was interrupted");
14:         }
15:
16:         System.out.println("Point D: t.isInterrupted()=" +
                                    ➡ t.isInterrupted());
17:     }
18: }
```

Running `InterruptCheck` produces the following output:

```
Point A: t.isInterrupted()=false
Point B: t.isInterrupted()=true
Point C: t.isInterrupted()=true
was interrupted
Point D: t.isInterrupted()=false
```

Initially, at Point A, the interrupted status is `false` (line 4), and it is set to `true` by invoking `interrupt()` (line 5). As a result, at Point B, `isInterrupted()` now returns `true` (line 6). At Point C, `isInterrupted()` still returns `true` and is unaffected by a previous call. Because the interrupted flag is `true`, `sleep()` immediately throws an `InterruptedException` (line 10). Execution jumps to the `catch` and prints a message indicating that the thread was interrupted (line 13). Finally, at Point D, `isInterrupted()` returns `false` because the interrupted flag was cleared by `sleep()` when it threw the exception.

Using Thread.interrupted()

You can use the `Thread.interrupted()` method to check (and implicitly reset to `false`) the interrupted status of the current thread:

```
public static boolean interrupted()
```

Because it is `static`, it cannot be invoked on a particular thread, but can only report the interrupted status of the thread that invoked it. This method returns `true` if the thread has been interrupted and its interrupted flag has not yet been cleared. Unlike `isInterrupted()`, it automatically resets the interrupted flag to `false`. Invoking `Thread.interrupted()` a second time would always return `false` unless the thread was reinterrupted. Listing 5.4 shows an example of how you can use `Thread.interrupted()`.

LISTING 5.4 InterruptReset.java—Using Thread.interrupted()

```
 1: public class InterruptReset extends Object {
 2:     public static void main(String[] args) {
 3:         System.out.println(
 4:             "Point X: Thread.interrupted()=" +
                  ➥ Thread.interrupted());
 5:         Thread.currentThread().interrupt();
 6:         System.out.println(
 7:             "Point Y: Thread.interrupted()=" +
                  ➥ Thread.interrupted());
 8:         System.out.println(
 9:             "Point Z: Thread.interrupted()=" +
                  ➥ Thread.interrupted());
10:     }
11: }
```

Running `InterruptReset` produces the following output:

```
Point X: Thread.interrupted()=false
Point Y: Thread.interrupted()=true
Point Z: Thread.interrupted()=false
```

Initially, at Point X, the interrupted status is `false` (lines 3–4). The current thread interrupts itself on line 5. At Point Y, the interrupted status is `true` and is automatically reset back to `false` by `Thread.interrupted()` (lines 6–7). The final check of the status at Point Z shows that it is indeed `false` again (lines 8–9).

Using InterruptedException

A method such as `Thread.sleep()` is kind enough to stop sleeping and throw an `InterruptedException` if it is interrupted. Another method commonly used in multithreaded programming is the `wait()` method of `Object`. It is involved with inter-thread communication and is covered in detail in Chapter 8, "Inter-thread Communication." Like `Thread.sleep()`, it, too, throws an `InterruptedException` if interrupted. Many other methods in the JDK will throw an `InterruptedException` if the thread that entered the method is interrupted before completing its work.

The pattern of throwing an `InterruptedException` when interrupted by another thread is a useful one to extend to other customized methods. For example, imagine that you need a method that performs a complex and long-running calculation. It would be nice if the calculation occasionally checked whether it had been interrupted and if it had, threw an `InterruptedException` to stop the calculation and indicate that it did not complete normally.

Listing 5.5 shows an example of how the interrupted status can be checked and used to throw an `InterruptedException` if necessary. When run, the class `PiInterrupt` proceeds to iterate continuously to calculate the special number pi until the desired level of accuracy is achieved—or until it is interrupted.

LISTING 5.5 PiInterrupt.java—Throwing InterruptedException When Necessary

```
 1: public class PiInterrupt extends Object implements Runnable {
 2:     private double latestPiEstimate;
 3:
 4:     public void run() {
 5:         try {
 6:             System.out.println("for comparison, Math.PI=" +
 7:                             Math.PI);
 8:             calcPi(0.000000001);
 9:             System.out.println("within accuracy, latest pi=" +
10:                             latestPiEstimate);
11:         } catch ( InterruptedException x ) {
12:             System.out.println("INTERRUPTED!! latest pi=" +
13:                             latestPiEstimate);
14:         }
15:     }
16:
17:     private void calcPi(double accuracy)
18:                 throws InterruptedException {
19:
20:         latestPiEstimate = 0.0;
21:         long iteration = 0;
22:         int sign = -1;
23:
24:         while ( Math.abs(latestPiEstimate - Math.PI) >
25:                 accuracy ) {
26:
27:             if ( Thread.interrupted() ) {
28:                 throw new InterruptedException();
29:             }
30:
31:             iteration++;
```

```
32:                sign = -sign;
33:                latestPiEstimate +=
34:                    sign * 4.0 / ( ( 2 * iteration ) - 1 );
35:            }
36:        }
37:
38:        public static void main(String[] args) {
39:            PiInterrupt pi = new PiInterrupt();
40:            Thread t = new Thread(pi);
41:            t.start();
42:
43:            try {
44:                Thread.sleep(10000);
45:                t.interrupt();
46:            } catch ( InterruptedException x ) {
47:                // ignore
48:            }
49:        }
50: }
```

In the main thread, a new `PiInterrupt` instance is constructed (line 39). Because `PiInterrupt` implements `Runnable`, an instance of it can be passed to the constructor for `Thread` (line 40). The new `Thread` object is started (line 41). The main thread then proceeds to sleep for 10 seconds (line 44) before interrupting the thread running inside `PiInterrupt`.

While the `main` thread is sleeping, the newly spawned thread enters the `run()` method (line 4). For comparison purposes, it prints out the value of pi held as a constant in the `Math` class (lines 6–7). It then proceeds to call `calcPi()`, specifying that it should continue to refine its calculation until it is within 0.000000001 of the constant `Math.PI` (line 8).

The `private` method `calcPi()` declares that it might throw an `InterruptedException` (line 18). It will do this if interrupted before getting within the specified accuracy. The technique used to calculate pi is to sum the terms of the infinite series

```
pi = 4/1 - 4/3 + 4/5 - 4/7 + 4/9 - 4/11 + 4/13 - 4/15 ...
```

for as long as necessary to get within the specified accuracy. The `while` loop continues as long as the absolute value of the difference between the calculated pi and the constant stored in `Math.PI` differ more than the desired accuracy (lines 24–25). Each time through the loop, the interrupted flag is checked and reset to `false` (line 27). If the flag was `true` before being reset, an `InterruptedException` is thrown (line 28) and the method stops calculating. If the flag was `false` before being reset, the estimate is further refined (lines 31–34) and the `while` loop continues.

If the desired accuracy is reached before the interrupt, flow returns to `run()`, and the estimated pi value is printed (lines 9–10). If the thread is interrupted before reaching the desired accuracy, the exception is thrown and flow jumps to the `catch` block (line 11) where the estimate pi value is printed (lines 12–13).

When `PiInterrupt` is run, output such as the following should be produced:

```
for comparison, Math.PI=3.141592653589793
INTERRUPTED!! latest pi=3.141592091246143
```

In this case, the calculation took too long and was interrupted after 10 seconds. If your machine is fast enough to get within the accuracy before 10 seconds has elapsed, reduce the sleep time (by perhaps 2 seconds), recompile, and run it again.

TIP

In long-running methods, consider using this technique of checking the interrupted status and throwing an `InterruptedException` when necessary. It is a nice way of allowing a long-running method to be "cancelled" by another thread.

Suspending and Resuming Thread Execution

Sometimes you might want to temporarily pause or suspend an executing thread and at a later time let it resume execution. As an example, consider a program that uses a thread to animate some images by flipping through them sequentially. When the animated window is not visible (minimized or covered by another window), there isn't any necessity to continue doing the work of animation until the window is visible again. In fact, continuing to animate the images when no one can see them is wasting valuable processor cycles. I'm sure that you will come across many other situations in which a thread should *temporarily* stop its work.

Using the Deprecated Methods suspend() and resume()

The `Thread` API contains two *deprecated* methods that are used to temporarily stop and later restart a thread:

```
public final void suspend()
public final void resume()
```

Although these methods are deprecated and shouldn't be used in new code, I'll show you an example of their use in case you inherit some older code that you have to maintain. The code for the class `VisualSuspendResume` is shown in Listing 5.6.

<table>
<tr><td>TIP</td><td></td></tr>
</table>

Methods and classes are deprecated by Sun Microsystems to indicate that developers should avoid using them. A deprecated method can still be used, but when the code is compiled, a warning is issued. Deprecation is used to indicate a method or class is obsolete or dangerous and may be removed from future releases of the JDK. Although you may still use deprecated methods, you should use them sparingly and only when absolutely necessary.

LISTING 5.6   VisualSuspendResume.java—Suspending and Resuming Animation Using the Deprecated Methods

```
 1: import java.awt.*;
 2: import java.awt.event.*;
 3: import javax.swing.*;
 4:
 5: public class VisualSuspendResume
 6:             extends JPanel
 7:             implements Runnable {
 8:
 9:     private static final String[] symbolList =
10:         { "|", "/", "-", "\\", "|", "/", "-", "\\" };
11:
12:     private Thread runThread;
13:     private JTextField symbolTF;
14:
15:     public VisualSuspendResume() {
16:         symbolTF = new JTextField();
17:         symbolTF.setEditable(false);
18:         symbolTF.setFont(new Font("Monospaced", Font.BOLD, 26));
19:         symbolTF.setHorizontalAlignment(JTextField.CENTER);
20:
21:         final JButton suspendB = new JButton("Suspend");
22:         final JButton resumeB = new JButton("Resume");
23:
24:         suspendB.addActionListener(new ActionListener() {
25:                 public void actionPerformed(ActionEvent e) {
26:                     suspendNow();
27:                 }
28:             });
29:
```

continues

LISTING 5.6   Continued

```
30:            resumeB.addActionListener(new ActionListener() {
31:                    public void actionPerformed(ActionEvent e) {
32:                        resumeNow();
33:                    }
34:                });
35:
36:            JPanel innerStackP = new JPanel();
37:            innerStackP.setLayout(new GridLayout(0, 1, 3, 3));
38:            innerStackP.add(symbolTF);
39:            innerStackP.add(suspendB);
40:            innerStackP.add(resumeB);
41:
42:            this.setLayout(new FlowLayout(FlowLayout.CENTER));
43:            this.add(innerStackP);
44:        }
45:
46:        private void suspendNow() {
47:            if ( runThread != null ) { // avoid NullPointerException
48:                runThread.suspend();
49:            }
50:        }
51:
52:        private void resumeNow() {
53:            if ( runThread != null ) { // avoid NullPointerException
54:                runThread.resume();
55:            }
56:        }
57:
58:        public void run() {
59:            try {
60:                // Store this for the suspendNow() and
61:                // resumeNow() methods to use.
62:                runThread = Thread.currentThread();
63:                int count = 0;
64:
65:                while ( true ) {
66:                    // each time through, show the next symbol
67:                    symbolTF.setText(
68:                        symbolList[ count % symbolList.length ]);
69:                    Thread.sleep(200);
70:                    count++;
71:                }
72:            } catch ( InterruptedException x ) {
73:                // ignore
```

```
74:        } finally {
75:            // The thread is about to die, make sure that the
76:            // reference to it is also lost.
77:            runThread = null;
78:        }
79:    }
80:
81:    public static void main(String[] args) {
82:        VisualSuspendResume vsr = new VisualSuspendResume();
83:        Thread t = new Thread(vsr);
84:        t.start();
85:
86:        JFrame f = new JFrame("Visual Suspend Resume");
87:        f.setContentPane(vsr);
88:        f.setSize(320, 200);
89:        f.setVisible(true);
90:        f.addWindowListener(new WindowAdapter() {
91:                public void windowClosing(WindowEvent e) {
92:                    System.exit(0);
93:                }
94:            });
95:    }
96: }
```

The VisualSuspendResume class subclasses JPanel and allows a thread to be run within it by implementing the Runnable interface (lines 5–7). A noneditable JTextField is created (lines 16–19) and used to sequentially display each character defined in the set of symbols (lines 9–10). The symbols are displayed in a continuous loop to create the illusion of a line spinning about its center in a clockwise rotation. A Suspend button is added that calls suspendNow() when clicked (lines 21 and 24–28). A Resume button is also added that calls resumeNow() when clicked (lines 22 and 30–34). These three components are stacked vertically in the panel (lines 36–43).

When a new thread enters run(), a reference to it is stored in runThread (line 62). Regardless of how the thread leaves the try block (lines 59–71), it will enter the finally block and set the runThread reference back to null (lines 74–78). This reference is used by suspendNow() and resumeNow() to control the thread.

As long as the thread is not suspended, it continues to execute the statements in the infinite while loop (lines 65–71). Each time through the loop, the next symbol is retrieved from the list, and the JTextField is updated through the setText() method (lines 67–68). After the thread sleeps for a bit (line 69), count is incremented (line 70) in preparation for retrieving the next symbol in the cycle.

When the Suspend button is clicked and the suspendNow() method is called, the thread pointed to by runThread is suspended (line 48). If runThread is not currently set, the request is simply ignored (line 47). Similarly, when the Resume button is clicked, resumeNow() is invoked and executes the resume() method of the Thread object (line 54) for the thread currently inside run().

Figure 5.1 shows a snapshot of how VisualSuspendResume looks when running.

FIGURE 5.1

A screen shot of VisualSuspendResume while running.

When you run this code, notice how the spinner stops when Suspend is clicked and how it starts again when Resume is clicked. Also note that clicking Suspend several times in a row has no adverse effects. It does no harm to suspend a thread that is already suspended. Likewise, clicking Resume several times in a row is also fine. It does no harm to resume a thread that is currently running.

The suspend() method is deprecated as of JDK 1.2 because if a thread is suspended at an inopportune time—such as when it is holding a lock for a shared resource—a deadlock condition may result. I explain and demonstrate deadlocks in Chapter 7, "Concurrent Access to Objects and Variables," but let it suffice to say for now that a deadlock is a very bad thing and can cause a program to freeze up on a user. Even when locks are not involved, a thread might be suspended while in the middle of a long procedure that really should not be left in a partially completed state. The resume() method is deprecated because without any use of suspend(), it is not needed.

TIP

Although suspend() and resume() are not deprecated in JDK 1.0 and 1.1, they should *not* be used for the same good reasons that they are deprecated in JDK 1.2. Alternative techniques to very closely simulate and safely replace the functionality of suspend() and resume() are presented next.

Suspending at a Bad Time

Although suspending a thread while it is holding a lock on a shared resource can be disastrous, suspending it while it's in the middle of long-running computation can also lead to problems. The sample class DeprecatedSuspendResume, shown in Listing 5.7, slows things down with some sleeps to make a thread more likely to be suspended at an inopportune time.

LISTING 5.7 DeprecatedSuspendResume.java—An Example of Suspension at a Bad Time

```
1: public class DeprecatedSuspendResume
2:         extends Object
3:         implements Runnable {
4:
5:     private volatile int firstVal;
6:     private volatile int secondVal;
7:
8:     public boolean areValuesEqual() {
9:         return ( firstVal == secondVal );
10:     }
11:
12:     public void run() {
13:         try {
14:             firstVal = 0;
15:             secondVal = 0;
16:             workMethod();
17:         } catch ( InterruptedException x ) {
18:             System.out.println(
19:                     "interrupted while in workMethod()");
20:         }
21:     }
22:
23:     private void workMethod() throws InterruptedException {
24:         int val = 1;
25:
26:         while ( true ) {
27:             stepOne(val);
28:             stepTwo(val);
29:             val++;
30:
31:             Thread.sleep(200);  // pause before looping again
32:         }
```

continues

LISTING 5.7   Continued

```
33:     }
34:
35:     private void stepOne(int newVal)
36:             throws InterruptedException {
37:
38:         firstVal = newVal;
39:         Thread.sleep(300);   // simulate some other long process
40:     }
41:
42:     private void stepTwo(int newVal) {
43:         secondVal = newVal;
44:     }
45:
46:     public static void main(String[] args) {
47:         DeprecatedSuspendResume dsr =
48:                 new DeprecatedSuspendResume();
49:         Thread t = new Thread(dsr);
50:         t.start();
51:
52:         // let the other thread get going and run for a while
53:         try { Thread.sleep(1000); }
54:         catch ( InterruptedException x ) { }
55:
56:         for ( int i = 0; i < 10; i++ ) {
57:             t.suspend();
58:             System.out.println("dsr.areValuesEqual()=" +
59:                                 dsr.areValuesEqual());
60:             t.resume();
61:             try {
62:                 // Pause for a random amount of time
63:                 // between 0 and 2 seconds.
64:                 Thread.sleep(
65:                         ( long ) (Math.random() * 2000.0) );
66:             } catch ( InterruptedException x ) {
67:                 // ignore
68:             }
69:         }
70:
71:         System.exit(0); // abruptly terminate application
72:     }
73: }
```

In main(), a new DeprecatedSuspendResume object is instantiated and a new thread is spawned to run it (lines 47–50). The main thread pauses for a second to let the new thread get up and running (line 53).

The newly spawned thread begins execution in run() (line 12) and then enters a try/catch block that catches any InterruptedException that might be thrown (lines 13–20). After making sure that both values are initially set to zero (lines 14–15), run() invokes workMethod(). In workMethod(), val is initially set to 1, incremented each time through the while loop, and passed as a parameter to both stepOne() and stepTwo(). In stepOne() (lines 35–40), firstVal is assigned its new value (line 38), and then a sleep() is used to simulate some other task that takes some time to execute (line 39). In stepTwo() (lines 42–44), secondVal is assigned its new value, and then it immediately returns (line 43). Back in workMethod(), a sleep() is used to slow things down before looping again (line 31).

Trouble arises when the new thread is suspended *after* it has set firstVal, but *before* it has set secondVal. Meanwhile, the main thread enters the for loop (lines 56–69). Each time through, the new thread is suspended (line 57) to check whether firstVal and secondVal are equal (lines 58–59). After the check, the thread is allowed to resume execution (line 60). The main thread then sleeps for a random amount of time between 0.0 and 2.0 seconds (lines 61–68) before jumping back up to the for. After 10 iterations, System.exit() is used to terminate all threads and exit the VM (line 71).

When this DeprecatedSuspendResume is run, output something like the following sample should be produced (your output will differ somewhat):

```
dsr.areValuesEqual()=true
dsr.areValuesEqual()=false
dsr.areValuesEqual()=false
dsr.areValuesEqual()=false
dsr.areValuesEqual()=true
dsr.areValuesEqual()=true
dsr.areValuesEqual()=false
dsr.areValuesEqual()=true
dsr.areValuesEqual()=true
dsr.areValuesEqual()=false
```

Notice that the value returned from areValuesEqual() is sometimes true and sometimes false. It is false when the new thread is suspended some time after stepOne() is called and before stepTwo() is completed. This is a bad time for the suspension to occur, but it cannot be avoided because the thread has no control over when its suspend method is called.

Suspending and Resuming Without Deprecated Methods

The method suspend() may be invoked on a particular thread at any time. In most programs, there are typically times when a thread is holding a lock or is in the middle of a long-running calculation and should not be suspended. In fact, suspending a thread while it is holding a lock can easily lead to a deadlock condition. Also, the suspend() and resume() methods have been wisely deprecated in the most recent JDK. In spite of all these reasons not to use suspend(), there are still situations where a thread's activities should be temporarily suspended. The AlternateSuspendResume class shown in Listing 5.8 demonstrates another way to achieve this.

LISTING 5.8   AlternateSuspendResume.java—Avoiding the Use of suspend() and resume()

```
 1: public class AlternateSuspendResume
 2:         extends Object
 3:         implements Runnable {
 4:
 5:     private volatile int firstVal;
 6:     private volatile int secondVal;
 7:     private volatile boolean suspended;
 8:
 9:     public boolean areValuesEqual() {
10:         return ( firstVal == secondVal );
11:     }
12:
13:     public void run() {
14:         try {
15:             suspended = false;
16:             firstVal = 0;
17:             secondVal = 0;
18:             workMethod();
19:         } catch ( InterruptedException x ) {
20:             System.out.println(
21:                 "interrupted while in workMethod()");
22:         }
23:     }
24:
25:     private void workMethod() throws InterruptedException {
26:         int val = 1;
27:
28:         while ( true ) {
29:             // blocks only if suspended is true
30:             waitWhileSuspended();
31:
32:             stepOne(val);
```

```
33:             stepTwo(val);
34:             val++;
35:
36:             // blocks only if suspended is true
37:             waitWhileSuspended();
38:
39:             Thread.sleep(200);   // pause before looping again
40:         }
41:     }
42:
43:     private void stepOne(int newVal)
44:                     throws InterruptedException {
45:
46:         firstVal = newVal;
47:
48:         // simulate some other lengthy process
49:         Thread.sleep(300);
50:     }
51:
52:     private void stepTwo(int newVal) {
53:         secondVal = newVal;
54:     }
55:
56:     public void suspendRequest() {
57:         suspended = true;
58:     }
59:
60:     public void resumeRequest() {
61:         suspended = false;
62:     }
63:
64:     private void waitWhileSuspended()
65:                     throws InterruptedException {
66:
67:         // This is an example of a "busy wait" technique.  It is
68:         // not the best way to wait for a condition to change
69:         // because it continually requires some processor
70:         // cycles to perform the checks.  A better technique
71:         // is to use Java's built-in wait-notify mechanism.
72:         while ( suspended ) {
73:             Thread.sleep(200);
74:         }
75:     }
```

continues

LISTING 5.8   Continued

```
76:
77:       public static void main(String[] args) {
78:           AlternateSuspendResume asr =
79:                   new AlternateSuspendResume();
80:
81:           Thread t = new Thread(asr);
82:           t.start();
83:
84:           // let the other thread get going and run for a while
85:           try { Thread.sleep(1000); }
86:           catch ( InterruptedException x ) { }
87:
88:           for ( int i = 0; i < 10; i++ ) {
89:               asr.suspendRequest();
90:
91:               // Give the thread a chance to notice the
92:               // suspension request.
93:               try { Thread.sleep(350); }
94:               catch ( InterruptedException x ) { }
95:
96:               System.out.println("dsr.areValuesEqual()=" +
97:                       asr.areValuesEqual());
98:
99:               asr.resumeRequest();
100:
101:              try {
102:                  // Pause for a random amount of time
103:                  // between 0 and 2 seconds.
104:                  Thread.sleep(
105:                          ( long ) (Math.random() * 2000.0) );
106:              } catch ( InterruptedException x ) {
107:                  // ignore
108:              }
109:          }
110:
111:          System.exit(0); // abruptly terminate application
112:      }
113: }
```

A new `volatile` member variable `suspended` is added (line 7) to keep track of a request to have the internal thread temporarily stop processing. This flag is initially `false` (line 15) in the beginning of `run()`. It is set to `true` every time the `suspendRequest()` method (lines 56–58) is invoked. It is set back to `false` every time `resumeRequest()` (lines 60–62) is invoked. The current value of suspended is checked in `waitWhileSuspended()` (lines 64–75), and if `true`, it will check (line 72) five times per second (every 200 milliseconds) to see whether the value has changed. Calls to `waitWhileSuspended()` do not return until suspended is `false`. If suspended was already `false`, calls return right away.

The loop inside `waitWhileSuspended()` is performing a *busy wait*. That is, the thread sleeps briefly between checks, but uses up processor cycles repeatedly performing these checks. If the sleep interval is reduced, even more processor resources are wasted. If the sleep interval is increased, it will be longer (on average) before it *notices* a change in the monitored value. (Later in this chapter, the class `BestReplacement` uses the wait/notify mechanism instead of a busy wait to provide the same functionality more efficiently.)

> **TIP**
>
> Busy waits are wasteful of processor resources and should be avoided. Using Java's wait/notify mechanism is a much better design decision in most cases. I'll show you how to use this mechanism in Chapter 8.

You can see that `waitWhileSuspended()` is invoked twice within the `while` loop of `workMethod()` (lines 30 and 37). Both these times, it would be all right for the thread to be suspended for a while. If it has not been suspended, these calls return right away.

> **TIP**
>
> If there is more than one safe place to suspend a thread in your code, you should add more `waitWhileSuspended()` method calls to all the safe places. Just make sure that you don't allow suspensions while holding a lock! Calls to `waitWhileSuspended()` should be done frequently to help the thread respond quickly to a suspend request. At the same time, keep in mind that invoking `waitWhileSuspended()` uses some processor resources, so don't use it *too* frequently. I'll provide you with a detailed explanation of locks in Chapter 7, "Concurrent Access to Objects and Variables."

In the `main()` method, instead of invoking `suspend()` on the `Thread` object, the `suspendRequest()` method is invoked on the `AlternateSuspendResume` object (line 89). As the name implies, this is only a *request* that the internal thread temporarily pause. It will continue to run until the next time that it calls `waitWhileSuspended()`, allowing any partially completed tasks to finish. After putting in the request, the `main` thread sleeps for 350 milliseconds (line 93) to allow the new thread enough time to get to its next `waitWhileSuspended()` call. The `areValuesEqual()` results are printed (lines 96–97), and then the `resumeRequest()` method is called (line 99) to signal the new thread that it can now return from `waitWhileSuspended()`.

When `AlternateSuspendResume` is run, output looks like this (your output should match):

```
dsr.areValuesEqual()=true
dsr.areValuesEqual()=true
dsr.areValuesEqual()=true
dsr.areValuesEqual()=true
dsr.areValuesEqual()=true
dsr.areValuesEqual()=true
dsr.areValuesEqual()=true
dsr.areValuesEqual()=true
dsr.areValuesEqual()=true
dsr.areValuesEqual()=true
```

The only way that it would not find values equal would be if `suspendRequest()` had been called by the `main` thread, and the internal thread had not yet called `waitWhileSuspended()`. The 350-millisecond sleep used before checking the values should be adequate in this case. If you need to be sure that the internal thread has entered `waitWhileSuspended()` before taking some sort of action, you could introduce another `boolean` member variable that is `true` only while the internal thread is inside `waitWhileSuspended()`. In the `BestReplacement` class at the end of this chapter, I will show you a way that this can be done.

This new way of suspending and resuming thread execution via requests is far safer than having a thread directly and abruptly suspended via the `suspend()` method of `Thread`.

Stopping a Thread

A thread is considered to be alive from just after the `start()` method of `Thread` is invoked until it dies. A thread may die by returning from `run()`—which is the case in the examples so far. A thread may also die when the `stop()` method of `Thread` is invoked. Like `suspend()` and `resume()`, `stop()` has been deprecated as of JDK 1.2.

Using the Deprecated Method stop()

At times, one of the additional threads spawned in a multithreaded program is no longer needed, but it continues to execute statements—perhaps in an infinite loop. The `Thread` API includes a `stop()` method to abruptly terminate a thread's execution:

```
public final void stop()
```

When this method is invoked on a thread, the thread immediately throws a
java.lang.ThreadDeath error (a subclass of java.lang.Error, which itself is a subclass of
java.lang.Throwable). This exception propagates up the method call stack, executing any
finally clauses present and releasing any locks that are currently held. Ultimately, this exception causes run() to abruptly return, and the thread dies.

The class DeprecatedStop, in Listing 5.9, shows a very simple example of how to use stop().

LISTING 5.9   DeprecatedStop.java—An Example Using the Deprecated stop() Method

```
 1: public class DeprecatedStop extends Object implements Runnable {
 2:
 3:     public void run() {
 4:         int count = 0;
 5:
 6:         while ( true ) {
 7:             System.out.println("Running ... count=" + count);
 8:             count++;
 9:
10:             try {
11:                 Thread.sleep(300);
12:             } catch ( InterruptedException x ) {
13:                 // ignore
14:             }
15:         }
16:     }
17:
18:
19:     public static void main(String[] args) {
20:         DeprecatedStop ds = new DeprecatedStop();
21:         Thread t = new Thread(ds);
22:         t.start();
23:
24:         try {
25:             Thread.sleep(2000);
26:         } catch ( InterruptedException x ) {
27:             // ignore
28:         }
29:
30:         // Abruptly stop the other thread in its tracks!
31:         t.stop();
32:     }
33: }
```

The `main` thread creates a new `DeprecatedStop` object (line 20) and a new `Thread` object (line 21) and starts the thread running (line 22). It then sleeps for two seconds while the new thread runs.

The new thread runs an infinite `while` loop (lines 6–15). In this loop, it prints a message with the latest `count` (line 7), increments `count`, and then sleeps for 300 milliseconds. This is done until the thread is stopped.

Back in the `main()` method, the `main` thread wakes up after its 2-second nap and abruptly stops the new thread (line 31).

When run, it produces the following output (your output should match):

```
Running ... count=0
Running ... count=1
Running ... count=2
Running ... count=3
Running ... count=4
Running ... count=5
Running ... count=6
```

The `stop()` method is deprecated as of JDK 1.2 because it can lead to corrupted data in objects. One problem is that when a thread is stopped abruptly, there is little opportunity to perform any cleanup work. Another problem is that when `stop()` is invoked on a thread, the thread releases all the locks it is currently holding. The locks are definitely being held for a good reason—probably to keep other threads from accessing data elements that are not yet in a consistent state. This sudden release of the locks may leave some data in some objects in an inconsistent state with no warning about the possible corruption. In many cases, there are other ways to have a thread return from `run()` in an orderly manner that leaves all objects in a consistent state.

TIP

Although `stop()` is not deprecated in JDK 1.0 and 1.1, it should *not* be used for the same good reasons that it is deprecated in JDK 1.2. Alternative techniques to very closely simulate and safely replace the functionality of `stop()` are presented next.

An Alternative to stop()

As an alternative to directly stopping a thread, a `boolean` indicator variable can be used to determine whether the thread should continue processing. In conjunction with this, the `interrupt()` method can be used to signal the thread that it should take a different course of action. Earlier in this chapter, the class `PiInterrupt` (refer to Listing 5.5) uses `interrupt()` to signal the new thread that it should stop refining its calculation and bail out.

The class `AlternateStop`, in Listing 5.10, shows how `interrupt()` and a boolean indicator can be used together to get a thread to safely stop.

LISTING 5.10   AlternateStop.java—Using interrupt() and a boolean Flag to Safely Stop a Thread

```
 1: public class AlternateStop extends Object implements Runnable {
 2:     private volatile boolean stopRequested;
 3:     private Thread runThread;
 4:
 5:     public void run() {
 6:         runThread = Thread.currentThread();
 7:         stopRequested = false;
 8:
 9:         int count = 0;
10:
11:         while ( !stopRequested ) {
12:             System.out.println("Running ... count=" + count);
13:             count++;
14:
15:             try {
16:                 Thread.sleep(300);
17:             } catch ( InterruptedException x ) {
18:                 Thread.currentThread().interrupt(); // reassert
19:             }
20:         }
21:     }
22:
23:     public void stopRequest() {
24:         stopRequested = true;
25:
26:         if ( runThread != null ) {
27:             runThread.interrupt();
28:         }
29:     }
30:
31:     public static void main(String[] args) {
32:         AlternateStop as = new AlternateStop();
33:         Thread t = new Thread(as);
34:         t.start();
35:
```

continues

LISTING 5.10 Continued

```
36:             try {
37:                 Thread.sleep(2000);
38:             } catch ( InterruptedException x ) {
39:                 // ignore
40:             }
41:
42:             as.stopRequest();
43:         }
44: }
```

In main(), a new thread is spawned (lines 32–34) to run inside an AlternateStop instance. The main thread then sleeps for two seconds to let the new thread run (lines 36–40).

The volatile member variable stopRequested (line 2) is used as the flag to indicate whether the thread should continue to run. The member variable runThread (line 3) is used to keep a reference to the thread that is currently running inside run().

When run() is invoked, the current thread is stored in runThread (line 6) for later use, and stopRequested is set to false. The while loop (lines 11–20) continues until stopRequested is true. Inside the while loop, any time a InterruptedException might be thrown, it should be caught (line 17) and reasserted (line 18). The interrupt flag should be reasserted in case any other statements yet to be executed in the loop have to be interrupted (in this example, it doesn't apply, but it's a good habit to get into). If there were more interruptible statements like sleep() or wait(), they would not throw an InterruptedException unless the interrupt had been reasserted. You do want them to throw an InterruptedException right away because the thread has been signaled to clean up and die.

Back in the main thread, after the two-second nap, the stopRequest() method of AlternateStop is invoked (line 42) to put in a *request* that the new thread die as soon as possible. When stopRequest() is invoked, stopRequested is set to true (line 24), and the thread that is running inside run() is interrupted (line 27).

When run, it produces the following output (your output should match):

```
Running ... count=0
Running ... count=1
Running ... count=2
Running ... count=3
Running ... count=4
Running ... count=5
Running ... count=6
```

The Best Replacement for stop(), suspend(), and resume()

The class BestReplacement presented in Listing 5.11 combines some techniques from other chapters to create a model class that effectively eliminates the need for the three deprecated methods stop(), suspend(), and resume().

LISTING 5.11   BestReplacement.java—Combined Alternative Techniques

```
 1: // uses BooleanLock from chapter 17
 2:
 3: public class BestReplacement extends Object {
 4:     private Thread internalThread;
 5:     private volatile boolean stopRequested;
 6:
 7:     private BooleanLock suspendRequested;
 8:     private BooleanLock internalThreadSuspended;
 9:
10:     public BestReplacement() {
11:         stopRequested = false;
12:
13:         suspendRequested = new BooleanLock(false);
14:         internalThreadSuspended = new BooleanLock(false);
15:
16:         Runnable r = new Runnable() {
17:                 public void run() {
18:                     try {
19:                         runWork();
20:                     } catch ( Exception x ) {
21:                         // in case ANY exception slips through
22:                         x.printStackTrace();
23:                     }
24:                 }
25:             };
26:
27:         internalThread = new Thread(r);
28:         internalThread.start();
29:     }
30:
31:     private void runWork() {
32:         int count = 0;
33:
```

continues

LISTING 5.11   Continued

```
34:            while ( !stopRequested ) {
35:                try {
36:                    waitWhileSuspended();
37:                } catch ( InterruptedException x ) {
38:                    // Reassert interrupt so that remaining code
39:                    // sees that an interrupt has been requested.
40:                    Thread.currentThread().interrupt();
41:
42:                    // Reevaluate while condition --probably
43:                    // false now.
44:                    continue;
45:                }
46:
47:                System.out.println("Part I - count=" + count);
48:
49:                try {
50:                    Thread.sleep(1000);
51:                } catch ( InterruptedException x ) {
52:                    Thread.currentThread().interrupt(); // reassert
53:                    // continue on as if sleep completed normally
54:                }
55:
56:                System.out.println("Part II - count=" + count);
57:
58:                try {
59:                    Thread.sleep(1000);
60:                } catch ( InterruptedException x ) {
61:                    Thread.currentThread().interrupt(); // reassert
62:                    // continue on as if sleep completed normally
63:                }
64:
65:                System.out.println("Part III - count=" + count);
66:
67:                count++;
68:            }
69:    }
70:
71:    private void waitWhileSuspended()
72:                    throws InterruptedException {
73:
74:        // only called by the internal thread - private method
75:
```

```
76:            synchronized ( suspendRequested ) {
77:                if ( suspendRequested.isTrue() ) {
78:                    try {
79:                        internalThreadSuspended.setValue(true);
80:                        suspendRequested.waitUntilFalse(0);
81:                    } finally {
82:                        internalThreadSuspended.setValue(false);
83:                    }
84:                }
85:            }
86:        }
87:
88:        public void suspendRequest() {
89:            suspendRequested.setValue(true);
90:        }
91:
92:        public void resumeRequest() {
93:            suspendRequested.setValue(false);
94:        }
95:
96:        public boolean waitForActualSuspension(long msTimeout)
97:                    throws InterruptedException {
98:
99:            // Returns 'true' if suspended, 'false' if the
100:           // timeout expired.
101:
102:           return internalThreadSuspended.waitUntilTrue(msTimeout);
103:       }
104:
105:       public void stopRequest() {
106:           stopRequested = true;
107:           internalThread.interrupt();
108:       }
109:
110:       public boolean isAlive() {
111:           return internalThread.isAlive();
112:       }
113:
114:       public static void main(String[] args) {
115:           try {
116:               BestReplacement br = new BestReplacement();
117:               System.out.println(
```

continues

LISTING 5.11   Continued

```
118:                         "--> just created, br.isAlive()=" +
119:                         br.isAlive());
120:            Thread.sleep(4200);
121:
122:            long startTime = System.currentTimeMillis();
123:            br.suspendRequest();
124:            System.out.println(
125:                    "--> just submitted a suspendRequest");
126:
127:            boolean suspensionTookEffect =
128:                    br.waitForActualSuspension(10000);
129:            long stopTime = System.currentTimeMillis();
130:
131:            if ( suspensionTookEffect ) {
132:                System.out.println(
133:                    "--> the internal thread took " +
134:                    (stopTime - startTime) + " ms to notice " +
135:                    "\n    the suspend request and is now " +
136:                    "suspended.");
137:            } else {
138:                System.out.println(
139:                    "--> the internal thread did not notice " +
140:                    "the suspend request " +
141:                    "\n    within 10 seconds.");
142:            }
143:
144:            Thread.sleep(5000);
145:
146:            br.resumeRequest();
147:            System.out.println(
148:                    "--> just submitted a resumeRequest");
149:            Thread.sleep(2200);
150:
151:            br.stopRequest();
152:            System.out.println(
153:                    "--> just submitted a stopRequest");
154:        } catch ( InterruptedException x ) {
155:            // ignore
156:        }
157:    }
158: }
```

In writing BestReplacement, I used some techniques from other chapters. It is a *self-running object* (for more details, see the technique in Chapter 11, "Self-Running Objects") in the sense that from outside the class, there is no indication that a thread will be running internally (although the class's documentation should mention this fact). A user of this class does not have to create a thread to run within it; one is created (line 27) and started (line 28) automatically in the constructor. The reference to this thread is held in a private member variable (line 4). The Runnable used by the internal thread is an inner class (lines 16–25). By using an inner class, the public void run() method is hidden and cannot be erroneously called by external code. Within this inner class, the private void runWork() method is invoked by the internal thread (line 19). In your design, if the thread should not be started in the constructor, you can include another method to allow the internalThread.start() operation to be performed when appropriate.

Additionally, the BooleanLock class is used from Chapter 17. BooleanLock encapsulates the wait/notify mechanism inside a class that holds a boolean value. The setValue() method is used to change the internal value and signal any and all threads waiting for the value to change. Other threads can wait for the value to be changed by invoking methods like waitUntilTrue() and waitUntilFalse(). In BestReplacement, two instances of BooleanLock are used. The suspendRequested instance (line 7) is used to track whether a suspend has been requested. The internalThreadSuspended instance (line 8) is used to determine if the internal thread has noticed a suspend request. Both are initially set to false (lines 13–14).

Inside the runWork() method, the while loop (lines 34–68) continues until stopRequested is true. Each time through, waitWhileSuspended() is called (line 36) to block, if currently suspended. This is a *safe place* for the internal thread to be suspended or stopped. If the internal thread is interrupted while waiting, it will throw an InterruptedException. The interrupt is used only to signal that the thread should die as soon as possible. This exception is caught, and the thread is reinterrupted (line 40) in case any other remaining statement becomes stuck and jumps back up to the top of the while because of the continue statement (line 44).

If not currently suspended, or after being resumed, the internal thread proceeds through the statements and prints various messages (lines 47, 56, and 65). Several sleeps are used and if interrupted, catch the exception and reassert the interrupted status (lines 52 and 61).

In suspendRequest(), the suspendRequested instance of BooleanLock has its value set to true (line 89). In resumeRequest(), suspendRequest is set to false (line 93). All of the synchronization and notification necessary for changing the value is encapsulated inside BooleanLock.

In waitWhileSuspended() (lines 71–86), a busy wait is avoided by using a BooleanLock instance (BooleanLock uses the wait/notify mechanism internally). First, the internal thread blocks until it can acquire exclusive access to the object-level lock on suspendRequested (line 76). If it is currently suspended, it enters the try/finally block (lines 77–84); otherwise, it simply returns. In the try/catch block, the internal thread indicates that it has noticed the suspend request by setting the state of internalThreadSuspened to true (line 79). The internal thread then invokes the waitUntilFalse() method of suspendRequested with a timeout of 0 to indicate that it should never timeout (line 80). No matter what happens, when the internal thread leaves the try section, it enters the finally section where the state of internalThreadSuspended is set back to false (line 82).

If an external thread wants to know if the internal thread has noticed the suspend request, the external thread can invoke waitForActualSuspension() (lines 96–103). This blocks waiting (up to the timeout) until internalThreadSuspended is set to true.

TIP

Don't worry if you don't fully understand the use of synchronized and the wait/notify mechanism encapsulated in BooleanLock at this time. I fully explain them in Chapters 7, 8, and 17.

The internal thread can be stopped by invoking stopRequest(). This method first sets the stopRequest boolean flag to true (line 106). It then interrupts the internal thread to "unstick" it from any blocking sleeps or waits (line 107). The isAlive() method is used to check whether the internal thread has died (line 111).

When run, output such as the following is produced:

```
--> just created, br.isAlive()=true
Part I - count=0
Part II - count=0
Part III - count=0
Part I - count=1
Part II - count=1
Part III - count=1
Part I - count=2
--> just submitted a suspendRequest
Part II - count=2
Part III - count=2
--> the internal thread took 1810 ms to notice
    the suspend request and is now suspended.
--> just submitted a resumeRequest
```

```
Part I - count=3
Part II - count=3
Part III - count=3
Part I - count=4
--> just submitted a stopRequest
Part II - count=4
Part III - count=4
```

Notice that when a suspend request is submitted, the loop continues until the suspend check at the top (waitWhileSuspended()). Also notice that when stopped, the internal thread does not immediately terminate, but instead finishes its tasks in an orderly manner.

> **CAUTION**
>
> Keep in mind that this stopping feature requires that a blocked statement respond to an interrupt. This is not always the case. For example, the read() method on an InputStream blocks until a new byte is available, the end of stream is reached, or an IOException is thrown. It does *not* throw an InterruptedException if the blocked thread is interrupted! A technique for dealing with this situation is offered in Chapter 15, "Breaking Out of a Blocked I/O State."

Daemon Threads

Threads that are marked as daemons stop in a whole new way. Daemon threads are used for background supporting tasks and are only needed while normal, nondaemon threads are still running. When the VM detects that the only remaining threads are daemon threads, it exits. If any *non*daemon thread is still alive, the VM will not exit. Daemon threads provide a nice way of managing some sort of behind-the-scenes processing that is only necessary to support other nondaemon threads.

The classes DaemonThread (see Listing 5.12) and DaemonThreadMain (see Listing 5.13) show how a daemon thread behaves.

LISTING 5.12   DaemonThread.java—The Daemon Thread Example

```
1: public class DaemonThread extends Object implements Runnable {
2:     public void run() {
3:         System.out.println("entering run()");
4:
5:         try {
```

continues

LISTING **5.12**   Continued

```
 6:                    System.out.println("in run() - currentThread()=" +
 7:                            Thread.currentThread());
 8:
 9:                    while ( true ) {
10:                        try { Thread.sleep(500); }
11:                        catch ( InterruptedException x ) {}
12:
13:                        System.out.println("in run() - woke up again");
14:                    }
15:                } finally {
16:                    System.out.println("leaving run()");
17:                }
18:        }
19: }
```

In this simple example, DaemonThread has only one method: run(). The message entering run() is printed when a thread begins (line 3). The while loop (lines 9–14) runs indefinitely, printing the woke up again message twice each second.

LISTING **5.13**   DaemonThreadMain.java—The Entry Point for the Daemon Thread Example

```
 1: public class DaemonThreadMain extends Object {
 2:     public static void main(String[] args) {
 3:         System.out.println("entering main()");
 4:
 5:         Thread t = new Thread(new DaemonThread());
 6:         t.setDaemon(true);
 7:         t.start();
 8:
 9:         try { Thread.sleep(3000); }
              ➥ catch ( InterruptedException x ) { }
10:
11:         System.out.println("leaving main()");
12:     }
13: }
```

In DaemonThreadMain, a new DaemonThread object is created and passed to one of Thread's constructors (line 5). Before the new thread is started, the daemon flag is set to true (line 6) to indicate that this thread should not keep the VM from exiting. Next, the thread is started (line 7). After letting the daemon thread run for three seconds (line 9), the main thread simply falls out of main() and dies. Very soon after this, the VM notices that the other thread is only a daemon thread and exits.

When DaemonThreadMain is run, something close to the following should be produced (your output might differ):

```
entering main()
entering run()
in run() - currentThread()=Thread[Thread-0,5,main]
in run() - woke up again
in run() - woke up again
in run() - woke up again
in run() - woke up again
in run() - woke up again
leaving main()
in run() - woke up again
```

One last woke up again message might be printed after the leaving main message. If the new thread was *not* a daemon thread, the woke up again messages would continue to be produced until the VM was terminated manually. Also notice that the daemon thread was abruptly stopped and never printed the message in its finally clause.

CAUTION

Although daemon threads can be very useful, care must be taken to ensure that it's not harmful for them to be stopped in their tracks when all the other nondaemon threads have died.

Summary

In this chapter, I showed you several ways to temporarily and permanently stop a thread's execution. Some of the lessons learned are

- interrupt() can be used to set a thread's interrupted status to true and break a thread out of a blocked sleeping or waiting state.
- InterruptedException is thrown to indicate that a thread has noticed that it has been interrupted.
- isInterrupted() can be used at any time on any thread to check whether it has been interrupted, without altering the interrupted status.

- `Thread.interrupted()` can be used to check whether the current thread has been interrupted, and if so, it automatically resets the interrupted status flag back to `false`.

- `suspend()`, `resume()`, and `stop()` are deprecated as of JDK 1.2 and should also be avoided in earlier releases.

- Alternative techniques are available to replace the functionality of the deprecated methods.

- Daemon threads automatically stop when all the nondaemon threads have died.

Thread Prioritization

IN THIS CHAPTER

Java allows you to give each of the threads running in a virtual machine a *priority*. Higher-priority threads generally get more of a chance to run than lower-priority threads, but exact thread-scheduling behavior varies by VM implementation and operating system. Thread prioritization can be used to provide suggestions to the VM as to how you would like the threads to take turns running on the processor relative to each other, increasing an application's responsiveness to relatively more important events.

System Thread Priorities

Back in Chapter 3, "Creating and Starting a Thread," Table 3.1 listed the threads that are normally started by the VM for applications with a graphical user interface. Tables 6.1, 6.2, and 6.3 show the priorities that are assigned to each of these system threads for each major release of Sun's JDK.

TABLE 6.1   System Thread Priorities—JDK 1.2

Priority	Thread Name
5	main
8	Finalizer
10	Reference Handler
5	Signal dispatcher
5	AWT-Windows
6	AWT-EventQueue-0
5	SunToolkit.PostEventQueue-0
4	Screen Updater

TABLE 6.2   System Thread Priorities—JDK 1.1

Priority	Thread Name
5	main
1	Finalizer thread
5	AWT-Windows
5	AWT-EventQueue-0
4	Screen Updater

TABLE 6.3   System Thread Priorities—JDK 1.0

Priority	Thread Name
5	main
1	Finalizer thread
5	AWT-Win32
5	AWT-Callback-Win32
4	Screen Updater

Chapter 3 provides descriptions of what these threads are used for and provides a cross-reference between the releases. The main thread is created by the VM and enters the main() method of applications. It runs at a middle-of-the-road priority of 5. The asynchronous garbage collection process uses the Finalizer thread. A notable change in JDK 1.2 is that the priority of the Finalizer thread was increased from 1 to 8 to help ensure that the garbage collector gets more of a chance to run and free up memory.

The AWT-EventQueue-0 thread is the event-handling thread. This thread invokes event-handling methods in response to GUI interactions with the user. In JDK 1.2, its priority is 6, just slighter higher than the priority of 5 that it had in JDK 1.1 and 1.0.

When assigning priorities to your threads, you should consider the relative priorities of the system threads to be sure your threads don't overwhelm their operations. By default, when a new Thread is constructed, it runs at the same priority as the thread that constructed it. Most new threads are constructed directly or indirectly by the main thread and will therefore run at a priority of 5. This works well under many scenarios, but there are times when you will want to raise or lower a thread's priority.

Thread Priority Constants

There are three public static final int member variables of Thread that indicate the range of priority values that can be passed to setPriority(). These constants should be used to determine the range of acceptable priorities.

Thread.MAX_PRIORITY

Thread.MAX_PRIORITY is the highest thread-scheduling priority that can be passed to setPriority() for a particular VM. Generally, it is 10. Threads running at this level might hog the processor and should be designed to block frequently to give other threads a chance to run.

Thread.MIN_PRIORITY

Thread.MIN_PRIORITY is the lowest thread-scheduling priority that can be passed to
setPriority() for a particular VM. Generally, it is 1. Threads running at this priority might
not get much processor time and might not get any if there are other higher-priority threads
running.

Thread.NORM_PRIORITY

Thread.NORM_PRIORITY is a not-too-high, not-too-low thread-scheduling priority for
setPriority(). Generally, it is 5. Threads running at this priority usually get a chance to run
without hogging the processor.

Determining the Current Priority: getPriority()

The getPriority() method of Thread returns an int representing the current priority of the
thread. Generally, a thread's priority does not change over its lifetime, but it can. The
GetPriority class shown in Listing 6.1 demonstrates the use of getPriority().

LISTING 6.1   GetPriority.java—Using getPriority()

```
 1: public class GetPriority extends Object {
 2:     private static Runnable makeRunnable() {
 3:         Runnable r =  new Runnable() {
 4:             public void run() {
 5:                 for ( int i = 0; i < 5; i++ ) {
 6:                     Thread t = Thread.currentThread();
 7:                     System.out.println(
 8:                         "in run() - priority=" +
 9:                         t.getPriority() +
10:                         ", name=" + t.getName());
11:
12:                     try {
13:                         Thread.sleep(2000);
14:                     } catch ( InterruptedException x ) {
15:                         // ignore
16:                     }
17:                 }
18:             }
19:         };
20:
21:         return r;
22:     }
23:
```

```
24:      public static void main(String[] args) {
25:          System.out.println(
26:              "in main() - Thread.currentThread().getPriority()=" +
27:              Thread.currentThread().getPriority());
28:
29:          System.out.println(
30:              "in main() - Thread.currentThread().getName()=" +
31:              Thread.currentThread().getName());
32:
33:          Thread threadA = new Thread(makeRunnable(), "threadA");
34:          threadA.start();
35:
36:          try { Thread.sleep(3000); }
37:          catch ( InterruptedException x ) { }
38:
39:          System.out.println("in main() - threadA.getPriority()=" +
40:                  threadA.getPriority());
41:      }
42: }
```

In main(), the name and priority of the thread running main() is printed (lines 25–31). Next, makeRunnable() is used to create a new Runnable object to pass to the constructor of Thread (line 33). In addition, the name of this new thread is designated as threadA (line 33). Next, this thread is started (line 34) and is allowed to run for 3 seconds (line 36). After the sleep, getPriority() is used to determine the current priority of threadA (lines 39–40).

The makeRunnable() method (lines 2–22) is used to create a new Runnable instance that prints the name and priority of the thread running it five times. Each time through the loop, the current thread is determined (line 6), and then the name and priority are extracted and printed (lines 7–10). Before looping again, the thread sleeps for two seconds (lines 12–16).

Listing 6.2 shows the output produced when GetPriority is run. Your output should match.

LISTING 6.2   Output from GetPriority

```
in main() - Thread.currentThread().getPriority()=5
in main() - Thread.currentThread().getName()=main
in run() - priority=5, name=threadA
in run() - priority=5, name=threadA
in main() - threadA.getPriority()=5
in run() - priority=5, name=threadA
in run() - priority=5, name=threadA
in run() - priority=5, name=threadA
```

Notice that the name of the thread running `main()` is `main` and that its priority is 5. Also note that `threadA` inherited the priority of 5 from `main`.

Changing the Priority of a Thread: setPriority()

The `setPriority()` method of `Thread` takes an `int` as a parameter indicating the new priority for the thread. The `setPriority()` method can be invoked either before the thread is started or once it is running. Some VMs might allow you to change the priority of the system threads, but this is not recommended—even if it is permitted.

The class `SetPriority`, shown in Listing 6.3, demonstrates how `setPriority()` can be used to specify a priority of a thread before it is started. It also shows how the priority of a running thread can be changed on-the-fly.

LISTING 6.3   SetPriority.java—Changing the Priority of a Thread with setPriority()

```
 1: public class SetPriority extends Object {
 2:     private static Runnable makeRunnable() {
 3:         Runnable r =  new Runnable() {
 4:             public void run() {
 5:                 for ( int i = 0; i < 5; i++ ) {
 6:                     Thread t = Thread.currentThread();
 7:                     System.out.println(
 8:                         "in run() - priority=" +
 9:                         t.getPriority() +
10:                         ", name=" + t.getName());
11:
12:                     try {
13:                         Thread.sleep(2000);
14:                     } catch ( InterruptedException x ) {
15:                         // ignore
16:                     }
17:                 }
18:             }
19:         };
20:
21:         return r;
22:     }
23:
24:     public static void main(String[] args) {
25:         Thread threadA = new Thread(makeRunnable(), "threadA");
26:         threadA.setPriority(8);
```

```
27:          threadA.start();
28:
29:          Thread threadB = new Thread(makeRunnable(), "threadB");
30:          threadB.setPriority(2);
31:          threadB.start();
32:
33:          Runnable r = new Runnable() {
34:                  public void run() {
35:                      Thread threadC =
36:                          new Thread(makeRunnable(), "threadC");
37:                      threadC.start();
38:                  }
39:              };
40:          Thread threadD = new Thread(r, "threadD");
41:          threadD.setPriority(7);
42:          threadD.start();
43:
44:          try { Thread.sleep(3000); }
45:          catch ( InterruptedException x ) { }
46:
47:          threadA.setPriority(3);
48:          System.out.println("in main() - threadA.getPriority()=" +
49:                  threadA.getPriority());
50:      }
51: }
```

The makeRunnable() method of SetPriority works the same as it did in GetPriority. This time several new threads are spawned inside main(). First, threadA is created and has its priority set to 8 before it is started (lines 25–27). Next, threadB is created and has its priority set to 2 before it is started (lines 29–31).

To demonstrate how a thread priority is inherited, threadD creates threadC (lines 33–42). The initial priority for threadD is set to 7 before it is started (line 41). When threadD runs, it executes the run() method inside r (lines 34–38). A new Thread is constructed by threadD and is called threadC. The priority of threadC is not changed, but is simply inherited from threadC's creator.

After launching the threads, the main thread sleeps for three seconds. When it wakes up, it invokes setPriority() on the already running thread threadA to change its priority to 3.

Listing 6.4 shows the output produced when SetPriority is run. Your output should be very similar, but might differ slightly.

LISTING 6.4   Possible Output from SetPriority

```
 1: in run() - priority=8, name=threadA
 2: in run() - priority=2, name=threadB
 3: in run() - priority=7, name=threadC
 4: in run() - priority=8, name=threadA
 5: in run() - priority=2, name=threadB
 6: in run() - priority=7, name=threadC
 7: in main() - threadA.getPriority()=3
 8: in run() - priority=3, name=threadA
 9: in run() - priority=2, name=threadB
10: in run() - priority=7, name=threadC
11: in run() - priority=3, name=threadA
12: in run() - priority=2, name=threadB
13: in run() - priority=7, name=threadC
14: in run() - priority=3, name=threadA
15: in run() - priority=2, name=threadB
16: in run() - priority=7, name=threadC
```

While examining the output from SetPriority, you can see that threadC is running with a priority of 7 (lines 3, 6, 10, 13, and 16). It was never directly set to 7, but was defaulted to that level when it was created by threadD. Also note that when the priority of threadA was reduced to 3 from 8, threadA printed the new priority the last three times through its for loop (lines 8, 11, and 14).

When setPriority() Might Not Work

Calls to setPriority can throw a SecurityException if the calling thread is not permitted to make the priority change. This will happen only if there is a SecurityManager installed and it rejects the change request. By default, applications do not have a SecurityManager.

An IllegalArgumentException will be thrown if the specified priority is greater than Thread.MAX_PRIORITY or less than Thread.MIN_PRIORITY.

The value passed to setPriority() can be silently reduced to the maximum priority allowed for the thread group. For example, in this code fragment

```
Thread t = //...
ThreadGroup tg = t.getThreadGroup();
int groupMax = tg.getMaxPriority();
```

the maximum value for the thread priority of thread t is groupMax. Usually, this is the same as Thread.MAX_PRIORITY. When groupMax is less than Thread.MAX_PRIORITY, calls to setPriority() still work, but will silently reduce the value passed to groupMax. If groupMax is 6 and setPriority(9) is called, the code will run as if setPriority(6) was called instead. See Chapter 10, "Thread Groups," for more on ThreadGroup.

CAUTION

The Java 1.1 VM inside Netscape's Navigator/Communicator (versions 4.0 through 4.5) silently ignores *all* calls to setPriority(). Even calls that would *lower* the priority of a thread are ignored! No exception is thrown, but the thread priority remains unchanged. Netscape implements an elaborate security scheme that requires a bunch of code to tell the VM to allow thread priorities to be changed. Future versions of Netscape might change this policy, but beware of the potential problems that applets might have running in this version of the browser. If thread prioritization is important in your applet, consider requiring the Java plug-in that Sun Microsystems supplies for free.

Thread States

While a thread is alive, it is in one of several states. On a single-processor system, only one thread is actually running at a time. The other threads are either blocked or are ready-to-run and waiting for a turn on the processor. Figure 6.1 lists the various states that an active thread can be in.

State	Blocked	Interruptible	Description
running			Currently running on the processor.
ready to run			Waiting for a turn on the processor.
sleeping	√	√	Will move to *ready to run* after a certain amount of time has elapsed or after being interrupted.
waiting	√	√	Will move to *ready to run* after being notified, after timing out, or after being interrupted.
blocked on I/O	√		Will move to *ready to run* after I/O condition changes (for example, a byte of data is read).
blocked on sync	√		Will move to *ready to run* when lock is acquired (passes synchronized statement).

FIGURE 6.1

Thread states.

The thread scheduler controls which one of the ready-to-run threads is actually running on the processor. Only one thread is actually in the running state at any given time. All the other threads that are ready-to-run wait to be picked by the thread scheduler. Thread priority helps the thread scheduler choose which of the ready-to-run threads should be run next.

Threads can be *blocked* in one of four states. When a thread executes `Thread.sleep()`, it blocks until the specified number of milliseconds passes or until it is interrupted by another thread. When a thread encounters a `wait()` statement (see Chapter 8, "Inter-thread Communication," for more on the wait/notify mechanism), it blocks until it is notified, interrupted, or the specified number of milliseconds elapses (if a timeout was specified).

There are many ways a thread can block waiting on different I/O methods. One common way is the `read()` method of `InputStream`. This method blocks until a byte of data is read from the stream. It can block indefinitely, and no timeout can be specified.

A thread can also block waiting to acquire exclusive access to an object's lock. The `synchronized` statement and `synchronized` method modifier (see Chapter 7, "Concurrent Access to Objects and Variables," for more on synchronization) are used to control concurrent access by more than one thread to a section of code. A thread will block on `synchronized` until it gets the specified lock. It can block indefinitely, and no timeout can be specified.

Notice that *not* all blocked states are interruptible. When a thread is blocked waiting to read a byte of data from an `InputStream`, it will not respond to interrupts (see Chapter 15, "Breaking Out of a Blocked I/O State," for some techniques for dealing with this). When a thread is blocked waiting to get the lock required by a `synchronized` statement, it also will not respond to interrupt requests (see Chapter 17, "BooleanLock Utility," for a technique that deals with long waits for locks).

When conditions change and a thread is no longer blocked, the thread moves to the ready-to-run state. It remains there until selected to run by the thread scheduler. Figure 6.2 shows how threads transition from one state to another.

Only one thread is actually running at a time, and it eventually blocks, yields, or is forcibly swapped off the processor by the thread scheduler. If it blocks, it remains blocked until some condition changes. When it finally unblocks, it moves to the ready-to-run state. When new threads are started, they are put into the ready-to-run state.

When the running state is open and there is at least one thread in the ready-to-run state, the thread scheduler chooses one from the pool of ready-to-run threads and transitions it to the running state. Threads of higher priority are more likely to be chosen than threads of lower priority, but the exact behavior is dependent on the VM and the operating system.

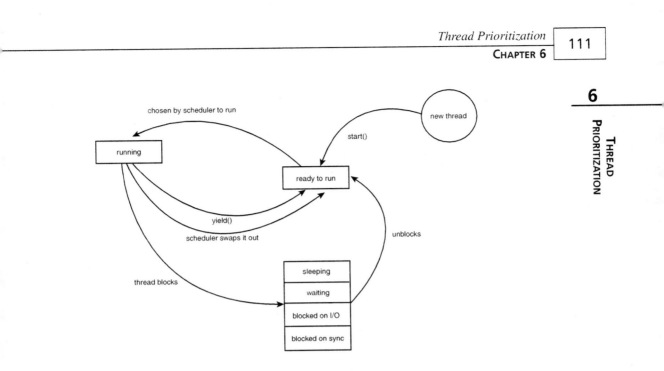

FIGURE 6.2

Thread state transition diagram.

TIP

These six states are not officially defined in Java, but are a useful tool for understanding thread behavior. The thread state transition diagram in Figure 6.2 is only a *model* that is helpful in imagining the inner workings of the VM. Most VM implementations use the underlying operating system's threads and thread scheduler. This model helps conceptualize what might be going on inside the VM, but it does not map directly to a real implementation.

Priorities and Scheduling

The virtual machine's thread scheduler determines which thread is currently running on the processor and how long it is allowed to run before being swapped off the processor to allow another thread to run. Thread priorities provide additional information to the thread scheduler as to which threads are more important to run.

Generally, higher-priority threads get more processor time than lower-priority threads. The *Java Language Specification* does not require any more specific scheduling selection than this.

In particular, a low-priority thread may not run until all of the threads with a higher priority are blocked (sleeping, waiting on I/O, or some other blocked condition). It is likely (but not guaranteed) that a low-priority thread will be swapped off the processor as soon as a higher-priority thread unblocks and becomes ready-to-run. Threads of equal priority may or may not share the processor with each other. In addition, most VM implementations use the underlying operating system's threads. Exact thread behavior varies from VM to VM, and you need to be careful that your designs do not critically depend on one particular implementation.

CAUTION

Thread priorities are only a *suggestion* to the thread scheduler and should not be used to guarantee program correctness. Write your programs in such a way that they would still produce correct results regardless of prioritization.

Voluntarily Relinquishing the Processor: Thread.yield()

To help ensure that other threads in the VM get a turn to run on the processor, a thread can voluntarily give up its turn early. If a thread invokes the static method Thread.yield(), the thread scheduler will swap it off the processor and allow another thread to run. It is likely (but not guaranteed) that only threads having a priority *equal to* or *greater than* the one that yielded control will be considered by the thread scheduler.

A thread implicitly yields the processor when it goes to sleep or otherwise blocks. The Thread.yield() method allows a thread to specify other times that are convenient for it to pause to allow other threads access to the processor. If you have a thread that frequently blocks on its own, there is no need to make Thread.yield() calls. But, if you have a thread that is performing a long non-blocking calculation, an occasional call to Thread.yield() can help split up the processor resources among the other threads. Be careful not to overuse Thread.yield() as some system overhead is incurred to perform a context switch between threads. As a rough guideline, try to avoid calling Thread.yield() more than five times per second.

The PriorityCompete class shown in Listing 6.5 creates three threads that all compete with each other to run nonblocking code. It runs once without using Thread.yield() and then a second time with voluntary yielding.

LISTING 6.5   PriorityCompete.java—Competing Threads of Different Priorities

```
 1: public class PriorityCompete extends Object {
 2:      private volatile int count;
 3:      private boolean yield;
 4:      private Thread internalThread;
 5:      private volatile boolean noStopRequested;
 6:
 7:      public PriorityCompete(
 8:                  String name,
 9:                  int priority,
10:                  boolean yield
11:              ) {
12:
13:          count = 0;
14:          this.yield = yield;
15:
16:          noStopRequested = true;
17:          Runnable r = new Runnable() {
18:                  public void run() {
19:                      try {
20:                          runWork();
21:                      } catch ( Exception x ) {
22:                          // in case ANY exception slips through
23:                          x.printStackTrace();
24:                      }
25:                  }
26:              };
27:
28:          internalThread = new Thread(r, name);
29:          internalThread.setPriority(priority);
30:      }
31:
32:      private void runWork() {
33:          Thread.yield();
34:
35:          while ( noStopRequested ) {
36:              if ( yield ) {
37:                  Thread.yield();
38:              }
39:
40:              count++;
```

continues

LISTING 6.5   Continued

```
41:
42:                     for ( int i = 0; i < 1000; i++ ) {
43:                         double x = i * Math.PI / Math.E;
44:                     }
45:                 }
46:         }
47:
48:         public void startRequest() {
49:             internalThread.start();
50:         }
51:
52:         public void stopRequest() {
53:             noStopRequested = false;
54:         }
55:
56:         public int getCount() {
57:             return count;
58:         }
59:
60:         public String getNameAndPriority() {
61:             return internalThread.getName() +
62:                 ": priority=" + internalThread.getPriority();
63:         }
64:
65:         private static void runSet(boolean yield) {
66:             PriorityCompete[] pc = new PriorityCompete[3];
67:             pc[0] = new PriorityCompete("PC0", 3, yield);
68:             pc[1] = new PriorityCompete("PC1", 6, yield);
69:             pc[2] = new PriorityCompete("PC2", 6, yield);
70:
71:             // let the dust settle for a bit before starting them up
72:             try { Thread.sleep(1000); }
73:             catch ( InterruptedException x ) { }
74:
75:             for ( int i = 0; i < pc.length; i++ ) {
76:                 pc[i].startRequest();
77:             }
78:
79:             long startTime = System.currentTimeMillis();
80:             try { Thread.sleep(10000); }
81:             catch ( InterruptedException x ) { }
82:
83:             for ( int i = 0; i < pc.length; i++ ) {
84:                 pc[i].stopRequest();
85:             }
86:
87:             long stopTime = System.currentTimeMillis();
```

```
88:
89:             // let things settle down again
90:             try { Thread.sleep(1000); }
91:             catch ( InterruptedException x ) { }
92:
93:             int totalCount = 0;
94:             for ( int i = 0; i < pc.length; i++ ) {
95:                 totalCount += pc[i].getCount();
96:             }
97:
98:             System.out.println("totalCount=" + totalCount +
99:                 ", count/ms=" + roundTo((((double) totalCount) /
100:                                 (stopTime - startTime), 3));
101:
102:            for ( int i = 0; i < pc.length; i++ ) {
103:                double perc = roundTo(100.0 * pc[i].getCount() /
104:                                 totalCount, 2);
105:                System.out.println(pc[i].getNameAndPriority() +
106:                     ", " + perc + "%, count=" + pc[i].getCount());
107:            }
108:        }
109:
110:        public static double roundTo(double val, int places) {
111:            double factor = Math.pow(10, places);
112:            return ( (int) ( ( val * factor ) + 0.5 ) ) / factor;
113:        }
114:
115:        public static void main(String[] args) {
116:            Runnable r = new Runnable() {
117:                    public void run() {
118:                        System.out.println(
119:                                "Run without using yield()");
120:                        System.out.println(
121:                                "=========================");
122:                        runSet(false);
123:
124:                        System.out.println();
125:                        System.out.println("Run using yield()");
126:                        System.out.println("=================");
127:                        runSet(true);
128:                    }
129:                };
130:
131:            Thread t = new Thread(r, "PriorityCompete");
132:            t.setPriority(Thread.MAX_PRIORITY - 1);
133:            t.start();
134:        }
135: }
```

In the main() method of PriorityCompete (lines 115–134), a new thread is created to run at a higher priority than the main thread normally does. This thread is named PriorityCompete (line 131) and runs at almost the maximum priority allowed (line 132). When it is started (line 133), the run() method (lines 117–128) is executed by the PriorityCompete thread. First it calls runSet(), passing false to indicate that the threads should not voluntarily yield to one another (line 122). After that completes, it calls runSet() again, this time passing in true to indicate that the threads *should* yield (line 127).

Each time the runSet() method (lines 65–108) is called, it creates three instances of PriorityCompete (lines 66–69). Two of them will run at a priority level of 6 and the third will run at a lower priority level of 3. The PriorityCompete thread then sleeps for a second (line 72) to allow the VM to settle down (making sure that the main thread has had an opportunity to leave main(), among other things). It starts each of the objects running (lines 75–77). Next, it takes note of the time (line 79), and then lets the objects compete for the processor for 10 seconds (line 80). After running for 10 seconds, they are stopped (lines 83–85), and the time is noted again (line 87). The time is requested because the sleep is usually a little longer than 10 seconds because of all the other processing activity.

Each of the PriorityCompete objects increments its internal counter. The final count that each achieved is retrieved and totaled (lines 93–96). The total count and the count increments per millisecond are printed (lines 98–100). Finally, the count for each PriorityCompete object is printed along with the percent of the total that its count represents (lines 102–107). The roundTo() method (lines 110–113) is simply used to round a double to the specified number of decimal places.

Each instance of PriorityCompete creates its own internal thread that will run at the specified priority (lines 7–30). PriorityCompete is roughly based on the self-running object technique shown in Chapter 11, "Self-Running Objects." The internal thread is created (line 28) and has its priority set (line 29), but is not started until startRequest() (lines 48–50) is called. The stopRequest() method (lines 52–54) simply changes an indicator variable so that the next time the internal thread checks, it returns from run(). The getCount() method (lines 56–58) and the getNameAndPriority() method (lines 60–63) are used in runSet() to retrieve information.

Each of the internal threads ends up invoking its own runWork() method (lines 32–46). Right away, it yields to allow all the threads to get a chance to start running (line 33). The while loop (lines 35–45) is executed until a stop request is received. Each time though the loop, if this instance is supposed to yield, it executes Thread.yield() (lines 36–38). Then it increments the internal counter (line 40). To slow down the progress through the loop, some busy work is done (lines 42–44). This busy work does not block, but keeps the processor working.

Listing 6.6 shows possible output when `PriorityCompete` is run. Your output is likely to differ significantly, as it is heavily dependent on how powerful the hardware is and how many other processes are running on the operating system.

LISTING 6.6   Possible Output from PriorityCompete

```
 1: Run without using yield()
 2: =========================
 3: totalCount=764469, count/ms=76.523
 4: PC0: priority=3, 4.65%, count=35510
 5: PC1: priority=6, 48.19%, count=368395
 6: PC2: priority=6, 47.17%, count=360564
 7:
 8: Run using yield()
 9: =================
10: totalCount=253523, count/ms=25.352
11: PC0: priority=3, 0.01%, count=31
12: PC1: priority=6, 49.99%, count=126739
13: PC2: priority=6, 50.0%, count=126753
```

In the first set (lines 1–6), the internal threads never block and only reluctantly relinquish the processor when the thread scheduler forces them into the ready-to-run state. Even though there is always a thread with a priority of 6 ready-to-run, the thread scheduler still gives the thread with a priority of 3 a chance to run now and then—just less than 5% of the time (line 4). Otherwise, the remaining percentage is roughly split between the two priority 6 threads (lines 5–6).

In the second set (lines 8–13), the internal threads yield each time though the loop. In this case, the lower-priority thread gets much less time (but not zero time) on the processor and gets only 0.01% of the processor resources. The high-priority threads split the time almost perfectly in half between themselves: 49.99% and 50.00%.

Also note that without yielding, the count/ms was about 76 (line 3), and when yielding was done, it was cut down to about 25 (line 10). This shows that the yielding caused a lot of context switches that brought with them some significant overhead. In this example, the excessive yielding wasted processor resources.

Thread-Scheduling Scenarios

There are many thread-scheduling algorithms that might be used on a particular platform. If you simultaneously consider the three following scenarios, you should end up with a good design that will work well on a wide variety of VM implementations.

Scenario I: One High-Priority Thread Hogs Processor

The highest-priority thread that is ready-to-run gets to run until it blocks, it yields the processor, or an even higher-priority thread becomes ready-to-run. In this case, the thread scheduler does not force the thread to move off the processor, but it waits for some condition to change. In this scenario, the following events can happen:

- Lower-priority threads may never get a chance to run and may become starved for processor time.
- Threads of equal priority don't get a chance to run until the running thread yields or blocks.
- If a thread of higher priority becomes ready-to-run, it will pre-empt the currently running thread.

Scenario II: All High-Priority Threads Hog Processor

This is a slight variation on Scenario I where the thread scheduler swaps threads of equal priority with each other. Now the running thread will continue to run until it blocks, it yields the processor, or a thread of higher *or equal* priority becomes ready-to-run:

- Lower-priority threads may never get a chance to run and may become starved for processor time.
- Threads of equal priority each get a chance to run.
- If a thread of higher priority becomes ready-to-run, it will pre-empt the currently running thread.

Scenario III: All Threads Get Some Time on the Processor

In this case, the thread scheduler makes sure that all threads get some time on the processor regardless of their priority. However, higher-priority threads will be scheduled for more processor time than lower-priority threads. This is the behavior observed in Listing 6.6:

- Lower-priority threads will get some processor time, although it will be less than higher-priority threads get.
- Threads of equal priority each get a chance to run.
- When higher-priority threads become ready-to-run, they will generally pre-empt a thread that is running at a lower priority. But, because all threads get some time on the processor, there might be short periods of time when a high-priority thread is ready-to-run, but is held back briefly while a lower-priority thread gets a small slice of time.

This last scenario is really the ideal case, but you will need to code with the other two in mind to be sure that each thread gets some time on the processor—regardless of the particular VM that the code is running on.

TIP

When assigning priorities to the threads in your application, use the higher priorities only for threads that block frequently (sleeping, waiting, I/O). CPU-intensive calculations should be done with a medium- to low-priority thread to ensure that the processor is not hogged. Avoid setting a priority to Thread.MAX_PRIORITY unless the thread spends nearly all of its time blocked or is very short-lived.

Summary

In this chapter I showed you how to use a few more parts of the Thread API:

- Thread.MAX_PRIORITY, Thread.NORM_PRIORITY, and Thread.MIN_PRIORITY
- getPriority()
- setPriority()
- Thread.yield()

The thread scheduler chooses which thread to move from the ready-to-run state to the running state. Thread priorities provide suggestions to the scheduler to help it pick the next thread to run. Generally, higher-priority threads get more processor time than lower-priority threads.

Thread scheduling varies from VM to VM and from operating system to operating system. Because of these differences, prioritization should only be used to try to improve responsiveness and efficiency, and should not be relied upon for program correctness.

Concurrent Access to Objects and Variables

IN THIS CHAPTER

When multiple threads are interacting with an object, controls need to be in place to ensure that the threads don't adversely affect one another. This chapter deals with issues that can introduce subtle errors in your application. An application that fails to safely control concurrent access can work properly most of the time—maybe nearly all the time—but will occasionally produce erroneous results. This makes the understanding and disciplined use of the information in this chapter critical to writing truly thread-safe applications that work properly all the time.

In this chapter, I'll show you when and how to use the synchronized and volatile keywords to control concurrent access to objects and variables.

volatile Member Variable Modifier

The volatile keyword is used as a modifier on member variables to force individual threads to reread the variable's value from shared memory every time the variable is accessed. In addition, individual threads are forced to write changes back to shared memory as soon as they occur. This way, two different threads always see the same value for a member variable at any particular time. Chances are that most of you expected this behavior from the Java VM already. In fact, many experienced Java developers don't understand when the use of volatile is necessary.

The *Java Language Specification* indicates that for optimal speed, individual threads are permitted to keep a working copy of shared member variables and only reconcile them with the shared original occasionally. To be more accurate, the word "occasionally" in the last sentence should be replaced with "when a thread enters or leaves a synchronized block of code." I'll tell you more about synchronized blocks later in this chapter. When only one thread is interacting with the member variables of an object, this optimization works very well and can allow for faster execution. When two (or more) threads are simultaneously working with an object, care must be taken to ensure that changes made to a shared member variable by one thread are seen by the other.

The volatile keyword is used to tell the VM that it should not keep a private copy of a variable and should instead interact directly with the shared copy. The class Volatile, shown in Listing 7.1, shows the behavior when the volatile keyword is and is not used.

LISTING 7.1 Volatile.java—Demonstration Showing How volatile Makes a Difference

```
1: public class Volatile extends Object implements Runnable {
2:     // not marked as 'volatile', but it should be!
3:     private int value;
4:
5:     private volatile boolean missedIt;
6:
```

Concurrent Access to Objects and Variables

CHAPTER 7

123

7

CONCURRENT
ACCESS TO OBJECTS
AND VARIABLES

```
 7:       // doesn't need to be volatile-doesn't change
 8:       private long creationTime;
 9:
10:       public Volatile() {
11:           value = 10;
12:           missedIt = false;
13:           creationTime = System.currentTimeMillis();
14:       }
15:
16:       public void run() {
17:           print("entering run()");
18:
19:           // each time, check to see if 'value' is different
20:           while ( value < 20 ) {
21:
22:               // Used to break out of the loop if change to
23:               // value is missed.
24:               if ( missedIt ) {
25:                   int currValue = value;
26:
27:                   // Simply execute a synchronized statement on an
28:                   // arbitrary object to see the effect.
29:                   Object lock = new Object();
30:                   synchronized ( lock ) {
31:                       // do nothing!
32:                   }
33:
34:                   int valueAfterSync = value;
35:
36:                   print("in run() - see value=" + currValue +
37:                       ", but rumor has it that it changed!");
38:                   print("in run() - valueAfterSync=" +
39:                       valueAfterSync);
40:
41:                   break;
42:               }
43:           }
44:
45:           print("leaving run()");
46:       }
47:
48:       public void workMethod() throws InterruptedException {
49:           print("entering workMethod()");
```

continues

LISTING 7.1 Continued

```
50:
51:             print("in workMethod() - about to sleep for 2 seconds");
52:             Thread.sleep(2000);
53:
54:             value = 50;
55:             print("in workMethod() - just set value=" + value);
56:
57:             print("in workMethod() - about to sleep for 5 seconds");
58:             Thread.sleep(5000);
59:
60:             missedIt = true;
61:             print("in workMethod() - just set missedIt=" + missedIt);
62:
63:             print("in workMethod() - about to sleep for 3 seconds");
64:             Thread.sleep(3000);
65:
66:             print("leaving workMethod()");
67:     }
68:
69:     private void print(String msg) {
70:             // This method could have been simplified by using
71:             // functionality present in the java.text package,
72:             // but did not take advantage of it since that package
73:             // is not present in JDK1.0.
74:
75:             long interval = System.currentTimeMillis() -
76:                             creationTime;
77:
78:             String tmpStr = "    " + ( interval / 1000.0 ) + "000";
79:
80:             int pos = tmpStr.indexOf(".");
81:             String secStr = tmpStr.substring(pos - 2, pos + 4);
82:
83:             String nameStr = "         " +
84:                     Thread.currentThread().getName();
85:
86:             nameStr = nameStr.substring(nameStr.length() - 8,
87:                                     nameStr.length());
88:
89:             System.out.println(secStr + " " + nameStr + ": " + msg);
90:     }
91:
```

```
 92:        public static void main(String[] args) {
 93:            try {
 94:                Volatile vol = new Volatile();
 95:
 96:                // slight pause to let some time elapse
 97:                Thread.sleep(100);
 98:
 99:                Thread t = new Thread(vol);
100:                t.start();
101:
102:                // slight pause to allow run() to go first
103:                Thread.sleep(100);
104:
105:                vol.workMethod();
106:            } catch ( InterruptedException x ) {
107:                System.err.println(
108:                    "one of the sleeps was interrupted");
109:            }
110:        }
111: }
```

In the `main()` method of `Volatile` (lines 92–110), the main thread creates a new instance of `Volatile` (line 94). It then sleeps for a fraction of a second (line 97) to allow the real-time clock to advance slightly so that the messages created in `print()` print an elapsed time greater than zero. The main thread then creates a new `Thread`, passing in the `Runnable` instance of `Volatile`, and starts it (lines 99–100). Another brief nap is taken to allow the new thread to get into the loop of the `run()` method (line 103). The main thread is then used to execute the code in the `workMethod()` of the `Volatile` object (line 105).

Meanwhile, the new thread enters the `run()` method (lines 16–46). It continues to execute the `while` loop (lines 20–43) as long as the non-`volatile` member variable `value` (line 3) is less than `20`. Earlier, when the main thread executed the constructor code (lines 10–14), `value` was initialized to `10`. The only place that `value` is changed is inside `workMethod()` (line 54). In case the new thread doesn't see the change to `value`, the volatile member variable `missedIt` (line 5) is used to provide another way out. If `missedIt` is true (line 24), the new thread captures its perception of `value` into the local variable `currValue` (line 25). Then a new object is created simply to use as a lock (line 29). The thread locks on this object and enters and exits the synchronized block (lines 30–32). It then records its new perception of `value` into the local variable `valueAfterSync` (line 34). The values recorded before and after the synchronized statement are then printed (lines 36–39). The `break` statement (line 41) is used to get out of the `while` loop, print a message (line 45), and allow the thread to return from `run()`.

While the new thread has been checking what it sees as the values of value and missedIt, the main thread has been slowly progressing through workMethod() (lines 48–67). After sleeping for two seconds (line 52), the main thread sets value to 50 (line 54). This is greater than 20 and should cause the thread inside run() to leave the while loop, but that thread might not see the change! After setting value, the main thread sleeps for five seconds to give the other thread a chance to notice the change (line 58). In case setting value to 50 was not noticed, it proceeds to set missedIt to true (line 60) and then sleeps for three seconds. Because value is not volatile and missedIt is volatile, you'll be able to see whether the use of volatile is important.

Listing 7.2 shows the possible output when Volatile is run. Your output should be a close match with only a couple of lines swapped.

LISTING 7.2   Possible Output from Volatile

```
 1:  0.170 Thread-0: entering run()
 2:  0.280     main: entering workMethod()
 3:  0.610     main: in workMethod() - about to sleep for 2 seconds
 4:  2.700     main: in workMethod() - just set value=50
 5:  2.700     main: in workMethod() - about to sleep for 5 seconds
 6:  7.750     main: in workMethod() - just set missedIt=true
 7:  7.750     main: in workMethod() - about to sleep for 3 seconds
 8:  7.750 Thread-0: in run() - see value=10, but rumor has it that
    ➥ it changed!
 9:  7.750 Thread-0: in run() - valueAfterSync=50
10:  7.750 Thread-0: leaving run()
11: 10.710     main: leaving workMethod()
```

Notice that 2.700 seconds after startup, the main thread sets value equal to 50 (line 4). Thread-0 does not notice this change in value. At 7.750 seconds, main sets the volatile variable missedIt to true (line 6). Thread-0 notices this change right away, but still sees value as 10 (line 8). After Thread-0 runs through the synchronized block, it finally sees that value is 50 (line 9).

Listing 7.2 shows the output when Volatile is run with the default command-line options in the VM included in Sun Microsystem's JDK 1.2. If the built-in Just-In-Time (JIT) compiler is turned off,

```
java -Djava.compiler=NONE Volatile
```

the code behaves as if value was declared to be volatile. Listing 7.3 shows the different output that this produces. Again, your output should match closely with only a message or two swapped.

LISTING 7.3   Possible Output from Volatile When the JIT Is Disabled

```
1:   0.110 Thread-0: entering run()
2:   0.220     main: entering workMethod()
3:   0.220     main: in workMethod() - about to sleep for 2 seconds
4:   2.200     main: in workMethod() - just set value=50
5:   2.200     main: in workMethod() - about to sleep for 5 seconds
6:   2.200 Thread-0: leaving run()
7:   7.200     main: in workMethod() - just set missedIt=true
8:   7.250     main: in workMethod() - about to sleep for 3 seconds
9: 10.220     main: leaving workMethod()
```

Notice that this time, when value is set to 50 by the main thread at 2.200 seconds (line 4), Thread-0 notices right away (line 6). In fact, the while loop of the run() method of Volatile exits normally (without the break) and simply prints the "leaving run()" message. With the JIT turned off, all threads read and write directly to shared memory and don't keep a private copy of variables. It is as if every member variable is declared to be volatile.

As Table 7.1 shows, volatile makes a difference only when JDK 1.1 or 1.2 is run with the Just-In-Time compiler turned on. JDK 1.0 did not include a JIT, so it can't be turned on or off. The JIT performs optimizations that make the use of volatile necessary.

TABLE 7.1   When the Use of volatile Makes a Difference

Version	Command Line	volatile Matters
JDK 1.2	java Volatile	Yes
JDK 1.2	java -Djava.compiler= NONE Volatile	No
JDK 1.1	java Volatile	Yes
JDK 1.1	java -nojit Volatile	No
JDK 1.0	java Volatile	No

Before Sun included a JIT with their VMs, volatile did not make a difference. In addition, even with the JIT, every time that a thread enters or leaves a synchronized block, it reconciles its private copy of a variable with the shared copy. Blocks of synchronized code are scattered throughout the java.* class libraries, so a developer might not even be aware that the private copy has been reconciled. For example, System.out.println() contains a synchronized block, so using it to print out the current value in Volatile would keep the private copy up to date, and the volatile modifier would seem to have no effect. Many developers have written code that *should have* used the volatile modifier on some of the member variables. But because of at least one of these reasons, the missing volatile failed to make a critical difference.

> **TIP**
>
> Use `volatile` on member variables that can be accessed by two or more threads unless *all* the threads access the variables within synchronized blocks of code. If a member variable remains constant after construction (it is read-only), there is no need for it to be `volatile`.

The `volatile` modifier exists to request that the VM always access the shared copy of the variable. This is less efficient than allowing the VM to perform optimizations by keeping a private copy. You should use `volatile` only when it is necessary; overuse will unnecessarily slow the application's execution.

synchronized Method Modifier

The addition of the `synchronized` modifier to a method declaration ensures that only one thread is allowed inside the method at a time. This can be useful in keeping out other threads while the state of an object is temporarily inconsistent.

Two Threads Simultaneously in the Same Method of One Object

As `BothInMethod` (see Listing 7.4) shows, normally more than one thread is allowed to be inside a method at a time.

LISTING 7.4   BothInMethod.java—Shows That More Than One Thread Can Be Inside a Method

```
 1: public class BothInMethod extends Object {
 2:     private String objID;
 3:
 4:     public BothInMethod(String objID) {
 5:         this.objID = objID;
 6:     }
 7:
 8:     public void doStuff(int val) {
 9:         print("entering doStuff()");
10:         int num = val * 2 + objID.length();
11:         print("in doStuff() - local variable num=" + num);
12:
13:         // slow things down to make observations
14:         try { Thread.sleep(2000); }
```

```
                          ➟ catch ( InterruptedException x ) { }
15:
16:         print("leaving doStuff()");
17:     }
18:
19:     public void print(String msg) {
20:         threadPrint("objID=" + objID + " - " + msg);
21:     }
22:
23:     public static void threadPrint(String msg) {
24:         String threadName = Thread.currentThread().getName();
25:         System.out.println(threadName + ": " + msg);
26:     }
27:
28:     public static void main(String[] args) {
29:         final BothInMethod bim = new BothInMethod("obj1");
30:
31:         Runnable runA = new Runnable() {
32:                 public void run() {
33:                     bim.doStuff(3);
34:                 }
35:             };
36:
37:         Thread threadA = new Thread(runA, "threadA");
38:         threadA.start();
39:
40:         try { Thread.sleep(200); }
                          ➟ catch ( InterruptedException x ) { }
41:
42:         Runnable runB = new Runnable() {
43:                 public void run() {
44:                     bim.doStuff(7);
45:                 }
46:             };
47:
48:         Thread threadB = new Thread(runB, "threadB");
49:         threadB.start();
50:     }
51: }
```

In main() (lines 28–50), one BothInMethod object is instantiated with an identifier of obj1 (line 29). Next, two threads are created to simultaneously access the doStuff() method. The first is named threadA, and the second threadB. After threadA is started (line 38), it invokes doStuff() and passes in 3 (line 33). About 200 milliseconds later, threadB is started (line 49) and invokes doStuff() on the same object, passing in 7 (line 44).

Both `threadA` and `threadB` will be inside `doStuff()` (lines 8–17) at the same time; `threadA` will enter first, and `threadB` will follow 200 milliseconds later. Inside `doStuff()`, the local variable `num` is calculated using the `int` passed in as parameter `val` and the member variable `objID` (line 10). Because `threadA` and `threadB` each pass in a different `val`, the local variable `num` will be different for each thread. A sleep is used inside `doStuff()` to slow things down enough to prove that both threads are simultaneously inside the same method of the same object (line 14).

> **NOTE**
>
> If two or more threads are simultaneously inside a method, each thread has its own copy of local variables.

Listing 7.5 shows the output produced when `BothInMethod` is run. Your output should match. Notice that `threadA` enters `doStuff()` first (line 1) and calculates that its local variable `num` is 10 (line 2). While `threadA` is still inside `doStuff()`, `threadB` also enters it (line 3) and calculates that its local variable `num` is 18 (line 4). Next, `threadA` reports that it is leaving `doStuff()` (line 5) and is followed closely by `threadB` (line 6).

LISTING 7.5 Output from BothInMethod (Your Output Should Match)

```
1: threadA: objID=obj1 - entering doStuff()
2: threadA: objID=obj1 - in doStuff() - local variable num=10
3: threadB: objID=obj1 - entering doStuff()
4: threadB: objID=obj1 - in doStuff() - local variable num=18
5: threadA: objID=obj1 - leaving doStuff()
6: threadB: objID=obj1 - leaving doStuff()
```

One Thread at a Time

More than one thread can be inside a method, and each thread keeps a copy of its own local variables. However, there are times when application constraints require that only one thread be permitted inside a method at a time. In `OnlyOneInMethod` (see Listing 7.6), the method modifier `synchronized` has been added to `doStuff()` (line 8). Other than this change, the rest of the class works the same as it did in `BothInMethod`.

LISTING 7.6 OnlyOneInMethod.java—Restricting Access to One Thread at a Time

```
1: public class OnlyOneInMethod extends Object {
2:     private String objID;
3:
4:     public OnlyOneInMethod(String objID) {
```

```
 5:            this.objID = objID;
 6:        }
 7:
 8:    public synchronized void doStuff(int val) {
 9:            print("entering doStuff()");
10:            int num = val * 2 + objID.length();
11:            print("in doStuff() - local variable num=" + num);
12:
13:            // slow things down to make observations
14:            try { Thread.sleep(2000); }
         ➥         catch ( InterruptedException x ) { }
15:
16:            print("leaving doStuff()");
17:        }
18:
19:    public void print(String msg) {
20:            threadPrint("objID=" + objID + " - " + msg);
21:        }
22:
23:    public static void threadPrint(String msg) {
24:            String threadName = Thread.currentThread().getName();
25:            System.out.println(threadName + ": " + msg);
26:        }
27:
28:    public static void main(String[] args) {
29:            final OnlyOneInMethod ooim = new OnlyOneInMethod("obj1");
30:
31:            Runnable runA = new Runnable() {
32:                    public void run() {
33:                        ooim.doStuff(3);
34:                    }
35:                };
36:
37:            Thread threadA = new Thread(runA, "threadA");
38:            threadA.start();
39:
40:            try { Thread.sleep(200); }
         ➥         catch ( InterruptedException x ) { }
41:
42:            Runnable runB = new Runnable() {
43:                    public void run() {
44:                        ooim.doStuff(7);
45:                    }
46:                };
47:
48:            Thread threadB = new Thread(runB, "threadB");
49:            threadB.start();
50:        }
51: }
```

Only one thread at a time will be allowed into `doStuff()` because it is now `synchronized`. Listing 7.7 shows the output when `OnlyOneInMethod` is run. Your output should match. Notice that this time, `threadA` enters (line 1) and leaves (line 3) the `doStuff()` method before `threadB` is allowed to enter (line 4). The addition of the `synchronized` modifier successfully guarded `doStuff()` and allowed only one thread to enter at a time.

LISTING 7.7   Output from OnlyOneInMethod (Your Output Should Match)

```
1: threadA: objID=obj1 - entering doStuff()
2: threadA: objID=obj1 - in doStuff() - local variable num=10
3: threadA: objID=obj1 - leaving doStuff()
4: threadB: objID=obj1 - entering doStuff()
5: threadB: objID=obj1 - in doStuff() - local variable num=18
6: threadB: objID=obj1 - leaving doStuff()
```

When a thread encounters a `synchronized` instance method, it blocks until it can get exclusive access to the object-level mutex lock. *Mutex* is short for mutual exclusion. A mutex lock can be held by only one thread at a time. Other threads waiting for the lock will block until it is released. When the lock is released, all the threads waiting for it compete for exclusive access. Only one will be successful, and the other threads will go back into a blocked state waiting for the lock to be released again.

If one `synchronized` method on an object invokes another `synchronized` method on that same object, it will not block trying to get the object-level lock because it already has exclusive access to the lock.

Two Threads, Two Objects

Every instance of a class has its *own* object-level lock. The `TwoObjects` class shown in Listing 7.8 demonstrates that each object has its own object-level lock.

LISTING 7.8   TwoObjects.java

```
1: public class TwoObjects extends Object {
2:     private String objID;
3:
4:     public TwoObjects(String objID) {
5:         this.objID = objID;
6:     }
7:
8:     public synchronized void doStuff(int val) {
9:         print("entering doStuff()");
```

```
10:           int num = val * 2 + objID.length();
11:           print("in doStuff() - local variable num=" + num);
12:
13:           // slow things down to make observations
14:           try { Thread.sleep(2000); }
                    ➡ catch ( InterruptedException x ) { }
15:
16:           print("leaving doStuff()");
17:       }
18:
19:       public void print(String msg) {
20:           threadPrint("objID=" + objID + " - " + msg);
21:       }
22:
23:       public static void threadPrint(String msg) {
24:           String threadName = Thread.currentThread().getName();
25:           System.out.println(threadName + ": " + msg);
26:       }
27:
28:       public static void main(String[] args) {
29:           final TwoObjects obj1 = new TwoObjects("obj1");
30:           final TwoObjects obj2 = new TwoObjects("obj2");
31:
32:           Runnable runA = new Runnable() {
33:                   public void run() {
34:                       obj1.doStuff(3);
35:                   }
36:               };
37:
38:           Thread threadA = new Thread(runA, "threadA");
39:           threadA.start();
40:
41:           try { Thread.sleep(200); }
                    ➡ catch ( InterruptedException x ) { }
42:
43:           Runnable runB = new Runnable() {
44:                   public void run() {
45:                       obj2.doStuff(7);
46:                   }
47:               };
48:
49:           Thread threadB = new Thread(runB, "threadB");
50:           threadB.start();
51:       }
52: }
```

This time, two different objects are created (lines 29–30). The `doStuff()` method of `obj1` is invoked by `threadA` (line 34). A fraction of a second later, the `doStuff()` method of `obj2` is invoked by `threadB` (line 45). The `doStuff()` method *is* synchronized (line 8), but this time there is no competition between `threadA` and `threadB` for exclusive access. Each thread gets exclusive access to the object-level lock of the instance it is working on. Listing 7.9 shows the output when `TwoObjects` is run. Your output should match.

LISTING 7.9 Output from TwoObjects (Your Output Should Match)

```
1: threadA: objID=obj1 - entering doStuff()
2: threadA: objID=obj1 - in doStuff() - local variable num=10
3: threadB: objID=obj2 - entering doStuff()
4: threadB: objID=obj2 - in doStuff() - local variable num=18
5: threadA: objID=obj1 - leaving doStuff()
6: threadB: objID=obj2 - leaving doStuff()
```

Although the `doStuff()` method is synchronized, there is no competition for exclusive access to the object-level lock. Each instance, `obj1` and `obj2`, has its own object-level lock. When `threadA` enters the `doStuff()` method of `obj1` (line 1), it acquires exclusive access to the object-level lock for `obj1`. When `threadB` enters the `doStuff()` method of `obj2` (line 3), it acquires exclusive access to the object-level lock for `obj2`.

Avoiding Accidental Corruption of an Object

`CorruptWrite`, shown in Listing 7.10, demonstrates the need to control concurrent access to a method. In this example, two strings are passed to a method for assignment into member variables. The trouble is that two threads are simultaneously trying to make assignments, and their assignments might get interleaved.

LISTING 7.10 CorruptWrite.java—Trouble Because of the Lack of Synchronization

```
1: public class CorruptWrite extends Object {
2:     private String fname;
3:     private String lname;
4:
5:     public void setNames(String firstName, String lastName) {
6:         print("entering setNames()");
7:         fname = firstName;
8:
9:         // A thread might be swapped out here, and may stay
10:        // out for a varying amount of time. The different
```

Concurrent Access to Objects and Variables

CHAPTER 7

135

7

CONCURRENT
ACCESS TO OBJECTS
AND VARIABLES

```
11:            // sleep times exaggerate this.
12:            if ( fname.length() < 5 ) {
13:                try { Thread.sleep(1000); }
14:                catch ( InterruptedException x ) { }
15:            } else {
16:                try { Thread.sleep(2000); }
17:                catch ( InterruptedException x ) { }
18:            }
19:
20:            lname = lastName;
21:
22:            print("leaving setNames() - " + lname + ", " + fname);
23:        }
24:
25:        public static void print(String msg) {
26:            String threadName = Thread.currentThread().getName();
27:            System.out.println(threadName + ": " + msg);
28:        }
29:
30:        public static void main(String[] args) {
31:            final CorruptWrite cw = new CorruptWrite();
32:
33:            Runnable runA = new Runnable() {
34:                    public void run() {
35:                        cw.setNames("George", "Washington");
36:                    }
37:                };
38:
39:            Thread threadA = new Thread(runA, "threadA");
40:            threadA.start();
41:
42:            try { Thread.sleep(200); }
43:            catch ( InterruptedException x ) { }
44:
45:            Runnable runB = new Runnable() {
46:                    public void run() {
47:                        cw.setNames("Abe", "Lincoln");
48:                    }
49:                };
50:
51:            Thread threadB = new Thread(runB, "threadB");
52:            threadB.start();
53:        }
54: }
```

In main() (lines 30–53), a single instance of CorruptWrite is created and referred to by cw (line 31). Two threads are started and both call the setNames() method passing in a first and last name. First, threadA executes cw.setNames("George", "Washington") (line 35) and 200 milliseconds later, threadB executes cw.setNames("Abe", "Lincoln") (line 47).

CorruptWrite has two member variables, fname and lname (lines 2–3), that hold the names passed to setNames(). Inside setNames() (lines 5–23), the first parameter passed is assigned to fname (line 7). Then, depending on the length of fname, the thread sleeps for either one or two seconds (lines 12–18). After the nap, the second parameter is assigned to the member variable lname (line 20).

I used the variable length sleep inside setNames() to exaggerate what might really happen. The exaggeration will help to land the object in an inconsistent state. Real-world code would look more like the following:

```
public void setNames(String firstName, String lastName) {
    fname = firstName;
    lname = lastName;
}
```

This revised and quick setNames() method is still subtly dangerous in a multithreaded environment. It is possible that threadA could be swapped off the processor by the thread scheduler just *after* making the fname assignment, and just *before* making the lname assignment. Although threadA is halfway complete with its work, threadB could come along and assign its parameters to both fname and lname. When threadA gets scheduled to run again, it finishes up by assigning its second parameter to lname. This leaves the object in an inconsistent state. Most of the time this code will run fine, but now and then it will corrupt the object. By adding the variable-length sleeps in the setNames() method used in CorruptWrite, I have guaranteed that the object will wind up corrupted for the purposes of demonstration. Table 7.2 summarizes the states of the object at various points in time.

TABLE 7.2   States of the Member Variables of CorruptWrite at Various Points in Time

fname	*lname*	*Point in Time*
null	null	Before either thread enters setNames()
George	null	After threadA sets fname
Abe	Lincoln	After threadB sets both
Abe	Washington	After threadA sets lname

Listing 7.11 shows the output produced when CorruptWrite is run. Your output should match. Before going to sleep, threadA reports that it has entered the setNames() method (line 1).

While threadA is sleeping, threadB comes along and enters setNames() (line 2). It assigns values to both member variables and just before returning, prints their values (line 3). When threadA wakes up, it assigns its second value and just before returning, prints the current values of the member variables (line 4) showing the inconsistent state. The name-pair "Abe" and "Washington" was never passed to setNames(), but this is the current (corrupted) state of the object.

LISTING 7.11   Output from CorruptWrite (Your Output Should Match)

```
1: threadA: entering setNames()
2: threadB: entering setNames()
3: threadB: leaving setNames() - Lincoln, Abe
4: threadA: leaving setNames() - Washington, Abe
```

FixedWrite (see Listing 7.12) corrects the dangerous code in CorruptWrite simply by adding the synchronized method modifier to the setNames() method (line 5). Otherwise, FixedWrite is basically the same as CorruptWrite.

LISTING 7.12   FixedWrite.java—Using synchronized to Control Concurrent Changes

```
 1: public class FixedWrite extends Object {
 2:     private String fname;
 3:     private String lname;
 4:
 5:     public synchronized void setNames(
 6:                 String firstName,
 7:                 String lastName
 8:             ) {
 9:
10:         print("entering setNames()");
11:         fname = firstName;
12:
13:         // A thread might be swapped out here, and may stay
14:         // out for a varying amount of time. The different
15:         // sleep times exaggerate this.
16:         if ( fname.length() < 5 ) {
17:             try { Thread.sleep(1000); }
18:             catch ( InterruptedException x ) { }
19:         } else {
20:             try { Thread.sleep(2000); }
```

continues

LISTING 7.12   Continued

```
21:                 catch ( InterruptedException x ) { }
22:         }
23:
24:         lname = lastName;
25:
26:         print("leaving setNames() - " + lname + ", " + fname);
27:     }
28:
29:     public static void print(String msg) {
30:         String threadName = Thread.currentThread().getName();
31:         System.out.println(threadName + ": " + msg);
32:     }
33:
34:     public static void main(String[] args) {
35:         final FixedWrite fw = new FixedWrite();
36:
37:         Runnable runA = new Runnable() {
38:                 public void run() {
39:                     fw.setNames("George", "Washington");
40:                 }
41:             };
42:
43:         Thread threadA = new Thread(runA, "threadA");
44:         threadA.start();
45:
46:         try { Thread.sleep(200); }
47:         catch ( InterruptedException x ) { }
48:
49:         Runnable runB = new Runnable() {
50:                 public void run() {
51:                     fw.setNames("Abe", "Lincoln");
52:                 }
53:             };
54:
55:         Thread threadB = new Thread(runB, "threadB");
56:         threadB.start();
57:     }
58: }
```

If you make setNames() a sychronized method, each thread that tries to enter this method
will block until it can get exclusive access to the object-level lock. Now when threadA goes to
sleep (or if the thread scheduler had otherwise decided to swap it out), threadB is prevented
from entering the method. When threadA finally completes its work inside setNames(), it

automatically releases the lock as it returns. Now, `threadB` is able to gain exclusive access to the lock and enters `setNames()`.

The variable-length sleeps are still inside `setNames()` to demonstrate that the addition of the `synchronized` method modifier solved the problem. Real-world code (that is truly safe) would look more like the following:

```
public synchronized void setNames(String firstName, String lastName) {
    fname = firstName;
    lname = lastName;
}
```

Listing 7.13 shows the output when `FixedWrite` is run. Your output should match. Notice that `threadB` doesn't enter `setNames()` (line 3) until `threadA` has left it (line 2). In this fixed version, both `threadA` and `threadB` print consistent name-pairs when they leave (lines 2, 4).

LISTING 7.13   Output from FixedWrite (Your Output Should Match)

```
1: threadA: entering setNames()
2: threadA: leaving setNames() - Washington, George
3: threadB: entering setNames()
4: threadB: leaving setNames() - Lincoln, Abe
```

Deferring Access to an Object While It Is Inconsistent

`FixedWrite` solved the problem by ensuring that the object was left in a consistent state by a call to `setNames()`. The object is consistent both before and after a thread invokes `setNames()`, but it is inconsistent while a thread is inside `setNames()`. If one thread is executing `setNames()` at the same time that a second thread is accessing the member variables, the second thread might occasionally see an inconsistent name-pair. `DirtyRead` (see Listing 7.14) demonstrates this problem.

LISTING 7.14   DirtyRead.java—Accessing Members Variables While in an Inconsistent State

```
1: public class DirtyRead extends Object {
2:     private String fname;
3:     private String lname;
4:
5:     public String getNames() {
6:         return lname + ", " + fname;
7:     }
8:
```

continues

LISTING 7.14   Continued

```
 9:    public synchronized void setNames(
10:                String firstName,
11:                String lastName
12:            ) {
13:
14:        print("entering setNames()");
15:        fname = firstName;
16:
17:        try { Thread.sleep(1000); }
18:        catch ( InterruptedException x ) { }
19:
20:        lname = lastName;
21:        print("leaving setNames() - " + lname + ", " + fname);
22:    }
23:
24:    public static void print(String msg) {
25:        String threadName = Thread.currentThread().getName();
26:        System.out.println(threadName + ": " + msg);
27:    }
28:
29:    public static void main(String[] args) {
30:        final DirtyRead dr = new DirtyRead();
31:        dr.setNames("George", "Washington"); // initially
32:
33:        Runnable runA = new Runnable() {
34:                public void run() {
35:                    dr.setNames("Abe", "Lincoln");
36:                }
37:            };
38:
39:        Thread threadA = new Thread(runA, "threadA");
40:        threadA.start();
41:
42:        try { Thread.sleep(200); }
43:        catch ( InterruptedException x ) { }
44:
45:        Runnable runB = new Runnable() {
46:                public void run() {
47:                    print("getNames()=" + dr.getNames());
48:                }
49:            };
50:
51:        Thread threadB = new Thread(runB, "threadB");
52:        threadB.start();
53:    }
54: }
```

DirtyRead is an evolution of FixedWrite. A new method called getNames() has been added (lines 5–7). This method constructs and returns a new String that is a combination of the lname and fname member variables (line 6).

The setNames() method (lines 9–22) is still synchronized (line 9). It has been simplified to just sleep for one second between the setting of the first name and last name.

Inside main() (lines 29–53), a few different actions are taken. First, just after the DirtyRead instance is created (line 30), setNames() is invoked by the main thread to initially set the names to "George" and "Washington" (line 31). After that, threadA invokes setNames(), passing in "Abe" and "Lincoln" (line 35). threadA runs for about 200 milliseconds before threadB is started (line 42).

The setNames() method is still slow, so while the names are in the process of being changed by threadA, threadB invokes the getNames() method (line 47). Listing 7.15 shows the output when DirtyRead is run. Your output should match.

Listing 7.15   Output from DirtyRead (Your Output Should Match)

```
1: main: entering setNames()
2: main: leaving setNames() - Washington, George
3: threadA: entering setNames()
4: threadB: getNames()=Washington, Abe
5: threadA: leaving setNames() - Lincoln, Abe
```

The setNames() method is invoked by threadA (line 3). Before it can finish setting both names, threadB invokes getNames() (line 4). It returns the combination of "Abe" and "Washington," catching the object in an inconsistent state. When threadA finishes executing setNames(), the object is back to a consistent state (line 5).

It's an unavoidable fact that the object must be in an inconsistent state for a brief period of time, even with everything except the assignments taken out:

```
public synchronized void setNames(String firstName, String lastName) {
    fname = firstName;
    lname = lastName;
}
```

No matter how fast the processor is, it's possible that the thread scheduler could swap out the thread making the changes after it has changed fname but before it has changed lname. Holding an object-level lock does not prevent a thread from being swapped out. And if it is swapped out, it continues to hold the object-level lock. Because of this, care must be taken to ensure that all reads are blocked when the data is in an inconsistent state. CleanRead (see Listing 7.16) simply adds the synchronized method modifier to getNames() to control concurrent reading and writing.

LISTING 7.16 CleanRead.java—Using synchronized to Control Concurrent Access While Changes Are Being Made

```
 1: public class CleanRead extends Object {
 2:     private String fname;
 3:     private String lname;
 4:
 5:     public synchronized String getNames() {
 6:         return lname + ", " + fname;
 7:     }
 8:
 9:     public synchronized void setNames(
10:                 String firstName,
11:                 String lastName
12:             ) {
13:
14:         print("entering setNames()");
15:         fname = firstName;
16:
17:         try { Thread.sleep(1000); }
18:         catch ( InterruptedException x ) { }
19:
20:         lname = lastName;
21:         print("leaving setNames() - " + lname + ", " + fname);
22:     }
23:
24:     public static void print(String msg) {
25:         String threadName = Thread.currentThread().getName();
26:         System.out.println(threadName + ": " + msg);
27:     }
28:
29:     public static void main(String[] args) {
30:         final CleanRead cr = new CleanRead();
31:         cr.setNames("George", "Washington"); // initially
32:
33:         Runnable runA = new Runnable() {
34:                 public void run() {
35:                     cr.setNames("Abe", "Lincoln");
36:                 }
37:             };
38:
39:         Thread threadA = new Thread(runA, "threadA");
40:         threadA.start();
41:
42:         try { Thread.sleep(200); }
43:         catch ( InterruptedException x ) { }
44:
```

```
45:            Runnable runB = new Runnable() {
46:                public void run() {
47:                    print("getNames()=" + cr.getNames());
48:                }
49:            };
50:
51:            Thread threadB = new Thread(runB, "threadB");
52:            threadB.start();
53:        }
54: }
```

Inside main() (lines 29–53), the same actions are taken as were for DirtyRead. First, just after the CleanRead instance is created (line 30), setNames() is invoked by the main thread to initially set the names to "George" and "Washington" (line 31). After that, threadA invokes setNames(), passing in "Abe" and "Lincoln" (line 35). threadA runs for about 200 milliseconds before threadB is started (line 42).

The setNames() method is still slow, so while the names are in the process of being changed by threadA, threadB invokes the getNames() method (line 47). Because getNames() is now synchronized, threadB blocks trying to get exclusive access to the object-level lock. When threadA returns from setNames(), it automatically releases the object-level lock. Then threadB proceeds to acquire the object-level lock and enters the getNames() method. Listing 7.17 shows the output when CleanRead is run. Your output should match.

LISTING 7.17   Output from CleanRead (Your Output Should Match)

```
1: main: entering setNames()
2: main: leaving setNames() - Washington, George
3: threadA: entering setNames()
4: threadA: leaving setNames() - Lincoln, Abe
5: threadB: getNames()=Lincoln, Abe
```

Although threadB invokes getNames() before threadA is finished with setNames(), it blocks waiting to get exclusive access to the object-level lock. This time, getNames() returns a valid name-pair (line 5).

TIP

If two or more threads might be simultaneously interacting with the member variables of an object, and at least one of those threads might change the values, it is generally a good idea to use synchronized to control concurrent access. If only one thread will be accessing an object, using synchronized is unnecessary and slows execution.

synchronized Statement Block

The synchronized block can be used when a whole method does not need to be synchronized or when you want the thread to get an object-level lock on a different object. The synchronized statement block looks like this:

```
synchronized ( obj ) {
    // block of code
}
```

where obj is a reference to the object whose object-level lock must be acquired before entering the block of code.

This setPoint() method

```
public synchronized void setPoint(int x, int y) {
    this.x = x;
    this.y = y;
}
```

can be rewritten to instead use a synchronized block:

```
public void setPoint(int x, int y) {
    synchronized ( this ) {
        this.x = x;
        this.y = y;
    }
}
```

The behavior of both versions of setPoint() is virtually the same. They do compile to different byte-code, but both of them make sure that they have exclusive access to the object-level lock for the instance before making changes to x and y.

Reducing the Time That the Lock Is Held

A synchronized block can be used to reduce the time that the object-level lock is held. If a method does a lot of other things that don't require access to the member variables, it can shorten the time that it holds the lock to just the critical portion:

```
public void setValues(int x, double ratio) {
    // Some other, long-running statements that don't work
    // with the member variables go here.
    // ...
    double processedValA = // ... long calculation ...
```

```
    double processedValB = // ... long calculation ...
    // ...
    synchronized ( this ) {
        a = processedValA;
        b = processedValB;
    }
}
```

In setValues(), exclusive access to the object-level lock is not needed until the time-consuming calculations have been made and the results are ready to be stored. At the bottom of the method, the object-level lock is acquired and held briefly to simply assign new values to the member variables a and b.

Locking an Object Other Than this

When a synchronized statement is used as follows,

```
synchronized ( mutex ) {
    // block of code
}
```

the reference mutex indicates the object whose object-level lock must be acquired before entering the statement block. It can be a reference to any object in the VM, not just this. Regardless of how a thread leaves a synchronized block, it automatically releases the lock. This includes a return statement, a throw statement, or just falling through to the next statement after the block. Calling a method from within the synchronized block does not constitute *leaving* the block (the lock is still held).

Sometimes you will need to call two synchronized methods on an object and be sure that no other thread sneaks in between the calls. Consider this code fragment from a class called Bucket:

```
public class Bucket extends Object {
    // ...
    public synchronized boolean isSpaceAvailable() { // ...
    public synchronized void add(BucketItem o)
                    throws NoSpaceAvailableException { // ...
    public synchronized BucketItem remove() { // ...
    // ...
}
```

All three methods use the synchronized modifier to control concurrent access by multiple threads. Items of the type BucketItem can be added and removed from Bucket. When using the object, a call should be made to isSpaceAvailable() before trying to add another

BucketItem, to prevent the NoSpaceAvailableException from being thrown. Of course, there are other ways to design Bucket, but imagine that you are stuck with this class as is. To add an item to Bucket, the following code fragment could be used:

```
Bucket b = // ...
// ...
if ( b.isSpaceAvailable() ) {
    b.add(item);
}
```

This is fine if only one thread is interacting with this instance of Bucket. But if multiple threads are potentially trying to add BucketItem objects to the same Bucket, a new approach has to be taken to avoid a race condition. Imagine that threadA checks and sees that space is available, but before it actually adds its item, threadB checks and also sees that space is available. Now threadA and threadB are racing to actually add an item. Only one can win the race, and that thread gets to add its item. The other thread will fail to add its item and will throw a NoSpaceAvailableException. To prevent this problem, a synchronized block should be wrapped around the two method calls:

```
Bucket b = // ...
// ...
synchronized ( b ) {
    if ( b.isSpaceAvailable() ) {
        b.add(item);
    }
}
```

The synchronized block uses the object-level lock on b, the Bucket instance. This is the same lock that must be acquired before entering the isSpaceAvailable() and add() methods. If a thread can get the object-level lock and enter the synchronized block, it is guaranteed to be able to invoke isSpaceAvailable() and add() without blocking. Because it already has the object-level lock for b, there is no delay or competition to enter the synchronized methods. In addition, no other thread can invoke these methods until the first thread leaves the synchronized block.

Imagine that threadA is able to get exclusive access to the object-level lock on b and enters the synchronized block. It checks to see if space is available, but before it actually adds its item, the thread scheduler swaps it out. threadB comes along and is blocked from acquiring the lock on b, so it is swapped out. Regardless of any particular thread scheduling, no other thread will be able to get the object-level lock on b until threadA releases it. When threadA is finally scheduled to run again, it will proceed to add its element to b and release the lock as it leaves the synchronized block. After threadA leaves the synchronized block, threadB can acquire the object-level lock on b.

Safely Copying the Contents of a Vector into an Array

The `Vector` class is used to hold an expandable array of objects. Some of its methods are shown following:

```
public final synchronized void addElement(Object o)
public final synchronized void insertElementAt(Object o, int pos)
public final synchronized void setElementAt(Object o, int pos)
public final synchronized void removeElementAt(int pos)
public final synchronized boolean removeElement(Object o)
public final synchronized void removeAllElements()
public final int size()
public final synchronized Object elementAt(int pos)
public final synchronized Object firstElement()
public final synchronized Object lastElement()
public final synchronized Enumeration elements()
public final boolean contains(Object obj)
public final int indexOf(Object obj)
```

I generated this information using reflection on the `Vector` class in JDK 1.1 (information on 1.2 and Collections is included later in this chapter). Notice that many of the methods are synchronized—particularly the ones used to add and remove elements from the `Vector`.

`SafeVectorCopy` in Listing 7.18 shows how a synchronized block can be used in conjunction with the synchronized methods of `Vector` to copy the current contents of the `Vector` into a `String[]`.

LISTING 7.18   SafeVectorCopy.java—Safely Copying the Contents of a Vector into an Array

```
 1: import java.util.*;
 2:
 3: public class SafeVectorCopy extends Object {
 4:     public static void main(String[] args) {
 5:         Vector vect = new Vector();
 6:         vect.addElement("Synchronization");
 7:         vect.addElement("is");
 8:         vect.addElement("important");
 9:
10:         String[] word;
11:
12:         synchronized ( vect ) {
13:             int size = vect.size();
```

continues

LISTING 7.18   Continued

```
14:                    word = new String[size];
15:
16:                    for ( int i = 0; i < word.length; i++ ) {
17:                        word[i] = (String) vect.elementAt(i);
18:                    }
19:                }
20:
21:            System.out.println("word.length=" + word.length);
22:            for ( int i = 0; i < word.length; i++ ) {
23:                System.out.println("word[" + i + "]=" + word[i]);
24:            }
25:        }
26: }
```

In SafeVectorCopy, three strings are added to a new Vector referred to by vect (lines 5–8). The synchronized block (lines 12–19) uses the object-level lock of vect to keep out other threads while the copying is taking place. Inside the block, the current number of elements in the Vector is used to allocate a new String[] (lines 13–14). One by one, each element is retrieved, cast into a String, and stored into the array (lines 16–18). If another thread had been trying to access vect to add or remove elements during this time, it would have been blocked until the thread doing the copying left the synchronized block.

CAUTION

> As of JDK 1.2, Vector and Hashtable have been incorporated into the Collections API. All the old methods are still present, but some new ones have been added that are *not* synchronized. The SafeVectorCopy example is only really safe for pre-1.2 code. Later in this chapter, I'll show you how to safely use Collections in a multi-threaded environment.

static synchronized Methods

In addition to the *object*-level lock that exists for each instance of a class, there is a *class*-level lock that all instances of a particular class share. Every class loaded by the VM has exactly one class-level lock. If a method is both static and synchronized, a thread must get exclusive access to the class-level lock before entering the method.

The class-level lock can be used to control concurrent access to `static` member variables. Just as the object-level lock was needed to prevent data corruption in non-`static` member variables, the class-level lock is needed to prevent corruption of `static` member variables. Even when no variables are involved, the `synchronized` modifier can be used on `static` methods simply to ensure that only one thread is inside the method at a time.

As you might guess from the name, the `StaticNeedSync` class in Listing 7.19 demonstrates a case where a `static` method would benefit from the addition of the `synchronized` modifier.

LISTING 7.19 StaticNeedSync.java—Demonstrating the Need for Static Synchronized Methods

```
1: public class StaticNeedSync extends Object {
2:      private static int nextSerialNum = 10001;
3:
4:      public static int getNextSerialNum() {
5:          int sn = nextSerialNum;
6:
7:          // Simulate a delay that is possible if the thread
8:          // scheduler chooses to swap this thread off the
9:          // processor at this point. The delay is exaggerated
10:         // for demonstration purposes.
11:         try { Thread.sleep(1000); }
12:         catch ( InterruptedException x ) { }
13:
14:         nextSerialNum++;
15:         return sn;
16:     }
17:
18:     private static void print(String msg) {
19:         String threadName = Thread.currentThread().getName();
20:         System.out.println(threadName + ": " + msg);
21:     }
22:
23:     public static void main(String[] args) {
24:         try {
25:             Runnable r = new Runnable() {
26:                 public void run() {
27:                     print("getNextSerialNum()=" +
28:                             getNextSerialNum());
29:                 }
```

continues

LISTING 7.19 Continued

```
30:                        };
31:
32:             Thread threadA = new Thread(r, "threadA");
33:             threadA.start();
34:
35:             Thread.sleep(1500);
36:
37:             Thread threadB = new Thread(r, "threadB");
38:             threadB.start();
39:
40:             Thread.sleep(500);
41:
42:             Thread threadC = new Thread(r, "threadC");
43:             threadC.start();
44:
45:             Thread.sleep(2500);
46:
47:             Thread threadD = new Thread(r, "threadD");
48:             threadD.start();
49:         } catch ( InterruptedException x ) {
50:             // ignore
51:         }
52:     }
53: }
```

The StaticNeedSync class has a private, static member variable, nextSerialNum, which is used to hold the next serial number that will be given out (line 2). The getNextSerialNum()method (lines 4–16) is both public and static. It is invoked when a unique serial number is needed. When called, it takes the current value of nextSerialNum and stores it in a local variable sn (line 5). Then, it puts the calling thread to sleep for one second to simulate the possibility that it could get swapped out at this point by the thread scheduler (line 11). When the thread gets a chance to run again, it increments the nextSerialNum member variable to prepare it for the next call (line 14). The locally stored serial number sn is returned to the caller (line 15).

The main thread starts four threads to interact with the getNextSerialNum() method. All four threads use the same Runnable (lines 25–30). Inside this Runnable, the results of calling getNextSerialNum() are printed along with the thread name (lines 27–28).

The main thread starts threadA (line 33) and then sleeps for 1.5 seconds. This is enough time for threadA to enter and return from getNextSerialNum(). Next, the main thread starts threadB (line 38) and then sleeps for 0.5 seconds (line 40) before starting threadC (line 43). Both threadB and threadC will be inside getNextSerialNum() at the same time—and this will cause some trouble.

After waiting 2.5 seconds (plenty of time for threadB and threadC to return), main starts threadD (lines 45–48). threadD invokes getNextSerialNum() one last time. Listing 7.20 shows the output produced when StaticNeedSync is run. Your output should match.

LISTING 7.20   Output from StaticNeedSync (Your Output Should Match)

```
threadA: getNextSerialNum()=10001
threadB: getNextSerialNum()=10002
threadC: getNextSerialNum()=10002
threadD: getNextSerialNum()=10004
```

When both threadB and threadC are allowed inside getNextSerialNum() at the same time, they *both* see 10002 for their number. Then each thread proceeds to increment the counter, and threadD sees 10004. Two callers get the same serial number, and no one gets 10003.

This code (without the sleep) is still vulnerable to duplicate serial numbers:

```
public static int getNextSerialNum() { // still dangerous
    int sn = nextSerialNum;
    nextSerialNum++;
    return sn;
}
```

Even this code has risks:

```
public static int getNextSerialNum() { // still dangerous
    return nextSerialNum++;
}
```

In both cases, a thread could be swapped out after reading the value of nextSerialNum but before incrementing it. This will happen only on rare occasions, but the risk should be eliminated.

StaticSync (see Listing 7.21) solves the problem by adding the synchronized method modifier (line 4) to the static method getNextSerialNum(). This ensures that only one thread is allowed into the method at a time and eliminates the problems of duplicate serial numbers.

LISTING 7.21   StaticSync.java—Using synchronized with static to Control Concurrent Access

```
 1: public class StaticSync extends Object {
 2:     private static int nextSerialNum = 10001;
 3:
 4:     public static synchronized int getNextSerialNum() {
 5:         int sn = nextSerialNum;
 6:
 7:         // Simulate a delay that is possible if the thread
 8:         // scheduler chooses to swap this thread off the
 9:         // processor at this point. The delay is exaggerated
10:         // for demonstration purposes.
11:         try { Thread.sleep(1000); }
12:         catch ( InterruptedException x ) { }
13:
14:         nextSerialNum++;
15:         return sn;
16:     }
17:
18:     private static void print(String msg) {
19:         String threadName = Thread.currentThread().getName();
20:         System.out.println(threadName + ": " + msg);
21:     }
22:
23:     public static void main(String[] args) {
24:         try {
25:             Runnable r = new Runnable() {
26:                     public void run() {
27:                         print("getNextSerialNum()=" +
28:                                 getNextSerialNum());
29:                     }
30:                 };
31:
32:             Thread threadA = new Thread(r, "threadA");
33:             threadA.start();
34:
35:             Thread.sleep(1500);
36:
37:             Thread threadB = new Thread(r, "threadB");
38:             threadB.start();
39:
40:             Thread.sleep(500);
41:
```

```
42:            Thread threadC = new Thread(r, "threadC");
43:            threadC.start();
44:
45:            Thread.sleep(2500);
46:
47:            Thread threadD = new Thread(r, "threadD");
48:            threadD.start();
49:        } catch ( InterruptedException x ) {
50:            // ignore
51:        }
52:    }
53: }
```

Listing 7.22 shows the output produced when StaticSync is run. Your output should match.

LISTING 7.22   Output from StaticSync (Your Output Should Match)

```
threadA: getNextSerialNum()=10001
threadB: getNextSerialNum()=10002
threadC: getNextSerialNum()=10003
threadD: getNextSerialNum()=10004
```

Note that this time, threadC gets the unique serial number of 10003. The addition of synchronized to the static method getNextSerialNum() solves the problem by blocking threadC from entering until threadB was finished.

Using the Class-Level Lock in a synchronized Statement

The synchronized statement can also use a class-level lock. This can be useful if a static method runs for a long period of time. Additionally, it can be used to ensure that two static method calls by one thread are not interleaved with a call by another thread.

To lock on the class-level lock, use the following code

```
synchronized ( ClassName.class ) {
    // body
}
```

where ClassName is replaced with the real name of the class you want to use. Class StaticBlock (see Listing 7.23) demonstrates this technique.

LISTING 7.23   StaticBlock.java—Using .class to Gain Access to the Class-Level Lock

```
 1: public class StaticBlock extends Object {
 2:     public static synchronized void staticA() {
 3:         System.out.println("entering staticA()");
 4:
 5:         try { Thread.sleep(5000); }
 6:         catch ( InterruptedException x ) { }
 7:
 8:         System.out.println("leaving staticA()");
 9:     }
10:
11:     public static void staticB() {
12:         System.out.println("entering staticB()");
13:
14:         synchronized ( StaticBlock.class ) {
15:             System.out.println(
16:                     "in staticB() - inside sync block");
17:
18:             try { Thread.sleep(2000); }
19:             catch ( InterruptedException x ) { }
20:         }
21:
22:         System.out.println("leaving staticB()");
23:     }
24:
25:     public static void main(String[] args) {
26:         Runnable runA = new Runnable() {
27:                 public void run() {
28:                     StaticBlock.staticA();
29:                 }
30:             };
31:
32:         Thread threadA = new Thread(runA, "threadA");
33:         threadA.start();
34:
35:         try { Thread.sleep(200); }
36:         catch ( InterruptedException x ) { }
37:
38:         Runnable runB = new Runnable() {
39:                 public void run() {
40:                     StaticBlock.staticB();
41:                 }
42:             };
43:
44:         Thread threadB = new Thread(runB, "threadB");
```

```
45:            threadB.start();
46:     }
47: }
```

In StaticBlock, the staticA() method (lines 2–9) is both static and synchronized. The staticB() method (lines 11–23) is static and contains a synchronized block (lines 14–20). The object used to control access to this block is the Class object for StaticBlock and is found by using StaticBlock.class (line 14).

In main() (lines 25–46), threadA is started and invokes staticA() (line 28). After a brief 200 millisecond break, threadB is started and invokes staticB(). While threadA is sleeping inside staticA(), threadB enters staticB(), prints a message, and blocks waiting to enter the synchronized statement block (line 14). When threadA returns from staticA(), threadB is able to get the class-level lock and completes staticB().

Listing 7.24 shows the output produced when StaticBlock is run. Your output should match.

LISTING 7.24   Output from StaticBlock (Your Output Should Match)

```
1: entering staticA()
2: entering staticB()
3: leaving staticA()
4: in staticB() - inside sync block
5: leaving staticB()
```

Notice that although threadB is able to enter staticB() (line 2), it can't enter the synchronized block (line 4) until threadA returns from staticA() (line 3). threadB blocks waiting for threadA to release the class-level lock.

Synchronization and the Collections API

The Collections API is new to JDK 1.2 and includes a number of interfaces and classes that facilitate the manipulation of *collections* of objects. Vector and Hashtable are now part of the Collections API, but have retained their old functionality for backward compatibility. Some of the new classes and interfaces include Collection, List, Map, Set, ArrayList, LinkedList, and HashMap.

Wrapping Collections to Make Them synchronized

Vector and Hashtable were originally designed to be multithread-safe. Take Vector, for example—the methods used to add and remove elements are synchronized. If only one thread will ever interact with an instance of Vector, the work required to acquire and release the object-level lock is wasted.

The designers of the Collections API wanted to avoid the overhead of synchronization when it wasn't necessary. As a result, none of the methods that alter the contents of a collection are synchronized. If a Collection or Map will be accessed by multiple threads, it should be wrapped by a class that synchronizes all the methods.

CAUTION

Collections are not inherently multithread-safe. Extra steps must be taken when more than one thread will be interacting with a collection to make it multithread-safe.

There are several static methods in the Collections class that are used to wrap unsynchronized collections with synchronized methods:

```
public static Collection synchronizedCollection(Collection c)
public static List synchronizedList(List l)
public static Map synchronizedMap(Map m)
public static Set synchronizedSet(Set s)
public static SortedMap synchronizedSortedMap(SortedMap sm)
public static SortedSet synchronizedSortedSet(SortedSet ss)
```

Basically, these methods return new classes that have synchronized versions of the collections' methods. To create a List that is multithread-safe and backed by an ArrayList, use the following:

```
List list = Collections.synchronizedList(new ArrayList());
```

Notice that the ArrayList instance was immediately wrapped and that no direct reference to the unsynchronized ArrayList exists. This is the safest approach. If another thread was to get a direct reference to the ArrayList instance, it could perform unsynchronized changes.

TIP

When synchronizing collections, do not keep any direct reference to the original unsynchronized collection. This will ensure that no other thread accidentally makes uncoordinated changes.

Safely Copying the Contents of a List into an Array

The SafeListCopy class in Listing 7.25 shows three different ways that the contents of a List can be safely copied into a String[] in a multithreaded environment.

LISTING 7.25   SafeListCopy.java—Safely Copying the Contents of a List into an Array

```
 1: import java.util.*;
 2:
 3: public class SafeListCopy extends Object {
 4:     public static void printWords(String[] word) {
 5:         System.out.println("word.length=" + word.length);
 6:         for ( int i = 0; i < word.length; i++ ) {
 7:             System.out.println("word[" + i + "]=" + word[i]);
 8:         }
 9:     }
10:
11:     public static void main(String[] args) {
12:         // To be safe, only keep a reference to the
13:         // *synchronized* list so that you are sure that
14:         // all accesses are controlled.
15:         List wordList =
16:                 Collections.synchronizedList(new ArrayList());
17:
18:         wordList.add("Synchronization");
19:         wordList.add("is");
20:         wordList.add("important");
21:
22:         // First technique (favorite)
23:         String[] wordA =
24:                 (String[]) wordList.toArray(new String[0]);
25:
26:         printWords(wordA);
27:
28:         // Second technique
29:         String[] wordB;
30:         synchronized ( wordList ) {
31:             int size = wordList.size();
32:             wordB = new String[size];
33:             wordList.toArray(wordB);
34:         }
35:
36:         printWords(wordB);
37:
38:         // Third technique (the 'synchronized' *is* necessary)
39:         String[] wordC;
40:         synchronized ( wordList ) {
41:             wordC = (String[]) wordList.toArray(
```

continues

LISTING 7.25   Continued

```
42:                                          new String[wordList.size()]);
43:           }
44:
45:           printWords(wordC);
46:       }
47: }
```

In SafeListCopy, a multithread-safe version of List is constructed using
Collections.synchronizedList() and is backed by an ArrayList instance (lines 15–16).
Three Strings are added to the List (lines 18–20).

The first technique for copying the contents of wordList into a String[] is the simplest and
exploits a convenient feature of collections. The toArray() method is used to copy the contents into an array of the type specified by the parameter (lines 23–24). Because the toArray()
method was synchronized by wrapping, this is all that is necessary to safely copy the contents.
If other threads were trying to add or remove elements during this operation, they would be
blocked until it completed.

The second technique uses a synchronized statement to keep other threads out while two steps
are performed (lines 29–34). The first step is to determine the exact length needed for the destination String[] and to allocate the array (lines 31–32). The second step is to pass this perfectly
sized array to the toArray() method (line 33). This second technique has a slight efficiency
advantage over the first one in that it does not create a throw-away, zero-length String[].

The third technique combines the steps of the second technique into one line (lines 39–43). It
still needs to be inside a synchronized block because another thread could intervene after the
size() method is called but before the toArray() method is called (line 42).

I would recommend that you stick with the first technique in most cases because it is the most
straightforward and least error-prone. Listing 7.26 shows the output when SafeListCopy is run.
Your output should match. Notice that in all three cases the proper set of strings is produced.

LISTING 7.26   Output from SafeListCopy (Your Output Should Match)

```
word.length=3
word[0]=Synchronization
word[1]=is
word[2]=important
word.length=3
word[0]=Synchronization
word[1]=is
word[2]=important
word.length=3
```

```
word[0]=Synchronization
word[1]=is
word[2]=important
```

Safely Iterating Through the Elements of a Collection

The elements of a Collection can be stepped through one by one by using an Iterator. In a multithreaded environment, you will generally want to block other threads from adding or removing elements while you are iterating through the current collection of elements.

The class SafeCollectionIteration shown in Listing 7.27 demonstrates how to block other threads while using an Iterator.

LISTING 7.27 SafeCollectionIteration.java—Safely Iterating Through the Elements of a Collection

```
 1: import java.util.*;
 2:
 3: public class SafeCollectionIteration extends Object {
 4:     public static void main(String[] args) {
 5:         // To be safe, only keep a reference to the
 6:         // *synchronized* list so that you are sure
 7:         // that all accesses are controlled.
 8:
 9:         // The collection *must* be synchronized
10:         // (a List in this case).
11:         List wordList =
12:                 Collections.synchronizedList(new ArrayList());
13:
14:         wordList.add("Iterators");
15:         wordList.add("require");
16:         wordList.add("special");
17:         wordList.add("handling");
18:
19:         // All of this must be in a synchronized block to
20:         // block other threads from modifying wordList while
21:         // the iteration is in progress.
22:         synchronized ( wordList ) {
23:             Iterator iter = wordList.iterator();
24:             while ( iter.hasNext() ) {
25:                 String s = (String) iter.next();
26:                 System.out.println("found string: " + s +
27:                     ", length=" + s.length());
28:             }
29:         }
30:     }
31: }
```

First, an `ArrayList` is wrapped in synchronization to ensure safe multithread access (lines 11–12). Next, four strings are added to the `List` (lines 14–17). A `synchronized` statement block is used to gain and hold the object-level lock for the `List` until the iteration is complete (lines 22–29). When the lock is safely held, an `Iterator` is retrieved by invoking the `iterator()` method (line 23) of `Collection` (`List` IS-A `Collection`). The `hasNext()` and `next()` methods of `Iterator` are used to traverse through the elements (lines 24–28). When the iteration is complete, the lock is released, and other threads (if there were any) are free to add and remove elements again.

Listing 7.28 shows the output produced when `SafeCollectionIteration` is run. Your output should match.

LISTING 7.28   Output from SafeCollectionIteration (Your Output Should Match)

```
found string: Iterators, length=9
found string: require, length=7
found string: special, length=7
found string: handling, length=8
```

Deadlocks

Using locks to control concurrent access to data is critical to avoid subtle race conditions within applications. However, trouble can arise when a thread needs to hold more than one lock at a time.

Imagine a situation where `threadA` currently has exclusive access to `lock1`. While `threadA` is holding its lock on `lock1`, `threadB` comes along and gets exclusive access to `lock2`. Next, while `threadA` still holds `lock1`, it tries to acquire `lock2`. Because `threadB` currently holds `lock2`, `threadA` blocks waiting for `threadB` to release it. So far, this is not a dangerous situation because when `threadB` releases `lock2`, `threadA` will unblock, acquire `lock2`, and complete its work.

A situation that *will* make trouble is if—while `threadB` is holding `lock2`—it needs to acquire `lock1`. Now `threadA` has exclusive access to `lock1` and is trying to get exclusive access to `lock2`. At the same time, `threadB` has exclusive access to `lock2` and is trying to get exclusive access to `lock1`. Both `threadA` and `threadB` will block forever waiting for the other to release its lock (see Figure 7.1). This situation is called a *deadlock* (it can also be called a *deadly embrace*).

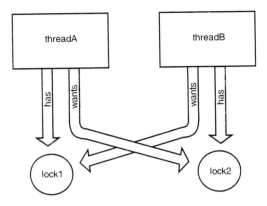

FIGURE 7.1

A deadlock scenario.

The class `Deadlock` in Listing 7.29 demonstrates a situation where two threads end up in a deadlock with each other. Because of this, you will have to manually terminate the application after the `main` thread prints its last message.

LISTING 7.29   Deadlock.java—Deadlock Between Two Threads

```
 1: public class Deadlock extends Object {
 2:     private String objID;
 3:
 4:     public Deadlock(String id) {
 5:         objID = id;
 6:     }
 7:
 8:     public synchronized void checkOther(Deadlock other) {
 9:         print("entering checkOther()");
10:
11:         // simulate some lengthy process
12:         try { Thread.sleep(2000); }
13:         catch ( InterruptedException x ) { }
14:
15:         print("in checkOther() - about to " +
16:                 "invoke 'other.action()'");
17:         other.action();
18:
```

continues

LISTING 7.29   Continued

```
19:             print("leaving checkOther()");
20:         }
21:
22:     public synchronized void action() {
23:         print("entering action()");
24:
25:         // simulate some work here
26:         try { Thread.sleep(500); }
27:         catch ( InterruptedException x ) { }
28:
29:         print("leaving action()");
30:     }
31:
32:     public void print(String msg) {
33:         threadPrint("objID=" + objID + " - " + msg);
34:     }
35:
36:     public static void threadPrint(String msg) {
37:         String threadName = Thread.currentThread().getName();
38:         System.out.println(threadName + ": " + msg);
39:     }
40:
41:     public static void main(String[] args) {
42:         final Deadlock obj1 = new Deadlock("obj1");
43:         final Deadlock obj2 = new Deadlock("obj2");
44:
45:         Runnable runA = new Runnable() {
46:                 public void run() {
47:                     obj1.checkOther(obj2);
48:                 }
49:             };
50:
51:         Thread threadA = new Thread(runA, "threadA");
52:         threadA.start();
53:
54:         try { Thread.sleep(200); }
55:         catch ( InterruptedException x ) { }
56:
57:         Runnable runB = new Runnable() {
58:                 public void run() {
59:                     obj2.checkOther(obj1);
60:                 }
61:             };
62:
```

Concurrent Access to Objects and Variables

CHAPTER 7

163

7

CONCURRENT
ACCESS TO OBJECTS
AND VARIABLES

```
63:          Thread threadB = new Thread(runB, "threadB");
64:          threadB.start();
65:
66:          try { Thread.sleep(5000); }
67:          catch ( InterruptedException x ) { }
68:
69:          threadPrint("finished sleeping");
70:
71:          threadPrint("about to interrupt() threadA");
72:          threadA.interrupt();
73:
74:          try { Thread.sleep(1000); }
75:          catch ( InterruptedException x ) { }
76:
77:          threadPrint("about to interrupt() threadB");
78:          threadB.interrupt();
79:
80:          try { Thread.sleep(1000); }
81:          catch ( InterruptedException x ) { }
82:
83:          threadPrint("did that break the deadlock?");
84:      }
85: }
```

In the main() method (lines 41–84), two instances of Deadlock are created and two threads are started—each one running one of the instances. The first instance has its objID set to obj1; the second is known as obj2 (lines 42–43). threadA is started and invokes the checkOther() method of obj1 passing in a reference to obj2 (line 47). After a quick 200 millisecond sleep, threadB is started and invokes the checkOther() method of obj2 passing in a reference to obj1 (line 59).

The checkOther() method (lines 8–20) is synchronized and requires a thread to get exclusive access to the instance's object-level lock before entering. After a thread gets inside, it prints a message (line 9) and then sleeps for two seconds to simulate a long-running task (line 12). After it wakes up, it prints a message and attempts to invoke the action() method of the *other* Deadlock instance (line 17). This will require that it get exclusive access to the object-level lock of the other instance because action() is synchronized (line 22).

Neither threadA nor threadB will ever get into the action() method of the other instance. While inside checkOther(), threadA is holding the object-level lock on obj1. threadB is simultaneously inside the checkOther() method of obj2 and is holding its object-level lock. When threadA tries to invoke the action() method on obj2, it will block waiting for threadB to release the lock. A fraction of a second later, threadB tries to invoke the action() method on obj1 and blocks waiting for threadA to release its lock. The two threads are deadlocked.

The `main` thread sleeps for five seconds while the deadlock is created (line 66). When it wakes up, it tries to break the deadlock by interrupting `threadA` (line 72). After one second, it tries to interrupt `threadB` (line 78). Unfortunately, this does not break the deadlock. When a thread is blocked waiting to acquire a lock, it does not respond to interrupts (refer to Chapter 6).

Listing 7.30 shows the output produced when `Deadlock` is run. Your output should match. Remember that you will have to manually terminate the application after about 15 seconds.

LISTING 7.30 Output Produced from Deadlock (Your Output Should Match)

```
1: threadA: objID=obj1 - entering checkOther()
2: threadB: objID=obj2 - entering checkOther()
3: threadA: objID=obj1 - in checkOther() - about to invoke 'other.action()'
4: threadB: objID=obj2 - in checkOther() - about to invoke 'other.action()'
5: main: finished sleeping
6: main: about to interrupt() threadA
7: main: about to interrupt() threadB
8: main: did that break the deadlock?
```

First `threadA` enters the `checkObject()` method of `obj1` (line 1). Shortly thereafter, `threadB` enters the `checkObject()` method of `obj2` (line 2). `threadA` wakes up first and tries to invoke the `action()` method of `obj2`, but blocks waiting for `threadB` to release the lock. Then `threadB` wakes up and tries to invoke the `action()` method of `obj1`, and also blocks waiting for the lock that is currently held by `threadA`. The attempts to interrupt the blocked threads have no effect (lines 6–7).

This is a bit of a contrived situation, but deadlocks are a very real problem and can arise in other ways too. Nothing limits a deadlock to only two threads. Any number of threads can get into a deadlock situation with each other.

Deadlock Avoidance

Deadlocks can be extremely difficult to track down. Generally, most of an application will continue to run, but a couple of threads will be stuck in a deadlock. To make matters worse, deadlocks can hide in code for quite a while, waiting for a rare condition to occur. An application can run fine 99 out of 100 times and only deadlock when the thread scheduler happens to run the threads in a slightly different order. Deadlock avoidance is a difficult task.

Most code is not vulnerable to deadlocks, but for the code that is, try following these guidelines to help avoid deadlocks:

- Hold locks for only the minimal amount of time necessary. Consider using `synchronized` statement blocks instead of synchronizing the whole method.

- Try to write code that does not need to hold more than one lock at a time. If this is unavoidable, try to make sure that threads hold the second lock only for a brief period of time.
- Create and use one *big* lock instead of several small ones. Use this lock for mutual exclusion instead of the object-level locks of the individual objects.
- Check out the `InterruptibleSyncBlock` class in Chapter 17. It uses another object to control concurrent access to a section of code. Additionally, instead of having a thread block on the `synchronized` statement, the thread is put into a wait-state that *is* interruptible. I'll tell you more about the wait-notify mechanism in Chapter 8.

Speeding Concurrent Access

Synchronization is critical to writing multithread-safe code. Synchronization does come at a cost. The simple task of acquiring and releasing a lock adds more work for the processor and slows execution. This extra processing cost is why the methods in the Collections API are not synchronized by default. When only one thread is working with a collection, synchronization is a waste of processor resources. However, many of the classes can be wrapped in synchronization when access by two or more threads makes it necessary.

To speed up execution, do not use `synchronized` unnecessarily. Be sure that it's really needed for proper functioning. If synchronization is necessary, see if using a `synchronized` statement block would work instead of a `synchronized` method. Although this won't decrease the cost of acquiring and releasing the lock, it will reduce contention for the lock among the other threads because the lock is held for a shorter period of time.

TIP

As you gain expertise in multithreaded programming, you'll begin to have a better feeling for where synchronization is and is not required. As you start out, you should err on the side of using *too much* synchronization (but watch out for deadlocks!). This way, the code might be slower than it could be, but it will be less likely to be missing synchronization where it is critically needed.

Summary

Having multiple threads running within an application can improve its performance and responsiveness to a user. Inevitably, these threads will have to interact with each other. Extra steps like synchronization have to be taken within the code to ensure that the threads do not corrupt any data and do not read any data that is in a temporarily inconsistent state.

In this chapter, I showed you:

- How to use `volatile` to force unsynchronized threads to work with the shared copy of a variable instead of a private working copy.
- How to use the `synchronized` method modifier on non-`static` methods to require a thread to get exclusive access to the object-level lock before entering the method.
- How to use the `synchronized` statement block to require a thread to get exclusive access to the object-level lock of the specified object before executing the code within the block.
- How to use the `synchronized` method modifier on `static` methods to require a thread to get exclusive access to the class-level lock before entering the method.
- How to work safely with the Collections API in a multithreaded environment.
- How to understand the causes of deadlocks, and how to try to avoid them.

Inter-thread Communication

When multiple threads are running inside an application, most of them will need to communicate with each other in some form. In Chapter 5, "Gracefully Stopping Threads," crude inter-thread communication was accomplished by one thread interrupting another thread. As a general guideline, the use of `interrupt()` should be reserved for situations where you want to interrupt a thread to signal it to die gracefully.

In the last chapter, you saw how the use of `synchronized` (or in some cases the use of `volatile`) is needed to be sure that one thread can safely write values that another thread can safely read. In this chapter, I'll show you how one thread can signal another thread that it has made a change.

In this chapter, I'll show you how to use the following:

- The `wait()`, `notify()`, and `notifyAll()` methods of `Object`
- The `join()` method of `Thread`
- The classes `PipedInputStream`, `PipedOutputStream`, `PipedReader`, and `PipedWriter`
- The classes `ThreadLocal` and `InheritableThreadLocal`

The Need for Inter-thread Signaling

Through synchronization, one thread can safely change values that another thread will read. How does the second thread know that the values have changed? What if the second thread is waiting for the values to change by rereading the values every few seconds?

One not-so-good way that a thread can wait for a value to change is by using a *busy/wait*:

```
while ( getValue() != desiredValue ) {
    Thread.sleep(500);
}
```

Such code is called a busy/wait because the thread is busy using up processor resources to continually check to see if the value has changed. To use fewer resources, the sleep time could be increased, but then the thread might not find out about the change for quite some time. On the other hand, if the sleep time is reduced, the thread will find out sooner, but will waste even more of the processor resources. In Java, there is a much better way to handle this kind of situation: the *wait/notify* mechanism.

The Wait/Notify Mechanism

The wait/notify mechanism allows one thread to wait for a notification from another thread that it may proceed. Typically, the first thread checks a variable and sees that the value is not yet what it needs. The first thread invokes `wait()` and goes to sleep (using virtually zero processor resources) until it is *notified* that something has changed. Eventually, the second thread comes along and changes the value of the variable and invokes `notify()` (or `notifyAll()`) to signal the sleeping thread that the variable has been changed.

The wait/notify mechanism does not *require* that a variable be checked by one thread and set by another. However, it is generally a good idea to use this mechanism in conjunction with at least one variable. Doing so helps in avoiding *missed notifications* and in detecting *early notifications* (I'll tell you about both later in this chapter).

Minimal Wait/Notify

At a bare minimum, you need an object to lock on and two threads to implement the wait/notify mechanism. For thread notification, two methods are available: `notify()` and `notifyAll()`. For simplicity, I'll use `notify()` here and explain the difference later in this chapter.

Imagine that there is a member variable, `valueLock`, that will be used for synchronization:

```
private Object valueLock = new Object();
```

The first thread comes along and executes this code fragment:

```
synchronized ( valueLock ) {
    try {
        valueLock.wait();
    } catch ( InterruptedException x ) {
        System.out.println("interrupted while waiting");
    }
}
```

The `wait()` method requires the calling thread to have previously acquired the object-level lock on the target object. In this case, the object that will be waited upon is `valueLock`, and two lines before the `valueLock.wait()` statement is the `synchronized(valueLock)` statement. The thread that invokes the `wait()` method releases the object-level lock and goes to sleep until notified or interrupted. If the waiting thread is interrupted, it competes with the other threads to reacquire the object-level lock and throws an `InterruptedException` from within `wait()`. If the waiting thread is notified, it competes with the other threads to reacquire the object-level lock and then returns from `wait()`.

Many times, a thread is interrupted to signal it that it should clean up and die (see Chapter 5). The statements used to wait can be slightly rearranged to allow the `InterruptedException` to propagate up further:

```
try {
    synchronized ( valueLock ) {
        valueLock.wait();
    }
} catch ( InterruptedException x ) {
    System.out.println("interrupted while waiting");
    // clean up, and allow thread to return from run()
}
```

Instead of catching `InterruptedException`, methods can simply declare that they `throw` it to pass the exception further up the call chain:

```java
public void someMethod() throws InterruptedException {
    // ...
    synchronized ( valueLock ) {
        valueLock.wait();
    }
    // ...
}
```

The thread doing the notification comes along and executes this code fragment:

```java
synchronized ( valueLock ) {
    valueLock.notify();  // notifyAll() might be safer...
}
```

This thread blocks until it can get exclusive access to the object-level lock for `valueLock`. After the lock is acquired, this thread notifies *one* of the waiting threads. If no threads are waiting, the notification effectively does nothing. If more than one thread is waiting on `valueLock`, the thread scheduler arbitrarily chooses *one* to receive the notification. The other waiting threads are not notified and continue to wait. To notify *all* waiting threads (instead of just one of them), use `notifyAll()` (discussed later in this chapter).

Typical Wait/Notify

In most cases, a member variable is checked by the thread doing the waiting and modified by the thread doing the notification. The checking and modification occur inside the `synchronized` blocks to be sure that no race conditions develop.

This time, two member variables are used:

```java
private boolean value = false;
private Object valueLock = new Object();
```

The `value` variable is checked by the thread doing the waiting and is set by the thread doing the notification. Synchronization on `valueLock` controls concurrent access to `value`.

The first thread comes along and executes this code fragment:

```java
try {
    synchronized ( valueLock ) {
        while ( value != true ) {
            valueLock.wait();
        }

        // value is now true
```

```
    }
} catch ( InterruptedException x ) {
    System.out.println("interrupted while waiting");
}
```

After acquiring the object-level lock for valueLock, the first thread checks value to see if it is true. If it is not, the thread executes wait(), releasing the object-level lock. When this thread is notified, it wakes up, reacquires the lock, and returns from wait(). To be sure that it was not falsely notified (see the "Early Notification" discussion later in this chapter), it re-evaluates the while expression. If value is still not true, the thread waits again. If it is true, the thread continues to execute the rest of the code inside the synchronized block.

While the first thread is waiting, a second thread comes along and executes this code fragment:

```
synchronized ( valueLock ) {
    value = true;
    valueLock.notify();  // notifyAll() might be safer...
}
```

When the first thread executes the wait() method on valueLock, it releases the object-level lock it was holding. This release allows the second thread to get exclusive access to the object-level lock on valueLock and enter the synchronized block. Inside, the second thread sets value to true and invokes notify() on valueLock to signal *one* waiting thread that value has been changed.

Wait/Notify with synchronized Methods

In the previous examples, valueLock was used with the synchronized statement to require that threads get exclusive access to the object-level lock associated with valueLock. Sometimes, the class is designed to synchronize on this instead of another object. In this case, the synchronized method modifier can be used instead of a synchronized statement. The following code fragments are an adaptation of the previous example.

As before, a member variable value is initially set to false:

```
private boolean value = false;
```

The first thread (threadA) comes along and invokes this waitUntilTrue() method:

```
public synchronized void waitUntilTrue()
                throws InterruptedException {

    while ( value == false ) {
        wait();
    }
}
```

While `threadA` is blocked on the `wait()`, a second thread (`threadB`) comes along and executes this method, passing in `true` for `newValue`:

```
public synchronized void setValue(boolean newValue) {
    if ( newValue != value ) {
        value = newValue;
        notify();  // notifyAll() might be safer...
    }
}
```

Note that both methods are `synchronized` and are members of the same class. In addition, both threads are invoking methods on the same *instance* of this class. The `waitUntilTrue()` method (with the `wait()` inside) declares that it might throw an `InterruptedException`. In this case, when `threadB` passes in `true`, `value` is changed and `notify()` is used to signal the waiting `threadA` that it may proceed. `threadA` wakes up, reacquires the object-level lock on `this`, returns from `wait()`, and re-evaluates the `while` expression. This time, `value` is `true`, and `threadA` will return from `waitUntilTrue()`.

Figure 8.1 shows a relative timeline of when everything occurs. When `threadA` wants to invoke `waitUntilTrue()`, it must first get exclusive access to the object-level lock on `this` (time T1). Just after `threadA` acquires the lock, it enters `waitUntilTrue()` (time T2). `threadA` determines that it must wait for `value` to change, so it invokes the `wait()` method on `this` (time T3). Just after `threadA` enters `wait()`, it releases the object-level lock on `this` (time T4).

Some time later, `threadB` acquires the lock (time T5) and enters the `setValue()` method (time T6). While inside `setValue()`, `threadB` sets `value` to `true` and invokes `notify()`. This action causes `threadA` to be notified, but `threadA` cannot return from `wait()` until it can get the lock, and `threadB` is still holding the lock. `threadB` then returns from `setValue()` (time T7) and releases the lock (time T8).

Soon after `threadB` releases the object-level lock on `this`, `threadA` is able to reacquire it (time T9) and returns from `wait()` (time T10). `threadA` sees that `value` is now `true` and proceeds to execute the rest of the `waitUntilTrue()` method. `threadA` returns from `waitUntilTrue()` (time T11) and releases the lock (time T12).

There are some particular points of interest in Figure 8.1. First, notice the small intervals of time between some events. For example, there is a very short, but non-zero interval between the time that `threadA` gets the lock (time T1) and the time that it is inside `waitUntilTrue()` (time T2). Also notice that `threadA` is inside `wait()` from time T3 through time T10, but releases the lock shortly after entering (time T4) and reacquires it just before returning (time T9). A thread might spend quite a bit of time inside a `wait()` method, but it is not holding the lock for most of that time. On the other hand, the time spent inside the `notify()` method is very brief, and the lock is held the whole time.

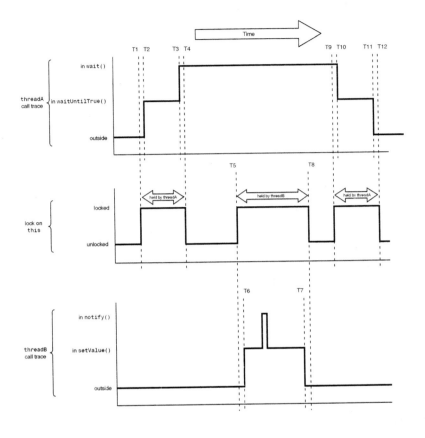

FIGURE 8.1
Timeline of events for wait/notify example.

Object API Used for Wait/Notify

The wait/notify mechanism is embedded deep in the heart of Java. Object, the superclass of all classes, has five methods that are the core of the wait/notify mechanism: notify(), notifyAll(), wait(), wait(long), and wait(long, int). All classes in Java inherit from Object, so all classes have these public methods available to them. Additionally, none of these methods can be overridden in a subclass as they are all declared final.

notify()

```
public final native void notify()
        throws IllegalMonitorStateException  // RuntimeException
```

The `notify()` method is used by a thread to signal any other threads that might be waiting on the object. If more than one thread is waiting on the object, the thread scheduler will arbitrarily choose exactly one to be notified, and the others will continue to wait. If no threads are currently waiting on the object, `notify()` has no effect. Before invoking `notify()`, a thread must get exclusive access to the object-level lock for the object. Unlike `wait()`, the invocation of `notify()` does *not* temporarily release the lock. If the proper lock is not held when `notify()` is called, an `IllegalMonitorStateException` is thrown. This exception is a subclass of `RuntimeException`, so a try-catch construct is not necessary and is rarely used.

notifyAll()

```
public final native void notifyAll()
        throws IllegalMonitorStateException  // RuntimeException
```

The `notifyAll()` method works the same as `notify()` (see above) with one important exception: When `notifyAll()` is invoked, *all* the threads waiting on the object are notified, not just one. The advantage of `notifyAll()` is that you don't have to be concerned about which *one* of the waiting threads will be notified—they will *all* be notified. The disadvantage is that it might be wasteful (in terms of processor resources) to notify all the waiting threads if only one will actually be able to proceed. When in doubt, err on the side of safety over speed and use `notifyAll()` instead of `notify()`.

wait()

```
public final void wait()
        throws InterruptedException,
            IllegalMonitorStateException  // RuntimeException
```

The `wait()` method is used to put the current thread to sleep until it is notified or interrupted. Before invoking `wait()`, a thread must get exclusive access to the object-level lock for the object. Just after entering `wait()`, the current thread *releases* the lock. Before returning from `wait()`, the thread competes with the other threads to reacquire the lock. If the proper lock is not held when `wait()` is called, an `IllegalMonitorStateException` is thrown. This exception is a subclass of `RuntimeException`, so a try-catch construct is not necessary and is rarely used.

If the waiting thread is interrupted, it competes to reacquire the lock and throws an `InterruptedException` from within `wait()`. This exception is *not* a subclass of `RuntimeException`, so a try-catch construct is required.

wait(long)

```
public final native void wait(long msTimeout)
        throws InterruptedException,
            IllegalMonitorStateException, // RuntimeException
            IllegalArgumentException      // RuntimeException
```

The wait(long) method is used to put the current thread to sleep until it is notified, interrupted, or the specified timeout elapses. Other than the timeout, wait(long) behaves the same as wait() (see above). The argument msTimeout specifies the maximum number of milliseconds that the thread should wait for notification. If msTimeout is 0, the thread will never time out (just like wait()). If the argument is less than 0, an IllegalArgumentException will be thrown. IllegalArgumentException is a subclass of RuntimeException, so a try-catch block is not required and is rarely used.

If the specified number of milliseconds elapses before the waiting thread is notified or interrupted, it competes to reacquire the lock and returns from wait(long). There is no way for the caller to determine whether a notification or a timeout occurred because no information (void) is returned from wait(long).

wait(long, int)

```
public final void wait(long msTimeout, int nanoSec)
        throws InterruptedException,
                IllegalMonitorStateException, // RuntimeException
                IllegalArgumentException      // RuntimeException
```

The wait(long, int) method works just like wait(long, int) (see above) with the exception that nanoseconds can be added to the timeout value. The argument nanoSec is added to msTimeout to determine the total amount of time that the thread will wait for notification before returning. A nanosecond is one-billionth of a second (10E-9), and most common implementations of the Java VM don't truly support this fine a resolution of time. For this reason, the use of the method is currently quite rare.

When to Use notifyAll() Instead of notify()

The fundamental difference between notify() and notifyAll() is that if more than one thread is simultaneously waiting for notification, notify() will provide notification to only one of the waiting threads, whereas notifyAll() will provide notification to all of them. If your code is well defended against early notifications (discussed later), notifyAll() is generally the better choice.

The major disadvantage of notifyAll() is that it is wasteful of processor resources if all but one of the notified threads will end up waiting again. This is a situation that is difficult to guarantee. If your code synchronizes on this either through synchronized blocks or the synchronized method modifier, you can't be sure that some code external to the class won't synchronize and wait on a reference to the object. If that happens, notify() might signal the thread running that external code instead of the thread that you intended. Consider a situation where you have a class, ClassX, with two methods:

```
public synchronized void waitUntilTrue()
```

```
                    throws InterruptedException {

    while ( value == false ) {
        wait();
    }
}


public synchronized void setValue(boolean newValue) {
    if ( newValue != value ) {
        value = newValue;
        notify();  // notifyAll() might be safer...
    }
}
```

In addition, there's an external class, ClassY, with this code in one of its methods:

```
ClassX cx = new ClassX();
cx.setValue(false);
// ...
synchronized ( cx ) {
    cx.wait(); // trouble
}
```

If threadA is running inside ClassY, it synchronizes on cx and invokes wait(). If threadB invokes waitUntilTrue(), it is now also waiting for notification. If threadC invokes setValue() and passes true (a new value), threadC will only notify one thread because notifyAll() wasn't used. There's no way to be sure whether threadA or threadB will be notified. In this situation, notifyAll() would have guaranteed that they would both be notified.

It is generally safe to use notify() only when you can guarantee that only one thread will ever be waiting for notification. This is a relatively unusual occurrence.

TIP

If you're not sure whether you need to use notify() or notifyAll(), use notifyAll(). It might be a little wasteful, but it's safer.

Missed Notification

A missed notification occurs when threadB tries to notify threadA, but threadA is not yet waiting for the notification. In a multithreaded environment like Java, you don't have much control over which thread runs and for how long. This uncertainty can lead to a situation in which most of the time an application is run, threadA is waiting before threadB does the notification. But occasionally, threadB does the notification before threadA is waiting. This missed notification scenario can be quite dangerous.

MissedNotify

MissedNotify (see Listing 8.1) demonstrates how a notification can be missed.

LISTING 8.1   MissedNotify.java—An Example of How a Notification Can Be Missed

```
 1: public class MissedNotify extends Object {
 2:     private Object proceedLock;
 3:
 4:     public MissedNotify() {
 5:         print("in MissedNotify()");
 6:         proceedLock = new Object();
 7:     }
 8:
 9:     public void waitToProceed() throws InterruptedException {
10:         print("in waitToProceed() - entered");
11:
12:         synchronized ( proceedLock ) {
13:             print("in waitToProceed() - about to wait()");
14:             proceedLock.wait();
15:             print("in waitToProceed() - back from wait()");
16:         }
17:
18:         print("in waitToProceed() - leaving");
19:     }
20:
21:     public void proceed() {
22:         print("in proceed() - entered");
23:
24:         synchronized ( proceedLock ) {
25:             print("in proceed() - about to notifyAll()");
26:             proceedLock.notifyAll();
27:             print("in proceed() - back from notifyAll()");
28:         }
29:
30:         print("in proceed() - leaving");
31:     }
```

continues

LISTING 8.1   Continued

```
32:
33:        private static void print(String msg) {
34:            String name = Thread.currentThread().getName();
35:            System.out.println(name + ": " + msg);
36:        }
37:
38:        public static void main(String[] args) {
39:            final MissedNotify mn = new MissedNotify();
40:
41:            Runnable runA = new Runnable() {
42:                    public void run() {
43:                        try {
44:                            Thread.sleep(1000);
45:                            mn.waitToProceed();
46:                        } catch ( InterruptedException x ) {
47:                            x.printStackTrace();
48:                        }
49:                    }
50:                };
51:
52:            Thread threadA = new Thread(runA, "threadA");
53:            threadA.start();
54:
55:            Runnable runB = new Runnable() {
56:                    public void run() {
57:                        try {
58:                            Thread.sleep(500);
59:                            mn.proceed();
60:                        } catch ( InterruptedException x ) {
61:                            x.printStackTrace();
62:                        }
63:                    }
64:                };
65:
66:            Thread threadB = new Thread(runB, "threadB");
67:            threadB.start();
68:
69:            try {
70:                Thread.sleep(10000);
71:            } catch ( InterruptedException x ) {
72:            }
73:
74:            print("about to invoke interrupt() on threadA");
75:            threadA.interrupt();
76:        }
77: }
```

The thread entering the waitToProceed() method (lines 9–19) blocks until it can get exclusive access to the object-level lock on proceedLock (line 12). After it does, it invokes wait() to go to sleep and await notification (line 14). The InterruptedException that might be thrown by wait() is passed along and is declared to be thrown from waitToProceed() (line 9).

The thread entering the proceed() method (lines 21–31) blocks until it gets the lock on proceedLock (line 24). It then invokes notifyAll() to signal any and all waiting threads (line 26).

In the main() method (lines 38–76), an instance of MissedNotify called mn is constructed (line 39) and two threads are spawned to interact with it. The first thread is threadA, which sleeps for one second (line 44) before invoking waitToProceed() (line 45). The second thread is threadB, which sleeps for 0.5 seconds (line 58) before invoking proceed() (line 59). Because threadB sleeps only half the time that threadA does, threadB will enter and exit proceed() while threadA is still sleeping. When threadA enters waitToProceed(), it will end up waiting indefinitely because it will have missed the notification.

After 10 seconds have elapsed (lines 69–72), the main thread invokes interrupt() on threadA (line 75) to get it to break out of wait(). Inside wait(), threadA throws an InterruptedException that causes waitToProceed() to abruptly terminate. The exception is caught (line 46) and a stack trace is printed (line 47).

Listing 8.2 shows the output produced when MissedNotify is run. Your output should match.

LISTING 8.2   Output from MissedNotify

```
1: main: in MissedNotify()
2: threadB: in proceed() - entered
3: threadB: in proceed() - about to notifyAll()
4: threadB: in proceed() - back from notifyAll()
5: threadB: in proceed() - leaving
6: threadA: in waitToProceed() - entered
7: threadA: in waitToProceed() - about to wait()
8: main: about to invoke interrupt() on threadA
9: java.lang.InterruptedException: operation interrupted
10:      at java.lang.Object.wait(Native Method)
11:      at java.lang.Object.wait(Object.java:424)
12:      at MissedNotify.waitToProceed(MissedNotify.java:14)
13:      at MissedNotify$1.run(MissedNotify.java:45)
14:      at java.lang.Thread.run(Thread.java:479)
```

You can see that threadB gets into proceed(), performs the notification, and leaves proceed() (lines 2–5). Long after threadB is finished, threadA enters waitToProceed() (line 6) and continues on to invoke wait() (line 7). threadA remains stuck here until the main thread interrupts it (lines 8–14).

Figure 8.2 shows the approximate sequence of events that occurs when `MissedNotify` is run. The lock on `proceedLock` is held by `threadB` from shortly after it enters `proceed()` until just before it returns from the method (from time T2 to T3). Soon after `threadB` leaves `proceed()` (time T4), `threadA` enters `waitToProceed()` (time T5). `threadA` acquires the lock on `proceedLock` (time T6) and invokes `wait()` (time T7). Just after entering the `wait()` method, it releases the lock (time T8). `threadA` remains inside `wait()` indefinitely because it has missed the notification.

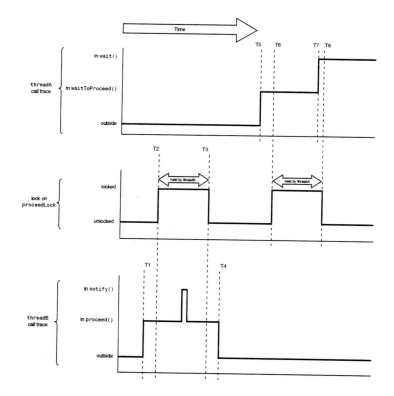

FIGURE 8.2

Timeline of events for a missed notification.

MissedNotifyFix

To fix `MissedNotify`, a `boolean` indicator variable should be added. The indicator is only accessed and modified inside `synchronized` blocks. This indicator will be initially `false` and will be set `true` *whenever* the `proceed()` method happens to be called. Inside `waitToProceed()`, the indicator will be checked to see if a wait is necessary or not. Listing 8.3 shows the code for `MissedNotifyFix`.

LISTING 8.3   MissedNotifyFix.java—A Fixed Version of MissedNotify

```
 1: public class MissedNotifyFix extends Object {
 2:     private Object proceedLock;
 3:     private boolean okToProceed;
 4:
 5:     public MissedNotifyFix() {
 6:         print("in MissedNotify()");
 7:         proceedLock = new Object();
 8:         okToProceed = false;
 9:     }
10:
11:     public void waitToProceed() throws InterruptedException {
12:         print("in waitToProceed() - entered");
13:
14:         synchronized ( proceedLock ) {
15:             print("in waitToProceed() - entered sync block");
16:
17:             while ( okToProceed == false ) {
18:                 print("in waitToProceed() - about to wait()");
19:                 proceedLock.wait();
20:                 print("in waitToProceed() - back from wait()");
21:             }
22:
23:             print("in waitToProceed() - leaving sync block");
24:         }
25:
26:         print("in waitToProceed() - leaving");
27:     }
28:
29:     public void proceed() {
30:         print("in proceed() - entered");
31:
32:         synchronized ( proceedLock ) {
33:             print("in proceed() - entered sync block");
34:
35:             okToProceed = true;
36:             print("in proceed() - changed okToProceed to true");
37:             proceedLock.notifyAll();
38:             print("in proceed() - just did notifyAll()");
39:
40:             print("in proceed() - leaving sync block");
41:         }
42:
```

continues

LISTING 8.3   Continued

```
43:             print("in proceed() - leaving");
44:         }
45:
46:     private static void print(String msg) {
47:         String name = Thread.currentThread().getName();
48:         System.out.println(name + ": " + msg);
49:     }
50:
51:     public static void main(String[] args) {
52:         final MissedNotifyFix mnf = new MissedNotifyFix();
53:
54:         Runnable runA = new Runnable() {
55:                 public void run() {
56:                     try {
57:                         Thread.sleep(1000);
58:                         mnf.waitToProceed();
59:                     } catch ( InterruptedException x ) {
60:                         x.printStackTrace();
61:                     }
62:                 }
63:             };
64:
65:         Thread threadA = new Thread(runA, "threadA");
66:         threadA.start();
67:
68:         Runnable runB = new Runnable() {
69:                 public void run() {
70:                     try {
71:                         Thread.sleep(500);
72:                         mnf.proceed();
73:                     } catch ( InterruptedException x ) {
74:                         x.printStackTrace();
75:                     }
76:                 }
77:             };
78:
79:         Thread threadB = new Thread(runB, "threadB");
80:         threadB.start();
81:
82:         try {
83:             Thread.sleep(10000);
84:         } catch ( InterruptedException x ) {
85:         }
86:
87:         print("about to invoke interrupt() on threadA");
88:         threadA.interrupt();
89:     }
90: }
```

MissedNotifyFix adds the private member variable okToProceed (line 3) to be used as the indicator. It is initially set to false in the constructor (line 8). The proceedLock object is used to control concurrent access to okToProceed and to facilitate the wait/notify implementation.

Inside the synchronized block (lines 32–41) of proceed() (lines 29–44), okToProceed is set true (line 35) just before notifyAll() is invoked. This way, if the notifyAll() method is ineffective because no threads are currently waiting, okToProceed indicates that proceed() has been called.

Inside the synchronized block (lines 14–24) of waitToProceed() (lines 11–27), okToProceed is checked to see if any waiting is necessary. Instead of just using an if statement to check, a while statement (lines 17–21) is used as a safeguard against early notifications (explained later in this chapter). As long as okToProceed is false, the calling thread (threadA) will wait() for notification (line 19). Even if threadA is notified while waiting, it will double-check okToProceed. If okToProceed is still false, threadA will wait() again.

In this particular case, okToProceed is set true by threadB long before threadA enters waitToProceed(). When threadA evaluates the while expression (line 17), it determines that no waiting is necessary and skips the body of the loop. The notification is still missed, but the indicator variable okToProceed prevents threadA from waiting.

Listing 8.4 shows the output produced when MissedNotifyFix is run. Your output should match. Notice that threadB gets in and out of proceed() (lines 2–7) before threadA enters waitToProceed() (line 8). With this indicator fix in place, threadA moves right through waitToProceed() (lines 8–11). Notice that none of the messages about wait() are printed. The indicator variable kept threadA from waiting for notification that would never come.

LISTING 8.4   Output from MissedNotifyFix

```
 1: main: in MissedNotify()
 2: threadB: in proceed() - entered
 3: threadB: in proceed() - entered sync block
 4: threadB: in proceed() - changed okToProceed to true
 5: threadB: in proceed() - just did notifyAll()
 6: threadB: in proceed() - leaving sync block
 7: threadB: in proceed() - leaving
 8: threadA: in waitToProceed() - entered
 9: threadA: in waitToProceed() - entered sync block
10: threadA: in waitToProceed() - leaving sync block
11: threadA: in waitToProceed() - leaving
12: main: about to invoke interrupt() on threadA
```

Figure 8.3 shows the sequence of events for MissedNotifyFix. The main difference to note is that threadA never calls wait().

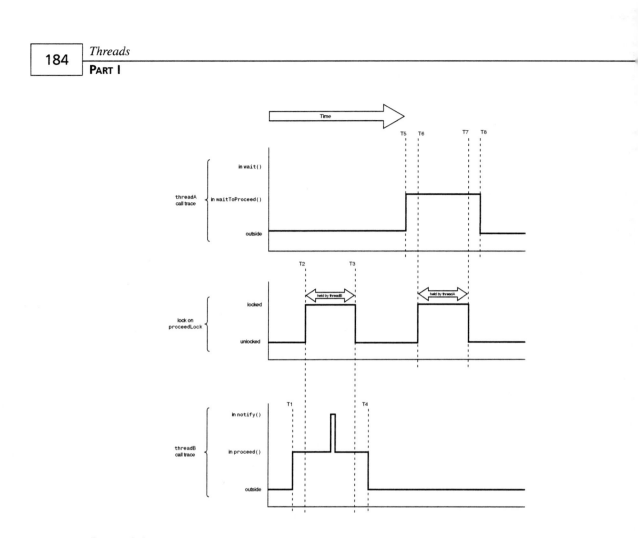

FIGURE 8.3
Timeline of events for MissedNotifyFix.

Early Notification

If a thread is notified while waiting, but the condition the thread is waiting for has not yet been met, the thread has received an *early notification*. An early notification can also occur if the condition is briefly met but quickly changes so it's no longer met. This might sound strange, but early notification can happen due to subtle errors in the code (generally when an `if` is used instead of a `while`).

EarlyNotify

`EarlyNotify` (see Listing 8.5) shows how an early notification can occur and the resulting problems it causes. Basically, two threads are waiting to remove an item, while another thread adds just one item.

LISTING 8.5   EarlyNotify.java—An Example of How a Notification Can Come Too Early

```
 1: import java.util.*;
 2:
 3: public class EarlyNotify extends Object {
 4:     private List list;
 5:
 6:     public EarlyNotify() {
 7:         list = Collections.synchronizedList(new LinkedList());
 8:     }
 9:
10:     public String removeItem() throws InterruptedException {
11:         print("in removeItem() - entering");
12:
13:         synchronized ( list ) {
14:             if ( list.isEmpty() ) {  // dangerous to use 'if'!
15:                 print("in removeItem() - about to wait()");
16:                 list.wait();
17:                 print("in removeItem() - done with wait()");
18:             }
19:
20:             // extract the new first item
21:             String item = (String) list.remove(0);
22:
23:             print("in removeItem() - leaving");
24:             return item;
25:         } // sync
26:     }
27:
28:     public void addItem(String item) {
29:         print("in addItem() - entering");
30:         synchronized ( list ) {
31:             // There'll always be room to add to this List
32:             // because it expands as needed.
33:             list.add(item);
34:             print("in addItem() - just added: '" + item + "'");
35:
36:             // After adding, notify any and all waiting
37:             // threads that the list has changed.
38:             list.notifyAll();
39:             print("in addItem() - just notified");
40:         } // sync
```

continues

LISTING 8.5 Continued

```
41:          print("in addItem() - leaving");
42:      }
43:
44:      private static void print(String msg) {
45:          String name = Thread.currentThread().getName();
46:          System.out.println(name + ": " + msg);
47:      }
48:
49:      public static void main(String[] args) {
50:          final EarlyNotify en = new EarlyNotify();
51:
52:          Runnable runA = new Runnable() {
53:                  public void run() {
54:                      try {
55:                          String item = en.removeItem();
56:                          print("in run() - returned: '" +
57:                                  item + "'");
58:                      } catch ( InterruptedException ix ) {
59:                          print("interrupted!");
60:                      } catch ( Exception x ) {
61:                          print("threw an Exception!!!\n" + x);
62:                      }
63:                  }
64:          };
65:
66:          Runnable runB = new Runnable() {
67:                  public void run() {
68:                      en.addItem("Hello!");
69:                  }
70:          };
71:
72:          try {
73:              Thread threadA1 = new Thread(runA, "threadA1");
74:              threadA1.start();
75:
76:              Thread.sleep(500);
77:
78:              // start a *second* thread trying to remove
79:              Thread threadA2 = new Thread(runA, "threadA2");
80:              threadA2.start();
81:
82:              Thread.sleep(500);
83:
84:              Thread threadB = new Thread(runB, "threadB");
```

```
85:                 threadB.start();
86:
87:                 Thread.sleep(10000); // wait 10 seconds
88:
89:                 threadA1.interrupt();
90:                 threadA2.interrupt();
91:             } catch ( InterruptedException x ) {
92:                 // ignore
93:             }
94:      }
95: }
```

In the constructor for EarlyNotify (lines 6–9), a multithread-safe List is created and used to hold the items added and removed. When a thread enters the removeItem() method (lines 10–26), it blocks until it can get exclusive access to the object-level lock for list (line 13). The thread checks to see if the list is empty (line 14). If the list is empty, the thread invokes wait() and sleeps until notified (line 16). If the thread is interrupted while waiting, it throws an InterruptedException (line 10) that is passed out of removeItem(). When notified, the thread removes the first item from the list and casts it into a String (line 21). This String is returned to the caller (line 24) and in the process of leaving the synchronized block, the lock is automatically released.

When a thread enters the addItem() method (lines 28–42), it blocks until it can get exclusive access to the object-level lock for list (line 30). The thread adds the item to list (line 33) and notifies any and all waiting threads with notifyAll() that list has been modified (line 38).

In the main() method (lines 49–94), three threads are started and simultaneously interact with one instance of EarlyNotify referred to by en (line 50). threadA1 is started (line 74) and invokes removeItem() (line 55). The list is initially empty, so threadA1 invokes wait() inside removeItem(). threadA2 is started (line 80) 0.5 seconds after threadA1. threadA2 invokes removeItem() and also finds the list is empty and blocks waiting for notification.

After another 0.5 seconds pass, threadB is started (line 85) and invokes addItem(), passing in Hello! (line 68). Both threadA1 and threadA2 have temporarily released the object-level lock on list while inside wait(), so threadB is free to acquire the lock. threadB adds the String to list and notifies any and all waiting threads with notifyAll().

The trouble arises from the fact that both threadA1 and threadA2 return from wait() and try to remove the added item from the list. Only one of the two will succeed. The other will end up trying to remove an item that has just disappeared from the list.

Listing 8.6 shows possible output when EarlyNotify is run. Your output might differ somewhat. In particular, whether threadA1 or threadA2 succeeds appears to be randomly determined and can change each time EarlyNotify is run.

LISTING 8.6   Possible Output from EarlyNotify

```
 1: threadA1: in removeItem() - entering
 2: threadA1: in removeItem() - about to wait()
 3: threadA2: in removeItem() - entering
 4: threadA2: in removeItem() - about to wait()
 5: threadB: in addItem() - entering
 6: threadB: in addItem() - just added: 'Hello!'
 7: threadB: in addItem() - just notified
 8: threadB: in addItem() - leaving
 9: threadA1: in removeItem() - done with wait()
10: threadA1: in removeItem() - leaving
11: threadA1: in run() - returned: 'Hello!'
12: threadA2: in removeItem() - done with wait()
13: threadA2: threw an Exception!!!
14: java.lang.IndexOutOfBoundsException: Index: 0, Size: 0
```

For this particular run of EarlyNotify, threadA1 returns from wait() first (line 9) and successfully removes the item from the list (lines 10–11). When threadA2 returns from wait() (line 12), it also tries to remove the item from the list. Because the list was just emptied by threadA1, threadA2 ends up causing an exception to be thrown when it tries to remove the nonexistent item (lines 13–14). In this case, threadA2 was notified too early and should not proceed to execute the rest of removeItem().

EarlyNotifyFix

This problem of early notification is fixed in EarlyNotifyFix (see Listing 8.7). Now, when a thread returns from wait(), it rechecks the condition it was waiting for to be sure that it has been met.

LISTING 8.7   EarlyNotifyFix.java—Managing Early Notifications to Avoid Errors

```
 1: import java.util.*;
 2:
 3: public class EarlyNotifyFix extends Object {
 4:     private List list;
 5:
 6:     public EarlyNotifyFix() {
 7:         list = Collections.synchronizedList(new LinkedList());
 8:     }
 9:
10:     public String removeItem() throws InterruptedException {
11:         print("in removeItem() - entering");
12:
```

```
13:         synchronized ( list ) {
14:             while ( list.isEmpty() ) {
15:                 print("in removeItem() - about to wait()");
16:                 list.wait();
17:                 print("in removeItem() - done with wait()");
18:             }
19:
20:             // extract the new first item
21:             String item = (String) list.remove(0);
22:
23:             print("in removeItem() - leaving");
24:             return item;
25:         }
26:     }
27:
28:     public void addItem(String item) {
29:         print("in addItem() - entering");
30:         synchronized ( list ) {
31:             // There'll always be room to add to this List
32:             // because it expands as needed.
33:             list.add(item);
34:             print("in addItem() - just added: '" + item + "'");
35:
36:             // After adding, notify any and all waiting
37:             // threads that the list has changed.
38:             list.notifyAll();
39:             print("in addItem() - just notified");
40:         }
41:         print("in addItem() - leaving");
42:     }
43:
44:     private static void print(String msg) {
45:         String name = Thread.currentThread().getName();
46:         System.out.println(name + ": " + msg);
47:     }
48:
49:     public static void main(String[] args) {
50:         final EarlyNotifyFix enf = new EarlyNotifyFix();
51:
52:         Runnable runA = new Runnable() {
53:                 public void run() {
54:                     try {
```

continues

8

INTER-THREAD
COMMUNICATION

LISTING 8.7   Continued

```
55:                             String item = enf.removeItem();
56:                             print("in run() - returned: '" +
57:                                   item + "'");
58:                         } catch ( InterruptedException ix ) {
59:                             print("interrupted!");
60:                         } catch ( Exception x ) {
61:                             print("threw an Exception!!!\n" + x);
62:                         }
63:                     }
64:             };
65:
66:         Runnable runB = new Runnable() {
67:                 public void run() {
68:                     enf.addItem("Hello!");
69:                 }
70:             };
71:
72:         try {
73:             Thread threadA1 = new Thread(runA, "threadA1");
74:             threadA1.start();
75:
76:             Thread.sleep(500);
77:
78:             // start a *second* thread trying to remove
79:             Thread threadA2 = new Thread(runA, "threadA2");
80:             threadA2.start();
81:
82:             Thread.sleep(500);
83:
84:             Thread threadB = new Thread(runB, "threadB");
85:             threadB.start();
86:
87:             Thread.sleep(10000); // wait 10 seconds
88:
89:             threadA1.interrupt();
90:             threadA2.interrupt();
91:         } catch ( InterruptedException x ) {
92:             // ignore
93:         }
94:     }
95: }
```

To properly protect the `removeItem()` method from early notifications, all that was necessary was to change the `if` to a `while` (line 14). Now, whenever a thread returns from `wait()` (line 16), it rechecks to see if it was notified early or if the list is really no longer empty (line 14). It is important that the code that checks to see if the list is empty, and the code that removes an item if it was not empty, all be within the same `synchronized` block.

TIP

As a general guideline for protection against early notifications, you should put your `wait()` statements inside `while` loops. This way, regardless of *why* the `wait()` statement returned, you can be sure that you proceed only when the proper conditions have been met.

Listing 8.8 shows the output produced from a particular run of `EarlyNotifyFix`. Your output might differ due to thread-scheduling randomness.

LISTING 8.8 Possible Output from EarlyNotifyFix

```
 1: threadA1: in removeItem() - entering
 2: threadA1: in removeItem() - about to wait()
 3: threadA2: in removeItem() - entering
 4: threadA2: in removeItem() - about to wait()
 5: threadB: in addItem() - entering
 6: threadB: in addItem() - just added: 'Hello!'
 7: threadB: in addItem() - just notified
 8: threadB: in addItem() - leaving
 9: threadA1: in removeItem() - done with wait()
10: threadA1: in removeItem() - leaving
11: threadA1: in run() - returned: 'Hello!'
12: threadA2: in removeItem() - done with wait()
13: threadA2: in removeItem() - about to wait()
14: threadA2: interrupted!
```

Notice that `threadA1` got to the list first and removed the item (lines 9–11). After `threadA2` returns from `wait()` (line 12), it rechecks the list and finds that the list is empty, so `threadA2` ignores the early notification and invokes `wait()` again (line 13). After the application has been running for about 10 seconds, the `main` thread interrupts `threadA1` and `threadA2`. In this case, `threadA1` has already died, but `threadA2` is blocked waiting inside `removeItem()`. When `threadA2` is interrupted, `wait()` throws an `InterruptedException` (line 14).

NOTE

If wait(long) is notified early, it is difficult to tell whether the method returned because it was notified too early or because it timed out. In Chapter 14, "Waiting for the Full Timeout," I'll show you a technique for waiting for the full timeout to elapse.

Missed notifications and early notifications can be tough bugs to track down in your code. Many times they are exposed only under rare conditions. It is important to be careful in your coding by using an indicator variable in addition to the wait/notify mechanism.

NOTE

I have incorporated the combination of a boolean variable and an associated object to use for locking into a class called BooleanLock (see Chapter 17, "The BooleanLock Utility"). BooleanLock encapsulates the details of the wait/notify mechanism and prevents both missed notifications and early notifications. It can be a very useful tool in simplifying the signaling between two or more threads.

CubbyHole Example

The class CubbyHole (see Listing 8.9) simulates a cubbyhole. A cubbyhole is a slot that can have only one item in it at a time. One thread puts an item into the slot and another thread takes it out. If a thread tries to put an item into a cubbyhole that is already occupied, the thread blocks until the slot is available. If a thread tries to remove an item from an empty cubbyhole, the thread blocks until an item is added. In this example, the slot is a reference to an object. This technique allows objects to be handed off from one thread to another in a thread-safe manner.

LISTING 8.9   CubbyHole.java—Object Passing from One Thread to Another

```
1: public class CubbyHole extends Object {
2:     private Object slot;
3:
4:     public CubbyHole() {
5:         slot = null; // null indicates empty
6:     }
```

```
 7:
 8:      public synchronized void putIn(Object obj)
 9:                          throws InterruptedException {
10:
11:          print("in putIn() - entering");
12:
13:          while ( slot != null ) {
14:              print("in putIn() - occupied, about to wait()");
15:              wait(); // wait while slot is occupied
16:              print("in putIn() - notified, back from wait()");
17:          }
18:
19:          slot = obj;  // put object into slot
20:          print("in putIn() - filled slot, about to notifyAll()");
21:          notifyAll(); // signal that slot has been filled
22:
23:          print("in putIn() - leaving");
24:      }
25:
26:      public synchronized Object takeOut()
27:                          throws InterruptedException {
28:
29:          print("in takeOut() - entering");
30:
31:          while ( slot == null ) {
32:              print("in takeOut() - empty, about to wait()");
33:              wait(); // wait while slot is empty
34:              print("in takeOut() - notified, back from wait()");
35:          }
36:
37:          Object obj = slot;
38:          slot = null; // mark slot as empty
39:          print(
40:              "in takeOut() - emptied slot, about to notifyAll()");
41:          notifyAll(); // signal that slot is empty
42:
43:          print("in takeOut() - leaving");
44:          return obj;
45:      }
46:
47:      private static void print(String msg) {
48:          String name = Thread.currentThread().getName();
49:          System.out.println(name + ": " + msg);
50:      }
51: }
```

CubbyHole has a `private` member variable slot (line 2) that is used to hold a reference to the object that is being passed between the threads. In the constructor, slot is set to null to indicate that it is empty (line 5).

The putIn() method (lines 8–24) is synchronized (line 8) and declares that it might throw an InterruptedException (line 9). A while loop (lines 13–17) is used to ensure that the thread that calls putIn() will not proceed until slot is empty. If slot is occupied, the calling thread invokes wait() on this (line 15) and releases the object-level lock it acquired just before entering putIn(). When slot is finally null, the thread proceeds to copy the passed parameter obj into slot (line 19) and invokes notifyAll() (line 21) to signal any and all waiting threads that data has become available.

The takeOut() method (lines 26–45) is synchronized (line 26) and declares that it might throw an InterruptedException (line 27). A while loop (lines 31–35) is used to ensure that the thread will not proceed until slot is occupied. If slot is currently empty, the thread sleeps, waiting for notification that something has changed (line 33). When slot is finally filled, the thread proceeds to copy the reference into obj (line 37), sets slot to null to indicate that it is again empty (line 38), and invokes notifyAll() (line 41) to signal any and all waiting threads that something has changed.

CubbyHoleMain (see Listing 8.10) creates an instance of CubbyHole and starts two threads to interact with it.

LISTING 8.10   CubbyHoleMain.java—Used to Demonstrate CubbyHole

```
 1: public class CubbyHoleMain extends Object {
 2:     private static void print(String msg) {
 3:         String name = Thread.currentThread().getName();
 4:         System.out.println(name + ": " + msg);
 5:     }
 6:
 7:     public static void main(String[] args) {
 8:         final CubbyHole ch = new CubbyHole();
 9:
10:         Runnable runA = new Runnable() {
11:             public void run() {
12:                 try {
13:                     String str;
14:                     Thread.sleep(500);
15:
16:                     str = "multithreaded";
17:                     ch.putIn(str);
18:                     print("in run() - just put in: '" +
19:                             str + "'");
20:
```

```
21:                              str = "programming";
22:                              ch.putIn(str);
23:                              print("in run() - just put in: '" +
24:                                       str + "'");
25:
26:                              str = "with Java";
27:                              ch.putIn(str);
28:                              print("in run() - just put in: '" +
29:                                       str + "'");
30:                          } catch ( InterruptedException x ) {
31:                              x.printStackTrace();
32:                          }
33:                     }
34:                 };
35:
36:         Runnable runB = new Runnable() {
37:                 public void run() {
38:                     try {
39:                          Object obj;
40:
41:                          obj = ch.takeOut();
42:                          print("in run() - just took out: '" +
43:                                   obj + "'");
44:
45:                          Thread.sleep(500);
46:
47:                          obj = ch.takeOut();
48:                          print("in run() - just took out: '" +
49:                                   obj + "'");
50:
51:                          obj = ch.takeOut();
52:                          print("in run() - just took out: '" +
53:                                   obj + "'");
54:                     } catch ( InterruptedException x ) {
55:                          x.printStackTrace();
56:                     }
57:                 }
58:             };
59:
60:         Thread threadA = new Thread(runA, "threadA");
61:         threadA.start();
62:
63:         Thread threadB = new Thread(runB, "threadB");
64:         threadB.start();
65:     }
66: }
```

In the `main()` method (lines 7–65), an instance of `CubbyHole` is constructed and assigned to `ch` (line 8). `threadA` initially sleeps for 0.5 seconds to give `threadB` a chance to get going (line 14). `threadA` then proceeds to invoke `putIn()` three times in a row. Three `String` objects are passed one at a time into `putIn()`: "multithreaded", "programming", and "with Java" (lines 17, 22, and 27). `CubbyHole` can hold only one item at a time, so the second and third calls to `putIn()` may block waiting for `threadB` to remove items.

When `threadB` is started, it immediately invokes `takeOut()` (line 41) and blocks waiting for `threadA` to add something. After removing the first item, `threadB` sleeps for 0.5 seconds (line 45) to give `threadA` time to put the second item into `slot` and to block waiting to put in the third item. `threadB` then proceeds to take out the second and third items (lines 47, 51).

Listing 8.11 shows the output from a particular run of `CubbyHoleMain`. Because of thread-scheduling issues, your output might differ a little.

LISTING 8.11   Possible Output from CubbyHoleMain

```
 1: threadB: in takeOut() - entering
 2: threadB: in takeOut() - empty, about to wait()
 3: threadA: in putIn() - entering
 4: threadA: in putIn() - filled slot, about to notifyAll()
 5: threadA: in putIn() - leaving
 6: threadA: in run() - just put in: 'multithreaded'
 7: threadA: in putIn() - entering
 8: threadA: in putIn() - occupied, about to wait()
 9: threadB: in takeOut() - notified, back from wait()
10: threadB: in takeOut() - emptied slot, about to notifyAll()
11: threadB: in takeOut() - leaving
12: threadB: in run() - just took out: 'multithreaded'
13: threadA: in putIn() - notified, back from wait()
14: threadA: in putIn() - filled slot, about to notifyAll()
15: threadA: in putIn() - leaving
16: threadA: in run() - just put in: 'programming'
17: threadA: in putIn() - entering
18: threadA: in putIn() - occupied, about to wait()
19: threadB: in takeOut() - entering
20: threadB: in takeOut() - emptied slot, about to notifyAll()
21: threadB: in takeOut() - leaving
22: threadB: in run() - just took out: 'programming'
23: threadB: in takeOut() - entering
24: threadB: in takeOut() - empty, about to wait()
25: threadA: in putIn() - notified, back from wait()
26: threadA: in putIn() - filled slot, about to notifyAll()
27: threadA: in putIn() - leaving
28: threadA: in run() - just put in: 'with Java'
29: threadB: in takeOut() - notified, back from wait()
```

```
30: threadB: in takeOut() - emptied slot, about to notifyAll()
31: threadB: in takeOut() - leaving
32: threadB: in run() - just took out: 'with Java'
```

Notice that sometimes a thread enters one of the methods and does not have to wait (lines 3–4), and other times it does have to wait (lines 1–2). This output shows both the case of a thread blocking waiting to put an item in (lines 7–8) and the case of a thread blocking waiting for an item to remove (lines 23–24). Even with all this complexity, the three `String` objects are delivered safely through the `CubbyHole` in the exact order that they were added.

Figure 8.4 shows the timeline of events from this run of `CubbyHoleMain`. The diagram reflects the internal workings that occurred to produce the output in Listing 8.11. Notice that both threads invoke `wait()` and `notifyAll()`. Both threads signal and listen for signals. Notice that to add and remove three items required 10 lock-unlock cycles on `this`. This kind of complexity is required to safely ensure that there are not any race conditions, missed notifications, or early notifications.

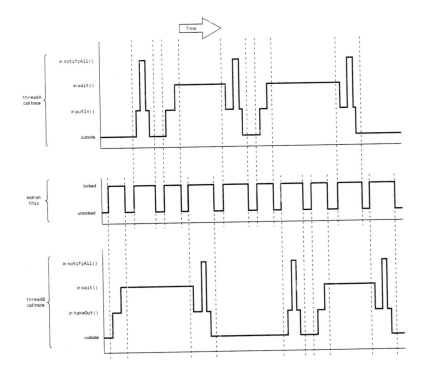

FIGURE 8.4
Timeline of events from a particular run of CubbyHoleMain.

Using join() to Wait for a Thread to Die

The join() method of Thread can be used to cause the current thread to block waiting for the specified thread to die. This is a relatively crude form of inter-thread communication, but on occasion it can be useful. If threadX runs the code

```
try {
    threadY.join()
} catch ( InterruptedException x ) {
}
```

threadX will block waiting for threadY to die. If threadX is interrupted while inside join(), it will throw an InterruptedException. There are three versions of the join() method available in Thread, all of which are public: join(), join(long), and join(long, int). Additionally, none of these methods can be overridden in a subclass because they are all declared final.

join()

```
public final void join()
        throws InterruptedException
```

The join() method causes the current thread to block and wait an unlimited amount of time for this thread to die. The current thread will throw an InterruptedException if interrupted while waiting for the specified thread to die.

join(long)

```
public final synchronized void join(long msTimeout)
        throws InterruptedException,
               IllegalArgumentException        // RuntimeException
```

The join(long) method causes the current thread to block and wait up to msTimeout milliseconds for the specified thread to die. If msTimeout is 0, the current thread will never time out and will wait forever for the specified thread to die (just like `join()`). If `msTimeout` is less than 0, an `IllegalArgumentException` is thrown. The current thread will throw an `InterruptedException` if interrupted while waiting for the specified thread to die.

join(long, int)

```
public final synchronized void join(long msTimeout, int nanoSec)
        throws InterruptedException,
              IllegalArgumentException      // RuntimeException
```

The `join(long, int)` method works just like `join(long)` (see above) with the exception that nanoseconds can be added to the timeout value. The argument `nanoSec` is added to `msTimeout` to determine the total amount of time that the thread will wait for the specified thread to die before returning. An `IllegalArgumentException` is thrown if `msTimeout` is less than 0 or if `nanoSec` is less than 0 or greater than **999999**. The current thread will throw an `InterruptedException` if interrupted while waiting for the specified thread to die.

JoinDemo

The class `JoinDemo` (see Listing 8.12) demonstrates how `join()` can be used to wait for threads to die. The `main` thread spawns three new threads and then waits for each of them to die. Each of the threads lives for a different amount of time.

LISTING 8.12   JoinDemo.java—Demonstration of the Use of join()

```
 1: public class JoinDemo extends Object {
 2:     public static Thread launch(String name, long napTime) {
 3:         final long sleepTime = napTime;
 4:
 5:         Runnable r = new Runnable() {
 6:             public void run() {
 7:                 try {
 8:                     print("in run() - entering");
 9:                     Thread.sleep(sleepTime);
10:                 } catch ( InterruptedException x ) {
11:                     print("interrupted!");
12:                 } finally {
13:                     print("in run() - leaving");
14:                 }
15:             }
```

continues

LISTING 8.12   Continued

```
16:                    };
17:
18:            Thread t = new Thread(r, name);
19:            t.start();
20:
21:            return t;
22:        }
23:
24:        private static void print(String msg) {
25:            String name = Thread.currentThread().getName();
26:            System.out.println(name + ": " + msg);
27:        }
28:
29:        public static void main(String[] args) {
30:            Thread[] t = new Thread[3];
31:
32:            t[0] = launch("threadA", 2000);
33:            t[1] = launch("threadB", 1000);
34:            t[2] = launch("threadC", 3000);
35:
36:            for ( int i = 0; i < t.length; i++ ) {
37:                try {
38:                    String idxStr = "t[" + i + "]";
39:                    String name = "[" + t[i].getName() + "]";
40:
41:                    print(idxStr + ".isAlive()=" +
42:                            t[i].isAlive() + " " + name);
43:                    print("about to do: " + idxStr +
44:                            ".join() " + name);
45:
46:                    long start = System.currentTimeMillis();
47:                    t[i].join(); // wait for the thread to die
48:                    long stop = System.currentTimeMillis();
49:
50:                    print(idxStr + ".join() - took " +
51:                            ( stop - start ) + " ms " + name);
52:                } catch ( InterruptedException x ) {
53:                    print("interrupted waiting on #" + i);
54:                }
55:            }
56:        }
57: }
```

In the static method launch() (lines 2–22) of JoinDemo, a new Runnable instance r is created. Inside the run() method of r, the thread prints an announcement (line 8), sleeps for the specified delay (line 9), and prints another message just before leaving `run()` (line 13). A new `Thread` is constructed and started for `r` and is given the name passed into `launch()` (lines 18–19). A reference to this new running `Thread` is returned to the caller (line 21).

In `main()` (lines 29–56), a `Thread[]` named `t` is created to hold three references (line 30). The `launch()` method is called three times with different parameters and the references returned are stored into `t` (lines 32–34):

- `t[0]` is named `threadA` and sleeps two seconds before dying.
- `t[1]` is named `threadB` and sleeps one seconds before dying.
- `t[2]` is named `threadC` and sleeps three seconds before dying.

All three threads are running concurrently. `threadB` finishes first, `threadA` finishes second, and `threadC` finishes last.

After launching all three threads, the `main` thread continues on into the `for` loop (lines 36–55). In this loop, `main` prints out some diagnostic information for each of the launched threads and then invokes `join()` on each of them to wait for each to die (line 47). Without all the extra information gathering and printing, the `for` loop boils down to this:

```
for ( int i = 0; i < t.length; i++ ) {
    try {
        t[i].join(); // wait for the thread to die
    } catch ( InterruptedException x ) {
    }
}
```

The `main` thread blocks for about two seconds waiting for `threadA` to die. Meanwhile, `threadB` has already died, so when the `main` thread invokes `join()` on `threadB`, `join()` returns right away. The `main` thread then proceeds to block for about one second waiting for `threadC` to die.

Listing 8.13 shows the output produced from a particular run of `JoinDemo`. Your output should match fairly closely. The only differences should be a little variation in the number of milliseconds that the `main` thread spends inside `join()` and perhaps a few lines of output swapped with each other.

LISTING 8.13 Output from JoinDemo

```
1: main: t[0].isAlive()=true [threadA]
2: threadA: in run() - entering
3: threadB: in run() - entering
4: threadC: in run() - entering
5: main: about to do: t[0].join() [threadA]
6: threadB: in run() - leaving
```

continues

LISTING 8.13 Continued

```
 7: threadA: in run() - leaving
 8: main: t[0].join() - took 1920 ms [threadA]
 9: main: t[1].isAlive()=false [threadB]
10: main: about to do: t[1].join() [threadB]
11: main: t[1].join() - took 0 ms [threadB]
12: main: t[2].isAlive()=true [threadC]
13: main: about to do: t[2].join() [threadC]
14: threadC: in run() - leaving
15: main: t[2].join() - took 990 ms [threadC]
```

The main thread finds threadA still alive (line 1), invokes join() on it (line 5), and waits 1920 milliseconds for it to die (line 8). Notice that threadB reported that it was leaving its run() method while the main thread was waiting on threadA (line 6). Therefore, the main thread finds threadB already dead (line 9) and when join() is invoked (line 10), the main thread returns right away (line 11). Next, the main thread finds threadC still alive (line 12), invokes join() on it (line 13), and waits 990 milliseconds for it to die (line 15).

Streaming Data Between Threads Using Pipes

The java.io package provides many classes for writing and reading data to and from streams. Most of the time, the data is written to or read from a file or network connection. Instead of streaming data to a file, a thread can stream it through a *pipe* to another thread. The first thread writes to the pipe, and the second thread reads from the pipe. A pipe is neither a file nor a network connection, but a structure in memory that holds the data that is written until it is read. Usually, a pipe has a fixed capacity. When the pipe is filled to this capacity, attempts to write more data will block waiting until some data is drained (read) from the pipe by another thread. Similarly, when a pipe is empty, attempts to read data from the pipe will block waiting until another thread writes some data into it.

There are four pipe-related classes in the java.io package that can be used to stream data between threads: PipedInputStream, PipedOutputStream, PipedReader, and PipedWriter. A PipedInputStream and a PipedOutputStream are hooked together to transfer bytes between threads. A PipedReader and a PipedWriter are hooked together to transfer character data between threads. Figure 8.5 shows the class diagram for these classes. The PipedOutputStream object keeps a reference to the PipedInputStream object it is connected to. Similarly, the PipedWriter object keeps a reference to the PipedReader object it is connected to.

A pipe made up of a PipedInputStream and a PipedOutputStream has a capacity to hold 1024 bytes. This means that the thread doing the writing can be up to 1024 bytes ahead of the thread doing the reading. This buffering makes the transfer of data more efficient than a single-byte handoff would be. A pipe made up of a PipedReader and a PipedWriter has a capacity to hold

1024 *characters*. Again, this buffering allows the thread doing the writing to work a little bit ahead of the thread doing the reading. I discovered the size of the pipes (1024 bytes and 1024 characters) by examining the source code from Sun Microsystems. The API documentation gives no information or guarantees regarding the internal pipe size. Therefore, you should not depend on 1024 being the universal size.

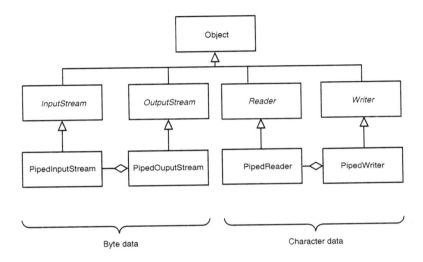

FIGURE 8.5
Class diagram for the pipe-related classes in java.io.

PipedInputStream and PipedOutputStream each represent an *end* of the pipe and need to be connected to each other before data can be sent. Both PipedInputStream and PipedOutputStream have a constructor that takes a reference to the other. It doesn't matter which is constructed first. You can write either

```
PipedInputStream pipeIn = new PipedInputStream();
PipedOutputStream pipeOut = new PipedOutputStream(pipeIn);
```

or

```
PipedOutputStream pipeOut = new PipedOutputStream();
PipedInputStream pipeIn = new PipedInputStream(pipeOut);
```

Additionally, both ends can be created with their zero-argument constructors and connected together with connect(). You can write either

```
PipedInputStream pipeIn = new PipedInputStream();
PipedOutputStream pipeOut = new PipedOutputStream();
pipeIn.connect(pipeOut);
```

or

```
PipedInputStream pipeIn = new PipedInputStream();
PipedOutputStream pipeOut = new PipedOutputStream();
pipeOut.connect(pipeIn);
```

If the ends of the pipe are not yet connected to each other, any attempt to read or write will cause an IOException to be thrown. Because of this, it's generally a good idea to connect the ends right away by using the constructor. PipedReader and PipedWriter connect to each other in the same ways that PipedInputStream and PipedOutputStream do, so the same rules and guidelines apply.

PipedBytes

The PipedBytes class (see Listing 8.14) shows how data can be sent through a pipe from one thread to another. Integers are written to a PipedOutputStream by one thread and are read from a PipedInputStream by another thread.

LISTING 8.14   PipedBytes.java—Sending Data Between Threads Using PipedInputStream and PipedOutputStream

```
 1: import java.io.*;
 2:
 3: public class PipedBytes extends Object {
 4:     public static void writeStuff(OutputStream rawOut) {
 5:         try {
 6:             DataOutputStream out = new DataOutputStream(
 7:                     new BufferedOutputStream(rawOut));
 8:
 9:             int[] data = { 82, 105, 99, 104, 97, 114, 100, 32,
10:                            72, 121, 100, 101 };
11:
12:             for ( int i = 0; i < data.length; i++ ) {
13:                 out.writeInt(data[i]);
14:             }
15:
16:             out.flush();
17:             out.close();
18:         } catch ( IOException x ) {
19:             x.printStackTrace();
20:         }
21:     }
22:
23:     public static void readStuff(InputStream rawIn) {
24:         try {
25:             DataInputStream in = new DataInputStream(
26:                     new BufferedInputStream(rawIn));
```

```
27:
28:                 boolean eof = false;
29:                 while ( !eof ) {
30:                     try {
31:                         int i = in.readInt();
32:                         System.out.println("just read: " + i);
33:                     } catch ( EOFException eofx ) {
34:                         eof = true;
35:                     }
36:                 }
37:
38:                 System.out.println("Read all data from the pipe");
39:             } catch ( IOException x ) {
40:                 x.printStackTrace();
41:             }
42:         }
43:
44:         public static void main(String[] args) {
45:             try {
46:                 final PipedOutputStream out =
47:                         new PipedOutputStream();
48:
49:                 final PipedInputStream in =
50:                         new PipedInputStream(out);
51:
52:                 Runnable runA = new Runnable() {
53:                     public void run() {
54:                         writeStuff(out);
55:                     }
56:                 };
57:
58:                 Thread threadA = new Thread(runA, "threadA");
59:                 threadA.start();
60:
61:                 Runnable runB = new Runnable() {
62:                     public void run() {
63:                         readStuff(in);
64:                     }
65:                 };
66:
67:                 Thread threadB = new Thread(runB, "threadB");
68:                 threadB.start();
69:             } catch ( IOException x ) {
70:                 x.printStackTrace();
71:             }
72:         }
73: }
```

In the main() method (lines 44–72), a data pipe is created and two threads are started to transfer data through it. First, the PipedOutputStream is constructed (lines 46–47). Next, the associated PipedInputStream is created by passing a reference to the PipedOutputStream that makes up the other end of the pipe (lines 49–50). threadA is started and executes the writeStuff() method, passing in a reference to the PipedOutputStream (line 54). threadB is started and executes the readStuff() method, passing in a reference to the PipedInputStream (line 63). threadA is writing data into one end of the pipe while threadB is simultaneously reading data from the other end of the pipe.

The writeStuff() method (lines 4–21) only expects an OutputStream to be passed to it and makes no special considerations for the fact that it might just happen to be a PipedOutputStream (line 4). When threadA invokes writeStuff(), it wraps the OutputStream in a DataOuputStream to be able to use the writeInt() method to put the integers into the pipe (lines 6–7). The integer data to be sent is stored into the int[] referred to by data (lines 9–10). Each of the integers in the array is written to the DataOutputStream (lines 12–14). Before returning, the stream is flushed and closed (lines 16–17).

Like writeStuff(), the readStuff() method (lines 23–42) only expects an InputStream to be passed to it and makes no special considerations for the fact that it might happen to be a PipedInputStream (line 23). This raw InputStream is wrapped in a DataInputStream to facilitate the reading of integers (lines 25–26). As long as the end-of-file is not detected, threadB continues to read integers from the stream (lines 28–36).

Listing 8.15 shows the output produced when PipedBytes is run. Your output should match. Notice that all the integers are read by threadB in exactly the same order as they are written by threadA.

LISTING 8.15   Output from PipedBytes

```
 1: just read: 82
 2: just read: 105
 3: just read: 99
 4: just read: 104
 5: just read: 97
 6: just read: 114
 7: just read: 100
 8: just read: 32
 9: just read: 72
10: just read: 121
11: just read: 100
12: just read: 101
13: Read all data from the pipe
```

PipedCharacters

The `PipedCharacters` class (see Listing 8.16) shows how character-based data can be sent through a pipe from one thread to another. Strings are written to a `PipedWriter` by one thread and are read from a `PipedReader` by another thread.

LISTING 8.16   PipedCharacters.java—Sending Characters Between Threads Using
PipedReader and PipedWriter

```
1: import java.io.*;
2:
3: public class PipedCharacters extends Object {
4:     public static void writeStuff(Writer rawOut) {
5:         try {
6:             BufferedWriter out = new BufferedWriter(rawOut);
7:
8:             String[][] line = {
9:                     { "Java", "has", "nice", "features." },
10:                    { "Pipes", "are", "interesting." },
11:                    { "Threads", "are", "fun", "in", "Java." },
12:                    { "Don't", "you", "think", "so?" }
13:                 };
14:
15:             for ( int i = 0; i < line.length; i++ ) {
16:                 String[] word = line[i];
17:
18:                 for ( int j = 0; j < word.length; j++ ) {
19:                     if ( j > 0 ) {
20:                         // put a space between words
21:                         out.write(" ");
22:                     }
23:
24:                     out.write(word[j]);
25:                 }
26:
27:                 // mark the end of a line
28:                 out.newLine();
29:             }
30:
31:             out.flush();
32:             out.close();
33:         } catch ( IOException x ) {
34:             x.printStackTrace();
```

continues

LISTING 8.16   Continued

```
35:           }
36:       }
37:
38:     public static void readStuff(Reader rawIn) {
39:         try {
40:             BufferedReader in = new BufferedReader(rawIn);
41:
42:             String line;
43:             while ( ( line = in.readLine() ) != null ) {
44:                 System.out.println("read line: " + line);
45:             }
46:
47:             System.out.println("Read all data from the pipe");
48:         } catch ( IOException x ) {
49:             x.printStackTrace();
50:         }
51:     }
52:
53:     public static void main(String[] args) {
54:         try {
55:             final PipedWriter out = new PipedWriter();
56:
57:             final PipedReader in = new PipedReader(out);
58:
59:             Runnable runA = new Runnable() {
60:                     public void run() {
61:                         writeStuff(out);
62:                     }
63:                 };
64:
65:             Thread threadA = new Thread(runA, "threadA");
66:             threadA.start();
67:
68:             Runnable runB = new Runnable() {
69:                     public void run() {
70:                         readStuff(in);
71:                     }
72:                 };
73:
74:             Thread threadB = new Thread(runB, "threadB");
75:             threadB.start();
76:         } catch ( IOException x ) {
77:             x.printStackTrace();
78:         }
79:     }
80: }
```

In the `main()` method (lines 53–79), a character-based data pipe is created and two threads are started to transfer data through it. First, a `PipedWriter` is constructed (line 55). Next, the associated `PipedReader` is constructed by passing a reference to the `PipedWriter` (line 57). `threadA` is started and executes the `writeStuff()` method, passing in a reference to the `PipedWriter` (line 61). `threadB` is started and executes the `readStuff()` method, passing in a reference to the `PipedReader` (line 70). `threadA` is writing characters into one end of the pipe while `threadB` is simultaneously reading characters from the other end of the pipe.

The `writeStuff()` method (lines 4–36) only expects a `Writer` to be passed to it and makes no special considerations for the fact that it might be a `PipedWriter` (line 4). When `threadA` invokes `writeStuff()`, it wraps the `Writer` in a `BufferedWriter` to be able to use the `newLine()` method to mark the end of each line (line 6). The sentences to be sent are stored in the `String[][]` referred to by `line` (lines 8–13). The two-dimensional array stores the sentences in one dimension and the individual words that make up each sentence in the other dimension. Each line (sentence) is stepped through using the outer `for` loop (lines 15–29). Each word in a line is stepped through using the inner `for` loop (lines 18–25). After the last word of each line is written, the `newLine()` method is used to mark the end-of-line (line 28). Before returning, the `BufferedWriter` is flushed and closed (lines 31–32).

The `readStuff()` method (lines 38–51) only expects a `Reader` to be passed to it and makes no special considerations for the fact that it might happen to be a `PipedReader` (line 38). This raw `Reader` is wrapped in a `BufferedReader` to facilitate the reading of whole lines at a time (line 40). Each line is read from the `BufferedReader` until the end-of-file is detected by a `null` return from `readLine()` (lines 42–45).

Listing 8.17 shows the output produced when `PipedCharacters` is run. Your output should match. Notice that all the lines (sentences) are read by `threadB` in exactly the same order that they are written by `threadA`.

LISTING 8.17   Output from PipedCharacters

```
1: read line: Java has nice features.
2: read line: Pipes are interesting.
3: read line: Threads are fun in Java.
4: read line: Don't you think so?
5: Read all data from the pipe
```

Using ThreadLocal and InheritableThreadLocal

Support for thread-specific variables has been added as of release 1.2 of the JDK. The value returned from the `get()` method `ThreadLocal` depends on which thread invokes the method. `InheritableThreadLocal` allows these values to be inherited from parent to child thread.

I'll just give you a quick, high-level overview on how the thread-specific variables are implemented. Figure 8.6 shows the class relationships for ThreadLocal and InheritableThreadLocal. ThreadLocal contains a reference to a WeakHashMap that holds key-value pairs. *Weak references* were introduced in JDK 1.2, and WeakHashMap takes advantage of them to automatically remove mappings for threads that have died and been de-referenced in all other places. This way, ThreadLocal does not keep track of values for threads that have long since died. In the WeakHashMap, the lookup key is the reference to the Thread and the value stored is a ThreadLocal.Entry object. ThreadLocal.Entry is an inner class to ThreadLocal and is used by ThreadLocal to store the thread-specific values.

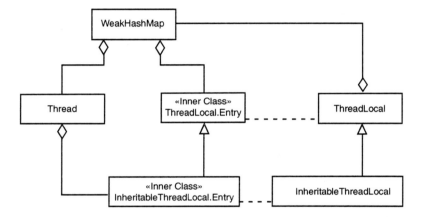

FIGURE 8.6
Class relationships for ThreadLocal and InheritableThreadLocal.

InheritableThreadLocal is a subclass of ThreadLocal that provides a mechanism for the thread-specific variable to be inherited from parent thread to child thread. InheritableThreadLocal.Entry is a subclass of ThreadLocal.Entry and is also an inner class. Thread contains a private reference to an InheritableThreadLocal.Entry object and uses it to pass the thread-specific variable down from parent thread to child thread when a new thread is created.

ThreadLocal API

ThreadLocal has two public methods. The first one is get():

```
public Object get()
```

get() is used to retrieve the thread-specific value. Internally, it looks up to see if the calling thread has a value stored. If is does, it returns that value. If not, it calls the protected method initialValue() to initialize a value for the calling thread, stores it in the internal WeakHashMap for future lookups, and returns the value to the caller. Typically, get() is the only method called on a ThreadLocal object.

However, on rare occasions, a thread can set its own value for future use by invoking the other public method of ThreadLocal directly:

public void set(Object value)

set() takes the value passed and stores it in the internal WeakHashMap for future lookups.

ThreadLocal is not abstract, but it generally needs to be subclassed to be useful. This protected method should be overridden in the subclass:

protected Object initialValue()

By default, initialValue() returns null, but in the subclass it can return a more meaningful value.

ThreadID

The class ThreadID (see Listing 8.18) is a subclass of ThreadLocal and creates a unique ID for every thread that invokes get(). If a thread comes back and invokes get() again, the same value is returned.

8

INTER-THREAD
COMMUNICATION

LISTING 8.18   ThreadID.java—Using ThreadLocal to Generate Unique Thread IDs

```
1: public class ThreadID extends ThreadLocal {
2:     private int nextID;
3:
4:     public ThreadID() {
5:         nextID = 10001;
6:     }
7:
8:     private synchronized Integer getNewID() {
9:         Integer id = new Integer(nextID);
10:        nextID++;
11:        return id;
12:    }
13:
14:    // override ThreadLocal's version
15:    protected Object initialValue() {
16:        print("in initialValue()");
17:        return getNewID();
```

continues

LISTING **8.18**   Continued

```
18:     }
19:
20:     public int getThreadID() {
21:         // Call get() in ThreadLocal to get the calling
22:         // thread's unique ID.
23:         Integer id = (Integer) get();
24:         return id.intValue();
25:     }
26:
27:     private static void print(String msg) {
28:         String name = Thread.currentThread().getName();
29:         System.out.println(name + ": " + msg);
30:     }
31: }
```

ThreadID is a subclass of ThreadLocal (line 1) and creates a unique ID for every thread that invokes the get() method. The next unique ID to be assigned is held in nextID (line 2) and is initialized to be 10001 (line 5). The getNewID() method (lines 8–12) is synchronized to ensure that only one thread is inside it at a time. The initialValue() method (lines 15–18) overrides the superclass's method and calls getNewID() to generate a new, unique ID.

The only public method is getThreadID() (lines 20–25). Inside, get() is invoked to look up the value for the calling thread (line 23). This action might indirectly cause initialValue() to be called if it is the first time that the calling thread has invoked get().

The class ThreadIDMain (see Listing 8.19) starts up three threads to demonstrate how ThreadID works. Each thread calls getThreadID() twice to show that the first call for each thread generates a new ID and that the second call simply returns the same value generated during the first call.

LISTING **8.19**   ThreadIDMain.java—Used to Demonstrate ThreadID

```
 1: public class ThreadIDMain extends Object implements Runnable {
 2:     private ThreadID var;
 3:
 4:     public ThreadIDMain(ThreadID var) {
 5:         this.var = var;
 6:     }
 7:
 8:     public void run() {
 9:         try {
10:             print("var.getThreadID()=" + var.getThreadID());
11:             Thread.sleep(2000);
```

```
12:            print("var.getThreadID()=" + var.getThreadID());
13:        } catch ( InterruptedException x ) {
14:            // ignore
15:        }
16:    }
17:
18:    private static void print(String msg) {
19:        String name = Thread.currentThread().getName();
20:        System.out.println(name + ": " + msg);
21:    }
22:
23:    public static void main(String[] args) {
24:        ThreadID tid = new ThreadID();
25:        ThreadIDMain shared = new ThreadIDMain(tid);
26:
27:        try {
28:            Thread threadA = new Thread(shared, "threadA");
29:            threadA.start();
30:
31:            Thread.sleep(500);
32:
33:            Thread threadB = new Thread(shared, "threadB");
34:            threadB.start();
35:
36:            Thread.sleep(500);
37:
38:            Thread threadC = new Thread(shared, "threadC");
39:            threadC.start();
40:        } catch ( InterruptedException x ) {
41:            // ignore
42:        }
43:    }
44: }
```

In main() (lines 23–43), one instance of ThreadID is constructed (line 24) and passed into the constructor for ThreadIDMain (line 25). The instance of ThreadIDMain is referred to by shared and implements the Runnable interface. The main thread proceeds to create three new threads (threadA, threadB, and threadC) that will all simultaneously run the one instance referenced by shared (lines 28–39).

When each thread runs, the thread invokes the run() method (lines 8–16). Inside run(), getThreadID() is invoked and the result is printed (line 10). After sleeping for two seconds (line 11), getThreadID() is invoked again and the result is printed (line 12).

Listing 8.20 shows the output produced when ThreadIDMain is run. Your output should match.

LISTING 8.20   Output from ThreadIDMain

```
1: threadA: in initialValue()
2: threadA: var.getThreadID()=10001
3: threadB: in initialValue()
4: threadB: var.getThreadID()=10002
5: threadC: in initialValue()
6: threadC: var.getThreadID()=10003
7: threadA: var.getThreadID()=10001
8: threadB: var.getThreadID()=10002
9: threadC: var.getThreadID()=10003
```

When threadA invokes getThreadID(), it indirectly causes initialValue() to be called (line 1). The unique ID for threadA is 10001 (line 2). When threadB and threadC invoke getThreadID(), they both get a new unique ID (lines 3–6). The second time that each of the threads invokes getThreadID(), a unique ID does *not* have to be generated and the same ID that was returned the first time is returned again (lines 7–9).

InheritableThreadLocal API

InheritableThreadLocal is a subclass of ThreadLocal and allows a thread-specific value to be inherited from the parent thread to the child thread. There are not any public methods on InheritableThreadLocal. It can be used directly as a special kind of ThreadLocal that passes its value from parent thread to child thread.

If you don't want to use the parent thread's value directly, you can override

```
protected Object childValue(Object parentValue)
```

to produce a customized child value at the time that the child thread is created. By default, childValue() simply returns parentValue.

InheritableThreadID

The class InheritableThreadID (see Listing 8.21) demonstrates three different ways that thread-specific variables can behave regarding inheritance from parent thread to child thread. First, a ThreadLocal variable is used to demonstrate that the child thread will have a different thread-specific value than its parent thread does. Second, an InheritableThreadLocal is used *without* overriding childValue() to demonstrate that the child thread will have the exact same thread-specific value as its parent. Third, an InheritableThreadLocal is used *with* the childValue() method overridden to demonstrate that the child's value can be based on the parent's value.

LISTING 8.21 InheritableThreadID.java—Demonstration of InheritableThreadLocal

```
 1: public class InheritableThreadID extends Object {
 2:     public static final int UNIQUE  = 101;
 3:     public static final int INHERIT = 102;
 4:     public static final int SUFFIX  = 103;
 5:
 6:     private ThreadLocal threadLocal;
 7:     private int nextID;
 8:
 9:     public InheritableThreadID(int type) {
10:         nextID = 201;
11:
12:         switch ( type ) {
13:             case UNIQUE:
14:                 threadLocal = new ThreadLocal() {
15:                         // override from ThreadLocal
16:                         protected Object initialValue() {
17:                             print("in initialValue()");
18:                             return getNewID();
19:                         }
20:                     };
21:                 break;
22:
23:             case INHERIT:
24:                 threadLocal = new InheritableThreadLocal() {
25:                         // override from ThreadLocal
26:                         protected Object initialValue() {
27:                             print("in initialValue()");
28:                             return getNewID();
29:                         }
30:                     };
31:                 break;
32:
33:             case SUFFIX:
34:                 threadLocal = new InheritableThreadLocal() {
35:                         // override from ThreadLocal
36:                         protected Object initialValue() {
37:                             print("in initialValue()");
38:                             return getNewID();
39:                         }
40:
```

continues

LISTING 8.21   Continued

```
41:                                // override from InheritableThreadLocal
42:                                protected Object childValue(
43:                                        Object parentValue
44:                                    ) {
45:
46:                                    print("in childValue() - " +
47:                                        "parentValue=" + parentValue);
48:
49:                                    return parentValue + "-CH";
50:                                }
51:                            };
52:                        break;
53:                    default:
54:                        break;
55:                }
56:        }
57:
58:        private synchronized String getNewID() {
59:            String id = "ID" + nextID;
60:            nextID++;
61:            return id;
62:        }
63:
64:        public String getID() {
65:            return (String) threadLocal.get();
66:        }
67:
68:        public static void print(String msg) {
69:            String name = Thread.currentThread().getName();
70:            System.out.println(name + ": " + msg);
71:        }
72:
73:        public static Runnable createTarget(InheritableThreadID id) {
74:            final InheritableThreadID var = id;
75:
76:            Runnable parentRun = new Runnable() {
77:                public void run() {
78:                    print("var.getID()=" + var.getID());
79:                    print("var.getID()=" + var.getID());
80:                    print("var.getID()=" + var.getID());
81:
82:                    Runnable childRun = new Runnable() {
83:                        public void run() {
84:                            print("var.getID()=" + var.getID());
```

```
85:                          print("var.getID()=" + var.getID());
86:                          print("var.getID()=" + var.getID());
87:                      }
88:                  };
89:
90:              Thread parentT = Thread.currentThread();
91:              String parentName = parentT.getName();
92:              print("creating a child thread of " +
93:                      parentName);
94:
95:              Thread childT = new Thread(childRun,
96:                      parentName + "-child");
97:              childT.start();
98:          }
99:      };
100:
101:      return parentRun;
102:  }
103:
104:  public static void main(String[] args) {
105:      try {
106:          System.out.println("======= ThreadLocal =======");
107:          InheritableThreadID varA =
108:              new InheritableThreadID(UNIQUE);
109:
110:          Runnable targetA = createTarget(varA);
111:          Thread threadA = new Thread(targetA, "threadA");
112:          threadA.start();
113:
114:          Thread.sleep(2500);
115:          System.out.println("\n======= " +
116:              "InheritableThreadLocal =======");
117:
118:          InheritableThreadID varB =
119:              new InheritableThreadID(INHERIT);
120:
121:          Runnable targetB = createTarget(varB);
122:          Thread threadB = new Thread(targetB, "threadB");
123:          threadB.start();
124:
125:          Thread.sleep(2500);
126:          System.out.println("\n======= " +
127:              "InheritableThreadLocal - custom childValue()" +
```

continues

8

INTER-THREAD
COMMUNICATION

LISTING 8.21   Continued

```
128:                   " =======");
129:
130:            InheritableThreadID varC =
131:                new InheritableThreadID(SUFFIX);
132:
133:            Runnable targetC = createTarget(varC);
134:            Thread threadC = new Thread(targetC, "threadC");
135:            threadC.start();
136:        } catch ( InterruptedException x ) {
137:            // ignore
138:        }
139:
140:    }
141: }
```

In the constructor for InheritableThreadID (lines 9–56), one of three different ThreadLocal instances is created. If type is UNIQUE (line 13), a plain ThreadLocal is used with its initialValue() method overridden to call getNewID() (lines 16–19). If type is INHERIT, an InheritableThreadLocal is used with its initialValue() method overridden to call getNewID() (lines 26–29). If type is SUFFIX, an InheritableThreadLocal is used with its initialValue() method overridden to call getNewID() (lines 36–39) *and* its childValue() method overridden to return the parent's value with "-CH" appended to it (lines 42–50).

Every time the synchronized method getNewID() is called, it generates a new String-based ID and returns it (lines 58–62).

When the getID() method (lines 64–66) is called, it invokes the get() method on whichever one of the three types of ThreadLocal variables was created in the constructor.

The static method createTarget() (lines 73–102) is used by main() to create a Runnable. When run() is invoked, the getID() method for the particular instance of InheritableThreadID is invoked three times (lines 78–80). Then this parent thread creates a new child thread (lines 95–97). The child thread is then started and invokes getID() three more times to see what value is returned to the child thread (lines 84–86).

In the main() method (lines 104–140), three different instances of InheritableThreadID are constructed and three different threads work with them.

First, varA refers to an InheritableThreadID that simply creates a unique ID for every thread—regardless of parent-child relationships (lines 107–108). A Runnable is created to use varA (line 110), and threadA is started to run it (lines 111–112).

Second, varB refers to an InheritableThreadID that allows the parent thread to pass its ID unmodified to the child thread—the child inherits the parent's value (lines 118–119). A Runnable is created to use varB (line 121), and threadB is started to run it (lines 122–123).

Third, varC refers to an InheritableThreadID that intercepts the passing of the value from the parent to child and adds a suffix to the child's value (lines 130–131). A Runnable is created to use varC (line 133), and threadC is started to run it (lines 134–135).

Listing 8.22 shows the output produced when InheritableThreadID is run. Your output should match.

LISTING 8.22   Output Produced When InheritableThreadID Is Run

```
 1: ======= ThreadLocal =======
 2: threadA: in initialValue()
 3: threadA: var.getID()=ID201
 4: threadA: var.getID()=ID201
 5: threadA: var.getID()=ID201
 6: threadA: creating a child thread of threadA
 7: threadA-child: in initialValue()
 8: threadA-child: var.getID()=ID202
 9: threadA-child: var.getID()=ID202
10: threadA-child: var.getID()=ID202
11:
12: ======= InheritableThreadLocal =======
13: threadB: in initialValue()
14: threadB: var.getID()=ID201
15: threadB: var.getID()=ID201
16: threadB: var.getID()=ID201
17: threadB: creating a child thread of threadB
18: threadB-child: var.getID()=ID201
19: threadB-child: var.getID()=ID201
20: threadB-child: var.getID()=ID201
21:
22: ======= InheritableThreadLocal - custom childValue() =======
23: threadC: in initialValue()
24: threadC: var.getID()=ID201
25: threadC: var.getID()=ID201
26: threadC: var.getID()=ID201
27: threadC: creating a child thread of threadC
28: threadC: in childValue() - parentValue=ID201
29: threadC-child: var.getID()=ID201-CH
30: threadC-child: var.getID()=ID201-CH
31: threadC-child: var.getID()=ID201-CH
```

8

INTER-THREAD
COMMUNICATION

Notice that when UNIQUE is used, the parent and child have completely different ID values: ID201 and ID202 (lines 1–10). When INHERIT is used, the parent and child have exactly the same ID values: ID201 (lines 12–20). When SUFFIX is used, the child's value is the same as the parent's with "-CH" added to the end: ID201 and ID201-CH (lines 22–31).

Summary

Threads can communicate and signal each other by several mechanisms in Java. The wait/notify mechanism (wait(), notify(), and notifyAll()) provides a multithread-safe way for one thread to signal another that a value has changed. I showed you that it is important to make sure to avoid missed notifications and early notifications.

In addition, threads can use the join() method of Thread to wait for other threads to die. A thread can also stream data through a pipe to another thread using the classes PipedInputStream, PipedOutputStream, PipedReader, and PipedWriter.

Threads can also use thread-specific variables that keep a different value for different threads by using the classes ThreadLocal and InheritableThreadLocal.

Threads and Swing

IN THIS CHAPTER

The Swing graphical toolkit brings a host of new components to the Java platform. There's a catch, though—Swing components are not designed for a multithreaded environment. In this chapter, I'll show how you how to safely interact with Swing components in a multithread-safe manner using `SwingUtilities.invokeAndWait()` and `SwingUtilities.invokeLater()`. I'll also show you some ways that animation can be achieved using Swing components and threads.

Why Isn't the Swing Toolkit Multithread-Safe?

After Swing components have been displayed on the screen, they should only be operated on by the event-handling thread. The event-handling thread (or just event thread) is started automatically by the Java VM when an application has a graphical interface. The event thread calls methods like `paint()` on `Component`, `actionPerformed()` on `ActionListener`, and all of the other event-handling methods.

Most of the time, modifications to Swing components are done in the event-handling methods. Because the event thread calls these methods, it is perfectly safe to directly change components in event-handling code. `SimpleEvent` (see Listing 9.1) shows safe Swing code.

LISTING 9.1 SimpleEvent.java—Safe Swing Code That Uses the Event Thread

```
 1: import java.awt.*;
 2: import java.awt.event.*;
 3: import javax.swing.*;
 4:
 5: public class SimpleEvent extends Object {
 6:     private static void print(String msg) {
 7:         String name = Thread.currentThread().getName();
 8:         System.out.println(name + ": " + msg);
 9:     }
10:
11:     public static void main(String[] args) {
12:         final JLabel label = new JLabel("— — — —");
13:         JButton button = new JButton("Click Here");
14:
15:         JPanel panel = new JPanel(new FlowLayout());
16:         panel.add(button);
17:         panel.add(label);
18:
19:         button.addActionListener(new ActionListener() {
20:             public void actionPerformed(ActionEvent e) {
21:                 print("in actionPerformed()");
22:                 label.setText("CLICKED!");
```

```
23:                    }
24:               });
25:
26:          JFrame f = new JFrame("SimpleEvent");
27:          f.setContentPane(panel);
28:          f.setSize(300, 100);
29:          f.setVisible(true);
30:     }
31: }
```

In `SimpleEvent`, two threads interact with the Swing components. First, the `main` thread creates the components (lines 12–15), adds them to `panel` (lines 16–17), and creates and configures a `JFrame` (lines 26–29). After `setVisible()` is invoked by `main` (line 29), it is no longer safe for any thread other than the event thread to make changes to the components.

When the button is clicked, the event thread invokes the `actionPerformed()` method (lines 20–23). In there, it prints a message to show which thread is running the code (line 21) and changes the text for `label` (line 22). This code is perfectly safe because it is the event thread that ends up calling `setText()`.

When `SimpleEvent` is run, the frame appears and the following output is printed to the console when the button is clicked:

```
AWT-EventQueue-0: in actionPerformed()
```

The thread named `AWT-EventQueue-0` is the event thread. This is the thread that can safely make changes through methods like `setText()`.

One of the goals for the developers of Swing was to make the toolkit as fast as possible. If the components had to be multithread-safe, there would need to be a lot of `synchronized` statements and methods. The extra overhead incurred acquiring and releasing locks all the time would have slowed the performance of the components. The developers made the choice for speed over safety. As a result, you need to be very careful when making modifications to Swing components that are initiated outside the event thread.

Using SwingUtilities.invokeAndWait()

The developers of the Swing toolkit realized that there would be times when an external thread would need to make changes to Swing components. They created a mechanism that puts a reference to a chunk of code on the event queue. When the event thread gets to this code block, it executes the code. This way, the GUI can be changed inside this block of code by the event thread.

The SwingUtilities class has a static invokeAndWait() method available to use to put references to blocks of code onto the event queue:

```
public static void invokeAndWait(Runnable target)
        throws InterruptedException,
                InvocationTargetException
```

The parameter target is a reference to an instance of Runnable. In this case, the Runnable will not be passed to the constructor of Thread. The Runnable interface is simply being used as a means to identify the entry point for the event thread. Just as a newly spawned thread will invoke run(), the event thread will invoke run() when it has processed all the other events pending in the queue.

An InterruptedException is thrown if the thread that called invokeAndWait() is interrupted before the block of code referred to by target completes. An InvocationTargetException (a class in the java.lang.reflect package) is thrown if an uncaught exception is thrown by the code inside run().

> **NOTE**
>
> A new thread is *not* created when Runnable is used with SwingUtilities.invokeAndWait(). The event thread will end up calling the run() method of the Runnable when its turn comes up on the event queue.

Suppose a JLabel component has been rendered on screen with some text:

```
label = new JLabel( // ...
```

Now, if a thread *other than the event thread* needs to call setText() on label to change it, the following should be done. First, create an instance of Runnable to do the work:

```
Runnable setTextRun = new Runnable() {
        public void run() {
            label.setText( // ...
        }
    };
```

Then pass the Runnable instance referred to by setTextRun to invokeAndWait():

```
try {
    SwingUtilities.invokeAndWait(setTextRun);
} catch ( InterruptedException ix ) {
    ix.printStackTrace();
} catch ( InvocationTargetException x ) {
    x.printStackTrace();
}
```

The try/catch block is used to catch the two types of exception that might be thrown while waiting for the code inside the run() method of setTextRun to complete.

InvokeAndWaitDemo (see Listing 9.2) is a complete example that demonstrates the use of SwingUtilities.invokeAndWait().

LISTING 9.2   InvokeAndWaitDemo.java—Using SwingUtilities.invokeAndWait()

```
 1: import java.awt.*;
 2: import java.awt.event.*;
 3: import java.lang.reflect.*;
 4: import javax.swing.*;
 5:
 6: public class InvokeAndWaitDemo extends Object {
 7:     private static void print(String msg) {
 8:         String name = Thread.currentThread().getName();
 9:         System.out.println(name + ": " + msg);
10:     }
11:
12:     public static void main(String[] args) {
13:         final JLabel label = new JLabel(" — — — — ");
14:
15:         JPanel panel = new JPanel(new FlowLayout());
16:         panel.add(label);
17:
18:         JFrame f = new JFrame("InvokeAndWaitDemo");
19:         f.setContentPane(panel);
20:         f.setSize(300, 100);
21:         f.setVisible(true);
22:
23:         try {
24:             print("sleeping for 3 seconds");
25:             Thread.sleep(3000);
26:
27:             print("creating code block for event thread");
28:             Runnable setTextRun = new Runnable() {
29:                     public void run() {
30:                         print("about to do setText()");
31:                         label.setText("New text!");
32:                     }
33:                 };
34:
```

continues

LISTING 9.2   Continued

```
35:                 print("about to invokeAndWait()");
36:                 SwingUtilities.invokeAndWait(setTextRun);
37:                 print("back from invokeAndWait()");
38:             } catch ( InterruptedException ix ) {
39:                 print("interrupted while waiting on invokeAndWait()");
40:             } catch ( InvocationTargetException x ) {
41:                 print("exception thrown from run()");
42:             }
43:         }
44: }
```

Note that the java.lang.reflect package is imported (line 3) solely for
InvocationTargetException. The main thread creates the GUI (lines 13–20) and invokes
setVisible() on the JFrame (line 21). *From that point on, only the event thread should make
changes to the GUI.*

After sleeping for 3 seconds (line 25), the main thread wants to change the text displayed in
label. To safely do this, the main thread must pass this work off to the event-handling thread.
The main thread creates a bundle of code in setTextRun, which is an instance of Runnable
(lines 28–33). Inside the run() method, the setText() method is invoked on label (line 31).
Ultimately, the event thread will end up invoking the setText() method inside this run()
method.

The main thread then calls SwingUtilities.invokeAndWait() passing in setTextRun (line
36). Inside invokeAndWait(), the setTextRun reference is put onto the event queue. When all
the events that were ahead of it in the queue have been processed, the event thread invokes the
run() method of setTextRun. When the event thread returns from run(), it notifies the main
thread that it has completed the work. The event thread then goes back to reading events from
the event queue. At the same time, the main thread returns from invokeAndWait(), indicating
that the code block inside setTextRun has been run by the event thread.

Listing 9.3 shows the output produced when InvokeAndWaitDemo is run. In addition, a GUI
frame appears, but that doesn't show anything other than the fact that the label changes when
setText() is invoked.

LISTING 9.3   Output from InvokeAndWaitDemo

```
1: main: sleeping for 3 seconds
2: main: creating code block for event thread
3: main: about to invokeAndWait()
4: AWT-EventQueue-0: about to do setText()
5: main: back from invokeAndWait()
```

The `main` thread announces that it is about to call `invokeAndWait()` (line 3). Next, the event thread (`AWT-EventQueue-0`) reports that it is indeed the thread that is invoking `setText()` (line 4). The `main` thread then reports that it is done blocking and has returned from `invokeAndWait()` (line 5).

> **CAUTION**
>
> Do not call `SwingUtilities.invokeAndWait()` from the event thread. Doing so causes an instance of `Error` to be thrown. Even if this call were allowed, it would put the event thread into a deadlocked state. The event thread does not need the services of `invokeAndWait()` because it can make the changes directly.

Using SwingUtilities.invokeLater()

The `SwingUtilities` class has another `static` method available to use to put references to blocks of code onto the event queue:

```
public static void invokeLater(Runnable target)
```

The `SwingUtilities.invokeLater()` method works like `SwingUtilities.invokeAndWait()` except for the fact that it puts the request on the event queue and *returns right away*. The `invokeLater()` method does not wait for the block of code inside the `Runnable` referred to by `target` to execute. This allows the thread that posted the request to move on to other activities.

> **NOTE**
>
> Just as with `invokeAndWait()`, a new thread is *not* created when `Runnable` is used with `SwingUtilities.invokeLater()`.

This example is just like the one used for `invokeAndWait()`, but instead shows the changes necessary to use `invokeLater()`. Suppose a `JLabel` component has been rendered on screen with some text:

```
label = new JLabel( // ...
```

If a thread *other than the event thread* needs to call `setText()` on `label` to change it, you should do the following. First, create an instance of `Runnable` to do the work:

```
Runnable setTextRun = new Runnable() {
        public void run() {
            try {
```

```
                        label.setText( // ...
                } catch ( Exception x ) {
                    x.printStackTrace();
                }
            }
        };
```

Be sure to catch all exceptions inside run() because unlike invokeAndWait(), invokeLater() does not have an automatic mechanism to propagate the exception back to the thread that called invokeLater(). Instead of simply printing a stack trace, you could have the event thread store the exception and notify another thread that an exception occurred.

Next, pass the Runnable instance referred to by setTextRun to invokeLater():

SwingUtilities.**invokeLater**(setTextRun);

This call returns right away and does not throw any exceptions. When the event thread has processed all of the pending events, it invokes the run() method of setTextRun.

InvokeLaterDemo (see Listing 9.4) is a complete example (based on InvokeAndWaitDemo) that demonstrates the use of SwingUtilities.invokeLater().

LISTING 9.4   InvokeLaterDemo.java—Using SwingUtilities.invokeLater()

```
 1: import java.awt.*;
 2: import java.awt.event.*;
 3: import javax.swing.*;
 4:
 5: public class InvokeLaterDemo extends Object {
 6:     private static void print(String msg) {
 7:         String name = Thread.currentThread().getName();
 8:         System.out.println(name + ": " + msg);
 9:     }
10:
11:     public static void main(String[] args) {
12:         final JLabel label = new JLabel(" — — — — ");
13:
14:         JPanel panel = new JPanel(new FlowLayout());
15:         panel.add(label);
16:
17:         JFrame f = new JFrame("InvokeLaterDemo");
18:         f.setContentPane(panel);
19:         f.setSize(300, 100);
20:         f.setVisible(true);
21:
```

```
22:            try {
23:                print("sleeping for 3 seconds");
24:                Thread.sleep(3000);
25:            } catch ( InterruptedException ix ) {
26:                print("interrupted while sleeping");
27:            }
28:
29:            print("creating code block for event thread");
30:            Runnable setTextRun = new Runnable() {
31:                    public void run() {
32:                        try {
33:                            Thread.sleep(100); // for emphasis
34:                            print("about to do setText()");
35:                            label.setText("New text!");
36:                        } catch ( Exception x ) {
37:                            x.printStackTrace();
38:                        }
39:                    }
40:                };
41:
42:            print("about to invokeLater()");
43:            SwingUtilities.invokeLater(setTextRun);
44:            print("back from invokeLater()");
45:        }
46: }
```

The main thread creates the GUI (lines 12–19) and invokes setVisible() on the JFrame (line 20). *From that point on, only the event thread should make changes to the GUI.*

After sleeping for 3 seconds (line 24), the main thread wants to change the text displayed in label. To safely do this, the main thread creates a bundle of code in setTextRun (lines 30–40). Inside the run() method, a try/catch block is used to capture any exceptions that might be thrown so that run() itself does not end up throwing any exceptions (lines 32–38). A very short sleep of 0.1 seconds (line 33) is used to momentarily slow the event thread to clearly show that the invokeLater() call returns right away. In real-world code there would not be any need for this sleep. Eventually, the event thread invokes the setText() method on label (line 35).

After setting up this code block, the main thread calls SwingUtilities.invokeLater(), passing in setTextRun (line 43). Inside invokeLater(), the setTextRun reference is put onto the event queue and then the main thread *returns right away*. When all of the events that were ahead of it in the queue have been processed, the event thread invokes the run() method of setTextRun.

Listing 9.5 shows the output produced when `InvokeLaterDemo` is run. Your output should match. In addition, a frame is drawn on the screen, but it doesn't show anything other than the fact that the label does indeed change.

LISTING 9.5 Output from InvokeLaterDemo

```
1: main: sleeping for 3 seconds
2: main: creating code block for event thread
3: main: about to invokeLater()
4: main: back from invokeLater()
5: AWT-EventQueue-0: about to do setText()
```

The `main` thread calls (line 3) and returns from (line 4) `invokeLater()` before the event thread gets a chance to invoke `setText()` (line 5). This is the exact asynchronous behavior that was desired.

NOTE

Unlike `SwingUtilities.invokeAndWait()`, the event thread *is* permitted to call `SwingUtilities.invokeLater()`. However, there isn't any value to doing so because the event thread can change the components directly.

Using SwingUtilities.isEventDispatchThread()

If you have code that must (or must not) be called by the event thread, you can use the `SwingUtilities.isEventDispatchThread()` method:

```
public static boolean isEventDispatchThread()
```

This `static` method returns `true` if the thread that invokes it is the event thread, and returns `false` if it is not.

If it is critical that only the event thread calls a particular method, you might want to put some code like this at the beginning of the method:

```
if ( SwingUtilities.isEventDispatchThread() == false ) {
    throw new RuntimeException(
        "only the event thread should invoke this method");
}
```

This way if any thread other than the event thread calls the method, a `RuntimeException` is thrown. This step can help safeguard against dangerous code that works *most* of the time when called by a thread other than the event thread.

A downside to this method is that it takes a little bit of time to execute. If you have some code where performance is critical, you might want to skip this check.

When invokeAndWait() and invokeLater() Are Not Needed

It is not always necessary to use invokeAndWait() and invokeLater() to interact with Swing components. Any thread can safely interact with the components before they have been added to a visible container. You have seen this already in the examples: The main thread constructs the GUI and then invokes setVisible(). After the components have been drawn to the screen, only the event thread should make further changes to their appearance.

There are a couple of exceptions to this restriction. The adding and removing of event listeners can safely be done by any thread at any time. Also, any thread can invoke the repaint() method. The repaint() method has always worked asynchronously to put a repaint request onto the event queue. And finally, any method that *explicitly* indicates that it does not have to be called by the event thread is safe. The API documentation for the setText() method of JTextComponent explicitly states that setText() can be safely called by any thread. The setText() method is inherited by JTextField (a subclass of JTextComponent), so any thread can safely invoke setText() on a JTextField component at any time.

TIP

If you aren't sure whether a particular method on a Swing component can be invoked by any thread, use the invokeAndWait() or invokeLater() mechanism to be safe.

The Need for Worker Threads in a GUI Setting

The event thread plays a critical role in an application with a graphical interface. Code that will be executed by the event-handling thread should be relatively brief and nonblocking. If the event-handling thread is blocked in a section of code for a while, no other events can be processed!

This is especially important in a client/server application (even more so in an n-tier application). Imagine a situation where the client is a graphical application with a Search button. When this button is clicked, a request is made over the network to the server for the results. The server produces the results and sends this information back down to the client. The client then displays this result information on the GUI. To be safe, the event thread needs to be the thread that gathers the information from the GUI for the search. The event thread also needs to be the thread that displays the results. But does the event thread have to send the request over the network? No, it does not, and should not.

The `BalanceLookupCantCancel` class (see Listing 9.6) shows what happens when the event thread is used to fulfill a request that takes a long time. This simple graphical client simulates a call over the network by sleeping for five seconds before returning the account balance.

LISTING 9.6   BalanceLookupCantCancel.java—Overusing the Event Thread

```
 1: import java.awt.*;
 2: import java.awt.event.*;
 3: import javax.swing.*;
 4:
 5: public class BalanceLookupCantCancel extends JPanel {
 6:     private JTextField acctTF;
 7:     private JTextField pinTF;
 8:     private JButton searchB;
 9:     private JButton cancelB;
10:     private JLabel balanceL;
11:
12:     public BalanceLookupCantCancel() {
13:         buildGUI();
14:         hookupEvents();
15:     }
16:
17:     private void buildGUI() {
18:         JLabel acctL = new JLabel("Account Number:");
19:         JLabel pinL = new JLabel("PIN:");
20:         acctTF = new JTextField(12);
21:         pinTF = new JTextField(4);
22:
23:         JPanel dataEntryP = new JPanel();
24:         dataEntryP.setLayout(new FlowLayout(FlowLayout.CENTER));
25:         dataEntryP.add(acctL);
26:         dataEntryP.add(acctTF);
27:         dataEntryP.add(pinL);
28:         dataEntryP.add(pinTF);
29:
30:         searchB = new JButton("Search");
31:         cancelB = new JButton("Cancel Search");
32:         cancelB.setEnabled(false);
33:
34:         JPanel innerButtonP = new JPanel();
35:         innerButtonP.setLayout(new GridLayout(1, -1, 5, 5));
```

```
36:            innerButtonP.add(searchB);
37:            innerButtonP.add(cancelB);
38:
39:            JPanel buttonP = new JPanel();
40:            buttonP.setLayout(new FlowLayout(FlowLayout.CENTER));
41:            buttonP.add(innerButtonP);
42:
43:            JLabel balancePrefixL = new JLabel("Account Balance:");
44:            balanceL = new JLabel("BALANCE UNKNOWN");
45:
46:            JPanel balanceP = new JPanel();
47:            balanceP.setLayout(new FlowLayout(FlowLayout.CENTER));
48:            balanceP.add(balancePrefixL);
49:            balanceP.add(balanceL);
50:
51:            JPanel northP = new JPanel();
52:            northP.setLayout(new GridLayout(-1, 1, 5, 5));
53:            northP.add(dataEntryP);
54:            northP.add(buttonP);
55:            northP.add(balanceP);
56:
57:            setLayout(new BorderLayout());
58:            add(northP, BorderLayout.NORTH);
59:        }
60:
61:        private void hookupEvents() {
62:            searchB.addActionListener(new ActionListener() {
63:                    public void actionPerformed(ActionEvent e) {
64:                        search();
65:                    }
66:                });
67:
68:            cancelB.addActionListener(new ActionListener() {
69:                    public void actionPerformed(ActionEvent e) {
70:                        cancelSearch();
71:                    }
72:                });
73:        }
74:
75:        private void search() {
76:            // better be called by event thread!
77:            searchB.setEnabled(false);
78:            cancelB.setEnabled(true);
```

9

THREADS AND SWING

continues

LISTING 9.6 Continued

```
79:            balanceL.setText("SEARCHING ...");
80:
81:        // get a snapshot of this info in case it changes
82:        String acct = acctTF.getText();
83:        String pin = pinTF.getText();
84:
85:        String bal = lookupBalance(acct, pin);
86:        setBalance(bal);
87:    }
88:
89:    private String lookupBalance(String acct, String pin) {
90:        try {
91:            // Simulate a lengthy search that takes 5 seconds
92:            // to communicate over the network.
93:            Thread.sleep(5000);
94:
95:            // result "retrieved", return it
96:            return "1,234.56";
97:        } catch ( InterruptedException x ) {
98:            return "SEARCH CANCELLED";
99:        }
100:    }
101:
102:    private void setBalance(String newBalance) {
103:        // better be called by event thread!
104:        balanceL.setText(newBalance);
105:        cancelB.setEnabled(false);
106:        searchB.setEnabled(true);
107:    }
108:
109:    private void cancelSearch() {
110:        System.out.println("in cancelSearch()");
111:        // Here's where the code to cancel would go if this
112:        // could ever be called!
113:    }
114:
115:    public static void main(String[] args) {
116:        BalanceLookupCantCancel bl =
117:                new BalanceLookupCantCancel();
118:
119:        JFrame f = new JFrame("Balance Lookup - Can't Cancel");
120:        f.addWindowListener(new WindowAdapter() {
121:            public void windowClosing(WindowEvent e) {
122:                System.exit(0);
123:            }
```

```
124:                });
125:
126:            f.setContentPane(bl);
127:            f.setSize(400, 150);
128:            f.setVisible(true);
129:        }
130: }
```

Most of `BalanceLookupCantCancel` (lines 1–73, 115–129) is dedicated to constructing the GUI. In `hookupEvents()` (lines 61–73), an event handler for each button is added. When the search button `searchB` is clicked, the `search()` method is called (lines 63–65). When the cancel button `cancelB` is clicked, `cancelSearch()` is called (lines 69–71).

Inside `search()` (lines 75–87), the Search button is disabled, the Cancel Search button is enabled, and the balance label is set to `SEARCHING ...` while the search is in progress (lines 77–78). The event thread is used to gather the account number and PIN number from the fields (lines 82–83). These strings are passed into `lookupBalance()`, and the balance found is returned and shown on the screen (lines 85–86).

The `lookupBalance()` method (lines 89–100) is used to simulate a lookup over a network connection. It sleeps for five seconds to simulate the delay for lookup and then returns `1,234.56` for every account. If the thread that called `lookupBalance()` is interrupted while the lookup is in progress (sleeping), it returns the `SEARCH CANCELLED` string instead of the balance. This is just a simulation; of course, a real system would do something more useful.

The `setBalance()` method (lines 102–107) is used to update the balance, disable the Cancel Search button, and enable the Search button again. The `cancelSearch()` method (lines 109–113) would normally be used to stop the search process, but in this example, it never gets called.

When the event thread calls `search()`, it blocks until the balance is retrieved and set. Keeping the event thread tied up for that long is a bad idea. And in this example, it prevents the Cancel Search button from being enabled.

Figure 9.1 shows how the application looks when it is first started. Notice that the Cancel Search button is disabled and that the balance label indicates that the balance is unknown.

After the user enters an account number and a PIN and clicks the Search button, the application looks like Figure 9.2. The window continues to look like that for about 5 seconds while the across-the-network lookup is simulated. Notice the following points:

- The `SEARCHING ...` message was not displayed in the balance label.
- The Cancel Search button was never enabled.
- The Search button stayed pressed in the whole time.

For the whole time that the lookup was going on, the GUI was unresponsive—the window couldn't even be closed. In particular, the Cancel Search button was never enabled. The event thread was tied up doing the long-running lookup and could not respond to user events. Obviously, this is not a good design.

Figure 9.3 shows what the application window looks like after the 5 seconds have elapsed. Here everything is as expected. The Search button is enabled, the Cancel Search button is disabled, and the balance label shows 1,234.56.

FIGURE 9.1
BalanceLookupCantCancel just after startup.

FIGURE 9.2
BalanceLookupCantCancel after the Search button is clicked.

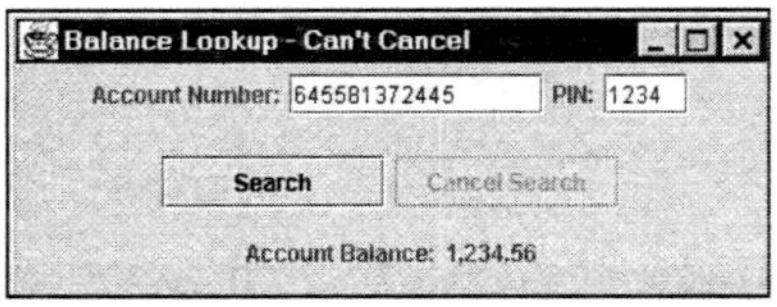

FIGURE 9.3
BalanceLookupCantCancel when the lookup finally completes.

Using a Worker Thread to Relieve the Event Thread

In BalanceLookupCantCancel, it became apparent that tying up the event thread to do an extensive operation was a bad idea. This was a problem especially because there was no way to signal that the search should be canceled. Another thread is needed to do the lookup so that the event thread can get back to the business of handling events.

BalanceLookup (see Listing 9.7) uses a worker thread to do the lengthy lookup and frees the event thread from this delay. This technique makes it possible to use the Cancel Search button to stop a search.

LISTING 9.7 BalanceLookup.java—Using a Worker Thread to Relieve the Event Thread

```
 1: import java.awt.*;
 2: import java.awt.event.*;
 3: import javax.swing.*;
 4:
 5: public class BalanceLookup extends JPanel {
 6:     private JTextField acctTF;
 7:     private JTextField pinTF;
 8:     private JButton searchB;
 9:     private JButton cancelB;
10:     private JLabel balanceL;
11:
12:     private volatile Thread lookupThread;
13:
14:     public BalanceLookup() {
15:         buildGUI();
16:         hookupEvents();
17:     }
18:
19:     private void buildGUI() {
20:         JLabel acctL = new JLabel("Account Number:");
21:         JLabel pinL = new JLabel("PIN:");
22:         acctTF = new JTextField(12);
23:         pinTF = new JTextField(4);
24:
25:         JPanel dataEntryP = new JPanel();
26:         dataEntryP.setLayout(new FlowLayout(FlowLayout.CENTER));
27:         dataEntryP.add(acctL);
28:         dataEntryP.add(acctTF);
29:         dataEntryP.add(pinL);
30:         dataEntryP.add(pinTF);
31:
32:         searchB = new JButton("Search");
33:         cancelB = new JButton("Cancel Search");
34:         cancelB.setEnabled(false);
35:
36:         JPanel innerButtonP = new JPanel();
```

9

continues

LISTING 9.7 Continued

```
37:          innerButtonP.setLayout(new GridLayout(1, -1, 5, 5));
38:          innerButtonP.add(searchB);
39:          innerButtonP.add(cancelB);
40:
41:          JPanel buttonP = new JPanel();
42:          buttonP.setLayout(new FlowLayout(FlowLayout.CENTER));
43:          buttonP.add(innerButtonP);
44:
45:          JLabel balancePrefixL = new JLabel("Account Balance:");
46:          balanceL = new JLabel("BALANCE UNKNOWN");
47:
48:          JPanel balanceP = new JPanel();
49:          balanceP.setLayout(new FlowLayout(FlowLayout.CENTER));
50:          balanceP.add(balancePrefixL);
51:          balanceP.add(balanceL);
52:
53:          JPanel northP = new JPanel();
54:          northP.setLayout(new GridLayout(-1, 1, 5, 5));
55:          northP.add(dataEntryP);
56:          northP.add(buttonP);
57:          northP.add(balanceP);
58:
59:          setLayout(new BorderLayout());
60:          add(northP, BorderLayout.NORTH);
61:      }
62:
63:      private void hookupEvents() {
64:          searchB.addActionListener(new ActionListener() {
65:                  public void actionPerformed(ActionEvent e) {
66:                      search();
67:                  }
68:              });
69:
70:          cancelB.addActionListener(new ActionListener() {
71:                  public void actionPerformed(ActionEvent e) {
72:                      cancelSearch();
73:                  }
74:              });
75:      }
76:
77:      private void search() {
78:          // better be called by event thread!
79:          ensureEventThread();
80:
```

```
81:            searchB.setEnabled(false);
82:            cancelB.setEnabled(true);
83:            balanceL.setText("SEARCHING ...");
84:
85:            // get a snapshot of this info in case it changes
86:            String acct = acctTF.getText();
87:            String pin = pinTF.getText();
88:
89:            lookupAsync(acct, pin);
90:        }
91:
92:        private void lookupAsync(String acct, String pin) {
93:            // Called by event thread, but can be safely
94:            // called by any thread.
95:            final String acctNum = acct;
96:            final String pinNum = pin;
97:
98:            Runnable lookupRun = new Runnable() {
99:                    public void run() {
100:                        String bal = lookupBalance(acctNum, pinNum);
101:                        setBalanceSafely(bal);
102:                    }
103:                };
104:
105:            lookupThread = new Thread(lookupRun, "lookupThread");
106:            lookupThread.start();
107:        }
108:
109:        private String lookupBalance(String acct, String pin) {
110:            // Called by lookupThread, but can be safely
111:            // called by any thread.
112:            try {
113:                // Simulate a lengthy search that takes 5 seconds
114:                // to communicate over the network.
115:                Thread.sleep(5000);
116:
117:                // result "retrieved", return it
118:                return "1,234.56";
119:            } catch ( InterruptedException x ) {
120:                return "SEARCH CANCELLED";
121:            }
122:        }
123:
```

9

THREADS AND
SWING

continues

LISTING 9.7 Continued

```
124:     private void setBalanceSafely(String newBal) {
125:         // Called by lookupThread, but can be safely
126:         // called by any thread.
127:         final String newBalance = newBal;
128:
129:         Runnable r = new Runnable() {
130:             public void run() {
131:                 try {
132:                     setBalance(newBalance);
133:                 } catch ( Exception x ) {
134:                     x.printStackTrace();
135:                 }
136:             }
137:         };
138:
139:         SwingUtilities.invokeLater(r);
140:     }
141:
142:     private void setBalance(String newBalance) {
143:         // better be called by event thread!
144:         ensureEventThread();
145:
146:         balanceL.setText(newBalance);
147:         cancelB.setEnabled(false);
148:         searchB.setEnabled(true);
149:     }
150:
151:     private void cancelSearch() {
152:         // better be called by event thread!
153:         ensureEventThread();
154:
155:         cancelB.setEnabled(false); //prevent additional requests
156:
157:         if ( lookupThread != null ) {
158:             lookupThread.interrupt();
159:         }
160:     }
161:
162:     private void ensureEventThread() {
163:         // throws an exception if not invoked by the
164:         // event thread.
165:         if ( SwingUtilities.isEventDispatchThread() ) {
166:             return;
```

```
167:            }
168:
169:            throw new RuntimeException("only the event " +
170:                "thread should invoke this method");
171:        }
172:
173:        public static void main(String[] args) {
174:            BalanceLookup bl = new BalanceLookup();
175:
176:            JFrame f = new JFrame("Balance Lookup");
177:            f.addWindowListener(new WindowAdapter() {
178:                    public void windowClosing(WindowEvent e) {
179:                        System.exit(0);
180:                    }
181:                });
182:
183:            f.setContentPane(bl);
184:            f.setSize(400, 150);
185:            f.setVisible(true);
186:        }
187: }
```

The code for `BalanceLookup` is based on `BalanceLookupCantCancel` but includes a few key changes to support a worker thread. Now, when the Search button is clicked and the `search()` method is called, `lookupAsync()` is invoked instead of looking up the balance directly.

The event thread invokes `lookupAsync()` (lines 92–107), passing in the account number and PIN strings. A new `Runnable` is created (lines 98–103). Inside the `run()` method, the slow `lookupBalance()` method is called. When `lookupBalance()` finally returns the balance, it is passed to the `setBalanceSafely()` method. A new `Thread` named `lookupThread` is constructed and started (lines 105–106). The event thread is now free to handle other events and `lookupThread` takes care of searching for the account information.

This time, the `lookupBalance()` method (lines 109–122) gets called by `lookupThread` instead of the event thread. `lookupThread` proceeds to sleep for 5 seconds to simulate the slow lookup on the server. If `lookupThread` is not interrupted while sleeping, it returns `1,234.56` for the balance (line 118). If it was interrupted, it returns `SEARCH CANCELLED` (line 120).

The `String` returned from `lookupBalance()` is taken by the `lookupThread` and passed to `setBalanceSafely()` (lines 124–140). Inside `setBalanceSafely()`, a `Runnable` is created that calls `setBalance()` inside its `run()` method (lines 129–137). This `Runnable` is passed to `SwingUtilities.invokeLater()` so that the event thread is the one that ultimately calls the `setBalance()` method.

Inside setBalance() (lines 142–149), a check is done by calling ensureEventThread() to be sure that it is indeed the event thread that has called the method. If it is, the balance label is updated with the information, the Cancel Search button is disabled again, and the Search button is enabled again.

The cancelSearch() method (lines 151–160) is called by the event thread when the Cancel Search button is clicked. Inside, it disables the Cancel Search button and interrupts lookupThread. This causes lookupThread to throw an InterruptedException and return the SEARCH CANCELLED message.

The ensureEventThread() method (lines 162–171) checks to see if the current thread is the event thread by using the SwingUtilities.isEventDispatchThread() method. If it is not, a RuntimeException is thrown. Several methods in BalanceLookup use ensureEventThread() to make sure that only the event thread is allowed to proceed.

Figure 9.4 shows how BalanceLookup looks just after startup. Notice that the Cancel Search button is disabled and that the balance label is BALANCE UNKNOWN.

After an account number and PIN are entered and the Search button is clicked, the application window looks like Figure 9.5. Notice that the Search button is disabled, the Cancel Search button is enabled, and the balance label is SEARCHING .... It remains like this for about 5 seconds while the lookup is simulated.

When the search finally completes, the application looks like Figure 9.6. Notice that the balance label is 1,234.56 (the fake balance), the Search button is enabled again, and the Cancel Search button is disabled again.

If you click on the Cancel Search button during the 5 seconds while the search is in progress, the window looks like Figure 9.7. Notice that that the balance label is SEARCH CANCELLED, indicating that the search did not get a chance to complete. As before, the Search button is enabled, and the Cancel Search button is disabled.

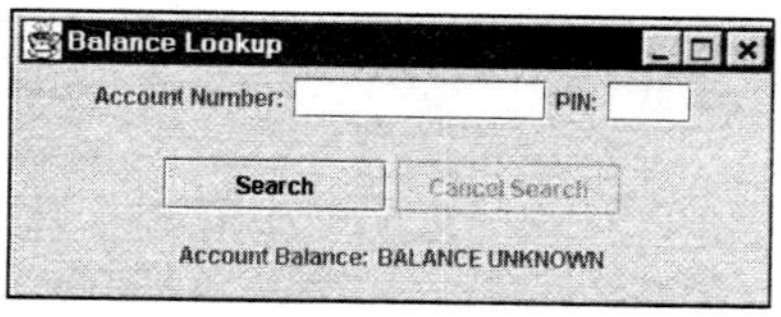

FIGURE 9.4

BalanceLookup just after startup.

FIGURE 9.5

BalanceLookup after the Search button is clicked.

FIGURE 9.6

BalanceLookup after the search has completed.

FIGURE 9.7

BalanceLookup after the Cancel Search button is clicked during a search.

TIP

Rather than spawning a new thread every time the Search button is clicked, a better design would be to have a thread up and running and waiting to do the work. The event thread would gather the information, pass it to the waiting worker thread using synchronization, and signal the worker through the wait-notify mechanism that a new request was pending. When the worker thread had fulfilled the request, it would update the GUI through the invokeLater() mechanism. The worker would then go back to waiting for another notification. To simplify the synchronization and notification of the handoff, an ObjectFIFO with a capacity of 1 could be used (see Chapter 18, "First-In-First-Out (FIFO) Queue"). Also look at the thread-pooling techniques in Chapter 13, "Thread Pooling," for an example of how to do this type of handoff from one thread to another through a First-In-First-Out queue.

Scrolling Text in a Custom Component

ScrollText (see Listing 9.8) is a custom JComponent that takes the text passed to its constructor and scrolls it from left to right across the face of the component. At the time of construction, an off-screen image is prepared with the specified text and an internal thread is started to scroll this image. ScrollText is a self-running object and uses some of the techniques from Chapter 11, "Self-Running Objects," to manage its internal thread.

LISTING 9.8   ScrollText.java—Scroll Text Across the Face of the Component

```
 1: import java.awt.*;
 2: import java.awt.image.*;
 3: import java.awt.font.*;
 4: import java.awt.geom.*;
 5: import javax.swing.*;
 6:
 7: public class ScrollText extends JComponent {
 8:     private BufferedImage image;
 9:     private Dimension imageSize;
10:     private volatile int currOffset;
11:
12:     private Thread internalThread;
13:     private volatile boolean noStopRequested;
14:
15:     public ScrollText(String text) {
16:         currOffset = 0;
17:         buildImage(text);
18:
19:         setMinimumSize(imageSize);
20:         setPreferredSize(imageSize);
21:         setMaximumSize(imageSize);
22:         setSize(imageSize);
23:
24:         noStopRequested = true;
25:         Runnable r = new Runnable() {
26:                 public void run() {
27:                     try {
28:                         runWork();
29:                     } catch ( Exception x ) {
30:                         x.printStackTrace();
31:                     }
32:                 }
33:             };
34:
```

```
35:          internalThread = new Thread(r, "ScrollText");
36:          internalThread.start();
37:      }
38:
39:      private void buildImage(String text) {
40:          // Request that the drawing be done with anti-aliasing
41:          // turned on and the quality high.
42:          RenderingHints renderHints = new RenderingHints(
43:              RenderingHints.KEY_ANTIALIASING,
44:              RenderingHints.VALUE_ANTIALIAS_ON);
45:
46:          renderHints.put(
47:              RenderingHints.KEY_RENDERING,
48:              RenderingHints.VALUE_RENDER_QUALITY);
49:
50:          // Create a scratch image for use in determining
51:          // the text dimensions.
52:          BufferedImage scratchImage = new BufferedImage(
53:                  1, 1, BufferedImage.TYPE_INT_RGB);
54:
55:          Graphics2D scratchG2 = scratchImage.createGraphics();
56:          scratchG2.setRenderingHints(renderHints);
57:
58:          Font font =
59:              new Font("Serif", Font.BOLD | Font.ITALIC, 24);
60:
61:          FontRenderContext frc = scratchG2.getFontRenderContext();
62:          TextLayout tl = new TextLayout(text, font, frc);
63:          Rectangle2D textBounds = tl.getBounds();
64:          int textWidth = (int) Math.ceil(textBounds.getWidth());
65:          int textHeight = (int) Math.ceil(textBounds.getHeight());
66:
67:          int horizontalPad = 10;
68:          int verticalPad = 6;
69:
70:          imageSize = new Dimension(
71:                  textWidth + horizontalPad,
72:                  textHeight + verticalPad
73:              );
74:
75:          // Create the properly-sized image
76:          image = new BufferedImage(
```

9

THREADS AND
SWING

continues

LISTING 9.8   Continued

```
77:                    imageSize.width,
78:                    imageSize.height,
79:                    BufferedImage.TYPE_INT_RGB);
80:
81:          Graphics2D g2 = image.createGraphics();
82:          g2.setRenderingHints(renderHints);
83:
84:          int baselineOffset =
85:              ( verticalPad / 2 ) - ( (int) textBounds.getY());
86:
87:          g2.setColor(Color.white);
88:          g2.fillRect(0, 0, imageSize.width, imageSize.height);
89:
90:          g2.setColor(Color.blue);
91:          tl.draw(g2, 0, baselineOffset);
92:
93:          // Free-up resources right away, but keep "image" for
94:          // animation.
95:          scratchG2.dispose();
96:          scratchImage.flush();
97:          g2.dispose();
98:      }
99:
100:     public void paint(Graphics g) {
101:         // Make sure to clip the edges, regardless of curr size
102:         g.setClip(0, 0, imageSize.width, imageSize.height);
103:
104:         int localOffset = currOffset; // in case it changes
105:         g.drawImage(image, -localOffset, 0, this);
106:         g.drawImage(
107:             image, imageSize.width - localOffset, 0, this);
108:
109:         // draw outline
110:         g.setColor(Color.black);
111:         g.drawRect(
112:             0, 0, imageSize.width - 1, imageSize.height - 1);
113:     }
114:
115:     private void runWork() {
116:         while ( noStopRequested ) {
117:             try {
118:                 Thread.sleep(100);  // 10 frames per second
119:
120:                 // adjust the scroll position
```

```
121:              currOffset =
122:                  ( currOffset + 1 ) % imageSize.width;
123:
124:              // signal the event thread to call paint()
125:              repaint();
126:          } catch ( InterruptedException x ) {
127:              Thread.currentThread().interrupt();
128:          }
129:      }
130:  }
131:
132:  public void stopRequest() {
133:      noStopRequested = false;
134:      internalThread.interrupt();
135:  }
136:
137:  public boolean isAlive() {
138:      return internalThread.isAlive();
139:  }
140:
141:  public static void main(String[] args) {
142:      ScrollText st =
143:          new ScrollText("Java can do animation!");
144:
145:      JPanel p = new JPanel(new FlowLayout());
146:      p.add(st);
147:
148:      JFrame f = new JFrame("ScrollText Demo");
149:      f.setContentPane(p);
150:      f.setSize(400, 100);
151:      f.setVisible(true);
152:  }
153: }
```

In main() (lines 141–152), a new ScrollText instance is constructed (lines 142–143) and put into a JPanel with a FlowLayout to let the instance of ScrollText take on its preferred size (lines 145–146). This JPanel is put into a JFrame and set visible.

Inside the constructor (lines 15–37), currOffset is set to initially be 0 pixels. currOffset is the x-position of the image relative to the component's coordinate system. Because currOffset is set by the internal thread and read by paint(), it is volatile (line 10). The buildImage() method is called to create the off-screen image that scrolls (line 17). The rest of the constructor sets the dimensions of the component and starts up the internal thread.

The `buildImage()` method (lines 39–98) is used to prepare the off-screen image with the desired text. Because the text will be drawn to the image only once, the rendering hints are set for quality and anti-alias (lines 42–48). A scratch image is created first and used in determining the exact pixel dimensions needed for the specified text (lines 52–65). A little bit of horizontal and vertical padding is added and the real off-screen image is created (lines 67–79). A graphics context is created from the image and used for drawing the text (lines 81–91).

Whenever the event-handling thread calls `paint()` (lines 100–113), the off-screen image is redrawn onto the component. The value of `currOffset` is captured in the local variable `localOffset` in case `currOffset` is changed while `paint()` is in progress (line 104). Actually, the image is drawn twice. It is drawn once off to the left of the component by the `localOffset` (line 105). And it is drawn a second time by the same offset from the right side of the component (lines 106–107). Parts of the images will be automatically clipped because they extend off the sides of the component (line 102). After the image is in place, a black outline is drawn around the edge (lines 110–112).

The `runWork()` method (lines 115–130) is invoked by the internal thread that was started in the constructor. It loops continuously until another thread invokes the `stopRequest()` method. In the `while` loop, the internal thread sleeps for 0.1 seconds (line 118), increments `currOffset` (lines 121–122), and puts a request onto the event queue for the `paint()` method to be called (line 125). The value of `currOffset` is kept between 0 and the width of the off-screen image (line 122). `currOffset` is `volatile` so that the event thread sees the changes in value being made by the internal thread.

Figure 9.8 shows a snapshot of `ScrollText` in action. Figure 9.9 shows the same component a few seconds later. The text "Java can do animation!" is scrolling from right to left across the component. The `main()` method of `ScrollText` is simply used for demonstration purposes. `ScrollText` can be used as a component anywhere. You might want to enhance `ScrollText` so that the colors, font, scroll rate, and size of the scroll window can be specified for a more real-world application. You can speed up the scrolling by moving more than one pixel at a time, or by moving more than 10 times per second. Keep in mind that increasing the number of advances per second will use more processor resources.

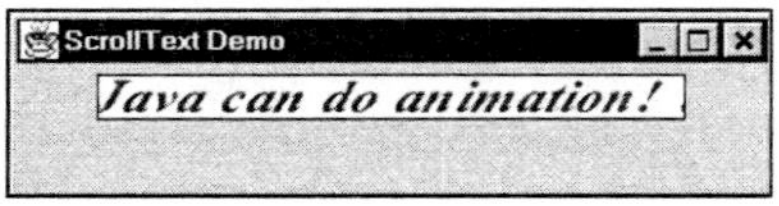

FIGURE 9.8

ScrollText—snapshot of text scrolling in progress.

FIGURE 9.9
ScrollText—another snapshot a few seconds later.

NOTE

Beginning with JDK 1.2, there is a class `javax.swing.Timer` that can be used to simplify animation. After being started, `Timer` calls the `actionPerformed()` method on the registered object at regular intervals. The event-handling thread is used to invoke `actionPerformed()`, so direct modification of visible components from within `actionPerformed()` is safe. If the action is nonblocking and brief, the use of `Timer` might be an appropriate substitute for the techniques I've shown you here.

Animating a Set of Images

Instead of scrolling one image across the face of a component as ScrollText does, a component can use an internal thread to step through a set of different images one image at a time. This set of images can be considered frames or slides. By flipping through the slides (or frames), the internal thread creates animation.

In SlideShow (see Listing 9.9), a set of images is created and an internal thread loops through them at a rate of 10 images per second. In this case, an expanding yellow circle is drawn on a blue background, but you could use any set of images.

LISTING 9.9 SlideShow.java—Animation of a Set of Images

```
1: import java.awt.*;
2: import java.awt.image.*;
3: import javax.swing.*;
4:
5: public class SlideShow extends JComponent {
6:     private BufferedImage[] slide;
7:     private Dimension slideSize;
8:     private volatile int currSlide;
9:
```

continues

LISTING 9.9   Continued

```
10:        private Thread internalThread;
11:        private volatile boolean noStopRequested;
12:
13:        public SlideShow() {
14:            currSlide = 0;
15:            slideSize = new Dimension(50, 50);
16:            buildSlides();
17:
18:            setMinimumSize(slideSize);
19:            setPreferredSize(slideSize);
20:            setMaximumSize(slideSize);
21:            setSize(slideSize);
22:
23:            noStopRequested = true;
24:            Runnable r = new Runnable() {
25:                    public void run() {
26:                        try {
27:                            runWork();
28:                        } catch ( Exception x ) {
29:                            // in case ANY exception slips through
30:                            x.printStackTrace();
31:                        }
32:                    }
33:                };
34:
35:            internalThread = new Thread(r, "SlideShow");
36:            internalThread.start();
37:        }
38:
39:        private void buildSlides() {
40:            // Request that the drawing be done with anti-aliasing
41:            // turned on and the quality high.
42:            RenderingHints renderHints = new RenderingHints(
43:                RenderingHints.KEY_ANTIALIASING,
44:                RenderingHints.VALUE_ANTIALIAS_ON);
45:
46:            renderHints.put(
47:                RenderingHints.KEY_RENDERING,
48:                RenderingHints.VALUE_RENDER_QUALITY);
49:
50:            slide = new BufferedImage[20];
51:
52:            Color rectColor = new Color(100, 160, 250);   // blue
53:            Color circleColor = new Color(250, 250, 150); // yellow
```

```
54:
55:            for ( int i = 0; i < slide.length; i++ ) {
56:                slide[i] = new BufferedImage(
57:                        slideSize.width,
58:                        slideSize.height,
59:                        BufferedImage.TYPE_INT_RGB);
60:
61:                Graphics2D g2 = slide[i].createGraphics();
62:                g2.setRenderingHints(renderHints);
63:
64:                g2.setColor(rectColor);
65:                g2.fillRect(0, 0, slideSize.width, slideSize.height);
66:
67:                g2.setColor(circleColor);
68:
69:                int diameter = 0;
70:                if ( i < ( slide.length / 2 ) ) {
71:                    diameter = 5 + ( 8 * i );
72:                } else {
73:                    diameter = 5 + ( 8 * ( slide.length - i ) );
74:                }
75:
76:                int inset = ( slideSize.width - diameter ) / 2;
77:                g2.fillOval(inset, inset, diameter, diameter);
78:
79:                g2.setColor(Color.black);
80:                g2.drawRect(
81:                    0, 0, slideSize.width - 1, slideSize.height - 1);
82:
83:                g2.dispose();
84:            }
85:        }
86:
87:        public void paint(Graphics g) {
88:            g.drawImage(slide[currSlide], 0, 0, this);
89:        }
90:
91:        private void runWork() {
92:            while ( noStopRequested ) {
93:                try {
94:                    Thread.sleep(100);   // 10 frames per second
95:
96:                    // increment the slide pointer
```

continues

9

THREADS AND SWING

LISTING 9.9   Continued

```
 97:                    currSlide = ( currSlide + 1 ) % slide.length;
 98:
 99:                    // signal the event thread to call paint()
100:                    repaint();
101:                } catch ( InterruptedException x ) {
102:                    Thread.currentThread().interrupt();
103:                }
104:            }
105:        }
106:
107:        public void stopRequest() {
108:            noStopRequested = false;
109:            internalThread.interrupt();
110:        }
111:
112:        public boolean isAlive() {
113:            return internalThread.isAlive();
114:        }
115:
116:        public static void main(String[] args) {
117:            SlideShow ss = new SlideShow();
118:
119:            JPanel p = new JPanel(new FlowLayout());
120:            p.add(ss);
121:
122:            JFrame f = new JFrame("SlideShow Demo");
123:            f.setContentPane(p);
124:            f.setSize(250, 150);
125:            f.setVisible(true);
126:        }
127: }
```

In main() (lines 116–126), a new SlideShow instance is constructed (line 117) and put into a JPanel with a FlowLayout to let the instance of SlideShow take on its preferred size (lines 119–120). This JPanel is put into a JFrame and set visible.

Inside the constructor (lines 13–37), currSlide is set to initially be 0. currSlide is the index into the BufferedImage[] referred to by slide indicating the current slide to display. Because currSlide is set by one thread (the internal thread) and read by another in paint() (the event thread), it must be volatile to ensure that the event thread sees the changes in value (line 8). The buildSlides() method is called to create the set of images used for the animation. The rest of the constructor sets the dimensions of the component and starts up the internal thread.

The buildSlides() method (lines 39–85) is used to construct an array of 20 images (line 50) to loop through. High-quality rendering hints are used because the images are drawn on only once and are displayed over and over (lines 42–48, 62). Each of the images is constructed and drawn on in the for loop (lines 55–84). First, a blue rectangle is filled in (lines 52, 64–65). Then a yellow circle of varying diameter is drawn in the center (lines 53, 67–77). The last shape drawn onto each image is a black rectangle to outline the slide (lines 79–81). Each graphics context is disposed of immediately when it is no longer needed (line 83).

Whenever the paint() method (lines 87–89) is called by the event thread, the current slide is drawn onto the component. Because currSlide is volatile, the event thread always sees the most recent index value.

The internal thread invokes the runWork() method (lines 91–105). Inside, it continues to execute the while loop until another thread comes along and invokes stopRequest(). Each time through, the internal thread sleeps for 0.1 seconds, increments the frame number, and requests that the event thread repaint the component as soon as possible (lines 94–100). The slide indexed by currSlide is kept in the range 0 to (slide.length - 1) (line 97). The internal thread loops through all of the slides over and over until stopRequest() is called.

Figure 9.10 catches SlideShow just as the yellow circle is beginning to expand. Figure 9.11 shows it when the yellow circle has expanded almost enough to touch the edges of the component. Figure 9.12 shows it when the yellow circle has grown to almost big enough to eclipse the entire blue region. After the yellow circle has grown to fill the component, it begins to shrink until it is a tiny circle again. This animation loop continues until stopRequest() is called. In this example I used simple drawing to keep the code size down, but you can feel free to use images of any complexity in this animation component.

FIGURE 9.10
SlideShow when the yellow circle is just beginning to expand.

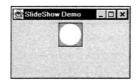

FIGURE 9.11
SlideShow when the yellow circle has almost expanded to the edges.

FIGURE 9.12
SlideShow when the yellow circle has almost engulfed the whole component.

Displaying Elapsed Time on a JLabel

DigitalTimer (see Listing 9.10) extends JLabel and uses an internal thread to update the text on the label with the elapsed time since the component was constructed. In this class it is important to use SwingUtilities.invokeAndWait() to have the event thread actually update the text on the label.

LISTING 9.10   DigitalTimer.java—Extending JLabel to Continually Display Elapsed Time

```
 1: import java.awt.*;
 2: import java.text.*;
 3: import java.lang.reflect.*;
 4: import javax.swing.*;
 5:
 6: public class DigitalTimer extends JLabel {
 7:     private volatile String timeText;
 8:
 9:     private Thread internalThread;
10:     private volatile boolean noStopRequested;
11:
12:     public DigitalTimer() {
13:         setBorder(BorderFactory.createLineBorder(Color.black));
14:         setHorizontalAlignment(SwingConstants.RIGHT);
```

```
15:            setFont(new Font("SansSerif", Font.BOLD, 16));
16:            setText("00000.0"); // use to size component
17:            setMinimumSize(getPreferredSize());
18:            setPreferredSize(getPreferredSize());
19:            setSize(getPreferredSize());
20:
21:            timeText = "0.0";
22:            setText(timeText);
23:
24:            noStopRequested = true;
25:            Runnable r = new Runnable() {
26:                    public void run() {
27:                        try {
28:                            runWork();
29:                        } catch ( Exception x ) {
30:                            x.printStackTrace();
31:                        }
32:                    }
33:                };
34:
35:        internalThread = new Thread(r, "DigitalTimer");
36:        internalThread.start();
37:    }
38:
39:    private void runWork() {
40:        long startTime = System.currentTimeMillis();
41:        int tenths = 0;
42:        long normalSleepTime = 100;
43:        long nextSleepTime = 100;
44:        DecimalFormat fmt = new DecimalFormat("0.0");
45:
46:        Runnable updateText = new Runnable() {
47:                public void run() {
48:                    setText(timeText);
49:                }
50:            };
51:
52:        while ( noStopRequested ) {
53:            try {
54:                Thread.sleep(nextSleepTime);
55:
56:                tenths++;
```

continues

LISTING 9.10 Continued

```
57:                         long currTime = System.currentTimeMillis();
58:                         long elapsedTime = currTime - startTime;
59:
60:                         nextSleepTime = normalSleepTime +
61:                             ( ( tenths * 100 ) - elapsedTime );
62:
63:                         if ( nextSleepTime < 0 ) {
64:                             nextSleepTime = 0;
65:                         }
66:
67:                         timeText = fmt.format(elapsedTime / 1000.0);
68:                         SwingUtilities.invokeAndWait(updateText);
69:                     } catch ( InterruptedException ix ) {
70:                         // stop running
71:                         return;
72:                     } catch ( InvocationTargetException x ) {
73:                         // If an exception was thrown inside the
74:                         // run() method of the updateText Runnable.
75:                         x.printStackTrace();
76:                     }
77:                 }
78:         }
79:
80:         public void stopRequest() {
81:             noStopRequested = false;
82:             internalThread.interrupt();
83:         }
84:
85:         public boolean isAlive() {
86:             return internalThread.isAlive();
87:         }
88:
89:         public static void main(String[] args) {
90:             DigitalTimer dt = new DigitalTimer();
91:
92:             JPanel p = new JPanel(new FlowLayout());
93:             p.add(dt);
94:
95:             JFrame f = new JFrame("DigitalTimer Demo");
96:             f.setContentPane(p);
97:             f.setSize(250, 100);
98:             f.setVisible(true);
99:         }
100: }
```

In `main()` (lines 89–99), a new `DigitalTimer` instance is constructed (line 90) and put into a `JPanel` with a `FlowLayout` to let it take on its preferred size (lines 92–93). This `JPanel` is put into a `JFrame` and set visible.

Inside the constructor (lines 12–37), the border, alignment, and font for the label are set. A sample text string of `00000.0` is used to initially size the component (lines 16–19). `timeText` is initialized to be `0.0`. `timeText` is declared to be `volatile` (line 7) because (after construction) it is set by the internal thread and read by the event thread. The rest of the constructor gets the internal thread up and running.

The internal thread invokes `runWork()` (lines 39–78) to keep track of time and update the label. Much of the work inside this method is done to keep the elapsed time as accurate as possible. (See Chapter 4, "Implementing Runnable Versus Extending Thread," for a more in-depth discussion of the accuracy issues and techniques used.) The `Runnable` instance referred to by `updateText` (lines 46–50) is used by `SwingUtilities.invokeAndWait()` to get the event thread to update the text on the label. Notice that the same `Runnable` instance is used over and over inside the `while` loop. The `Runnable` reads the `volatile` member variable `timeText` to find out what text should be displayed.

In the `while` loop (lines 52–77), the internal thread sleeps for a while (about 0.1 seconds), increments the `tenths` counter, and calculates the elapsed time (lines 54–58). The `nextSleepTime` is calculated to keep the clock from running too fast or too slow (lines 60–65). The elapsed time is converted into seconds (from milliseconds) and formatted into a `String` that is stored in `timeText` (line 67). Next, `SwingUtilities.invokeAndWait()` is used to get the event thread to update the text currently displayed on the label (line 68). `SwingUtilities.invokeAndWait()` was used instead of `SwingUtilities.invokeLater()` so that the internal thread would not get ahead of the event thread.

Figure 9.13 shows how `DigitalTimer` appears after 15.5 seconds have elapsed.

FIGURE 9.13
DigitalTimer after 15.5 seconds have elapsed.

Floating Components Around Inside a Container

`CompMover` (see Listing 9.11) is a utility that takes a component and an initial position and moves the component around inside its container. This is basically a demonstration of how animation can be achieved by moving components.

LISTING 9.11 CompMover.java—A Utility to Float Components Around Inside a Container

```
 1: import java.awt.*;
 2: import javax.swing.*;
 3:
 4: public class CompMover extends Object {
 5:     private Component comp;
 6:     private int initX;
 7:     private int initY;
 8:     private int offsetX;
 9:     private int offsetY;
10:     private boolean firstTime;
11:     private Runnable updatePositionRun;
12:
13:     private Thread internalThread;
14:     private volatile boolean noStopRequested;
15:
16:     public CompMover(Component comp,
17:                 int initX, int initY,
18:                 int offsetX, int offsetY
19:             ) {
20:
21:         this.comp = comp;
22:         this.initX = initX;
23:         this.initY = initY;
24:         this.offsetX = offsetX;
25:         this.offsetY = offsetY;
26:
27:         firstTime = true;
28:
29:         updatePositionRun = new Runnable() {
30:                 public void run() {
31:                     updatePosition();
32:                 }
33:             };
34:
35:         noStopRequested = true;
36:         Runnable r = new Runnable() {
37:                 public void run() {
38:                     try {
39:                         runWork();
40:                     } catch ( Exception x ) {
41:                         // in case ANY exception slips through
42:                         x.printStackTrace();
43:                     }
```

```
44:                    }
45:                };
46:
47:            internalThread = new Thread(r);
48:            internalThread.start();
49:        }
50:
51:        private void runWork() {
52:            while ( noStopRequested ) {
53:                try {
54:                    Thread.sleep(200);
55:                    SwingUtilities.invokeAndWait(updatePositionRun);
56:                } catch ( InterruptedException ix ) {
57:                    // ignore
58:                } catch ( Exception x ) {
59:                    x.printStackTrace();
60:                }
61:            }
62:        }
63:
64:        public void stopRequest() {
65:            noStopRequested = false;
66:            internalThread.interrupt();
67:        }
68:
69:        public boolean isAlive() {
70:            return internalThread.isAlive();
71:        }
72:
73:        private void updatePosition() {
74:            // should only be called by the *event* thread
75:
76:            if ( !comp.isVisible() ) {
77:                return;
78:            }
79:
80:            Component parent = comp.getParent();
81:            if ( parent == null ) {
82:                return;
83:            }
84:
85:            Dimension parentSize = parent.getSize();
86:            if ( ( parentSize == null ) &&
```

continues

Listing 9.11 Continued

```
 87:                ( parentSize.width < 1 ) &&
 88:                ( parentSize.height < 1 )
 89:            ) {
 90:
 91:             return;
 92:        }
 93:
 94:        int newX = 0;
 95:        int newY = 0;
 96:
 97:        if ( firstTime ) {
 98:            firstTime = false;
 99:            newX = initX;
100:            newY = initY;
101:        } else {
102:            Point loc = comp.getLocation();
103:            newX = loc.x + offsetX;
104:            newY = loc.y + offsetY;
105:        }
106:
107:        newX = newX % parentSize.width;
108:        newY = newY % parentSize.height;
109:
110:        if ( newX < 0 ) {
111:            // wrap around other side
112:            newX += parentSize.width;
113:        }
114:
115:        if ( newY < 0 ) {
116:            // wrap around other side
117:            newY += parentSize.height;
118:        }
119:
120:        comp.setLocation(newX, newY);
121:        parent.repaint();
122:    }
123:
124:    public static void main(String[] args) {
125:        Component[] comp = new Component[6];
126:
127:        comp[0] = new ScrollText("Scrolling Text");
128:        comp[1] = new ScrollText("Java Threads");
129:        comp[2] = new SlideShow();
130:        comp[3] = new SlideShow();
131:        comp[4] = new DigitalTimer();
```

```
132:            comp[5] = new DigitalTimer();
133:
134:            JPanel p = new JPanel();
135:            p.setLayout(null); // no layout manager
136:
137:            for ( int i = 0; i < comp.length; i++ ) {
138:                p.add(comp[i]);
139:
140:                int x = (int) ( 300 * Math.random() );
141:                int y = (int) ( 200 * Math.random() );
142:                int xOff = 2 - (int) ( 5 * Math.random() );
143:                int yOff = 2 - (int) ( 5 * Math.random() );
144:
145:                new CompMover(comp[i], x, y, xOff, yOff);
146:            }
147:
148:            JFrame f = new JFrame("CompMover Demo");
149:            f.setContentPane(p);
150:            f.setSize(400, 300);
151:            f.setVisible(true);
152:        }
153: }
```

The constructor for CompMover (lines 16–49) takes a component, an initial position, and x and y offset information. A Runnable is created (lines 29–33) to be passed to SwingUtilities.invokeAndWait(). This Runnable is referred to by updatePositionRun and invokes the updatePosition() when called by the event thread. The rest of the constructor gets the internal thread up and running.

The internal thread invokes runWork() (lines 51–62), where it loops inside the while until another thread invokes stopRequest(). Inside the while loop, the thread sleeps for 0.2 seconds and then invokes SwingUtilities.invokeAndWait() passing in updatePositionRun (lines 54–55). updatePositionRun causes the event thread to invoke updatePosition().

Each time that the event thread calls updatePosition() (lines 73–122), the event thread attempts to move the component a little. Several checks are done to be sure that the parent container is accessible (lines 76–92). The current location of the component is retrieved and the x and y offsets are added to determine the new location (lines 97–118). The event thread proceeds to invoke setLocation() on the component to move it to its new position (line 120). The event thread then invokes repaint() on the parent container to get the move to show up (line 121).

In main() (lines 124–152), a number of components are constructed: two instances of ScrollText, two instances of SlideShow, and two instances of DigitalTimer (lines 125–132). A panel is created to house these components, and it has its layout manager set to null because `CompMover` is taking care of component positions (lines 134–135). Inside the `for` loop (lines 137–146), each component is added to the panel (line 138) and has its initial position and x and y offsets randomly determined (lines 140–143). Each component also gets handed off to a new instance of `CompMover` to handle its positioning (line 145).

Each of the six components has an internal thread running within it to handle its animation. In addition, each of the six instances of `CompMover` also has an internal thread running to handle the component movement. All 12 of these threads perform many operations per second and can bog down the processor. If you don't have a really fast machine, you might notice some sluggishness when you run this example. As you can see, animation is very processor-intensive.

Figure 9.14 shows how `CompMover` looks after running for about 75 seconds. Figure 9.15 shows how it looks after about 136 seconds. Each of the components travels around in a different direction. When a component moves off one side of the screen, it returns on the other side. Your output will differ significantly because the initial positions and directions of movement for the components are randomly determined.

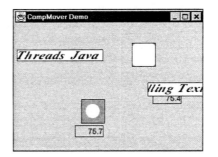

FIGURE 9.14

A snapshot of CompMover in action.

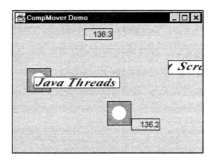

FIGURE 9.15

Another snapshot of CompMover after more time has passed.

Summary

In this chapter, you saw how it is important that the event thread be the only thread that makes direct modifications to Swing components after they have been added to a visible container. The `SwingUtilities.invokeAndWait()` and `SwingUtilities.invokeLater()` methods provide a mechanism for any thread to put a block of code onto the event queue. When the event thread gets to the block of code, it executes it and safely makes changes to Swing components. Using these tools, threads were added to components to provide animation capabilities. Additionally, a worker thread was able to take the results of a long-running search and safely update the graphical interface of an application.

Thread Groups

IN THIS CHAPTER

In Java, threads can be grouped together and associated with an instance of `ThreadGroup`. In this chapter, I'll show you how to use some of the methods of `ThreadGroup`. At the end of the chapter, I'll show you how to use the class `ThreadViewer` to visually display the status of all the threads running in the Java VM.

In addition to the information in this chapter, a detailed description of the `ThreadGroup` API can be found in Appendix B at the end of this book.

What Are Thread Groups?

In Java, all threads belong to an instance of the `ThreadGroup` class. A thread group has a name and some properties associated with it and can be used to facilitate the management of threads within it as a group. Thread groups allow the threads of the VM to be organized and can provide some inter-group security. A `ThreadGroup` can contain other `ThreadGroups`. Figure 10.1 shows a sample containment tree for `Thread` and `ThreadGroup` objects. There is only one root thread group, and it contains all the other threads and groups. Each subgroup can contain other groups and threads. All threads belong to exactly one thread group. All thread groups (except for the root thread group) have exactly one parent thread group.

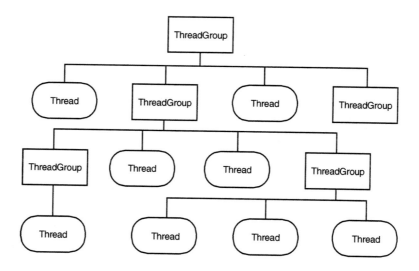

FIGURE 10.1

An example containment hierarchy for threads and thread groups.

When a new `ThreadGroup` is constructed, it is added as a member of an existing `ThreadGroup`. If `threadX` is in the `groupA` thread group and it executes the code

```
ThreadGroup groupB = new ThreadGroup("groupB");
```

the newly formed thread group `groupB` has `groupA` as its parent group. If you want a parent thread group other than the default, you can specify the parent thread group at the time of construction. If `threadX` is in `groupA` and it executes the code

```
ThreadGroup groupD = new ThreadGroup(groupC, "groupD");
```

the newly formed `groupD` has `groupC` as its parent thread group, not `groupA`.

Like `Thread`, instances of `ThreadGroup` have names associated with them. Unlike `Thread`, a name must be specified—there is no option for names to be automatically generated. If `threadX` executes the code

```
ThreadGroup group = new ThreadGroup("comm subsystem");
```

a new `ThreadGroup` is created and named `comm subsystem`. To retrieve the name of a particular group, the `getName()` method is used. If you run the code

```
String groupName = group.getName();
```

`groupName` is the name passed to the constructor when group is instantiated: that is, `comm subsystem`.

New `Thread` objects default to be in the same thread group as the thread that does the construction. If `threadX` is in `groupA` and it executes the code

```
Thread threadY = new Thread(target);
```

`threadY` is in `groupA`, just like the thread (`threadX`) that constructed it. If a new thread should be in another group, the desired thread group can be passed to the constructor for `Thread`. If `threadX` is in `groupA` and it executes the code

```
Thread threadZ = new Thread(groupC, target);
```

`threadZ` is a member of `groupC`, not `groupA`.

Using getParent()

If you need to know which thread group a particular thread group belongs to, you can use the `getParent()` method on `ThreadGroup`. Suppose at some time in the past, this code was executed:

```
ThreadGroup groupD = new ThreadGroup(groupC, "groupD");
```

Then, later in the application, the following code is used:

```
ThreadGroup parentOfGroupD = groupD.getParent();
```

The reference returned and stored in `parentOfGroupD` refers to the same `ThreadGroup` instance as groupC does.

If `getParent()` is invoked on the root thread group, `null` is returned. In the VM, only one instance of `ThreadGroup` does not have a parent group, and that is the root group.

Finding the Subgroups of a Thread Group

The `activeGroupCount()` method returns the number of active thread groups in a particular `ThreadGroup` *and all of its subgroups*. Keep in mind that this can be dynamically changing, but it's an accurate snapshot at a moment in time.

To get a reference to all of the groups and subgroups of a `ThreadGroup`, the `enumerate(ThreadGroup[])` method can be used. If you don't want to include a recursive search of the subgroups, use `enumerate(ThreadGroup[], false)` instead. Both methods return the number of groups copied into the array that is passed. If the array is not big enough, the extra groups are silently ignored. To get an idea of how big the destination array needs to be, you can use the value returned from `activeGroupCount()`. This code tries to capture all of the groups and subgroups of group:

```
ThreadGroup group = // ...
int estimatedSize = 2 * group.activeGroupCount();
ThreadGroup[] dest = new ThreadGroup[estimatedSize];
int actualSize = group.enumerate(dest);
```

The count returned from `activeGroupCount()` is doubled in an attempt to be sure that the destination array is large enough. Based on `estimatedSize`, a destination array for the groups is allocated and referred to by `dest`. The `enumerate(ThreadGroup[])` method copies up to `dest.length` groups into `dest`. The number of groups copied is returned and stored in `actualSize`. If `actualSize` is equal to `dest.length`, there is a good chance that `dest` was not big enough. Generally, `actualSize` is less than `dest.length` and indicates the number of valid groups in `dest`.

Using the getThreadGroup() Method of Thread

If you need to know which thread group a thread belongs to, you can use the `getThreadGroup()` method on `Thread`. To find out which thread group `threadX` belongs to, use this code:

```
ThreadGroup groupForThreadX = threadX.getThreadGroup();
```

groupForThreadX is a reference to the ThreadGroup that threadX belongs to. If a thread is no longer alive, getThreadGroup() returns null instead of a ThreadGroup.

To determine which thread group the thread executing a block of code belongs to, use:

```
ThreadGroup group = Thread.currentThread().getThreadGroup();
```

Finding All the Threads in a Thread Group

The activeCount() method returns the number of active threads in a particular ThreadGroup *and all of its subgroups*. Keep in mind that this can be dynamically changing, as new threads might be created and existing threads might be dying.

To get a reference to all of the threads in a ThreadGroup and all of its subgroups, the enumerate(Thread[]) method can be used. If you don't want to include a recursive search of the subgroups, use enumerate(Thread[], false) instead. Both methods return the number of threads copied into the passed array. If the array is not big enough, the extra threads are silently ignored. To get an idea of how big the destination array needs to be, you can use the value returned from activeCount(). This code tries to capture all of the threads in group and its subgroups:

```
ThreadGroup group = // ...
int estimatedSize = 2 * group.activeCount();
Thread[] dest = new Thread[estimatedSize];
int actualSize = group.enumerate(dest);
```

The count returned from activeCount() is doubled in an attempt to be sure that the destination array is large enough. Based on estimatedSize, a destination array for the threads is allocated and referred to by dest. The enumerate(Thread[]) method copies up to dest.length threads into dest. The number of threads copied is returned and stored in actualSize. If actualSize is equal to dest.length, there is a good chance that dest was not big enough. Generally, actualSize is less than dest.length and indicates the number of valid threads in dest.

Understanding Thread Group Security

The checkAccess() method of ThreadGroup is called internally by many of the other ThreadGroup methods. It checks to see if a SecurityManager exists for a VM. By default, applications do not have a SecurityManager installed. Applets, on the other hand, might have one.

If a SecurityManager exists and it determines that a particular thread is not permitted to take an action, it throws a SecurityException. SecurityException is a subclass of RuntimeException, so try/catch blocks are typically not used. If no SecurityManager is installed, or if the SecurityManager approves of the access, checkAccess() silently returns.

A full discussion of security in Java is beyond the scope of this book. You just need to be aware that a SecurityException might be thrown from most of the methods of ThreadGroup. If you are writing an application, you can usually safely ignore these checkAccess() issues.

Using setMaxPriority() and getMaxPriority()

The setMaxPriority() method sets the maximum priority that all threads in a particular thread group and all of its subgroups can have. Threads that are already running at a higher priority are not affected. This method has an effect when new threads are constructed or when the setPriority() method of Thread is invoked.

If setPriority() is called with a priority higher than the maximum allowed for the group that a thread is in, the priority is silently lowered to the maximum allowed. The getMaxPriority() method returns the current maximum priority permitted for threads in a particular thread group.

Using interrupt()

The interrupt() method of ThreadGroup can be used to signal an interrupt to all the threads in the group and subgroups. This method can be useful if several threads have been spawned to handle a task, and it's time to signal all of them to shut down. (See Chapter 5, "Gracefully Stopping Threads," for more on signaling threads to die by interrupting them.)

Deprecated Methods: stop(), suspend(), and resume()

The stop(), suspend(), and resume() methods of ThreadGroup have all been deprecated as of JDK 1.2 and should not be used. The stop() method stops all the threads in the specified thread group and subgroups. The suspend() method suspends execution of all of the threads in the specified thread group and subgroups. The resume() method resumes execution of all of the threads in the specified thread group and subgroups. These methods are deprecated at the ThreadGroup level for the same good reasons that they are deprecated at the Thread level. See Chapter 5 for more information about why these methods are deprecated and ways that you can safely implement similar behavior.

Class ThreadViewer

The class ThreadViewer (see Listing 10.1) graphically displays all of the threads currently running in the Java VM. It automatically refreshes itself every 5 seconds to keep current. ThreadViewer can be a handy tool to have around during the development and debugging of multithreaded applications.

LISTING 10.1 ThreadViewer.java—Displays All of the Currently Running Threads in a Table

```
 1: import java.awt.*;
 2: import java.awt.event.*;
 3: import javax.swing.*;
 4: import javax.swing.table.*;
 5:
 6: public class ThreadViewer extends JPanel {
 7:     private ThreadViewerTableModel tableModel;
 8:
 9:     public ThreadViewer() {
10:         tableModel = new ThreadViewerTableModel();
11:
12:         JTable table = new JTable(tableModel);
13:         table.setAutoResizeMode(JTable.AUTO_RESIZE_LAST_COLUMN);
14:
15:         TableColumnModel colModel = table.getColumnModel();
16:         int numColumns = colModel.getColumnCount();
17:
18:         // manually size all but the last column
19:         for ( int i = 0; i < numColumns - 1; i++ ) {
20:             TableColumn col = colModel.getColumn(i);
21:
22:             col.sizeWidthToFit();
23:             col.setPreferredWidth(col.getWidth() + 5);
24:             col.setMaxWidth(col.getWidth() + 5);
25:         }
26:
27:         JScrollPane sp = new JScrollPane(table);
28:
29:         setLayout(new BorderLayout());
30:         add(sp, BorderLayout.CENTER);
31:     }
32:
33:     public void dispose() {
34:         tableModel.stopRequest();
35:     }
36:
37:     protected void finalize() throws Throwable {
38:         dispose();
39:     }
40:
41:     public static JFrame createFramedInstance() {
42:         final ThreadViewer viewer = new ThreadViewer();
```

continues

LISTING 10.1   Continued

```
43:
44:            final JFrame f = new JFrame("ThreadViewer");
45:            f.addWindowListener(new WindowAdapter() {
46:                    public void windowClosing(WindowEvent e) {
47:                        f.setVisible(false);
48:                        f.dispose();
49:                        viewer.dispose();
50:                    }
51:                });
52:
53:            f.setContentPane(viewer);
54:            f.setSize(500, 300);
55:            f.setVisible(true);
56:
57:            return f;
58:        }
59:
60:        public static void main(String[] args) {
61:            JFrame f = ThreadViewer.createFramedInstance();
62:
63:            // For this example, exit the VM when the viewer
64:            // frame is closed.
65:            f.addWindowListener(new WindowAdapter() {
66:                    public void windowClosing(WindowEvent e) {
67:                        System.exit(0);
68:                    }
69:                });
70:
71:            // Keep the main thread from exiting by blocking
72:            // on wait() for a notification that never comes.
73:            Object lock = new Object();
74:            synchronized ( lock ) {
75:                try {
76:                    lock.wait();
77:                } catch ( InterruptedException x ) {
78:                }
79:            }
80:        }
81: }
```

ThreadViewer extends JPanel (line 6) so that it can be placed in any container. Typically, you would invoke the static method ThreadViewer.createFramedInstance() (lines 41–58) to have a new instance of ThreadViewer be automatically put into a JFrame and displayed.

In the constructor (lines 9–31), a new `ThreadViewerTableModel` (see Listing 10.2) is created and passed to the constructor for `JTable` (lines 10–12). The rest of the constructor takes care of setting the column sizing options and puts the `JTable` into a `JScrollPane` in case it gets quite large.

The `dispose()` method (lines 33–35) should be called when you are done with an instance of `ThreadViewer`. It sends a message to the thread running inside the model to stop soon. I'll explain more about the model and the thread running within it later.

The `static` method `createFramedInstance()` (lines 41–58) creates an instance of `ThreadViewer` and puts it into a `JFrame`. The `JFrame` is sized, displayed, and returned to the caller (lines 54–57). When the user closes the frame, the frame is hidden and disposed, and the `dispose()` method of `ThreadViewer` is also called (lines 46–50).

In `main()` (lines 60–80), a framed instance of `ThreadViewer` is created. To keep the `main` thread from exiting the `main()` method, the thread waits on an arbitrary object for notification that will never come (lines 73–79). This is only done for demonstration purposes so that the `main` thread is listed in the `ThreadViewer` window.

The `JTable` in `ThreadViewer` gets its data from a `ThreadViewerTableModel` (see Listing 10.2).

LISTING 10.2   ThreadViewerTableModel.java—Represents the Current List of Threads as a TableModel for JTable

```
 1: import java.awt.*;
 2: import java.lang.reflect.*;
 3: import javax.swing.*;
 4: import javax.swing.table.*;
 5:
 6: public class ThreadViewerTableModel extends AbstractTableModel {
 7:     private Object dataLock;
 8:     private int rowCount;
 9:     private Object[][] cellData;
10:     private Object[][] pendingCellData;
11:
12:     // the column information remains constant
13:     private final int columnCount;
14:     private final String[] columnName;
15:     private final Class[] columnClass;
16:
17:     // self-running object control variables
18:     private Thread internalThread;
```

continues

LISTING 10.2 Continued

```
19:      private volatile boolean noStopRequested;
20:
21:      public ThreadViewerTableModel() {
22:          rowCount = 0;
23:          cellData = new Object[0][0];
24:
25:          // JTable uses this information for the column headers
26:          String[] names = {
27:              "Priority", "Alive",
28:              "Daemon", "Interrupted",
29:              "ThreadGroup", "Thread Name" };
30:          columnName = names;
31:
32:          // JTable uses this information for cell rendering
33:          Class[] classes = {
34:              Integer.class, Boolean.class,
35:              Boolean.class, Boolean.class,
36:              String.class, String.class };
37:          columnClass = classes;
38:
39:          columnCount = columnName.length;
40:
41:          // used to control concurrent access
42:          dataLock = new Object();
43:
44:          noStopRequested = true;
45:          Runnable r = new Runnable() {
46:                  public void run() {
47:                      try {
48:                          runWork();
49:                      } catch ( Exception x ) {
50:                          // in case ANY exception slips through
51:                          x.printStackTrace();
52:                      }
53:                  }
54:              };
55:
56:          internalThread = new Thread(r, "ThreadViewer");
57:          internalThread.setPriority(Thread.MAX_PRIORITY - 2);
58:          internalThread.setDaemon(true);
59:          internalThread.start();
60:      }
61:
62:      private void runWork() {
```

```
63:
64:            // The run() method of transferPending is called by
65:            // the event handling thread for safe concurrency.
66:            Runnable transferPending = new Runnable() {
67:                    public void run() {
68:                        transferPendingCellData();
69:
70:                        // Method of AbstractTableModel that
71:                        // causes the table to be updated.
72:                        fireTableDataChanged();
73:                    }
74:                };
75:
76:            while ( noStopRequested ) {
77:                try {
78:                    createPendingCellData();
79:                    SwingUtilities.invokeAndWait(transferPending);
80:                    Thread.sleep(5000);
81:                } catch ( InvocationTargetException tx ) {
82:                    tx.printStackTrace();
83:                    stopRequest();
84:                } catch ( InterruptedException x ) {
85:                    Thread.currentThread().interrupt();
86:                }
87:            }
88:        }
89:
90:        public void stopRequest() {
91:            noStopRequested = false;
92:            internalThread.interrupt();
93:        }
94:
95:        public boolean isAlive() {
96:            return internalThread.isAlive();
97:        }
98:
99:        private void createPendingCellData() {
100:            // this method is called by the internal thread
101:            Thread[] thread = findAllThreads();
102:            Object[][] cell = new Object[thread.length][columnCount];
103:
104:            for ( int i = 0; i < thread.length; i++ ) {
105:                Thread t = thread[i];
```

continues

LISTING 10.2 Continued

```
106:                  Object[] rowCell = cell[i];
107:
108:                      rowCell[0] = new Integer(t.getPriority());
109:                      rowCell[1] = new Boolean(t.isAlive());
110:                      rowCell[2] = new Boolean(t.isDaemon());
111:                      rowCell[3] = new Boolean(t.isInterrupted());
112:                      rowCell[4] = t.getThreadGroup().getName();
113:                      rowCell[5] = t.getName();
114:              }
115:
116:          synchronized ( dataLock ) {
117:              pendingCellData = cell;
118:          }
119:      }
120:
121:      private void transferPendingCellData() {
122:          // this method is called by the event thread
123:          synchronized ( dataLock ) {
124:              cellData = pendingCellData;
125:              rowCount = cellData.length;
126:          }
127:      }
128:
129:      public int getRowCount() {
130:          // this method is called by the event thread
131:          return rowCount;
132:      }
133:
134:      public Object getValueAt(int row, int col) {
135:          // this method is called by the event thread
136:          return cellData[row][col];
137:      }
138:
139:      public int getColumnCount() {
140:          return columnCount;
141:      }
142:
143:      public Class getColumnClass(int columnIdx) {
144:          return columnClass[columnIdx];
145:      }
146:
147:      public String getColumnName(int columnIdx) {
148:          return columnName[columnIdx];
149:      }
```

```
150:
151:        public static Thread[] findAllThreads() {
152:            ThreadGroup group =
153:                Thread.currentThread().getThreadGroup();
154:
155:            ThreadGroup topGroup = group;
156:
157:            // traverse the ThreadGroup tree to the top
158:            while ( group != null ) {
159:                topGroup = group;
160:                group = group.getParent();
161:            }
162:
163:            // Create a destination array that is about
164:            // twice as big as needed to be very confident
165:            // that none are clipped.
166:            int estimatedSize = topGroup.activeCount() * 2;
167:            Thread[] slackList = new Thread[estimatedSize];
168:
169:            // Load the thread references into the oversized
170:            // array. The actual number of threads loaded
171:            // is returned.
172:            int actualSize = topGroup.enumerate(slackList);
173:
174:            // copy into a list that is the exact size
175:            Thread[] list = new Thread[actualSize];
176:            System.arraycopy(slackList, 0, list, 0, actualSize);
177:
178:            return list;
179:        }
180: }
```

ThreadViewerTableModel extends AbstractTableModel (line 6) and holds the data to be displayed in the JTable. The event thread comes in and invokes various methods to determine what should be drawn on the screen. The model has an internal thread that refreshes the list of threads every 5 seconds and updates the model data to reflect the new state. To control concurrent access by the internal thread and the event thread, the dataLock object (lines 7, 42) is used for synchronization. rowCount reflects the most recent polling of the number of threads (line 8). The two-dimensional array cellData (line 9) is read by the event thread to determine what to draw for each cell of the table. The other two-dimensional array pendingCellData (line 10) is populated by the internal thread and copied into cellData by the event thread when it is complete.

In the constructor (lines 21–60), the number of rows is initialized to 0 and a zero-sized `cellData` is created. This step is necessary in case the event thread starts calling methods on the model before a list of threads has been formatted. The names of the columns are constant and are stored in `columnName` (lines 26–30). The datatypes for each column are stored in `columnClass` (lines 32–37). These types are queried by the event thread and are used to determine how to render the cell data in the table. An internal thread is started to refresh the data every 5 seconds (lines 44–59). The priority of the internal thread is set at 8 so that it is a relatively high-priority thread (line 57). The internal thread spends most of its time sleeping anyway. This internal thread is set to be a daemon thread because there is no point of it running if every other nondaemon thread is done (line 58).

The internal thread invokes `runWork()` (lines 62–88). A `Runnable` is constructed and referred by `transferPending` (lines 66–74). `transferPending` is used to bundle code for the event thread and is passed to `SwingUtilities.invokeAndWait()` (line 79). Inside `transferPending`, the event thread calls `transferPendingCellData()` followed by `fireTableDataChanged()` to get the table to display the new values. The internal thread loops (lines 76–87) in the `while` until another thread invokes the `stopRequest()` method. Inside the `while` loop, `createPendingCellData()` is called to check the running threads again and build up the new cell data (line 78). Then `SwingUtilities.invokeAndWait()` is called to get the event thread to read the new data (line 79). Before looping again, the internal thread sleeps for 5 seconds (line 80).

When the internal thread invokes `createPendingCellData()` (lines 99–119), the current list of threads is built by calling `findAllThreads()` (line 101). The new data is first put into the local variable `cell` (line 102). The dimensions of `cell` are based on the number of columns (fixed) and the number of threads that were just found. For each thread found, the thread's priority, alive status, daemon status, interrupted status, thread group name, and thread name are gathered and stored into `cell` (lines 104–114). After locking on `dataLock`, `pendingData` is set to refer to the two-dimensional array referred to by `cell` (lines 116–118).

Next, the event thread invokes `transferPendingCellData()` (lines 121–127). After locking on `dataLock`, `cellData` is set to refer to `pendingCellData` and `rowCount` is updated to match the number of cells. The most recent data is now accessible through the `cellData` reference.

The `public` and `static` method `findAllThreads()` (lines 151–179) can be used from anywhere to return a `Thread[]` with the most recent list of running threads. In `ThreadViewer`, the internal thread invokes `findAllThreads()` every 5 seconds to update the table model. First, the `ThreadGroup` of the invoking thread is determined (lines 152–153). From this starting point, the `ThreadGroup` containment tree is traversed to the root thread group (lines 155–161). After `topGroup` is determined, the number of threads is retrieved using `activeCount()` (line 166). This count is doubled to get an estimate that should be large enough (line 166). A new array of

Thread objects (slackList) is allocated based on the estimated count (line 167). The enumerate() method is invoked on topGroup and fills slackList with all the threads it finds (line 172). The actual number of threads found is returned by enumerate(). A new Thread[] of the exact size is allocated (line 175), and the Thread references are copied into it from slackList (line 176). Finally, the exact-sized array is returned to the caller (line 178).

Figure 10.2 shows a sample screenshot produced when ThreadViewer is run. You can see that quite a few threads are running in the VM. The row for the internal thread is highlighted. Its name is ThreadViewer, and you can see that its priority is 8 and that it is a daemon thread. Because main is blocked and still running, you can see its entry too. Currently, none of the threads is interrupted. Generally, a thread only has interrupted status briefly before it is reset and an InterruptedException is thrown.

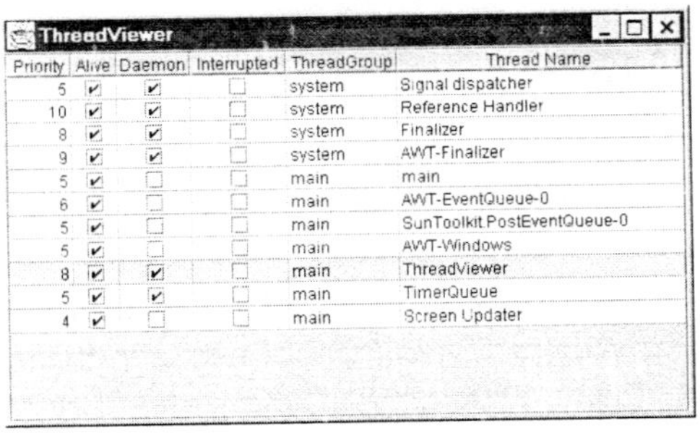

FIGURE 10.2
ThreadViewer in action.

Summary

ThreadGroup can help to organize the threads of a VM into groups. In this chapter, I showed you some of the methods that are available to work on thread groups. In particular, the getParent(), getName(), activeCount(), and enumerate() methods of ThreadGroup were used along with the getThreadGroup() method of Thread to produce the data for ThreadViewer. ThreadViewer can be a very useful tool for code development and debugging.

Techniques

IN THIS PART

Self-Running Objects

IN THIS CHAPTER

In an object-based application, most objects are *passive*. A passive object just sits there waiting for one of its methods to be invoked. A passive object's `private` member variables can only be changed by the code in its own methods, so its state remains constant until one of its methods is invoked. In a multithreaded environment like Java, threads can run within objects to make the objects *active*. Objects that are active make autonomous changes to themselves.

Sometimes in modeling a system, it becomes apparent that if some of the objects were active, the model would be simplified. Earlier in this book, classes that implemented `Runnable` were instantiated, passed to one of the constructors of `Thread`, and then `start()` was invoked. This style required a user of a class to know that a thread needed to be started to run within it, creating a burden on the user of the class. In addition, because the user of the class created the `Thread` object for it, a reference to `Thread` was available for misuse. The user of the class could erroneously set the priority of the thread, suspend it at a bad time, or outright stop the thread when the object it was running in was in an inconsistent state. Having to activate objects externally is both inconvenient and potentially hazardous. In this chapter, I'll show you how to have an active object transparently create and start up its own internal thread.

Simple Self-Running Class

The class `SelfRun`, shown in Listing 11.1, demonstrates a simple example of an active object. During construction, it automatically starts an internal thread running.

LISTING 11.1   SelfRun.java—A Simple Self-Running Class

```
1: public class SelfRun extends Object implements Runnable {
2:     private Thread internalThread;
3:     private volatile boolean noStopRequested;
4:
5:     public SelfRun() {
6:         // other constructor stuff should appear here first ...
7:         System.out.println("in constructor - initializing...");
8:
9:         // Just before returning, the thread should be
10:        // created and started.
11:        noStopRequested = true;
12:        internalThread = new Thread(this);
13:        internalThread.start();
14:     }
15:
16:     public void run() {
17:         // Check that no one has erroneously invoked
18:         // this public method.
19:         if ( Thread.currentThread() != internalThread ) {
```

```
20:              throw new RuntimeException("only the internal " +
21:                  "thread is allowed to invoke run()");
22:          }
23:
24:          while ( noStopRequested ) {
25:              System.out.println("in run() - still going...");
26:
27:              try {
28:                  Thread.sleep(700);
29:              } catch ( InterruptedException x ) {
30:                  // Any caught interrupts should be habitually
31:                  // reasserted for any blocking statements
32:                  // which follow.
33:                  Thread.currentThread().interrupt();
34:              }
35:          }
36:      }
37:
38:      public void stopRequest() {
39:          noStopRequested = false;
40:          internalThread.interrupt();
41:      }
42:
43:      public boolean isAlive() {
44:          return internalThread.isAlive();
45:      }
46: }
```

SelfRun implements Runnable (line 1), as did the earlier examples. The two member variables are used to maintain and control the internal thread. The private variable internalThread (line 2) holds a reference to the thread that is used to run the object. The private variable noStopRequested (line 3) is used as a flag to indicate whether or not the internal thread should continue processing. The internal thread continues to process code as long as noStopRequested is true. It is marked volatile because two different threads access it: the internal thread reads it, and an external thread will change it.

In the constructor (lines 5-14), after the class-specific initialization activities have all been completed (lines 6-7), the noStopRequested flag is initially set to true (line 11). A new Thread object is constructed by passing in this, the reference to the SelfRun object being created. This thread is used as the internal thread for this object and is automatically started (line 13). By the time the constructor returns, an internal thread has been created and has been started. We don't know if run() has been called yet by this internal thread, but the correctness of the design should not depend on its being called before the constructor returns. You should keep in mind that run() might be invoked before the constructor returns, right after it returns, or some time after it returns. The timing is dependent on the whims of the thread scheduler.

In run() (lines 16–36), the very first thing done is a check that run() was only invoked by the internal thread (lines 19–22). This is necessary to ensure that no one mistakenly invokes run() from outside this class, something that is completely possible because run() is public. If any other thread invokes run(), a RuntimeException is thrown to indicate the error (lines 20–21).

The while loop within run() (lines 24–35) continues until noStopRequested becomes false. In this example, a simple message is printed each time through just to show the internal activities (line 25). The internal thread then sleeps briefly before looping again (line 28). If this sleep() is interrupted, its InterruptedException is caught right away (line 29). After catching the exception, the internal thread reinterrupts itself (line 33) in case any other interrupt-detecting statements (such as wait(), or another sleep()) are present before the orderly shutdown can complete. This is a good habit to get into when interrupting a thread is used as a signaling mechanism for stopping.

To request that the internal thread gracefully die as soon as possible, the stopRequest() method is used (lines 38–41). When invoked, it sets noStopRequested to false (line 39). stopRequest() then interrupts the internal thread in case it is blocked on an interruptible statement (such as wait() or sleep()) so that it gets a chance to notice that noStopRequested is now false.

Because a stopRequest() is only a *request* that the thread die as soon as it has completed any cleanup activities, another method is needed to determine if the thread has died yet. The isAlive() method (lines 43–45) is used to proxy the query to the internal thread to determine if it is still alive.

The SelfRunMain class is used to demonstrate the SelfRun class in action. The code for it is in Listing 11.2.

LISTING 11.2 SelfRunMain.java—Demonstration Code for SelfRun

```
1: public class SelfRunMain extends Object {
2:     public static void main(String[] args) {
3:         SelfRun sr = new SelfRun();
4:
5:         try { Thread.sleep(3000); }
                  ➥catch ( InterruptedException x ) { }
6:
7:         sr.stopRequest();
8:     }
9: }
```

`SelfRunMain` simply constructs a `SelfRun` (line 3), lets it run for 3 seconds (line 5), and then requests that it stop soon (line 7). The main feature to note is that all I had to do was to construct a `SelfRun`. The hassle of creating a `Thread` and starting it is gone. In fact, if I don't have a need to ever stop it, I don't even have to be aware that it has a thread running within it!

When `SelfRunMain` is run, the following output will be produced (your output should match):

```
in constructor - initializing...
in run() - still going...
in run() - still going...
in run() - still going...
in run() - still going...
in run() - still going...
```

Using an Inner Class to Hide run()

In the previous example, steps had to be taken to protect the class from erroneous invocations of `run()`. Although the class is adequately protected from external intrusion, a user of the class can still fall prey to the lure of calling `run()`. Or perhaps a user might notice that the class implements `Runnable` and be tempted to create a `Thread` and start it. In both cases, a quite unexpected `RuntimeException` will be thrown.

A better approach available to JDK 1.1 and later developers is to use an inner class to hide the implementation of `run()` from external code. The class `InnerSelfRun`, shown in Listing 11.3, demonstrates how this can be done.

LISTING 11.3   InnerSelfRun.java—Hiding the run() Method in an Inner Class

```
 1: public class InnerSelfRun extends Object {
 2:     private Thread internalThread;
 3:     private volatile boolean noStopRequested;
 4:
 5:     public InnerSelfRun() {
 6:         // other constructor stuff should appear here first ...
 7:         System.out.println("in constructor - initializing...");
 8:
 9:         // before returning, the thread should be started.
10:         noStopRequested = true;
11:
12:         Runnable r = new Runnable() {
13:             public void run() {
14:                 try {
15:                     runWork();
```

continues

LISTING 11.3   Continued

```
16:                              } catch ( Exception x ) {
17:                                  // in case ANY exception slips through
18:                                  x.printStackTrace();
19:                              }
20:                          }
21:                      };
22:
23:              internalThread = new Thread(r);
24:              internalThread.start();
25:          }
26:
27:          private void runWork() {
28:              while ( noStopRequested ) {
29:                  System.out.println("in runWork() - still going...");
30:
31:                  try {
32:                      Thread.sleep(700);
33:                  } catch ( InterruptedException x ) {
34:                      // Any caught interrupts should be reasserted
35:                      // for any blocking statements which follow.
36:                      Thread.currentThread().interrupt();
37:                  }
38:              }
39:          }
40:
41:          public void stopRequest() {
42:              noStopRequested = false;
43:              internalThread.interrupt();
44:          }
45:
46:          public boolean isAlive() {
47:              return internalThread.isAlive();
48:          }
49: }
```

Most of InnerSelfRun is the same as SelfRun, but there are a few key differences. The biggest change is that InnerSelfRun does not implement Runnable (line 1), but instead uses an anonymous, inner class (lines 12–21) to create a Runnable. The Runnable that is created is passed as a parameter to the constructor of Thread (line 23). In the inner class, run() is implemented (lines 13–20). The private method runWork() is called (line 15) from within a try/catch block. Any exception that slips all the way up through runWork() is caught (line 16) and has its stack trace printed (line 18). Because run() is implemented in an inner class, it is not accessible from the outside, and there is no danger of its being accidentally called. This inner class's run() method can access the private method runWork() of its enclosing class, but no code outside of InnerSelfRun can accidentally call runWork().

There is no longer any need to check which thread is calling runWork() because it cannot be called from outside this class (no checking between lines 27 and 28). The message printed in the while loop is slightly different (line 29) than before. Otherwise, the remainder of the InnerSelfRun class definition is the same as SelfRun.

InnerSelfRunMain (Listing 11.4) simply creates an InnerSelfRun (line 3), lets it run for 3 seconds (line 5), and then requests that it stop soon (line 7). As before, all that I had to do was instantiate an InnerSelfRun. I didn't have, nor did I need to have, any knowledge that it was an active object.

LISTING 11.4 InnerSelfRunMain.java—Demonstration Code for InnerSelfRun

```
1: public class InnerSelfRunMain extends Object {
2:      public static void main(String[] args) {
3:          InnerSelfRun sr = new InnerSelfRun();
4:
5:          try { Thread.sleep(3000); }
                     ➥catch ( InterruptedException x ) { }
6:
7:          sr.stopRequest();
8:      }
9: }
```

When InnerSelfRunMain is run, it produces the following output (your output should be the same):

```
in constructor - initializing...
in runWork() - still going...
in runWork() - still going...
in runWork() - still going...
in runWork() - still going...
in runWork() - still going...
```

Additional Functionality to Consider

You can extend the concept of a self-running object to allow more details about the internal thread to be specified:

- A ThreadGroup for the internal thread can be passed to the class's constructor and then passed to the Thread constructor.

- A name for the internal thread can be passed to the class's constructor and then passed to the `Thread` constructor.

- The methods `getInternalThreadName()` and `setInternalThreadName()` can be added if desired. They would simply proxy the request to the underlying thread `internalThread`.

- A priority for the internal thread can be passed to the class's constructor and then `internalThread.setPriority()` can be invoked before the thread is started.

- The methods `getInternalThreadPriority()` and `setInternalThreadPriority()` can be added if desired. They would simply proxy the request to `internalThread`.

- If it's inappropriate for the internal thread to be started in the constructor, a new method can be added to allow it to be started later:

```
public void start() {
    if ( neverStarted ) {
        neverStarted = false;
        internalThread.start();
    }
}
```

- The `suspendRequest()` and `resumeRequest()` techniques of Chapter 5, "Gracefully Stopping Threads," can be added if needed.

Example: Animated Images on a JComponent

In this example, I'll show you how to animate a set of images using a customized `JComponent` that automatically runs a thread inside itself to flip through the images. The images are generated at construction time, but you can modify this design to animate images from any source: computer-generated or from a set of files.

The customized component `Squish`, shown in Listing 11.5, draws the top half of an ellipse with successively smaller heights. It appears that a mound is being squished down until it is flat. Then the cycle starts over with the full-height, top-half ellipse. The work to animate the images is transparent to the user of the class as the component creates its own internal thread to flip through the images.

LISTING 11.5   Squish.java—The Animated Image Component

```
1: import java.awt.*;
2: import java.awt.image.*;
3: import java.awt.geom.*;
4: import javax.swing.*;
5:
6: public class Squish extends JComponent {
7:     private Image[] frameList;
```

```
 8:        private long msPerFrame;
 9:        private volatile int currFrame;
10:
11:        private Thread internalThread;
12:        private volatile boolean noStopRequested;
13:
14:        public Squish(
15:                    int width,
16:                    int height,
17:                    long msPerCycle,
18:                    int framesPerSec,
19:                    Color fgColor
20:                ) {
21:
22:            setPreferredSize(new Dimension(width, height));
23:
24:            int framesPerCycle =
25:                    (int) ( ( framesPerSec * msPerCycle ) / 1000 );
26:            msPerFrame = 1000L / framesPerSec;
27:
28:            frameList =
29:                buildImages(width, height, fgColor, framesPerCycle);
30:            currFrame = 0;
31:
32:            noStopRequested = true;
33:            Runnable r = new Runnable() {
34:                    public void run() {
35:                        try {
36:                            runWork();
37:                        } catch ( Exception x ) {
38:                            // in case ANY exception slips through
39:                            x.printStackTrace();
40:                        }
41:                    }
42:                };
43:
44:            internalThread = new Thread(r);
45:            internalThread.start();
46:        }
47:
48:        private Image[] buildImages(
49:                    int width,
50:                    int height,
51:                    Color color,
```

continues

LISTING 11.5   Continued

```
52:                  int count
53:            ) {
54:
55:        BufferedImage[] im = new BufferedImage[count];
56:
57:        for ( int i = 0; i < count; i++ ) {
58:            im[i] = new BufferedImage(
59:                    width, height, BufferedImage.TYPE_INT_ARGB);
60:
61:            double xShape = 0.0;
62:            double yShape =
63:                ( (double) ( i * height ) ) / (double) count;
64:
65:            double wShape = width;
66:            double hShape = 2.0 * ( height - yShape );
67:            Ellipse2D shape = new Ellipse2D.Double(
68:                    xShape, yShape, wShape, hShape);
69:
70:            Graphics2D g2 = im[i].createGraphics();
71:            g2.setColor(color);
72:            g2.fill(shape);
73:            g2.dispose();
74:        }
75:
76:        return im;
77:    }
78:
79:    private void runWork() {
80:        while ( noStopRequested ) {
81:            currFrame = ( currFrame + 1 ) % frameList.length;
82:            repaint();
83:
84:            try {
85:                Thread.sleep(msPerFrame);
86:            } catch ( InterruptedException x ) {
87:                // reassert interrupt
88:                Thread.currentThread().interrupt();
89:                // continue on as if sleep completed normally
90:            }
91:        }
92:    }
93:
94:    public void stopRequest() {
95:        noStopRequested = false;
```

```
 96:            internalThread.interrupt();
 97:        }
 98:
 99:        public boolean isAlive() {
100:            return internalThread.isAlive();
101:        }
102:
103:        public void paint(Graphics g) {
104:            g.drawImage(frameList[currFrame], 0, 0, this);
105:        }
106: }
```

Squish extends JComponent so that it can inherit the functionality of a generic Swing component (line 6). Notice that although it will be running an internal thread, it does not implement
the Runnable interface (line 6). This example uses the technique of hiding run() in an anonymous, inner class.

The set of images to animate is held in Image array frameList (line 7). The number of milliseconds that each frame should be shown before flipping to the next one is held in
msPerFrame (line 8). The current index into the frameList is held in the volatile member
variable currFrame (line 9). It is marked as volatile because it is modified by the internal
thread inside runWork() (line 81), and read by the event-handling thread inside paint() (line
104). The thread running inside this component is referenced by internalThread (line 11).
The flag indicating whether or not a stop has been requested is held in noStopRequested
(line 12).

The constructor (lines 14–46) takes several parameters. The component's width in pixels is
passed in through width (line 15). Its height is passed in through height (line 16). The number
of milliseconds it should take for the mound to be squished down from its full height is specified through msPerCycle (line 17). The number of frames to be flipped though per second is
framesPerSec (line 18). The higher the frames per second rate is (up to about 30 fps), the
smoother the animation appears, but the greater the demand on the processor. The last parameter fgColor (line 19) is simply the color with which the mound should be drawn.

The preferred size for this component is simply the combination of the width and height
passed in (line 22). The number of images to generate for a full cycle from tall to flat is calculated based on the passed-in parameters (lines 24–25). The time that each frame should be
shown for is calculated (line 26). The images to use are computer generated and stored in
frameList (lines 28–29), and the index into this list is initialized to be 0 (line 30). The rest of
the constructor (lines 32–45) implements the standard internal thread pattern I showed you earlier in this chapter.

The `buildImages` method (lines 48–77) creates all of the frames to be flipped though during animation. A set of `BufferedImage` objects is created and drawn onto using `Graphics2D` methods. This set of images is returned to the caller, which in this case is the constructor.

Control of which frame to display is managed inside `runWork()` (lines 79–92). Each time through the `while` loop, a check is done to see if a stop has been requested (line 80). If not, the frame number is incremented and wrapped around back to `0` if the last frame has been shown (line 81). After the frame number advances, a repaint request is submitted to the event queue so that the new frame is drawn as soon as possible (line 82). Before looping again, the internal thread sleeps for the interframe interval (line 85). If this sleep is interrupted (probably by `stopRequest()`), the `InterruptedException` is caught (line 86). As a matter of good style, the internal thread is reinterrupted (line 88) in case any other interruptible, blocking statements are encountered before the thread gets a chance to die.

The `stopRequest()` method simply sets the `noStopRequested` flag to `false` (line 95) and interrupts the internal thread (line 96) in case it is blocked on an interruptible statement. In this example, the internal thread spends most of its time blocked sleeping, and the interrupt will wake it up early to take notice of the stop request. The `isAlive()` method is used after a `stopRequest()` call to check if the thread has died yet.

The `paint()` method (lines 103–105) is invoked by the event handling thread whenever there has been a request to repaint the component. In this case, paint simply draws the image indicated by `currFrame` onto the component (line 104).

The class `SquishMain`, shown in Listing 11.6, creates support containers to demonstrate the functionality of two `Squish` components.

LISTING 11.6   SquishMain.java—Code to Demonstrate the Use of Squish

```
 1: import java.awt.*;
 2: import java.awt.event.*;
 3: import javax.swing.*;
 4:
 5: public class SquishMain extends JPanel {
 6:     public SquishMain() {
 7:         Squish blueSquish =
                     ➥new Squish(150, 150, 3000L, 10, Color.blue);
 8:         Squish redSquish =
                     ➥new Squish(250, 200, 2500L, 10, Color.red);
 9:
10:         this.setLayout(new FlowLayout());
11:         this.add(blueSquish);
12:         this.add(redSquish);
13:     }
```

```
14:
15:     public static void main(String[] args) {
16:         SquishMain sm = new SquishMain();
17:
18:         JFrame f = new JFrame("Squish Main");
19:         f.setContentPane(sm);
20:         f.setSize(450, 250);
21:         f.setVisible(true);
22:         f.addWindowListener(new WindowAdapter() {
23:             public void windowClosing(WindowEvent e) {
24:                 System.exit(0);
25:             }
26:         });
27:     }
28: }
```

In main() (lines 15–27), a new SquishMain object is constructed (line 16) and placed into the content pane of a JFrame (line 19). The frame is sized and made visible (lines 20–21). Event-handling code is added to the frame so that when its Close control is clicked, the VM will exit (lines 22–26).

The SquishMain class is a subclass of JPanel (line 5) so that it can have components added to it. In the constructor (lines 6–13), two Squish components are constructed: one blue, and one red (lines 7–8). Because the Squish components each automatically start an internal thread to animate themselves, no further action is required to use them other than simply constructing them! The objects are a subclass of JComponent and are simply added to the panel within a FlowLayout (lines 10–12).

Figures 11.1 and 11.2 show two snapshots of SquishMain in action.

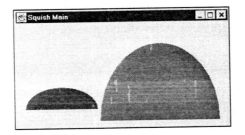

FIGURE 11.1
Snapshot of SquishMain running with both mounds relatively tall.

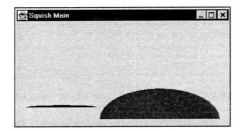

FIGURE 11.2
Another snapshot of SquishMain running, this time with both mounds a bit flatter.

Summary

In this chapter, I showed you a technique for creating active classes that are self-running. Self-running classes automatically create an internal thread that runs inside the object. This thread is usually started in the constructor, but can be started later if necessary. Users of self-running objects do not need to concern themselves with the details of creating and starting a thread for an object—in fact, they don't even need to know that a thread is running inside it at all. Additionally, because the users of a self-running object do not have a reference to the internal thread, they cannot erroneously use deprecated methods to suspend or stop the thread at a bad time.

Of the two self-running designs presented, I recommend that you use the one that hides run() within an anonymous, inner class. This design has the advantage of preventing a user from mistakenly invoking run() directly, or from mistakenly creating a new thread that invokes run().

Exception Callback

IN THIS CHAPTER

Exceptions can be thrown just about anywhere in a Java program. Methods must declare all of the exceptions they might throw except for RuntimeException and its subclasses. A RuntimeException can occur on just about every line of code (just think of the fact that NullPointerException can be thrown anytime a method is invoked if the object reference is null!).

When an exception occurs and is not immediately caught, it propagates up the call stack until it either is caught by one of the invoking methods, or remains uncaught. For methods called from the main() method, the exception can potentially float all the way back up to main() and get reported there. However, when a new thread is spawned, a brand new call stack is created. This call stack starts with the run() method. The run() method does not declare that it throws any exceptions and should therefore catch all of them.

Many times Java developers are frustrated by the fact that they cannot catch exceptions that occur in other threads. In this chapter, I'll show you a way to pass exceptions that occur inside an active class to another class to signal it that a potential problem has occurred.

ExceptionListener Interface

Classes that want to be notified when an exception occurs in an active class can implement the ExceptionListener interface shown in Listing 12.1.

LISTING 12.1   ExceptionListener.java—The Interface to Be Implemented for Exception Callback

```
1: public interface ExceptionListener {
2:     public void exceptionOccurred(Exception x, Object source);
3: }
```

This interface declares that classes of the type ExceptionListener must implement an exceptionOccurred() method. An active class will invoke this method on the listener whenever a notable exception should be relayed. The first parameter, x, is a reference to the actual exception. The second parameter, source, is a reference to the active class that caught the exception. Having a reference to the source object allows one ExceptionListener to monitor more than one active object and take a different course of action for each object monitored. If this is not necessary, the source parameter can simply be ignored.

Additional Methods to Support ExceptionListener

In the monitored class, three new methods are needed to support the existence of optional external ExceptionListener observers:

```
public void addExceptionListener(ExceptionListener l)
public void removeExceptionListener(ExceptionListener l)
private void sendException(Exception x)
```

The method addExceptionListener() adds a new listener for exceptions within the active object. The method removeExceptionListener() is used to clear out the current listener, if it exists, without setting a new one so that there are no longer any listeners.

Inside the active object, the private method sendException() should be invoked whenever an exception occurs that should be noted. Not all exceptions should be reported. For example, when InterruptedException is caught, it is generally not reported but used as a signal that someone has requested that the internal thread clean up and die soon.

For those exceptions that are reported, sendException() passes the exception on to all of the ExceptionListeners that have been added. If no listeners have been added, it is generally a good idea to instead print a stack trace to the console for the exception.

After the exception is reported, the internal thread can take different actions. If the exception was not very serious and can be worked around, the internal thread should proceed. If the exception is a critical error, the thread should clean up and return from run() soon.

The class ExceptionCallback, shown in Listing 12.2, supports monitoring by an ExceptionListener.

LISTING 12.2   ExceptionCallback.java—An Active Object That Supports Monitoring by an ExceptionListener

```
 1: import java.io.*;
 2: import java.util.*;
 3:
 4: public class ExceptionCallback extends Object {
 5:     private Set exceptionListeners;
 6:     private Thread internalThread;
 7:     private volatile boolean noStopRequested;
 8:
 9:     public ExceptionCallback(ExceptionListener[] initialGroup) {
10:         init(initialGroup);
11:     }
12:
13:     public ExceptionCallback(ExceptionListener initialListener) {
14:         ExceptionListener[] group = new ExceptionListener[1];
15:         group[0] = initialListener;
16:         init(group);
17:     }
```

continues

LISTING 12.2   Continued

```
18:
19:        public ExceptionCallback() {
20:            init(null);
21:        }
22:
23:        private void init(ExceptionListener[] initialGroup) {
24:            System.out.println("in constructor - initializing...");
25:
26:            exceptionListeners =
27:                    Collections.synchronizedSet(new HashSet());
28:
29:            // If any listeners should be added before the internal
30:            // thread starts, add them now.
31:            if ( initialGroup != null ) {
32:                for ( int i = 0; i < initialGroup.length; i++ ) {
33:                    addExceptionListener(initialGroup[i]);
34:                }
35:            }
36:
37:            // Just before returning from the constructor,
38:            // the thread should be created and started.
39:            noStopRequested = true;
40:
41:            Runnable r = new Runnable() {
42:                    public void run() {
43:                        try {
44:                            runWork();
45:                        } catch ( Exception x ) {
46:                            // in case ANY exception slips through
47:                            sendException(x);
48:                        }
49:                    }
50:                };
51:
52:            internalThread = new Thread(r);
53:            internalThread.start();
54:        }
55:
56:        private void runWork() {
57:            try {
58:                makeConnection(); // will throw an IOException
59:            } catch ( IOException x ) {
60:                sendException(x);
61:                // Probably in a real scenario, a "return"
```

```
62:                    // statement should be here.
63:            }
64:
65:            String str = null;
66:            int len = determineLength(str); // NullPointerException
67:        }
68:
69:        private void makeConnection() throws IOException {
70:            // A NumberFormatException will be thrown when
71:            // this String is parsed.
72:            String portStr = "j20";
73:            int port = 0;
74:
75:            try {
76:                port = Integer.parseInt(portStr);
77:            } catch ( NumberFormatException x ) {
78:                sendException(x);
79:                port = 80; // use default;
80:            }
81:
82:            connectToPort(port); // will throw an IOException
83:        }
84:
85:        private void connectToPort(int portNum) throws IOException {
86:            throw new IOException("connection refused");
87:        }
88:
89:        private int determineLength(String s) {
90:            return s.length();
91:        }
92:
93:        public void stopRequest() {
94:            noStopRequested = false;
95:            internalThread.interrupt();
96:        }
97:
98:        public boolean isAlive() {
99:            return internalThread.isAlive();
100:       }
101:
102:       private void sendException(Exception x) {
103:           if ( exceptionListeners.size() == 0 ) {
104:               // If there aren't any listeners, dump the stack
```

continues

LISTING 12.2 Continued

```
105:                    // trace to the console.
106:                    x.printStackTrace();
107:                    return;
108:                }
109:
110:                // Used "synchronized" to make sure that other threads
111:                // do not make changes to the Set while iterating.
112:                synchronized ( exceptionListeners ) {
113:                    Iterator iter = exceptionListeners.iterator();
114:                    while ( iter.hasNext() ) {
115:                        ExceptionListener l =
116:                                (ExceptionListener) iter.next();
117:
118:                        l.exceptionOccurred(x, this);
119:                    }
120:                }
121:        }
122:
123:        public void addExceptionListener(ExceptionListener l) {
124:            // Silently ignore a request to add a "null" listener.
125:            if ( l != null ) {
126:                // If a listener was already in the Set, it will
127:                // silently replace itself so that no duplicates
128:                // accumulate.
129:                exceptionListeners.add(l);
130:            }
131:        }
132:
133:        public void removeExceptionListener(ExceptionListener l) {
134:            // Silently ignore a request to remove a listener
135:            // that is not in the Set.
136:            exceptionListeners.remove(l);
137:        }
138:
139:        public String toString() {
140:            return getClass().getName() +
141:                "[isAlive()=" + isAlive() + "]";
142:        }
143: }
```

This class uses the self-running, anonymous inner class pattern explained in Chapter 11, "Self-Running Objects." It expands on it to include support for monitoring by an ExceptionListener.

There are three constructors and they all invoke init(). The first constructor (lines 9–11) takes an ExceptionListener[] as a parameter. All of the listeners in the array will be added before the internal thread is started to ensure that no exceptions are missed. The second constructor (lines 13–17) takes a single ExceptionListener as a parameter. This listener will be added before the internal thread is started. The third constructor (lines 19–21) is used when no initial listeners are needed.

All three constructors end up calling init() (lines 23–54) to finish up the object initialization. The member variable exceptionListeners refers to a Set that is holding the group of current ExceptionListeners (line 5). I used a Set to automatically keep out duplicate listeners. Specifically, a HashSet is used and wrapped in synchronization for multithread safety (lines 26–27). For more information on using the Collections API in a multithreaded environment, see Chapter 7. If any ExceptionListeners should be added before the internal thread is started, they are passed one by one to addExceptionListener() (lines 31–35). Inside the anonymous inner class, if any exception slips through from runWork() (line 44), it is caught (line 45) and sent to sendException() (line 47).

Inside runWork() (lines 56–67), a few methods are called to produce some mock exceptions. First, makeConnection() is invoked. It declares that it might throw an IOException, so a try/catch block is used and if an IOException is thrown, it will be passed to sendException() (line 60). In the real world, this might be a serious enough error that a return should be used to let the thread die, but in this scenario, I'll let it proceed to create a null String reference (line 65). This reference is passed to determineLength() (line 66). Although determineLength() might throw a NullPointerException (and in this case it does!), no try/catch clause is required because NullPointerException is a subclass of RuntimeException. If the exception occurs, it will propagate up the call stack to run() in the inner class, and there it will be caught (line 45) and passed to sendException() (line 47).

The makeConnection() method (lines 69–83) first tries to parse the string "j20" (line 72) into an integer (line 76). It will fail because of the *j* in the string, and a NumberFormatException will be thrown. This exception is caught (line 77) and passed off to sendException() for logging purposes, and a default port number of 80 is used instead, and then processing proceeds. This might be more representative of a real-world situation: one where you want to report the error, but also want to continue with a reasonable default value. This default port number is then passed to the connectToPort() method (line 82). The connectToPort() method (lines 85–87) simply throws a new IOException with the message *connection refused*. This exception will propagate up to runWork(), will be caught there (line 59), and reported (line 60).

All that determineLength() (lines 89–91) does is to return the length of the string passed into it. In this case, it will be passed null, which will cause a NullPointerException to be thrown. This exception will propagate all the way back up to run() and be caught there (line 45).

The `private` method `sendException()` (lines 102–121) first checks to see if there are any listeners (line 103). If there currently are no listeners, a stack trace of the exception is printed to the console (line 106) and the method returns right away (line 107). If there are listeners in the set, each one has its `exceptionOccurred()` method invoked passing in the exception and a reference to `this` in case the listener needs to know in which object the exception occurred (lines 112–120).

The `addExceptionListener()` method (lines 123–131) is used to add an `ExceptionListener` to the set of listeners that will be called if an exception occurs. If `null` is passed in, it is silently ignored (line 125). Otherwise, the new listener is added to the set of current listeners. Because `Set` does not allow duplicates, if the new listener is already in the `Set`, it is silently replaced with itself (line 129). In addition, because the `Set` was wrapped in synchronization (lines 26–27), adding elements is thread-safe and will temporarily block if `sendException()` is currently notifying the listeners.

The `removeExceptionListener()` method (lines 133–137) is used to stop a specific `ExceptionListener` from receiving any more exceptions. If the specified listener is not in the `Set`, the request to remove it is silently ignored. In addition, because the `Set` was wrapped in synchronization (lines 26–27), removing elements is thread-safe and will temporarily block if `sendException()` is currently notifying the listeners.

`ExceptionCallbackMain` in Listing 12.3 demonstrates how `ExceptionCallback` can be monitored.

LISTING 12.3   ExceptionCallbackMain.java—Used to Demonstrate ExceptionCallback

```
 1: public class ExceptionCallbackMain
 2:         extends Object
 3:         implements ExceptionListener {
 4:
 5:     private int exceptionCount;
 6:
 7:     public ExceptionCallbackMain() {
 8:         exceptionCount = 0;
 9:     }
10:
11:     public void exceptionOccurred(Exception x, Object source) {
12:         exceptionCount++;
13:         System.err.println("EXCEPTION #" + exceptionCount +
14:                 ", source=" + source);
15:         x.printStackTrace();
```

```
16:      }
17:
18:      public static void main(String[] args) {
19:          ExceptionListener xListener = new ExceptionCallbackMain();
20:          ExceptionCallback ec = new ExceptionCallback(xListener);
21:      }
22: }
```

ExceptionCallbackMain implements the ExceptionListener interface (line 3) so that it will have its exceptionOccurred() method called when an object that it is monitoring throws an exception. The variable exceptionCount (line 5) is simply used to keep track of how many exceptions are reported.

When the exceptionOccurred() method is called, exceptionCount is incremented and a header message is printed along with the results of invoking toString() on the source object (lines 13–14). After that, the stack trace of the exception is printed (line 15).

In main(), an ExceptionListener reference is created by constructing an ExceptionCallbackMain (line 19). This reference is passed into the constructor of ExceptionCallback so that exceptions are reported right away (line 20). ExceptionCallback is a self-running object, so no further action is necessary to get things going.

When ExceptionCallbackMain is run, the following output occurs (your output should match):

```
 1: in constructor - initializing...
 2: EXCEPTION #1, source=ExceptionCallback[isAlive()=true]
 3: java.lang.NumberFormatException: j20
 4:     at java.lang.Integer.parseInt(Compiled Code)
 5:     at java.lang.Integer.parseInt(Integer.java:458)
 6:     at ExceptionCallback.makeConnection(ExceptionCallback.java:76)
 7:     at ExceptionCallback.runWork(ExceptionCallback.java:58)
 8:     at ExceptionCallback.access$0(ExceptionCallback.java:56)
 9:     at ExceptionCallback$1.run(ExceptionCallback.java:44)
10:     at java.lang.Thread.run(Thread.java:479)
11: EXCEPTION #2, source=ExceptionCallback[isAlive()=true]
12: java.io.IOException: connection refused
13:     at ExceptionCallback.connectToPort(ExceptionCallback.java:86)
14:     at ExceptionCallback.makeConnection(ExceptionCallback.java:82)
15:     at ExceptionCallback.runWork(ExceptionCallback.java:58)
16:     at ExceptionCallback.access$0(ExceptionCallback.java:56)
17:     at ExceptionCallback$1.run(ExceptionCallback.java:44)
18:     at java.lang.Thread.run(Thread.java:479)
19: EXCEPTION #3, source=ExceptionCallback[isAlive()=true]
20: java.lang.NullPointerException
```

```
21:      at ExceptionCallback.determineLength(ExceptionCallback.java:90)
22:      at ExceptionCallback.runWork(ExceptionCallback.java:66)
23:      at ExceptionCallback.access$0(ExceptionCallback.java:56)
24:      at ExceptionCallback$1.run(ExceptionCallback.java:44)
25:      at java.lang.Thread.run(Thread.java:479)
```

All of the rigged exceptions are passed back to ExceptionCallbackMain and printed.

Summary

It is very likely that you will write code for an active object that can throw exceptions. A typical case would be when worker threads are used to communicate across a network. Exceptions are important and should not be frivolously discarded, but the run() method cannot throw any exceptions back to another thread because it has its own call stack. The exception callback technique I showed you in this chapter can be used to pass any exceptions that might occur back to an object that can monitor them.

Thread Pooling

IN THIS CHAPTER

When design situations arise that could benefit by using many short-lived threads, thread *pooling* is a useful technique. Rather than create a brand new thread for each task, you can have one of the threads from the thread pool pulled out of the pool and assigned to the task. When the thread is finished with the task, it adds itself back to the pool and waits for another assignment.

In this chapter, I present two examples that use thread pooling. One creates a pool of threads that can be generically used to run Runnable objects. The other creates a pool of threads for servicing requests that come into a simple Hypertext Transfer Protocol (HTTP) server (a Web page server).

Benefits of Thread Pooling

Thread pooling saves the virtual machine the work of creating brand new threads for every short-lived task. In addition, it minimizes overhead associated with getting a thread started and cleaning it up after it dies. By creating a pool of threads, a single thread from the pool can be recycled over and over for different tasks.

With the thread pooling technique, you can reduce response time because a thread is already constructed and started and is simply waiting for its next task. In the case of an HTTP server, an available thread in the pool can deliver each new file requested. Without pooling, a brand new thread would have to be constructed and started before the request could be serviced.

Another characteristic of the thread pools discussed in this chapter is that they are fixed in size at the time of construction. All the threads are started, and then each goes into a wait state (which uses very few processor resources) until a task is assigned to it. This fixed size characteristic holds the number of assigned tasks to an upper limit. If all the threads are currently assigned a task, the pool is empty. New service requests can simply be rejected or can be put into a wait state until one of the threads finishes its task and returns itself to the pool. In the case of an HTTP server, this limit prevents a flood of requests from overwhelming the server to the point of servicing everyone very slowly or even crashing. You can expand on the designs presented in this chapter to include a method to support *growing* the size of the pool at runtime if you need this kind of dynamic tuning.

Considerations and Costs of Thread Pooling

Thread pooling works only when the tasks are relatively short-lived. An HTTP server fulfilling a request for a particular file is a perfect example of a task that is done best in another thread and does not run for very long. By using another thread to service each request, the server can simultaneously deliver multiple files. For tasks that run indefinitely, a normal thread is usually a better choice.

A cost of thread pooling is that all the threads in the pool are constructed and started in hopes that they will be needed. It is possible that the pool will have capacity far greater than necessary. Care should be taken to measure the utilization of the threads in the pool and tune the capacity to an optimal level.

The thread pool might also be too small. If tasks are rejected when the pool is empty (as is the case in the HTTP server example later in this chapter), a high rejection rate might be unacceptable. If the tasks are not rejected, but are held in a wait state, the waiting time could become too long. When the waiting time is long, response time worsens.

Also, some risk exists that one of the tasks assigned to a thread could cause it to deadlock or die. If thread pooling is not being used, this is still a problem. It is an even bigger problem if threads leave the pool and never return. Eventually, the pool will become empty and remain empty. You should code as carefully as possible to avoid this pitfall.

A Generic Thread Pool: ThreadPool

The class `ThreadPool`, shown in Listing 13.1, is used to pool a set of threads for generic tasks. The worker threads are running inside `ThreadPoolWorker` objects, shown in Listing 13.2. When a `ThreadPool` object is constructed, it constructs as many `ThreadPoolWorker` objects as are specified. To run a task, `ThreadPool` is passed a `Runnable` object through its `execute()` method. If a `ThreadPoolWorker` object is available, the `execute()` method removes it from the pool and hands off the `Runnable` to it for execution. If the pool is empty, the `execute()` method blocks until a worker becomes available. When the `run()` method of the `Runnable` task passed in returns, the `ThreadPoolWorker` has completed the task and puts itself back into the pool of available workers. There is no other signal that the task has been completed. If a signal is necessary, it should be coded in the task's `run()` method just before it returns.

NOTE

The `Runnable` interface is being used here in a slightly different manner than you've seen before. Earlier in the book, it was required that a `Runnable` object reference be passed to the constructor of `Thread`, and the `run()` method was the entry point for the new thread. The `run()` method was never called directly.

Here, instead of creating a new interface for thread pooling, the use of the existing `Runnable` interface is being expanded a little. Now, one of the worker threads will invoke the `run()` method directly (see line 72 of `ThreadPoolWorker` in Listing 13.2) when it is assigned to execute the `Runnable` task. I chose to use `Runnable` in this design so that passing a task to `execute()` would cause the `run()` method to be called by another thread in much the same way as `Thread`'s `start()` method causes a new thread to invoke `run()`.

LISTING 13.1   ThreadPool.java—A Thread Pool Used to Run Generic Tasks

```
1: // uses ObjectFIFO from chapter 18
2:
3: public class ThreadPool extends Object {
4:     private ObjectFIFO idleWorkers;
5:     private ThreadPoolWorker[] workerList;
6:
7:     public ThreadPool(int numberOfThreads) {
8:         // make sure that it's at least one
9:         numberOfThreads = Math.max(1, numberOfThreads);
10:
11:         idleWorkers = new ObjectFIFO(numberOfThreads);
12:         workerList = new ThreadPoolWorker[numberOfThreads];
13:
14:         for ( int i = 0; i < workerList.length; i++ ) {
15:             workerList[i] = new ThreadPoolWorker(idleWorkers);
16:         }
17:     }
18:
19:     public void execute(Runnable target)
                        ➥throws InterruptedException {
20:         // block (forever) until a worker is available
21:         ThreadPoolWorker worker =
                        ➥(ThreadPoolWorker) idleWorkers.remove();
22:         worker.process(target);
23:     }
24:
25:     public void stopRequestIdleWorkers() {
26:         try {
27:             Object[] idle = idleWorkers.removeAll();
28:             for ( int i = 0; i < idle.length; i++ ) {
29:                 ( (ThreadPoolWorker) idle[i] ).stopRequest();
30:             }
31:         } catch ( InterruptedException x ) {
32:             Thread.currentThread().interrupt(); // re-assert
33:         }
34:     }
35:
36:     public void stopRequestAllWorkers() {
37:         // Stop the idle one's first
38:         // productive.
39:         stopRequestIdleWorkers();
40:
41:         // give the idle workers a quick chance to die
42:         try { Thread.sleep(250); }
```

```
                   ➥catch ( InterruptedException x ) { }
43:
44:              // Step through the list of ALL workers.
45:              for ( int i = 0; i < workerList.length; i++ ) {
46:                  if ( workerList[i].isAlive() ) {
47:                      workerList[i].stopRequest();
48:                  }
49:              }
50:          }
51: }
```

ThreadPool serves as the central point of control for managing the worker threads. It holds a list of all the workers created in workerList (line 5). The current pool of idle ThreadPoolWorker objects is kept in a FIFO queue, idleWorkers (line 4).

NOTE

First-In-First-Out (FIFO) queues allow items to be *added* to one end of the queue and *removed* from the other end. Items are removed in the exact same order as they were added (the first item *in* is the first item *out*). A FIFO queue has a fixed capacity. If a thread invokes the add() method when the FIFO is full, it blocks waiting until another thread removes an item. If a thread invokes the remove() method when the FIFO is empty, it blocks waiting until another thread adds an item.

FIFO queues are explained and demonstrated in Chapter 18, "First-In-First-Out (FIFO) Queue." You can skip ahead to look at that technique at this time if you want to know more.

13

THREAD POOLING

The constructor (lines 7–17) takes as its only parameter an int specifying the number of worker threads that should be created for this pool (line 7). The number of threads is silently forced to be at least 1 (line 9). A new ObjectFIFO is created with a capacity large enough to hold the entire pool of worker threads (line 11). This queue holds all the workers currently available for assignment to new tasks. A ThreadPoolWorker[] is created to keep a handle on all the workers—regardless of whether they are currently idle (line 12). The for loop (lines 14–16) is used to construct each of the ThreadPoolWorker objects. Each has a reference to the pool of available workers passed to its constructor (line 15). Each one will use this reference to add itself back to the pool when it is ready to service a new task.

When an external thread wants to run a task using one of the threads in the pool, it invokes the execute() method (lines 19–23). The execute() method takes a Runnable object as a parameter. This object will have its run() method invoked by the next available worker thread. The external thread blocks waiting until an idle `ThreadPoolWorker` becomes available (line 21). When one is ready, the external thread passes the `Runnable` to the worker's `process()` method (line 22), which returns right away. The external thread returns from `execute()` and is free to continue with whatever else it has to do while the worker thread runs the `target`.

The `stopRequestIdleWorkers()` method (lines 25–34) is used to request that the internal threads of the idle workers stop as soon as possible. First, all the currently idle workers are removed from the queue (line 27). Each worker then has its `stopRequest()` method invoked (line 29). You should keep in mind that as other tasks finish, more idle workers could be added to the pool and will not be stopped until another `stopRequestIdleWorkers()` invocation occurs.

The `stopRequestAllWorkers()` method (lines 36–50) is used to request that all the workers stop as soon as possible, regardless of whether they are currently idle. First, a call to `stopRequestIdleWorkers()` is done because they can be stopped right away with negligible impact (line 39). A quarter-second break is taken to give the idle workers a chance to shut down. Next, the list of all the workers is stepped through using a `for` loop (lines 45–49). Each worker that is still alive (line 46) has its `stopRequest()` method invoked (line 47). It's possible that one or more of the idle threads will not have a chance to die before the `isAlive()` check. In this case, the `stopRequest()` method will be called twice, which should be harmless.

The `ThreadPoolWorker` class, shown in Listing 13.2, is in charge of providing the thread to run the specified task. In a real-world setting, this class should probably not be `public`, but should have package scope or be an inner class to `ThreadPool`. It is never accessed directly because `ThreadPool` acts as the sole interface to external code.

LISTING 13.2   ThreadPoolWorker.java—The Internal Assistant to ThreadPool Used to Run a Task

```
 1: // uses class ObjectFIFO from chapter 18
 2:
 3: public class ThreadPoolWorker extends Object {
 4:     private static int nextWorkerID = 0;
 5:
 6:     private ObjectFIFO idleWorkers;
 7:     private int workerID;
 8:     private ObjectFIFO handoffBox;
 9:
10:     private Thread internalThread;
11:     private volatile boolean noStopRequested;
12:
13:     public ThreadPoolWorker(ObjectFIFO idleWorkers) {
14:         this.idleWorkers = idleWorkers;
```

```
15:
16:            workerID = getNextWorkerID();
17:            handoffBox = new ObjectFIFO(1); // only one slot
18:
19:            // just before returning, the thread should be created.
20:            noStopRequested = true;
21:
22:            Runnable r = new Runnable() {
23:                    public void run() {
24:                        try {
25:                            runWork();
26:                        } catch ( Exception x ) {
27:                            // in case ANY exception slips through
28:                            x.printStackTrace();
29:                        }
30:                    }
31:                };
32:
33:            internalThread = new Thread(r);
34:            internalThread.start();
35:        }
36:
37:        public static synchronized int getNextWorkerID() {
38:            // notice: sync'd at the class level to ensure uniqueness
39:            int id = nextWorkerID;
40:            nextWorkerID++;
41:            return id;
42:        }
43:
44:        public void process(Runnable target)
                            ➥throws InterruptedException {
45:            handoffBox.add(target);
46:        }
47:
48:        private void runWork() {
49:            while ( noStopRequested ) {
50:                try {
51:                    System.out.println("workerID=" + workerID +
52:                            ", ready for work");
53:                    // Worker is ready work. This will never block
54:                    // because the idleWorker FIFO queue has
55:                    // enough capacity for all the workers.
56:                    idleWorkers.add(this);
57:
```

continues

LISTING 13.2   Continued

```
58:                          // wait here until the server adds a request
59:                          Runnable r = (Runnable) handoffBox.remove();
60:
61:                          System.out.println("workerID=" + workerID +
62:                              ", starting execution of new Runnable: " + r);
63:                          runIt(r); // catches all exceptions
64:                      } catch ( InterruptedException x ) {
65:                          Thread.currentThread().interrupt(); // re-assert
66:                      }
67:                  }
68:          }
69:
70:      private void runIt(Runnable r) {
71:          try {
72:              r.run();
73:          } catch ( Exception runex ) {
74:              // catch any and all exceptions
75:              System.err.println(
                      ➥"Uncaught exception fell through from run()");
76:              runex.printStackTrace();
77:          } finally {
78:              // Clear the interrupted flag (in case it comes back
79:              // set) so that if the loop goes again, the
80:              // handoffBox.remove() does not mistakenly
81:              // throw an InterruptedException.
82:              Thread.interrupted();
83:          }
84:      }
85:
86:      public void stopRequest() {
87:          System.out.println("workerID=" + workerID +
88:                  ", stopRequest() received.");
89:          noStopRequested = false;
90:          internalThread.interrupt();
91:      }
92:
93:      public boolean isAlive() {
94:          return internalThread.isAlive();
95:      }
96: }
```

`ThreadPoolWorker` uses the active object technique discussed in Chapter 11, "Self-Running Objects." Each worker constructed is assigned a unique `workerID` (line 7) to help clarify the output messages. In a real-world setting, individual identity tracking is not always necessary.

At the class level, the next worker ID is held in a static member variable, nextWorkerID (line 4). This variable is retrieved and incremented inside the getNextWorkerID() method (lines 37–42). It is static and synchronized so that the class-level lock is acquired before changes are made (line 37). This ensures that no two instances of ThreadPoolWorker are accidentally assigned the same workerID value.

A reference to the list of currently unused workers is held in idleWorkers (line 6). This is a reference to an ObjectFIFO queue, and the worker adds itself back to idleWorkers when it is available for assignment. The handoffBox FIFO queue (line 8) is used to pass Runnable objects to the worker in a thread-safe manner.

In the constructor (lines 13–35), the passed reference to the pool of available workers is assigned to a member variable for later access (line 14). The getNextWorkerID() method is used to obtain a unique int to store in workerID (line 16). An ObjectFIFO with a capacity of only 1 is created to be used for handing off the next Runnable task to the internal thread. The rest of the code in the constructor uses the standard pattern for an active object (see Chapter 11).

The process() method (lines 44–46) is invoked by code inside the execute() method of ThreadPool. It is used to pass the Runnable task in to the worker for processing. It is put into the handoff box to be noticed and picked up by the internal thread (line 45). Although add() declares that it will throw an InterruptedException if it is interrupted while waiting for space, this should never happen in this scenario. The handoffBox FIFO queue should be empty when the worker is available and waiting for another assignment. I chose to use an ObjectFIFO here to encapsulate the wait-notify mechanism that is necessary to signal the internal thread that a new task has arrived. It's a simpler approach and uses well-tested code.

The runWork() method (lines 48–68) follows the active object pattern of looping using the internal thread as long as no stop has been requested (line 49). Each time through the loop, the internal thread adds itself to the pool of available workers (line 56). It then waits indefinitely for an external thread to invoke the process() method and put a Runnable into the handoff box. When assigned a request, the internal thread removes it from handoffBox and casts it down from Object to Runnable (line 59). The internal thread then passes the task to the runIt() method.

The private method runIt() (lines 70–84) takes the Runnable passed (line 70) and invokes its run() method (line 72). If any exceptions slip through—especially RuntimeExceptions such as NullPointerException that can occur unexpectedly just about anywhere—they are caught to protect the worker thread (line 73). Instances of Error (and its subclasses, such as OutOfMemoryError) will break the worker, but all instances of Exception (and its subclasses) will be safely caught. If one is caught, a message and a stack trace are printed to the console (lines 75–76). Regardless of how the internal thread returns from run(), the finally clause (lines 77–83) ensures that the thread's interrupted flag is cleared (line 82) before returning to runWork(). This is important because if the flag comes back set, and noStopRequested is still true, an erroneous InterruptedException will be thrown by the remove() method on line 59.

If the interrupted flag was set by stopRequest(), no harm will be done by clearing it. This is because, after runIt() returns (line 63), the very next action is a check of the noStopRequested flag (line 49). Because stopRequest() sets this false, runWork() will return (line 25), and the worker thread will die quietly as requested. I give a full explanation of stopRequest() and isAlive() in Chapter 11.

ThreadPoolMain, shown in Listing 13.3, is used to demonstrate how ThreadPool can be used to run several tasks and then recycle its threads to run more tasks.

LISTING 13.3   ThreadPoolMain.java—Used to Demonstrate ThreadPool

```
 1: public class ThreadPoolMain extends Object {
 2:
 3:     public static Runnable makeRunnable(
 4:                 final String name,
 5:                 final long firstDelay
 6:             ) {
 7:
 8:         return new Runnable() {
 9:             public void run() {
10:                 try {
11:                     System.out.println(name +": starting up");
12:                     Thread.sleep(firstDelay);
13:                     System.out.println(
                              ➥name + ": doing some stuff");
14:                     Thread.sleep(2000);
15:                     System.out.println(name + ": leaving");
16:                 } catch ( InterruptedException ix ) {
17:                     System.out.println(
                              ➥name + ": got interrupted!");
18:                     return;
19:                 } catch ( Exception x ) {
20:                     x.printStackTrace();
21:                 }
22:             }
23:
24:             public String toString() {
25:                 return name;
26:             }
27:         };
28:     }
29:
30:     public static void main(String[] args) {
```

```
31:           try {
32:               ThreadPool pool = new ThreadPool(3);
33:
34:               Runnable ra = makeRunnable("RA", 3000);
35:               pool.execute(ra);
36:
37:               Runnable rb = makeRunnable("RB", 1000);
38:               pool.execute(rb);
39:
40:               Runnable rc = makeRunnable("RC", 2000);
41:               pool.execute(rc);
42:
43:               Runnable rd = makeRunnable("RD", 60000);
44:               pool.execute(rd);
45:
46:               Runnable re = makeRunnable("RE", 1000);
47:               pool.execute(re);
48:
49:               pool.stopRequestIdleWorkers();
50:               Thread.sleep(2000);
51:               pool.stopRequestIdleWorkers();
52:
53:               Thread.sleep(5000);
54:               pool.stopRequestAllWorkers();
55:           } catch ( InterruptedException ix ) {
56:               ix.printStackTrace();
57:           }
58:       }
59: }
```

ThreadPoolMain creates five Runnable objects and passes them to the execute() method of ThreadPool. The static method makeRunnable() (lines 3–28) is used to manufacture Runnable objects that are similar. It takes two parameters, the first being the name to use in output messages to differentiate the Runnable from the others (line 4). The second is the number of milliseconds to wait between printing the first and second messages (line 5). These two parameters are declared final so that they can be accessed from the anonymous inner class that is created (lines 8-27).

The Runnable interface is implemented on-the-fly. The two methods that are defined are toString() (lines 24–26) and run() (lines 9–22). The toString() method simply prints out name. The run() method prints several messages, all of which include the name to clarify the output (lines 11, 13, 15, and 17). The delay factor passed in is used to control the length of the first sleep() (line 12). If either sleep() is interrupted, a message is printed and the method returns (lines 16–18). If any other exception occurs, a stack trace is printed and the method returns (lines 19–21).

In main(), a ThreadPool object is constructed with the specification that it should create 3 instances of ThreadPoolWorker (line 32). The makeRunnable() method is invoked 5 times, and the results of each are passed to the execute() method (lines 34–47). All 5 will not be able to run at the same time because the pool has only 3 workers. The fourth and fifth calls to execute() will block briefly until a worker becomes available. After all 5 have been started (and at least 2 will have finished), the stopRequestIdleWorkers() method is invoked (line 49) on the pool to remove and shut down any and all workers that are currently not processing a request. After 2 seconds (line 50), another request is issued to stop all idle workers (line 51). After an additional 5 seconds have elapsed, the stopRequestAllWorkers() method is called to shut down any and all remaining workers, regardless of whether they are currently busy servicing a request (line 54).

Listing 13.4 shows possible output from running ThreadPoolMain. Your output should differ a bit because of the whims of the thread scheduler.

LISTING 13.4   Possible Output from ThreadPoolMain

```
 1: workerID=0, ready for work
 2: workerID=2, ready for work
 3: workerID=1, ready for work
 4: workerID=0, starting execution of new Runnable: RA
 5: RA: starting up
 6: workerID=2, starting execution of new Runnable: RB
 7: RB: starting up
 8: workerID=1, starting execution of new Runnable: RC
 9: RC: starting up
10: RB: doing some stuff
11: RC: doing some stuff
12: RA: doing some stuff
13: RB: leaving
14: workerID=2, ready for work
15: workerID=2, starting execution of new Runnable: RD
16: RD: starting up
17: RC: leaving
18: workerID=1, ready for work
19: workerID=1, starting execution of new Runnable: RE
20: RE: starting up
21: RA: leaving
22: workerID=0, ready for work
23: RE: doing some stuff
24: workerID=0, stopRequest() received.
25: RE: leaving
26: workerID=1, ready for work
27: workerID=1, stopRequest() received.
28: workerID=2, stopRequest() received.
29: RD: got interrupted!
```

Notice that the workers add themselves to the idle list in just about any order (output lines 1–3). However, the tasks are started in the requested order (lines 4–9). When the RB task is done (line 13), the worker that was running it, 2, adds itself back to the idle queue (line 14). Task RD was blocked inside execute(), waiting for a worker to become available. As soon as 2 puts itself on the idle queue, it is recycled and removed to run task RD (line 15). When worker 1 finishes running task RC (line 17), it is recycled to run task RE (lines 18–19). Next, worker 0 finishes task RA and adds itself to the idle queue (line 22).

The first request to stop the currently idle threads gets idle worker 0 to stop (line 24). The next request gets idle worker 1 to stop. Task RD was started with a 60-second delay and is still running. When the request to stop all the threads comes in (line 28), task RD is interrupted during its long sleep (line 29), but then returns to allow the thread to die.

A Specialized Worker Thread Pool: HttpServer

In this section, I'll show you how a simple Web page server can utilize thread-pooling techniques to service requests. In this case, the workers are specialized to handle requests for files from Web browsers.

Web browsers and Web servers communicate with each other using the Hypertext Transfer Protocol (HTTP). HTTP 1.0 (older, but simpler for this example than HTTP 1.1) is fully specified in RFC 1945, which is available at this URL:

```
http://www.w3.org/Protocols/rfc1945/rfc1945
```

The basics of this protocol consist of a *request* from the Web browser client, and a *response* from the Web server. The communication occurs over the InputStream and OutputStream pair available from a TCP/IP socket. The socket connection is initiated by the client and accepted by the server. The request-response cycle occurs while the socket is open. After the response is sent, the socket is closed. Each request uses a new socket. The client Web browser may make several simultaneous requests to a single server, each over its own socket.

The request consists of a required request line, followed by optional header lines, followed by a required blank line, followed by an optional message body. In this example, only the request line will be parsed. The request line consists of a request method, a space, the requested resource, a space, and finally the HTTP protocol version being used by the client. The only request method supported here is GET, so a sample request line would be

```
GET /dir1/dir2/file.html HTTP/1.0
```

The response consists of a required status line, followed by optional header lines, followed by a required blank line, followed by an optional message body. In this example, if the file is found, the server will return the status line, one header line with the content length, another header line with the content type, and a message body with the bytes of the requested file. The status line consists of the HTTP protocol version, a space, a response code, a space, and finally a textual explanation of the response code. In response to a GET request, a response such as the following would be produced:

```
HTTP/1.0 200 OK
Content-Length: 1967
Content-Type: text/html
<blank line>
<the 1,967 bytes of the requested file>
```

This simple Web server supports three response status lines:

```
HTTP/1.0 200 OK
HTTP/1.0 404 Not Found
HTTP/1.0 503 Service Unavailable
```

The first is used when the requested file is found, the second if the file could not be found, and the third if the server is too busy to service the request properly.

Class HttpServer

The HttpServer class, shown in Listing 13.5, serves as the main interface to the Web server and creates several HttpWorker objects (see Listing 13.6). The HttpServer object and the HttpWorker objects each have their own internal thread. The workers add themselves to a pool when they are ready to accept another HTTP request. When a request comes in, the server checks the pool for available workers and if one is available, assigns it to the connection. If none are available, the terse Service Unavailable response is returned to the client.

LISTING 13.5   HttpServer.java—A Simple Web Page Server

```
 1: import java.io.*;
 2: import java.net.*;
 3:
 4: // uses ObjectFIFO from chapter 18
 5:
 6: public class HttpServer extends Object {
 7:
 8:     // currently available HttpWorker objects
 9:     private ObjectFIFO idleWorkers;
10:
11:     // all HttpWorker objects
12:     private HttpWorker[] workerList;
13:     private ServerSocket ss;
14:
15:     private Thread internalThread;
```

```
16:        private volatile boolean noStopRequested;
17:
18:        public HttpServer(
19:                    File docRoot,
20:                    int port,
21:                    int numberOfWorkers,
22:                    int maxPriority
23:               ) throws IOException {
24:
25:            // Allow a max of 10 sockets to queue up
26:            // waiting for accpet().
27:            ss = new ServerSocket(port, 10);
28:
29:            if ( ( docRoot == null ) ||
30:                 !docRoot.exists() ||
31:                 !docRoot.isDirectory()
32:               ) {
33:
34:                throw new IOException("specified docRoot is null " +
35:                    "or does not exist or is not a directory");
36:            }
37:
38:            // ensure that at least one worker is created
39:            numberOfWorkers = Math.max(1, numberOfWorkers);
40:
41:            // Ensure:
42:            // (minAllowed + 2) <= serverPriority <= (maxAllowed - 1)
43:            // which is generally:
44:            //   3 <= serverPriority <= 9
45:            int serverPriority = Math.max(
46:                    Thread.MIN_PRIORITY + 2,
47:                    Math.min(maxPriority, Thread.MAX_PRIORITY - 1)
48:                );
49:
50:            // Have the workers run at a slightly lower priority so
51:            // that new requests are handled with more urgency than
52:            // in-progress requests.
53:            int workerPriority = serverPriority - 1;
54:
55:            idleWorkers = new ObjectFIFO(numberOfWorkers);
56:            workerList = new HttpWorker[numberOfWorkers];
57:
58:            for ( int i = 0; i < numberOfWorkers; i++ ) {
59:                // Workers get a reference to the FIFO to add
```

continues

LISTING 13.5   Continued

```
60:                    // themselves back in when they are ready to
61:                    // handle a new request.
62:                    workerList[i] = new HttpWorker(
63:                            docRoot, workerPriority, idleWorkers);
64:            }
65:
66:        // Just before returning, the thread should be
67:        // created and started.
68:        noStopRequested = true;
69:
70:        Runnable r = new Runnable() {
71:                public void run() {
72:                    try {
73:                        runWork();
74:                    } catch ( Exception x ) {
75:                        // in case ANY exception slips through
76:                        x.printStackTrace();
77:                    }
78:                }
79:            };
80:
81:        internalThread = new Thread(r);
82:        internalThread.setPriority(serverPriority);
83:        internalThread.start();
84:    }
85:
86:    private void runWork() {
87:        System.out.println(
88:                "HttpServer ready to receive requests");
89:
90:        while ( noStopRequested ) {
91:            try {
92:                Socket s = ss.accept();
93:
94:                if ( idleWorkers.isEmpty() ) {
95:                    System.out.println(
96:                        "HttpServer too busy, denying request");
97:
98:                    BufferedWriter writer =
99:                        new BufferedWriter(
100:                            new OutputStreamWriter(
101:                                s.getOutputStream()));
102:
103:                    writer.write("HTTP/1.0 503 Service " +
```

```
104:                              "Unavailable\r\n\r\n");
105:
106:                     writer.flush();
107:                     writer.close();
108:                     writer = null;
109:                 } else {
110:                     // No need to be worried that idleWorkers
111:                     // will suddenly be empty since this is the
112:                     // only thread removing items from the queue.
113:                     HttpWorker worker =
114:                             (HttpWorker) idleWorkers.remove();
115:
116:                     worker.processRequest(s);
117:                 }
118:             } catch ( IOException iox ) {
119:                 if ( noStopRequested ) {
120:                     iox.printStackTrace();
121:                 }
122:             } catch ( InterruptedException x ) {
123:                 // re-assert interrupt
124:                 Thread.currentThread().interrupt();
125:             }
126:         }
127:     }
128:
129:     public void stopRequest() {
130:         noStopRequested = false;
131:         internalThread.interrupt();
132:
133:         for ( int i = 0; i < workerList.length; i++ ) {
134:             workerList[i].stopRequest();
135:         }
136:
137:         if ( ss != null ) {
138:             try { ss.close(); } catch ( IOException iox ) { }
139:             ss = null;
140:         }
141:     }
142:
143:     public boolean isAlive() {
144:         return internalThread.isAlive();
145:     }
146:
```

13

THREAD POOLING

continues

LISTING 13.5   Continued

```
147:     private static void usageAndExit(String msg, int exitCode) {
148:         System.err.println(msg);
149:         System.err.println("Usage: java HttpServer <port> " +
150:                             "<numWorkers> <documentRoot>");
151:         System.err.println("   <port> - port to listen on " +
152:                             "for HTTP requests");
153:         System.err.println("   <numWorkers> - number of " +
154:                             "worker threads to create");
155:         System.err.println("   <documentRoot> - base " +
156:                             "directory for HTML files");
157:         System.exit(exitCode);
158:     }
159:
160:     public static void main(String[] args) {
161:         if ( args.length != 3 ) {
162:             usageAndExit("wrong number of arguments", 1);
163:         }
164:
165:         String portStr = args[0];
166:         String numWorkersStr = args[1];
167:         String docRootStr = args[2];
168:
169:         int port = 0;
170:
171:         try {
172:             port = Integer.parseInt(portStr);
173:         } catch ( NumberFormatException x ) {
174:             usageAndExit("could not parse port number from '" +
175:                     portStr + "'", 2);
176:         }
177:
178:         if ( port < 1 ) {
179:             usageAndExit("invalid port number specified: " +
180:                     port, 3);
181:         }
182:
183:         int numWorkers = 0;
184:
185:         try {
186:             numWorkers = Integer.parseInt(numWorkersStr);
187:         } catch ( NumberFormatException x ) {
188:             usageAndExit(
189:                     "could not parse number of workers from '" +
190:                     numWorkersStr + "'", 4);
```

```
191:            }
192:
193:            File docRoot = new File(docRootStr);
194:
195:            try {
196:                new HttpServer(docRoot, port, numWorkers, 6);
197:            } catch ( IOException x ) {
198:                x.printStackTrace();
199:                usageAndExit("could not construct HttpServer", 5);
200:            }
201:        }
202: }
```

HttpServer keeps a pool of idle workers in idleWorkers by using an ObjectFIFO (line 9). In addition, it keeps a list of all the HttpWorker objects it created in an array (line 12). It also uses the self-running object pattern shown in Chapter 11.

The constructor (lines 18–84) takes four parameters. The docRoot parameter (line 19) is a File referring to the directory on the server machine that is the base directory for all HTTP file requests. The port parameter (line 20) is the TCP/IP port that the Web server will be listening to for new sockets (requests). The numberOfWorkers parameter (line 21) indicates the number of HttpWorker objects that should be created to service requests. The maxPriority parameter (line 22) is used to indicate the thread priority for the thread running inside HttpServer. The threads running inside the HttpWorker objects will run at a slightly lower priority: (maxPriority - 1).

Inside the constructor, a ServerSocket is created to listen on port (line 27). It also specifies that the VM should accept up to 10 sockets more than what has been returned from the accept() method of ServerSocket. If there are any problems setting up the ServerSocket, an IOException will be thrown and will propagate out of the constructor (line 23). The docRoot parameter is then checked to be sure that it refers to an existing file and that it is also a directory (lines 29–36). The numberOfWorkers parameter is silently increased to 1 if it was less than that before (line 39). The priorities for the server thread and the worker threads are silently forced into a valid range (lines 45–53), so that

```
Thread.MIN_PRIORITY < workerPriority <
                            ↪serverPriority < Thread.MAX_PRIORITY
```

where workerPriority is just 1 less than serverPriority.

An ObjectFIFO is created with enough capacity to hold all the workers (line 55). A list of all the workers, idle or busy, is created (line 56), and each of the HttpWorker objects is constructed and added to this list (lines 58–64). Each HttpWorker is passed a reference to the idleWorkers FIFO queue so that it can add itself to the queue when it is ready to process a new request.

The rest of the constructor (lines 68–83) follows the pattern in Chapter 11, with just one minor addition: The priority of the internal thread is set before it is started (line 82).

The runWork() method (lines 86–127) is invoked by the internal thread. As long as no stop has been requested (line 90), the method continues to accept new sockets (line 92). When a socket is accepted, runWork() checks whether any idle workers are available to process the request (line 94). If the pool is empty, the request is denied, and a minimal response is created and sent back over the socket connection (lines 98–108). In HTTP message headers, an end-of-line is marked by a carriage-return, line-feed pair: "\r\n".

If an idle worker is found in the pool, it is removed (lines 113–114). The processRequest() method of that HttpWorker is invoked, and the socket that was just accepted is passed to it for servicing (line 116). If an IOException occurs in the process of accepting a socket and handing it off to be processed, and no stop has been requested, the exception will have its stack trace dumped (lines 118–121). If an InterruptedException occurs, it is caught, and the interrupt is reasserted (lines 122–124).

The stopRequest() method (lines 129–141) follows the pattern of Chapter 11, but adds another two steps. After signaling the internal thread to stop, it invokes stopRequest() on each of the HttpWorker objects. Because the internal thread may be blocked on the accept() method of ServerSocket (line 92), steps have to be taken to unblock it. It does *not* respond to being interrupted, so if the internal thread is blocked on accept(), the interrupt() call (line 131) is ineffective. To unblock the accept() method, the ServerSocket is closed (line 138), which causes accept() to throw an IOException. This IOException is caught (line 118), and if a stop has been requested, the exception is ignored. In this case, a stop was requested, so the exception thrown by forcibly closing the ServerSocket is silently ignored. This technique can be used to unblock various I/O methods that do not respond to interrupts. I explain it in detail in Chapter 15, "Breaking Out of a Blocked I/O State."

The static method usageAndExit() (lines 147–158) assists main() in reporting command-line mistakes and printing the proper command usage. For example, if HttpServer is run with no command-line arguments,

```
java HttpServer
```

the following output is produced:

```
wrong number of arguments
Usage: java HttpServer <port> <numWorkers> <documentRoot>
    <port> - port to listen on for HTTP requests
    <numWorkers> - number of worker threads to create
    <documentRoot> - base directory for HTML files
```

After the error message (line 148) and the usage lines (lines 149–156) are printed, usageAndExit() causes the VM to exit with the exit code that was passed to it (line 157).

The main() method (lines 160–201) is used to parse and validate the command-line options and to construct an HttpServer instance. HttpServer can simply be used as a class in a larger application, or it can be run as its own application using main(). First, the port number passed on the command line is converted to an int (lines 169–176) and is checked to be a positive number (lines 178–181). If either step fails, usageAndExit() is used to halt the application with an appropriate message. Second, the number of HttpWorker objects to create is parsed and validated (lines 183–191). Third, the document root directly passed on the command line is converted into a platform-independent File object (line 193). Finally, an attempt is made to construct an HttpServer object with these parameters and a maximum thread priority of 6 (line 196).

The HttpServer object's internal thread will run at a priority of 6, and each of the HttpWorker objects' internal threads will run at a priority of 5 (line 53). Constructing an HttpServer object might throw an IOException, especially if the port is already in use. If this or another problem occurs, a message is printed and the VM exits (lines 197–199). If all goes well, the constructor returns after starting the internal thread, and the main() method completes.

Class HttpWorker

HttpWorker objects, shown in Listing 13.6, are used as the specialized pool of threaded resources accessed from HttpServer. HttpWorker is similar to ThreadPoolWorker (refer to Listing 13.2), and I'll point out only the major differences.

LISTING 13.6   HttpWorker.java—The Helper Class for HttpServer

```
1: import java.io.*;
2: import java.net.*;
3: import java.util.*;
4:
5: // uses class ObjectFIFO from chapter 18
6:
7: public class HttpWorker extends Object {
8:     private static int nextWorkerID = 0;
9:
10:     private File docRoot;
11:     private ObjectFIFO idleWorkers;
12:     private int workerID;
13:     private ObjectFIFO handoffBox;
14:
15:     private Thread internalThread;
16:     private volatile boolean noStopRequested;
```

continues

LISTING 13.6   Continued

```
17:
18:      public HttpWorker(
19:              File docRoot,
20:              int workerPriority,
21:              ObjectFIFO idleWorkers
22:            ) {
23:
24:          this.docRoot = docRoot;
25:          this.idleWorkers = idleWorkers;
26:
27:          workerID = getNextWorkerID();
28:          handoffBox = new ObjectFIFO(1); // only one slot
29:
30:          // Just before returning, the thread should be
31:          // created and started.
32:          noStopRequested = true;
33:
34:          Runnable r = new Runnable() {
35:                  public void run() {
36:                      try {
37:                          runWork();
38:                      } catch ( Exception x ) {
39:                          // in case ANY exception slips through
40:                          x.printStackTrace();
41:                      }
42:                  }
43:              };
44:
45:          internalThread = new Thread(r);
46:          internalThread.setPriority(workerPriority);
47:          internalThread.start();
48:      }
49:
50:      public static synchronized int getNextWorkerID() {
51:          // synchronized at the class level to ensure uniqueness
52:          int id = nextWorkerID;
53:          nextWorkerID++;
54:          return id;
55:      }
56:
57:      public void processRequest(Socket s)
58:              throws InterruptedException {
59:
60:          handoffBox.add(s);
```

```
61:      }
62:
63:      private void runWork() {
64:          Socket s = null;
65:          InputStream in = null;
66:          OutputStream out = null;
67:
68:          while ( noStopRequested ) {
69:              try {
70:                  // Worker is ready to receive new service
71:                  // requests, so it adds itself to the idle
72:                  // worker queue.
73:                  idleWorkers.add(this);
74:
75:                  // Wait here until the server puts a request
76:                  // into the handoff box.
77:                  s = (Socket) handoffBox.remove();
78:
79:                  in = s.getInputStream();
80:                  out = s.getOutputStream();
81:                  generateResponse(in, out);
82:                  out.flush();
83:              } catch ( IOException iox ) {
84:                  System.err.println(
85:                      "I/O error while processing request, " +
86:                      "ignoring and adding back to idle " +
87:                      "queue - workerID=" + workerID);
88:              } catch ( InterruptedException x ) {
89:                  // re-assert the interrupt
90:                  Thread.currentThread().interrupt();
91:              } finally {
92:                  // Try to close everything, ignoring
93:                  // any IOExceptions that might occur.
94:                  if ( in != null ) {
95:                      try {
96:                          in.close();
97:                      } catch ( IOException iox ) {
98:                          // ignore
99:                      } finally {
100:                         in = null;
101:                     }
102:                 }
103:
104:                 if ( out != null ) {
```

continues

LISTING 13.6 Continued

```
105:                    try {
106:                        out.close();
107:                    } catch ( IOException iox ) {
108:                        // ignore
109:                    } finally {
110:                        out = null;
111:                    }
112:                }
113:
114:                if ( s != null ) {
115:                    try {
116:                        s.close();
117:                    } catch ( IOException iox ) {
118:                        // ignore
119:                    } finally {
120:                        s = null;
121:                    }
122:                }
123:            }
124:        }
125:    }
126:
127:    private void generateResponse(
128:            InputStream in,
129:            OutputStream out
130:        ) throws IOException {
131:
132:        BufferedReader reader =
133:            new BufferedReader(new InputStreamReader(in));
134:
135:        String requestLine = reader.readLine();
136:
137:        if ( ( requestLine == null ) ||
138:            ( requestLine.length() < 1 )
139:          ) {
140:
141:            throw new IOException("could not read request");
142:        }
143:
144:        System.out.println("workerID=" + workerID +
145:                ", requestLine=" + requestLine);
146:
147:        StringTokenizer st = new StringTokenizer(requestLine);
148:        String filename = null;
```

```
149:
150:        try {
151:            // request method, typically 'GET', but ignored
152:            st.nextToken();
153:
154:            // the second token should be the filename
155:            filename = st.nextToken();
156:        } catch ( NoSuchElementException x ) {
157:            throw new IOException(
158:                    "could not parse request line");
159:        }
160:
161:        File requestedFile = generateFile(filename);
162:
163:        BufferedOutputStream buffOut =
164:                new BufferedOutputStream(out);
165:
166:        if ( requestedFile.exists() ) {
167:            System.out.println("workerID=" + workerID +
168:                    ", 200 OK: " + filename);
169:
170:            int fileLen = (int) requestedFile.length();
171:
172:            BufferedInputStream fileIn =
173:                new BufferedInputStream(
174:                    new FileInputStream(requestedFile));
175:
176:            // Use this utility to make a guess obout the
177:            // content type based on the first few bytes
178:            // in the stream.
179:            String contentType =
180:                URLConnection.guessContentTypeFromStream(
181:                    fileIn);
182:
183:            byte[] headerBytes = createHeaderBytes(
184:                    "HTTP/1.0 200 OK",
185:                    fileLen,
186:                    contentType
187:                );
188:
189:            buffOut.write(headerBytes);
190:
191:            byte[] buf = new byte[2048];
```

continues

LISTING 13.6 Continued

```
192:               int blockLen = 0;
193:
194:             while ( ( blockLen = fileIn.read(buf) ) != -1 ) {
195:                 buffOut.write(buf, 0, blockLen);
196:             }
197:
198:             fileIn.close();
199:         } else {
200:             System.out.println("workerID=" + workerID +
201:                     ", 404 Not Found: " + filename );
202:
203:             byte[] headerBytes = createHeaderBytes(
204:                     "HTTP/1.0 404 Not Found",
205:                     -1,
206:                     null
207:                 );
208:
209:             buffOut.write(headerBytes);
210:         }
211:
212:         buffOut.flush();
213:     }
214:
215:     private File generateFile(String filename) {
216:         File requestedFile = docRoot; // start at the base
217:
218:         // Build up the path to the requested file in a
219:         // platform independent way. URL's use '/' in their
220:         // path, but this platform may not.
221:         StringTokenizer st = new StringTokenizer(filename, "/");
222:         while ( st.hasMoreTokens() ) {
223:             String tok = st.nextToken();
224:
225:             if ( tok.equals("..") ) {
226:                 // Silently ignore parts of path that might
227:                 // lead out of the document root area.
228:                 continue;
229:             }
230:
231:             requestedFile =
232:                 new File(requestedFile, tok);
233:         }
234:
235:         if ( requestedFile.exists() &&
```

```
236:                requestedFile.isDirectory()
237:            ) {
238:
239:            // If a directory was requested, modify the request
240:            // to look for the "index.html" file in that
241:            // directory.
242:            requestedFile =
243:                new File(requestedFile, "index.html");
244:        }
245:
246:        return requestedFile;
247:    }
248:
249:    private byte[] createHeaderBytes(
250:                String resp,
251:                int contentLen,
252:                String contentType
253:            ) throws IOException {
254:
255:        ByteArrayOutputStream baos = new ByteArrayOutputStream();
256:        BufferedWriter writer = new BufferedWriter(
257:                new OutputStreamWriter(baos));
258:
259:        // Write the first line of the response, followed by
260:        // the RFC-specified line termination sequence.
261:        writer.write(resp + "\r\n");
262:
263:        // If a length was specified, add it to the header
264:        if ( contentLen != -1 ) {
265:            writer.write(
266:                "Content-Length: " + contentLen + "\r\n");
267:        }
268:
269:        // If a type was specified, add it to the header
270:        if ( contentType != null ) {
271:            writer.write(
272:                "Content-Type: " + contentType + "\r\n");
273:        }
274:
275:        // A blank line is required after the header.
276:        writer.write("\r\n");
277:        writer.flush();
278:
```

13

THREAD POOLING

continues

LISTING 13.6 Continued

```
279:            byte[] data = baos.toByteArray();
280:            writer.close();
281:
282:            return data;
283:        }
284:
285:        public void stopRequest() {
286:            noStopRequested = false;
287:            internalThread.interrupt();
288:        }
289:
290:        public boolean isAlive() {
291:            return internalThread.isAlive();
292:        }
293: }
```

The constructor of `HttpWorker` (lines 18–48) is passed `docRoot`, the base directory for files (line 19), the priority to use for the internal thread (line 20), and a reference to the idle worker pool. The internal thread priority is set just before the thread is started (line 46). A one-slot handoff box is created (line 28) for passing the socket accepted in the `HttpServer` thread to this worker's internal thread.

The `processRequest()` method (lines 57–61) is invoked by the `HttpServer` object and puts the reference to the new socket into the handoff box. It should never block because a worker will add itself to the idle pool only when it is ready to process a new request. Also, the server will invoke the `processRequest()` methods only on workers it just removed from the idle pool.

The `runWork()` method (lines 63–125) is where the internal thread does the bulk of the processing. Basically, the internal thread loops until a stop is requested (lines 68–124). Each time through, the worker adds itself to the server's list of idle workers (line 73). It then blocks, indefinitely waiting for an assignment to be dropped off in its handoff box (line 77). When a `Socket` reference is picked up, the worker retrieves the `InputStream` and `OutputStream` from the reference and passes them to the `generateResponse()` method (lines 79–81). After `generateResponse()` has read the request from the `InputStream` and written the proper response to the `OutputStream`, the `OutputStream` is flushed to ensure that the data is pushed through any buffering (line 82). If an `IOException` occurs during any of this, a message is printed (lines 83–87). Whether or not an `IOException` occurs, the `finally` clause is used to ensure that the streams and socket are closed properly (lines 91–112). Next, the `while` expression is re-evaluated (line 68). If no stop request has been made, the worker adds itself back to the idle queue and waits for its next assignment.

The generateResponse() method (lines 127–213) is used to analyze the HTTP request on the InputStream and generate an appropriate HTTP response on the OutputStream. The raw OutputStream from the socket is wrapped in a BufferedOutputStream to data transfer efficiently (lines 163–164). The raw InputStream from the socket is wrapped in a BufferedReader (lines 132–133). The first line is read from the request (line 135–142) and broken up into tokens to pick out the filename (lines 147–159). The generateFile() method is used to create a new File instance that refers to the requested file (line 161).

Inside generateFile() (lines 215–247), the request is parsed on the '/' character to build up a new File object starting from docRoot. When the parsing is complete, a check is done to see if the requested file is a directory (lines 235–236). If a directory was requested, "index.html" is appended as the default file to return from a directory (lines 242–243).

If the requested file is found, it is sent back to the client (lines 166–198). First, the length of the file in bytes is determined for the response header (line 170). Next, the content type for the file is guessed by the use of the static method guessContentTypeFromStream() on the class java.net.URLConnection (lines 179–181). Then the createHeaderBytes() method (see the following description) is used to format the response header and convert it to an array of bytes (lines 183–187). This header information is written to the stream (line 189), followed by the contents of the file (lines 191–198).

If the requested file is not found, a brief response indicating that this is sent back to the client (lines 199–209). The createHeaderBytes() method is used to format a 404 Not Found response (lines 203–207). These bytes are written back to the client (line 209).

The createHeaderBytes() method (lines 249–283) is used to format a response header and write it to an array of bytes. The resp string passed in is written as is (lines 255–261). If a valid content length is passed in, the Content-Length: header field is appended (lines 264–267). If a content type is specified, the Content-Type: header field is appended (lines 270–273). All headers end with a blank line (line 276). The resulting byte[] is passed back to the caller (lines 185–188).

Sample Files to Be Served

To demonstrate this simple Web server, I created a directory named htmldir, with the following files and subdirectory:

```
./htmldir/index.html
./htmldir/images/five.gif
./htmldir/images/four.gif
./htmldir/images/one.gif
./htmldir/images/three.gif
./htmldir/images/two.gif
```

The `index.html` file is the main file served, and it makes references to the graphics stored in the `images` subdirectory. When the server is launched, `htmldir` will be used as the document root directory.

The `index.html` file, shown in Listing 13.7, uses the Hypertext Markup Language (HTML) to specify the layout of a Web page. You can read more about it at this URL:

`http://www.w3.org/TR/REC-html32.html`

LISTING 13.7   index.html—An HTML File for Demonstrating HttpServer

```
 1: <html>
 2: <head><title>Thread Pooling - 1</title></head>
 3: <body bgcolor="#FFFFFF">
 4: <center>
 5: <table border="2" cellspacing="5" cellpadding="2">
 6: <tr>
 7:    <td valign="top"><img src="./images/one.gif"></td>
 8:    <td>Thread pooling helps to save the VM the work of creating and
 9:        destroying threads when they can be easily recycled.</td>
10: </tr>
11: <tr>
12:    <td valign="top"><img src="./images/twoDOESNOTEXIST.gif"></td>
13:    <td>Thread pooling reduces response time because the worker
14:        thread is already created, started, and running. It's only
15:        only waiting for the signal to <b><i>go</i></b>!</td>
16: </tr>
17: <tr>
18:    <td valign="top"><img src="./images/three.gif"></td>
19:    <td>Thread pooling holds resource usage to a predetermined upper
20:        limit. Instead of starting a new thread for every request
21:        received by an HTTP server, a set of workers is available to
22:        service requests. When this set is being completely used by
23:        other requests, the server does not increase its load, but
24:        rejects requests until a worker becomes available.</td>
25: </tr>
26: <tr>
27:    <td valign="top"><img src="./images/four.gif"></td>
28:    <td>Thread pooling generally works best when a thread is
29:        needed for only a brief period of time.</td>
30: </tr>
31: <tr>
32:    <td valign="top"><img src="./images/five.gif"></td>
33:    <td>When using the thread pooling technique, care must
34:        be taken to reasonably ensure that threads don't become
35:        deadlocked or die.<td>
36: </tr>
```

```
37: </table>
38: </body>
39: </html>
```

This HTML file makes references to 5 images that will subsequently be requested by the Web browser. All but one of them exists. Instead of `two.gif`, `twoDOESNOTEXIST.gif` is requested (line 12) to cause the simple server to generate a `404 Not Found` response.

Running HttpServer with 3 Workers

First, I'll show you what happens when the `HttpServer` application is run with only 3 workers in the pool:

```
java HttpServer 2001 3 htmldir
```

The Web server will be listening on port `2001` for connections. If you can't use this port on your system, specify a different one. (Generally, Web servers listen to port `80`, but on some systems, only privileged users can run processes that listen to ports less than `1024`.) The second command-line argument indicates that 3 workers should be created to service requests. The third argument is the directory where the HTML files are located. On my machine they are in `htmldir`, which is a subdirectory of the current directory. You can use a fully qualified pathname if necessary.

Possible output from this simple Web server application is shown in Listing 13.8.

LISTING 13.8 Possible Output from HttpServer with 3 Threads

```
 1: HttpServer ready to receive requests
 2: workerID=0, requestLine=GET / HTTP/1.0
 3: workerID=0, 200 OK: /index.html
 4: HttpServer too busy, denying request
 5: HttpServer too busy, denying request
 6: workerID=1, requestLine=GET /images/one.gif HTTP/1.0
 7: workerID=0, requestLine=GET /images/five.gif HTTP/1.0
 8: workerID=2, requestLine=GET /images/twoDOESNOTEXIST.gif HTTP/1.0
 9: workerID=1, 200 OK: /images/one.gif
10: workerID=0, 200 OK: /images/five.gif
11: workerID=2, 404 Not Found: /images/twoDOESNOTEXIST.gif
12: workerID=1, requestLine=GET / HTTP/1.0
13: workerID=1, 200 OK: /index.html
14: workerID=0, requestLine=GET /images/twoDOESNOTEXIST.gif HTTP/1.0
15: workerID=2, requestLine=GET /images/three.gif HTTP/1.0
16: workerID=1, requestLine=GET /images/four.gif HTTP/1.0
17: workerID=0, 404 Not Found: /images/twoDOESNOTEXIST.gif
18: workerID=2, 200 OK: /images/three.gif
19: workerID=1, 200 OK: /images/four.gif
```

When the server is up and running and ready to received requests, it prints a message (line 1). I used Netscape 4.5 to request the following URL:

```
http://localhost:2001/
```

> **NOTE**
>
> The hostname `localhost` is used in TCP/IP networking to generically refer to the current machine. If you don't have `localhost` defined on your system, you can supply another hostname or an IP address. Additionally, you can consider adding the following line to your machine's hosts file (it may be `/etc/hosts`, `C:\windows\hosts`, or something else):
>
> ```
> 127.0.0.1    localhost
> ```

The Web browser requests a connection on port `2001` of `localhost`. Then, it asks for filename `/`. This request is handed off to worker `0` (line 2). The worker responds with `/index.html` (line 3). When the browser parses this HTML file, it very quickly requests the 5 graphic files referenced. Only 3 workers are available, so when the server is flooded with these requests, it denies 2 of them (lines 4–5). Worker 1 is assigned to `/images/one.gif` (line 6), finds it, and sends it (line 9). Worker 0 is assigned to `/images/five.gif` (line 7), finds it, and sends it (line 10). Worker 2 looks for the nonexistent file `/images/twoDOESNOTEXIST.gif` (line 8), can't find it, and sends back the `404 Not Found` response (line 11).

After this, the browser looks like Figure 13.1. Notice that the graphics for 2, 3, and 4 are missing. The graphic for 2 does not exist and looks slightly different than the surrogate images supplied by Netscape for 3 and 4.

To attempt to get the other graphics to load, I clicked on the Location field in the Web browser and pressed the Enter key to retrieve the page again. Referring back to Listing 13.8, you can see that the `/` file is requested again (line 12) and served back by worker 1 (line 13). This time, only 3 images are requested because the other 2 are already loaded. The `twoDOESNOTEXIST.gif` image is requested again (line 14) by the Web browser in the hope that the image is now there. It is not, and the `404 Not Found` response is sent again (line 17). Workers are available this time to send `three.gif` and `four.gif` (lines 15–16 and 18–19).

After this second try, the browser looks like Figure 13.2. Notice that everything is drawn, except for the missing `twoDOESNOTEXIST.gif` image.

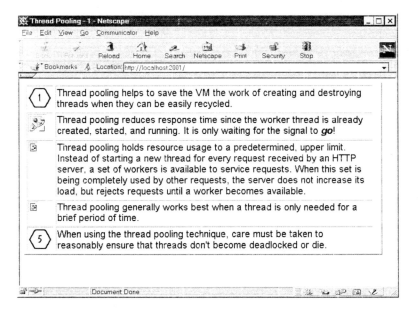

FIGURE 13.1

The first attempt to retrieve the page, with only 3 worker threads.

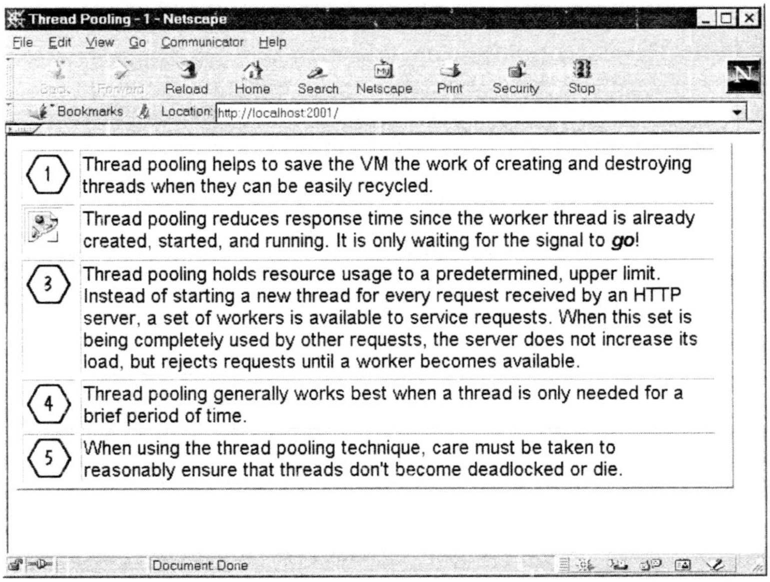

FIGURE 13.2

The second attempt to retrieve the page.

Running HttpServer with 10 Workers

If, instead, `HttpServer` is started with 10 workers,

```
java HttpServer 2001 10 htmldir
```

more resources are available to meet the demands. The Web browser is closed and restarted, and the same URL is requested. This time, the server output is shown in Listing 13.9. The Web browser looks like Figure 13.2 on the first try.

LISTING 13.9   Possible Output from HttpServer with 10 Threads

```
 1: HttpServer ready to receive requests
 2: workerID=0, requestLine=GET / HTTP/1.0
 3: workerID=0, 200 OK: /index.html
 4: workerID=4, requestLine=GET /images/four.gif HTTP/1.0
 5: workerID=1, requestLine=GET /images/one.gif HTTP/1.0
 6: workerID=2, requestLine=GET /images/twoDOESNOTEXIST.gif HTTP/1.0
 7: workerID=3, requestLine=GET /images/three.gif HTTP/1.0
 8: workerID=4, 200 OK: /images/four.gif
 9: workerID=1, 200 OK: /images/one.gif
10: workerID=3, 200 OK: /images/three.gif
11: workerID=2, 404 Not Found: /images/twoDOESNOTEXIST.gif
12: workerID=6, requestLine=GET /images/five.gif HTTP/1.0
13: workerID=6, 200 OK: /images/five.gif
```

With 10 workers running, none of the requests are denied—the simple Web server has idle workers to spare. When you run the server, you are likely to see slightly different ordering of requests and responses.

You can expand on this design to include a short wait before requests are denied. This would allow some time for a worker to finish up and put itself back into the idle queue.

Summary

Thread pooling can be used when a thread is needed for a relatively short time. Thread pooling allows a thread to be assigned to a task and, when the task completes, to be recycled for use in another task. Because threads in the pool are already up and running, response time is usually reduced. The number of threads in the pool can be fixed to an upper limit to prevent a sudden overloading of the application.

I showed you how to create a generic pool of threads to execute the `run()` method of objects that implement the `Runnable` interface. Then, I showed you how to create a specialized pool of threads to service HTTP requests. Both these techniques can be elaborated on to provide more specialized and robust solutions in your code.

Waiting for the Full Timeout

IN THIS CHAPTER

In Java, two threads can communicate with each other through the wait-notify mechanism (see Chapter 8, "Inter-thread Communication"). When a thread invokes one of the wait() methods of Object, an optional timeout value can be specified. The thread does not return from the wait(long msTimeout) call until it is notified by another thread, the specified millisecond timeout has elapsed, or it is interrupted. It is obvious when it has been interrupted as an InterruptedException is thrown. But other than that, wait() does not return any information as to whether it was notified or just timed out.

There will be times when you'll want to write code that waits up to a specified amount of time for a condition to be met. The waiting thread might be notified many times before the condition is met. Imagine that you want a thread to wait for an integer value to increase from 5 to a minimum of 20. Every time the value is changed by another thread, the waiting thread is notified. The notification doesn't necessarily mean that value being waited for has been met, but simply that the value has been changed. The thread waiting for the condition to be met will return from wait(long msTimeout) either because the timeout has expired, or because it has been notified. In this chapter, I'll show you a technique for differentiating between these two possibilities to ensure that the full timeout elapses when required.

Accidentally Returning Early

In EarlyReturn, shown in Listing 14.1, one thread blocks waiting for the internal value to reach a specified minimum while a second thread changes the value. Every time the second thread changes the value, it notifies any waiting threads. The first thread is waiting (up to the timeout) for a particular value to be reached. In this example, the first thread will accidentally return before the value is reached *and* before the timeout occurs.

LISTING 14.1   EarlyReturn.java—An Example of an Accidental Early Return

```
 1: public class EarlyReturn extends Object {
 2:     private volatile int value;
 3:
 4:     public EarlyReturn(int initialValue) {
 5:         value = initialValue;
 6:     }
 7:
 8:     public synchronized void setValue(int newValue) {
 9:         if ( value != newValue ) {
10:             value = newValue;
11:             notifyAll();
12:         }
13:     }
```

```
14:
15:     public synchronized boolean waitUntilAtLeast(
16:               int minValue,
17:               long msTimeout
18:           ) throws InterruptedException {
19:
20:         System.out.println("entering waitUntilAtLeast() - " +
21:               "value=" + value +
22:               ",minValue=" + minValue);
23:
24:         if ( value < minValue ) {
25:             wait(msTimeout);
26:         }
27:
28:         System.out.println("leaving waitUntilAtLeast() - " +
29:               "value=" + value +
30:               ",minValue=" + minValue);
31:
32:         // May have timed out, or may have met value,
33:         // calc return value.
34:         return ( value >= minValue );
35:     }
36:
37:     public static void main(String[] args) {
38:         try {
39:             final EarlyReturn er = new EarlyReturn(0);
40:
41:             Runnable r = new Runnable() {
42:                     public void run() {
43:                         try {
44:                             Thread.sleep(1500);
45:                             er.setValue(2);
46:                             Thread.sleep(500);
47:                             er.setValue(3);
48:                             Thread.sleep(500);
49:                             er.setValue(4);
50:                         } catch ( Exception x ) {
51:                             x.printStackTrace();
52:                         }
53:                     }
54:                 };
55:
56:             Thread t = new Thread(r);
```

continues

LISTING 14.1   Continued

```
57:                t.start();
58:
59:                System.out.println(
60:                        "about to: waitUntilAtLeast(5, 3000)");
61:                long startTime = System.currentTimeMillis();
62:                boolean retVal = er.waitUntilAtLeast(5, 3000);
63:                long elapsedTime =
64:                        System.currentTimeMillis() - startTime;
65:
66:                System.out.println("after " + elapsedTime +
67:                        " ms, retVal=" + retVal);
68:            } catch ( InterruptedException ix ) {
69:                ix.printStackTrace();
70:            }
71:        }
72: }
```

EarlyReturn holds the last value set in the private member variable value (line 2). The constructor (lines 4–6) simply sets value to some initial state. The setValue() method (lines 8–13) is synchronized so it blocks until it can acquire the lock on this (the EarlyReturn instance). After the lock is acquired, setValue() checks to see if newValue is really new (line 9) to avoid unnecessary notifications. If it is different, setValue() sets value (line 10) and then notifies any and all threads waiting on this object for a change (line 11).

The waitUntilAtLeast() method (lines 15–35) is used by threads that want to block—up to a specified amount of time—waiting for value to increase to the minimum specified. Any number of threads can be blocked simultaneously inside waitUntilAtLeast() as notifyAll() is used inside setValue() to be sure that all waiters are notified of the change. If the minimum value has not yet been met (line 24), the thread waits for up to msTimeout milliseconds for it to increase (line 25). Regardless of whether the minimum was achieved or the wait timed out, the boolean returned is calculated based on the current setting of value. If value is at least minValue, true is returned. Otherwise, false is returned to indicate a timeout.

The main() method (lines 37–71) is used to create a new thread to call setValue(), while the main thread continues to block on waitUntilAtLeast(). A new EarlyReturn object is created with an initial value of 0 (line 39). It is final so that it can be accessed from the anonymous inner class. A new Runnable is declared (lines 41–54) to alternately sleep and call setValue() with new values (lines 44–49). Next, the Thread for this Runnable is created and started (lines 56–57).

The main thread then takes note of the current time to be able to measure how long waitUntilAtLeast() blocks (line 61). The waitUntilAtLeast() method is invoked with a minimum value to wait for of 5, and a maximum time to wait of three seconds (line 60). The boolean returned from `waitUntilAtLeast()` is captured into `retVal`. The elapsed time that the thread was blocked inside `waitUntilAtLeast()` is calculated (lines 63–64) and printed along with `retVal` (lines 66–67).

When `EarlyReturn` is run, output much like the following is produced (your output should almost match except for slightly different times):

```
about to: waitUntilAtLeast(5, 3000)
entering waitUntilAtLeast() - value=0,minValue=5
leaving waitUntilAtLeast() - value=2,minValue=5
after 1370 ms, retVal=false
```

The problem with this is that `waitUntilAtLeast()` returns before the minimum value of 5 is reached *and* before the timeout of 3000 milliseconds has elapsed. This isn't what `waitUntilAtLeast()` was designed to do!

What's going on here is that after the new thread sleeps for 1500 milliseconds, it invokes `er.setValue(2)` (line 45). Inside `setValue()`, the `notifyAll()` (line 11) causes any and all waiting threads to return from `wait()`. By the time this happens, the `main` thread has been waiting for a little more than one second (line 25). The `main` thread returns from `wait()`, prints the current values, and calculates the `boolean` to return. In this case, `false` is returned because it was waiting for a minimum of 5 and `value` was only set to 2. What is needed here is a way to tell if `wait()` returned because the timeout was reached, or if it returned because it was notified. If it returned because it was notified, a check needs to be added to see if `minValue` has been met yet. If it hasn't been met, `wait()` should be invoked again. If it returned because it timed out, no more waiting should be done.

Determining If wait() Should Be Invoked Again

When `wait()` returns, it could be because the timeout was reached or because it was notified. In fact, in the `EarlyReturn` example there are four ways that a thread blocked on `wait()` becomes unblocked. They are listed in Table 14.1.

TABLE 14.1   What To Do After wait() Returns

State	Action
`InterruptedException` thrown	Pass on `InterruptedException`
Timed out	Return `false` right away
Notified, minimum is met	Return `true` right away
Notified, minimum not met	Calculate time remaining, wait again

The `InterruptedException` is obvious and should be allowed to propagate up to indicate that the `wait()` call was terminated early—probably because someone wants this thread to clean up and die as soon as possible. Other than that, `wait()` is declared to return `void` so there is no direct indication as to whether the thread timed out or was notified. If it was notified, it's possible that the condition has not yet been met and more time is available to wait again. When the thread returns from `wait()`, two calculations need to be done: one to see if the condition has been met, and another to see how much more time remains before the timeout value has been reached. If the condition has not been met and there is some time remaining, the thread should wait again. For this second call to `wait()`, a revised (shorter) timeout value needs to be passed.

`EarlyReturnFix`, shown in Listing 14.2, is basically the same as `EarlyReturn` except with a new `waitUntilAtLeast()` method (lines 15–42). It deals with all of the issues listed in Table 14.1.

LISTING 14.2   EarlyReturnFix.java—Waiting for the Full Timeout

```
 1: public class EarlyReturnFix extends Object {
 2:     private volatile int value;
 3:
 4:     public EarlyReturnFix(int initialValue) {
 5:         value = initialValue;
 6:     }
 7:
 8:     public synchronized void setValue(int newValue) {
 9:         if ( value != newValue ) {
10:             value = newValue;
11:             notifyAll();
12:         }
13:     }
14:
15:     public synchronized boolean waitUntilAtLeast(
16:                     int minValue,
17:                     long msTimeout
18:                 ) throws InterruptedException {
19:
20:         System.out.println("entering waitUntilAtLeast() - " +
21:                 "value=" + value + ",minValue=" + minValue);
22:
23:         long endTime = System.currentTimeMillis() + msTimeout;
24:         long msRemaining = msTimeout;
25:
26:         while ( ( value < minValue ) && ( msRemaining > 0L ) ) {
27:             System.out.println("in waitUntilAtLeast() - " +
28:                     "about to: wait(" + msRemaining + ")");
29:             wait(msRemaining);
30:             msRemaining = endTime - System.currentTimeMillis();
31:             System.out.println("in waitUntilAtLeast() - " +
```

```
32:                          "back from wait(), new msRemaining=" +
33:                          msRemaining);
34:           }
35:
36:         System.out.println("leaving waitUntilAtLeast() - " +
37:                  "value=" + value + ",minValue=" + minValue);
38:
39:         // May have timed out, or may have met value,
40:         // calc return value.
41:         return ( value >= minValue );
42:     }
43:
44:     public static void main(String[] args) {
45:         try {
46:             final EarlyReturnFix er = new EarlyReturnFix(0);
47:
48:             Runnable r = new Runnable() {
49:                     public void run() {
50:                         try {
51:                             Thread.sleep(1500);
52:                             er.setValue(2);
53:                             Thread.sleep(500);
54:                             er.setValue(3);
55:                             Thread.sleep(500);
56:                             er.setValue(4);
57:                         } catch ( Exception x ) {
58:                             x.printStackTrace();
59:                         }
60:                     }
61:                 };
62:
63:             Thread t = new Thread(r);
64:             t.start();
65:
66:             System.out.println(
67:                     "about to: waitUntilAtLeast(5, 3000)");
68:             long startTime = System.currentTimeMillis();
69:             boolean retVal = er.waitUntilAtLeast(5, 3000);
70:             long elapsedTime =
71:                     System.currentTimeMillis() - startTime;
72:
73:             System.out.println("after " + elapsedTime +
74:                     " ms, retVal=" + retVal);
75:         } catch ( InterruptedException ix ) {
76:             ix.printStackTrace();
77:         }
78:     }
79: }
```

The waitUntilAtLeast() method declares that it might throw an InterruptedException (line 18) if one occurs while it is blocked waiting. This way, no action is assumed if the thread is interrupted, but the method passes on the exception to signal that it did not complete normally.

Inside waitUntilAtLeast(), the current time is added to the timeout value specified to determine endTime (line 23). This time limit will be used to determine if the thread should wait again. The number of milliseconds left before endTime is held in the local variable msRemaining. It is initially the full timeout value (line 24), but is recalculated each time wait() returns (line 30).

The while loop is entered only if the minimum value has not already been met *and* a positive timeout value was passed in (line 26). Inside the loop, after printing an informational message, the thread waits for the current msRemaining (line 29). Regardless of whether it returns from wait() because it was notified or because it timed out, a new msRemaining is calculated based on the difference between the time limit and the current system clock time (line 30).

After another informational message is printed, the while loop expression is re-evaluated (line 26). If the minimum value *has been* reached, the body of the while loop will not be re-executed. If the minimum value has still not been met, either the thread was notified early, or the wait() timed out. If the wait() timed out, msRemaining should be less than or equal to 0, and the body of the loop will not be re-executed. If it was early notification, the body of the loop will be re-executed.

CAUTION

It is important to be careful that 0 is not *accidentally* passed to wait(). A timeout of 0 indicates that the wait() should *never time out*. Line 26 in the EarlyReturnFix example checks that the new timeout value is greater than 0.

When the while is done (or if it was skipped altogether), an informational message is printed (lines 36–37). The boolean value returned is calculated based on whether or not the minimum was reached (line 41). The waitUntilAtLeast() method can return for many reasons:

- A negative or zero timeout was specified.
- The waiting exceeded the limit specified by the timeout.
- The minimum had been met or exceeded *before* the method was invoked.
- The minimum was reached before the timeout.

Regardless of why waitUntilAtLeast() is returning, the return value is true if the minimum is currently met, and is false otherwise.

Listing 14.3 shows possible output from running EarlyReturnFix. Your output is likely to differ slightly on the exact millisecond figures.

LISTING 14.3   Output from a Particular Run of EarlyReturnFix (with Line Numbers Added)

```
 1: about to: waitUntilAtLeast(5, 3000)
 2: entering waitUntilAtLeast() - value=0,minValue=5
 3: in waitUntilAtLeast() - about to: wait(3000)
 4: in waitUntilAtLeast() - back from wait(), new msRemaining=1570
 5: in waitUntilAtLeast() - about to: wait(1570)
 6: in waitUntilAtLeast() - back from wait(), new msRemaining=1080
 7: in waitUntilAtLeast() - about to: wait(1080)
 8: in waitUntilAtLeast() - back from wait(), new msRemaining=590
 9: in waitUntilAtLeast() - about to: wait(590)
10: in waitUntilAtLeast() - back from wait(), new msRemaining=-20
11: leaving waitUntilAtLeast() - value=4,minValue=5
12: after 3020 ms, retVal=false
```

Each time through the loop and just before the wait(), the number of milliseconds passed to wait() is displayed (output lines 3, 5, 7, and 9). The "main" thread keeps calling setValue() with a new value, but it never gets up to 5. Each time setValue() is called, the waiting thread is notified, returns from wait(), recalculates the number of milliseconds remaining, and determines if it should loop again. Finally, msRemaining is non-positive, and the loop breaks (line 10). The minimum has not been met in 3020 milliseconds, so false is returned (line 12).

The next section shows a more complete example that allows a timeout value of 0 to be passed in and removes all the clutter of the main() method.

A General-Purpose Wait-Until Pattern

In this section, I'll show you a more complete example that can be used as a model and expanded to fit your real-world needs when a wait-until scenario is needed. The main enhancement is to allow a timeout of 0 to be passed in just as wait() allows.

On Object, a call to

```
public final void wait() throws InterruptedException
```

behaves as if 0 was passed into

```
public final void wait(long timeout) throws InterruptedException
```

in the sense that it waits until notified, regardless of how much real time elapses. FullWait, shown in Listing 14.4, expands upon EarlyNotifyFix to allow msTimeout to be 0 when invoking waitUntilAtLeast() to indicate that the thread should not return until the minimum is reached—regardless of how much time elapses.

LISTING 14.4   FullWait.java—A Good Base Design Pattern to Use for Wait-Until Situations

```
 1: public class FullWait extends Object {
 2:     private volatile int value;
 3:
 4:     public FullWait(int initialValue) {
 5:         value = initialValue;
 6:     }
 7:
 8:     public synchronized void setValue(int newValue) {
 9:         if ( value != newValue ) {
10:             value = newValue;
11:             notifyAll();
12:         }
13:     }
14:
15:     public synchronized boolean waitUntilAtLeast(
16:                 int minValue,
17:                  long msTimeout
18:             ) throws InterruptedException {
19:
20:         if ( msTimeout == 0L ) {
21:             while ( value < minValue ) {
22:                 wait();  // wait indefinitely until notified
23:             }
24:
25:             // condition has finally been met
26:             return true;
27:         }
28:
29:         // only wait for the specified amount of time
30:         long endTime = System.currentTimeMillis() + msTimeout;
31:         long msRemaining = msTimeout;
32:
33:         while ( ( value < minValue ) && ( msRemaining > 0L ) ) {
34:             wait(msRemaining);
35:             msRemaining = endTime - System.currentTimeMillis();
36:         }
37:
```

```
38:          // May have timed out, or may have met value,
39:          // calc return value.
40:          return ( value >= minValue );
41:      }
42:
43:      public String toString() {
44:          return getClass().getName() + "[value=" + value + "]";
45:      }
46: }
```

FullWait is based upon EarlyReturnFix with the main() method and the informational messages removed. The waitUntilAtLeast() method (lines 15–41) has been expanded to support a timeout of 0.

If msTimeout is equal to 0 (line 20), the while loop continues to wait() until the minimum value has been met (lines 21–23). If the minimum was met before waitUntilAtLeast() was invoked, the while loop's body is never executed, and true is returned. Otherwise, the body of the while loop is executed and the thread waits until notified (line 22). Every time setValue() is called with a new value, any and all waiting threads are notified—regardless of what value was set. This means that the wait() (line 22) might be notified before the minimum is met. If this happens, the while loop will simply execute again, causing the thread to go into another wait-until-notified state. If the minimum is ever met, the while loop will terminate and true will be returned (line 26).

If msTimeout is non-zero, waitUntilAtLeast() will behave exactly as it did in EarlyReturnFix (see detailed description earlier). It will continually wait until either the timeout has been reached, or the minimum has been met (lines 30–40).

FullWaitMain in Listing 14.5 constructs a FullWait and demonstrates different scenarios.

LISTING 14.5   FullWaitMain.java—Code to Demonstrate FullWait

```
1: public class FullWaitMain extends Object {
2:      private FullWait fullwait;
3:      private Thread internalThread;
4:      private volatile boolean noStopRequested;
5:
6:      public FullWaitMain(FullWait fw) {
7:          fullwait = fw;
8:
9:          noStopRequested = true;
```

continues

LISTING 14.5 Continued

```
10:            Runnable r = new Runnable() {
11:                public void run() {
12:                    try {
13:                        runWork();
14:                    } catch ( Exception x ) {
15:                        x.printStackTrace();
16:                    }
17:                }
18:            };
19:
20:            internalThread = new Thread(r);
21:            internalThread.start();
22:        }
23:
24:        private void runWork() {
25:            int count = 6;
26:
27:            while ( noStopRequested ) {
28:                fullwait.setValue(count);
29:                System.out.println("just set value to " + count);
30:                count++;
31:
32:                try {
33:                    Thread.sleep(1000);
34:                } catch ( InterruptedException x ) {
35:                    // reassert interrupt
36:                    Thread.currentThread().interrupt();
37:                }
38:            }
39:        }
40:
41:        public void stopRequest() {
42:            noStopRequested = false;
43:            internalThread.interrupt();
44:        }
45:
46:        public boolean isAlive() {
47:            return internalThread.isAlive();
48:        }
49:
50:        public static void waitfor(FullWait fw, int val, long limit)
51:                    throws InterruptedException {
52:
53:            System.out.println("about to waitUntilAtLeast(" +
```

```
54:                    val + ", " + limit + ") ... ");
55:
56:        long startTime = System.currentTimeMillis();
57:        boolean retVal = fw.waitUntilAtLeast(val, limit);
58:        long endTime = System.currentTimeMillis();
59:
60:        System.out.println("waited for " +
61:                ( endTime - startTime ) +
62:                " ms, retVal=" + retVal + "\n--------------");
63:    }
64:
65:    public static void main(String[] args) {
66:        try {
67:            FullWait fw = new FullWait(5);
68:            FullWaitMain fwm = new FullWaitMain(fw);
69:
70:            Thread.sleep(500);
71:
72:            // should return true before 10 seconds
73:            waitfor(fw, 10, 10000L);
74:
75:            // should return true right away --already >= 6
76:            waitfor(fw, 6, 5000L);
77:
78:            // should return true right away
79:            //    --already >= 6 (negative time ignored)
80:            waitfor(fw, 6, -1000L);
81:
82:            // should return false right away --not there
83:            // yet & negative time
84:            waitfor(fw, 15, -1000L);
85:
86:            // should return false after 5 seconds
87:            waitfor(fw, 999, 5000L);
88:
89:            // should eventually return true
90:            waitfor(fw, 20, 0L);
91:
92:            fwm.stopRequest();
93:        } catch ( InterruptedException x ) {
94:            System.err.println("*unexpectedly* interrupted " +
95:                    "somewhere in main()");
96:        }
97:    }
98: }
```

In main(), a FullWait object is constructed with an initial value of 5 (line 67). This object is passed as a parameter to the constructor of FullWaitMain (line 68). The main thread then sleeps to let the internal thread get up and going (line 70). This sleep is not a critical step, but helps ensure that the other thread has a chance to run for a little bit (about half a second) before the waiting begins.

The constructor for FullWaitMain (lines 6–22) stores the reference to the FullWait object, starts the internal thread running, and then returns. The internal thread invokes runWork() (lines 24–39). In the while loop inside runWork(), the thread invokes the setValue() method on the FullWait object (line 28). Initially, it passes 6 to setValue() and then sleeps for one second (line 33). Each time through the while loop, the value passed is incremented by 1 (line 30). The internal thread continues to increment the value once per second until a stop request is received.

Back in main(), several calls to the static method waitFor() are made. The waitFor() method (lines 50–63) is used to call waitUntilAtLeast() on the FullWait object. Each time informational messages are printed, the time spent inside waitUntilAtLeast() is measured, and the return value is captured.

The first waitFor() call (line 73) waits for up to 10 seconds for the value to reach 10. The value should be at about 6 when this is called, and because it increments once each second, it should easily reach a minimum value of 10 before the timeout.

The next call (line 76) waits for the value to reach 6, but it is already at least 10, so it returns true right away. The next call (line 80) passes a negative timeout value, but because the minimum value passed is 6 and it has already been reached, it should return true right away and ignore the negative timeout. The next call (line 84) passes in a minimum of 15 (which has not yet been reached) and a negative timeout. The negative timeout causes it to return right away, and because the minimum was not reached, false is returned. The next call (line 87) will only wait five seconds for the value to reach 999. This won't happen in that time, so after five seconds, it returns false. The last call (line 90) specifies a minimum of 20 and a timeout of 0. A timeout of 0 will cause it to wait indefinitely until the minimum value is reached. A few seconds later, 20 is reached, and true is returned.

For cleanup purposes, stopRequest() is called (line 92) to shut down the internal thread. Most of main() is in a try/catch block (lines 66–96) because an InterruptedException might be thrown. In this case, this occurrence is quite unexpected and a message to that effect is printed if it happens (lines 94–95).

Listing 14.6 shows output from a particular run of FullWaitMain. Your times will probably vary from this a bit, but the true and false return values should match exactly for each of the scenarios.

LISTING 14.6   Sample Output from Running FullWaitMain (Your Output Will Differ)

```
 1: just set value to 6
 2: about to waitUntilAtLeast(10, 10000) ...
 3: just set value to 7
 4: just set value to 8
 5: just set value to 9
 6: just set value to 10
 7: waited for 3630 ms, retVal=true
 8: ---------------
 9: about to waitUntilAtLeast(6, 5000) ...
10: waited for 0 ms, retVal=true
11: ---------------
12: about to waitUntilAtLeast(6, -1000) ...
13: waited for 0 ms, retVal=true
14: ---------------
15: about to waitUntilAtLeast(15, -1000) ...
16: waited for 0 ms, retVal=false
17: ---------------
18: about to waitUntilAtLeast(999, 5000) ...
19: just set value to 11
20: just set value to 12
21: just set value to 13
22: just set value to 14
23: waited for 5000 ms, retVal=false
24: ---------------
25: about to waitUntilAtLeast(20, 0) ...
26: just set value to 15
27: just set value to 16
28: just set value to 17
29: just set value to 18
30: just set value to 19
31: just set value to 20
32: waited for 5050 ms, retVal=true
33: ---------------
```

Summary

As you build larger applications in Java, you will sometimes need to specify limits as to how long you want one thread to wait for a certain condition to be met. Because the wait() method returns when notified and returns when it times out, steps need to be taken to keep track of how much more time (if any) should be spent waiting for the condition to be met. In this chapter, I showed you a technique for doing this by calculating an ending time before waiting, and then waiting again if this time has not yet been reached.

Breaking Out of a Blocked I/O State

Unfortunately, as of Java 1.2, most blocking I/O statements in the JDK still ignore interrupt requests. This presents a problem when you want to have a thread stop waiting on the I/O operation and do something else—typically to clean up and die. This problem generally arises in situations where data is read from a stream intermittently. A common case is a conversation between a client and server over a socket's streams. Typically in this scenario, a thread blocks for long periods of time on a stream waiting for another request to come across the line.

In this chapter, I'll present some techniques that you can use to get a thread to break out of a blocked I/O state. I'll begin by demonstrating the blocking problem with an example.

The read() Method Ignores Interrupts and Stop Requests

The read() methods of most subclasses of InputStream in the JDK ignore interrupts and don't even respond when the blocked thread is *stopped*. One notable exception is the PipedInputStream class, whose read() method does respond to interrupts by throwing an InterruptedIOException.

The class DefiantStream (see Listing 15.1) shows that when a thread is blocked waiting to read data from the keyboard, it does not respond to an interrupt or a stop request.

LISTING 15.1   DefiantStream.java—Demonstration of interrupt() and stop() Being Ignored

```
 1: import java.io.*;
 2:
 3: public class DefiantStream extends Object {
 4:     public static void main(String[] args) {
 5:         final InputStream in = System.in;
 6:
 7:         Runnable r = new Runnable() {
 8:             public void run() {
 9:                 try {
10:                     System.err.println(
11:                         "about to try to read from in");
12:                     in.read();
13:                     System.err.println("just read from in");
14:                 } catch ( InterruptedIOException iiox ) {
15:                     iiox.printStackTrace();
16:                 } catch ( IOException iox ) {
17:                     iox.printStackTrace();
18:                 //} catch ( InterruptedException ix ) {
```

```
19:                    //  InterruptedException is never thrown!
20:                    //  ix.printStackTrace();
21:                } catch ( Exception x ) {
22:                    x.printStackTrace();
23:                } finally {
24:                    Thread currThread =
25:                            Thread.currentThread();
26:                    System.err.println("inside finally:\n" +
27:                        "  currThread=" + currThread + "\n" +
28:                        "  currThread.isAlive()=" +
29:                        currThread.isAlive());
30:                }
31:            }
32:        };
33:
34:        Thread t = new Thread(r);
35:        t.start();
36:
37:        try { Thread.sleep(2000); }
38:        catch ( InterruptedException x ) { }
39:
40:        System.err.println("about to interrupt thread");
41:        t.interrupt();
42:        System.err.println("just interrupted thread");
43:
44:        try { Thread.sleep(2000); }
45:        catch ( InterruptedException x ) { }
46:
47:        System.err.println("about to stop thread");
48:        // stop() is being used here to show that the extreme
49:        // action of stopping a thread is also ineffective.
50:        // Because stop() is deprecated, the compiler issues
51:        // a warning.
52:        t.stop();
53:        System.err.println("just stopped thread, t.isAlive()=" +
54:                t.isAlive());
55:
56:        try { Thread.sleep(2000); }
57:        catch ( InterruptedException x ) { }
58:
59:        System.err.println("t.isAlive()=" + t.isAlive());
60:        System.err.println("leaving main()");
61:    }
62: }
```

The `InputStream` used in this example is `System.in` (line 5). It simply passes lines of input from the keyboard to the stream. Input is passed a line at a time from the keyboard to `System.in` so the Enter key must be pressed to send the characters typed. A new `Runnable` and a new `Thread` are created (lines 7–35) to block trying to read bytes from `in` (`System.in`). This new thread will block on `read()` until a line is typed in on the keyboard and the Enter key is pressed (line 12). If any of several types of `Exception` are thrown, a stack trace is printed (lines 14–22). Regardless of how the thread leaves the `try` block, it will jump into the `finally` block and print some information (lines 23–30).

After the new thread is spawned, it is given a chance (two seconds) to get to the `read()` by the main thread (lines 37–38). Next, the `main` thread interrupts the new thread (lines 40–42) to see if this has any effect. After another two seconds pass (lines 44–45), the `main` thread takes a harsher approach and *tries* to stop the new thread (lines 47–53). Just in case the thread takes a while to notice, the `main` thread sleeps for yet another two seconds (lines 56–57) before checking again (line 59).

Listing 15.2 shows the output produced when `DefiantStream` is run. A few seconds after the "leaving main()" message was printed, I typed the "INPUT FROM KEYBOARD" line to supply the blocked thread with some data.

LISTING 15.2   Output from DefiantStream

```
 1: about to try to read from in
 2: about to interrupt thread
 3: just interrupted thread
 4: about to stop thread
 5: just stopped thread, t.isAlive()=false
 6: t.isAlive()=false
 7: leaving main()
 8: --------->INPUT FROM KEYBOARD
 9: inside finally:
10:    currThread=Thread[Thread-0,5,main]
11:    currThread.isAlive()=false
```

The `interrupt()` was ignored (lines 2–3), and quite surprisingly, so was the `stop()` (lines 4–5). Notice that `isAlive()` returns `false`, but the thread remains blocked on the `read()`! Even after the `main` thread dies (line 7), the blocked thread continues to wait for input. After a few more seconds, I typed line 8 to supply data to the `System.in` stream. Sure enough, the `read()` was no longer blocked, and the *dead* thread printed the last three lines! The *somewhat dead* thread is able to print that it is not alive (line 11). The thread is *somewhat dead* in the sense that it returns `false` from `isAlive()`, but it continues to execute code! Note that `read()` probably threw an instance of `ThreadDeath` (a subclass of `Error`) after it got some data, so that only the `finally` block was executed as the thread shut down.

> **NOTE**
>
> The example shows the behavior as of JDK 1.2 on the Win32 platform. As of this writing, there are several bug reports/requests for enhancement (depending on your perspective) pending on these issues. Future releases of the JDK might change this behavior. You can always use `DefiantStream` to check to see how a particular JavaVM responds.

Closing a Stream to Break Out of the Blocked State

Although `interrupt()` and `stop()` are ignored by a thread blocked on `read()`, the thread can usually be unblocked by closing the stream with another thread.

The next series of examples presents three classes: `CalcServer`, `CalcWorker`, and `CalcClient`. These classes work with each other to demonstrate in a somewhat realistic client/server configuration the technique of closing a blocked stream with another thread.

`CalcServer` is started first and waits for socket connections on port `2001`. When a connection is received, `CalcServer` creates a new `CalcWorker` to handle the detailed communications with the client. In a separate VM on the same machine, `CalcClient` is launched and creates a connection to `CalcServer`. `CalcClient` makes one request of the server, and then leaves the line open. The server (through `CalcWorker`) responds to the first request and then blocks on a socket `read()` waiting for an additional request—a request that never comes. After running for 15 seconds, the server shuts down and uses the stream closing technique to get the thread inside `CalcWorker` to break out of its blocked state.

Class CalcServer and Breaking Out of a Blocked accept()

The class `CalcServer` (see Listing 15.3) waits for socket connections from `CalcClient`. It passes the socket to a new instance of `CalcWorker` to manage the server side of the client session. When `CalcServer` is shut down, it uses another closing technique to break the internal thread out of its blocked state on the `accept()` method of `ServerSocket`.

LISTING 15.3   CalcServer.java—Listens for Connections from CalcClient

```
 1: import java.io.*;
 2: import java.net.*;
 3: import java.util.*;
 4:
 5: public class CalcServer extends Object {
 6:     private ServerSocket ss;
 7:     private List workerList;
 8:
 9:     private Thread internalThread;
10:     private volatile boolean noStopRequested;
11:
12:     public CalcServer(int port) throws IOException {
13:         ss = new ServerSocket(port);
14:         workerList = new LinkedList();
15:
16:         noStopRequested = true;
17:         Runnable r = new Runnable() {
18:                 public void run() {
19:                     try {
20:                         runWork();
21:                     } catch ( Exception x ) {
22:                         // in case ANY exception slips through
23:                         x.printStackTrace();
24:                     }
25:                 }
26:             };
27:
28:         internalThread = new Thread(r);
29:         internalThread.start();
30:     }
31:
32:     private void runWork() {
33:         System.out.println(
34:                 "in CalcServer - ready to accept connections");
35:
36:         while ( noStopRequested ) {
37:             try {
38:                 System.out.println(
39:                         "in CalcServer - about to block " +
40:                         "waiting for a new connection");
41:                 Socket sock = ss.accept();
42:                 System.out.println(
43:                     "in CalcServer - received new connection");
```

```
44:                workerList.add(new CalcWorker(sock));
45:            } catch ( IOException iox ) {
46:                if ( noStopRequested ) {
47:                    iox.printStackTrace();
48:                }
49:            }
50:        }
51:
52:        // stop all the workers that were created
53:        System.out.println("in CalcServer - putting in a " +
54:                "stop request to all the workers");
55:        Iterator iter = workerList.iterator();
56:        while ( iter.hasNext() ) {
57:            CalcWorker worker = (CalcWorker) iter.next();
58:            worker.stopRequest();
59:        }
60:
61:        System.out.println("in CalcServer - leaving runWork()");
62:    }
63:
64:    public void stopRequest() {
65:        System.out.println(
66:                "in CalcServer - entering stopRequest()");
67:        noStopRequested = false;
68:        internalThread.interrupt();
69:
70:        if ( ss != null ) {
71:            try {
72:                ss.close();
73:            } catch ( IOException x ) {
74:                // ignore
75:            } finally {
76:                ss = null;
77:            }
78:        }
79:    }
80:
81:    public boolean isAlive() {
82:        return internalThread.isAlive();
83:    }
84:
```

continues

LISTING 15.3 Continued

```
85:     public static void main(String[] args) {
86:         int port = 2001;
87:
88:         try {
89:             CalcServer server = new CalcServer(port);
90:             Thread.sleep(15000);
91:             server.stopRequest();
92:         } catch ( IOException x ) {
93:             x.printStackTrace();
94:         } catch ( InterruptedException x ) {
95:             // ignore
96:         }
97:     }
98: }
```

CalcServer is a self-running object, and 15 seconds after it is created, its stopRequest() method is called (lines 89–91). CalcServer creates a ServerSocket to listen to port 2001 for client connections (line 13). In its runWork() method, the internal thread blocks on the accept() method of ServerSocket waiting for new socket connections (line 41). When a connection is received, the socket is passed to a new instance of CalcWorker, and a reference to this CalcWorker is added to workerList (line 44).

When stopRequest() is invoked, noStopRequested is set to false (line 67) and the internal thread is interrupted (line 68). Much like a blocked read(), the accept() method ignores interrupts. To get the accept() method to throw an exception, the ServerSocket is closed (lines 70–78). Back in runWork(), the internal thread jumps down to the catch block (lines 45–49) because of this IOException. A stack trace is printed only if a stop has *not* been requested (lines 46–48) and in this case, no trace is printed because the closing of the ServerSocket caused the exception. The internal thread continues on and invokes stopRequest() on each of the CalcWorker objects (lines 55–59).

Class CalcWorker and Breaking Out of a Blocked read()

The class CalcWorker (see Listing 15.4) handles the server-side portion of a client session. It creates streams off the socket and communicates with CalcClient over them. When it is shut down, it uses a closing technique to break the internal thread out of its blocked state on the read() method of InputStream.

LISTING 15.4   CalcWorker.java—The Server-Side Portion of a Client Session

```
 1: import java.io.*;
 2: import java.net.*;
 3:
 4: public class CalcWorker extends Object {
 5:     private InputStream sockIn;
 6:     private OutputStream sockOut;
 7:     private DataInputStream dataIn;
 8:     private DataOutputStream dataOut;
 9:
10:     private Thread internalThread;
11:     private volatile boolean noStopRequested;
12:
13:     public CalcWorker(Socket sock) throws IOException {
14:         sockIn = sock.getInputStream();
15:         sockOut = sock.getOutputStream();
16:
17:         dataIn = new DataInputStream(
18:                 new BufferedInputStream(sockIn));
19:         dataOut = new DataOutputStream(
20:                 new BufferedOutputStream(sockOut));
21:
22:         noStopRequested = true;
23:         Runnable r = new Runnable() {
24:                 public void run() {
25:                     try {
26:                         runWork();
27:                     } catch ( Exception x ) {
28:                         // in case ANY exception slips through
29:                         x.printStackTrace();
30:                     }
31:                 }
32:             };
33:
34:         internalThread = new Thread(r);
35:         internalThread.start();
36:     }
37:
38:     private void runWork() {
39:         while ( noStopRequested ) {
40:             try {
```

continues

LISTING 15.4 Continued

```
41:                          System.out.println("in CalcWorker - about to " +
42:                                  "block waiting to read a double");
43:                      double val = dataIn.readDouble();
44:                      System.out.println(
45:                              "in CalcWorker - read a double!");
46:                  dataOut.writeDouble(Math.sqrt(val));
47:                  dataOut.flush();
48:              } catch ( IOException x ) {
49:                  if ( noStopRequested ) {
50:                      x.printStackTrace();
51:                      stopRequest();
52:                  }
53:              }
54:          }
55:
56:          // In real-world code, be sure to close other streams and
57:          // the socket as part of the clean-up. Omitted here for
58:          // brevity.
59:
60:          System.out.println("in CalcWorker - leaving runWork()");
61:      }
62:
63:      public void stopRequest() {
64:          System.out.println(
65:                  "in CalcWorker - entering stopRequest()");
66:          noStopRequested = false;
67:          internalThread.interrupt();
68:
69:          if ( sockIn != null ) {
70:              try {
71:                  sockIn.close();
72:              } catch ( IOException iox ) {
73:                  // ignore
74:              } finally {
75:                  sockIn = null;
76:              }
77:          }
78:
79:          System.out.println(
80:                  "in CalcWorker - leaving stopRequest()");
81:      }
82:
83:      public boolean isAlive() {
84:          return internalThread.isAlive();
85:      }
86: }
```

`CalcWorker` is a self-running object that spends most of its time with its internal thread blocked waiting to read a new request from the client. It keeps a reference to the raw `InputStream` retrieved from the socket for use in closing (line 14). It then wraps the raw streams with `DataInputStream` and `DataOutputStream` to get the desired functionality (lines 17–20).

TIP

When using the closing technique to try to get a blocked `read()` to unblock, always attempt to close the *rawest* stream possible. In this example, the rawest `InputStream` is the one returned by the `getInputStream()` method on `Socket`. This maximizes the chances that the stream will throw an exception.

Inside `runWork()`, the internal thread blocks waiting to read a `double` from the client (line 43). When the thread reads a `double`, it calculates the mathematical square root of the `double` and sends the resulting `double` back down to the client (lines 46–47). The thread then goes back to its blocked state waiting to read more data from the client.

When `stopRequest()` is invoked, `noStopRequested` is set to `false` (line 66) and the internal thread is interrupted (line 67). A blocked `read()` does not respond to an interrupt, so the socket's input stream is closed (lines 69–77) causing the blocked `read()` to throw an `IOException`. Back up in `runWork()`, the internal thread jumps down to the catch block (lines 48–53). A stack trace is printed only if a stop has *not* been requested (lines 49–52), and in this case, no trace is printed because the closing of the stream caused the exception.

CAUTION

Invoking `close()` on an `InputStream` can sometimes block. This can occur if both `read()` and `close()` are synchronized. The thread blocked on the `read()` has the instance lock. Meanwhile, another thread is trying to invoke `close()` and blocks trying to get exclusive access to the lock. As of JDK 1.2, `BufferedInputStream` has added the synchronized modifier to its `close()` method (it wasn't present in 1.0 and 1.1). This is not indicated in the Javadoc, but is shown in the source code and through reflection. If this is the case, the closing technique will not work unless done on the underlying stream.

Class CalcClient

The class `CalcClient` (see Listing 15.5) is run in a different VM than `CalcServer`, but on the same machine. It creates a connection to the server and makes only one request. After that, it keeps the connection open, but does no further communication.

LISTING 15.5   CalcClient.java—Code to Test CalcWorker

```
 1: import java.io.*;
 2: import java.net.*;
 3:
 4: public class CalcClient extends Object {
 5:     public static void main(String[] args) {
 6:         String hostname = "localhost";
 7:         int port = 2001;
 8:
 9:         try {
10:             Socket sock = new Socket(hostname, port);
11:
12:             DataInputStream in = new DataInputStream(
13:                 new BufferedInputStream(sock.getInputStream()));
14:             DataOutputStream out = new DataOutputStream(
15:                 new BufferedOutputStream(sock.getOutputStream()));
16:
17:             double val = 4.0;
18:             out.writeDouble(val);
19:             out.flush();
20:
21:             double sqrt = in.readDouble();
22:             System.out.println("sent up " + val +
                           ➡", got back " + sqrt);
23:
24:             // Don't ever send another request, but stay alive in
25:             // this eternally blocked state.
26:             Object lock = new Object();
27:             while ( true ) {
28:                 synchronized ( lock ) {
29:                     lock.wait();
30:                 }
31:             }
32:         } catch ( Exception x ) {
33:             x.printStackTrace();
34:         }
35:     }
36: }
```

`CalcClient` is crudely written to simply show the minimal communication necessary. It creates a socket connection to the server, extracts the data streams, and wraps them to get a `DataInputStream` and a `DataOutputStream` (lines 10–15). Then it writes a `double` over to the server and waits for a different `double` to be returned (lines 17–21). After that, `CalcClient` keeps the socket connection up, but does not communicate with the server any more. Instead, it goes into an infinite wait state (lines 26–31).

Output When Run

When `CalcClient` is run, it produces one line of output and waits to be killed:

```
sent up 4.0, got back 2.0
```

On the server side, `CalcServer` and `CalcWorker` produce the output shown in Listing 15.6. Notice that when the stop request comes in, no exceptions are printed and the worker and server shut down in an orderly manner.

LISTING 15.6   Output from CalcServer and CalcWorker

```
 1: in CalcServer - ready to accept connections
 2: in CalcServer - about to block waiting for a new connection
 3: in CalcServer - received new connection
 4: in CalcServer - about to block waiting for a new connection
 5: in CalcWorker - about to block waiting to read a double
 6: in CalcWorker - read a double!
 7: in CalcWorker - about to block waiting to read a double
 8: in CalcServer - entering stopRequest()
 9: in CalcServer - putting in a stop request to all the workers
10: in CalcWorker - entering stopRequest()
11: in CalcWorker - leaving stopRequest()
12: in CalcServer - leaving runWork()
13: in CalcWorker - leaving runWork()
```

Throwing InterruptedIOException When Interrupted

The `read()` method on `PipedInputStream` will throw a subclass of `IOException` called `InterruptedIOException` if the blocked thread is interrupted while waiting for bytes to arrive. This is very useful functionality that I would like to see implemented across the whole `java.io` package. Until that happens, other techniques have to be used to get out of the blocked state. The next example illustrates such a technique.

Class ThreadedInputStream

The class `ThreadedInputStream` (see Listing 15.7) is a subclass of `FilterInputStream` and responds to interrupts by throwing an `InterruptedIOException`. It uses an internal thread to read from the underlying stream and loads the bytes into a `ByteFIFO` (discussed in Chapter 18, "First-In-First-Out (FIFO) Queue"). This read-ahead mechanism can help speed performance but does carry the cost of an extra thread running in the VM. Although very useful, instances of `ThreadedInputStream` are not particularly lightweight and should be used sparingly in an application.

LISTING 15.7   ThreadedInputStream.java—Interruptible read() Capability

```
 1: import java.io.*;
 2:
 3: // uses SureStop from chapter 16
 4: // uses ByteFIFO from chapter 18
 5:
 6: public class ThreadedInputStream extends FilterInputStream {
 7:     private ByteFIFO buffer;
 8:
 9:     private volatile boolean closeRequested;
10:     private volatile boolean eofDetected;
11:     private volatile boolean ioxDetected;
12:     private volatile String ioxMessage;
13:
14:     private Thread internalThread;
15:     private volatile boolean noStopRequested;
16:
17:     public ThreadedInputStream(InputStream in, int bufferSize) {
18:         super(in);
19:
20:         buffer = new ByteFIFO(bufferSize);
21:
22:         closeRequested = false;
23:         eofDetected = false;
24:         ioxDetected = false;
25:         ioxMessage = null;
26:
27:         noStopRequested = true;
28:         Runnable r = new Runnable() {
29:                 public void run() {
30:                     try {
31:                         runWork();
32:                     } catch ( Exception x ) {
```

```
33:                         // in case ANY exception slips through
34:                         x.printStackTrace();
35:                     }
36:                 }
37:             };
38:
39:         internalThread = new Thread(r);
40:         internalThread.setDaemon(true);
41:         internalThread.start();
42:     }
43:
44:     public ThreadedInputStream(InputStream in) {
45:         this(in, 2048);
46:     }
47:
48:     private void runWork() {
49:         byte[] workBuf = new byte[buffer.getCapacity()];
50:
51:         try {
52:             while ( noStopRequested ) {
53:                 int readCount = in.read(workBuf);
54:
55:                 if ( readCount == -1 ) {
56:                     signalEOF();
57:                     stopRequest();
58:                 } else if ( readCount > 0 ) {
59:                     addToBuffer(workBuf, readCount);
60:                 }
61:             }
62:         } catch ( IOException iox ) {
63:             if ( !closeRequested ) {
64:                 ioxMessage = iox.getMessage();
65:                 signalIOX();
66:             }
67:         } catch ( InterruptedException x ) {
68:             // ignore
69:         } finally {
70:             // no matter what, make sure that eofDetected is set
71:             signalEOF();
72:         }
73:     }
74:
```

continues

LISTING 15.7   Continued

```
75:        private void signalEOF() {
76:            synchronized ( buffer ) {
77:                eofDetected = true;
78:                buffer.notifyAll();
79:            }
80:        }
81:
82:        private void signalIOX() {
83:            synchronized ( buffer ) {
84:                ioxDetected = true;
85:                buffer.notifyAll();
86:            }
87:        }
88:
89:        private void signalClose() {
90:            synchronized ( buffer ) {
91:                closeRequested = true;
92:                buffer.notifyAll();
93:            }
94:        }
95:
96:        private void addToBuffer(byte[] workBuf, int readCount)
97:                throws InterruptedException {
98:
99:            // Create an array exactly as large as the number of
100:           // bytes read and copy the data into it.
101:           byte[] addBuf = new byte[readCount];
102:           System.arraycopy(workBuf, 0, addBuf, 0, addBuf.length);
103:
104:           buffer.add(addBuf);
105:        }
106:
107:        private void stopRequest() {
108:            if ( noStopRequested ) {
109:                noStopRequested = false;
110:                internalThread.interrupt();
111:            }
112:        }
113:
114:        public void close() throws IOException {
115:            if ( closeRequested ) {
116:                // already closeRequested, just return
117:                return;
118:            }
```

```
119:            signalClose();
120:
121:            SureStop.ensureStop(internalThread, 10000);
122:            stopRequest();
123:
124:            // Use a new thread to close "in" in case it blocks
125:            final InputStream localIn = in;
126:            Runnable r = new Runnable() {
127:                    public void run() {
128:                        try {
129:                            localIn.close();
130:                        } catch ( IOException iox ) {
131:                            // ignore
132:                        }
133:                    }
134:                };
135:
136:            Thread t = new Thread(r, "in-close");
137:            // give up when all other non-daemon threads die
138:            t.setDaemon(true);
139:            t.start();
140:        }
141:
142:        private void throwExceptionIfClosed() throws IOException {
143:            if ( closeRequested ) {
144:                throw new IOException("stream is closed");
145:            }
146:        }
147:
148:        // Throws InterruptedIOException if the thread blocked on
149:        // read() is interrupted while waiting for data to arrive.
150:        public int read()
151:                throws InterruptedIOException, IOException {
152:
153:            // Using read(byte[]) to keep code in one place —makes
154:            // single-byte read less efficient, but simplifies
155:            // the coding.
156:            byte[] data = new byte[1];
157:            int ret = read(data, 0, 1);
158:
159:            if ( ret != 1 ) {
160:                return -1;
161:            }
162:
```

continues

LISTING 15.7 Continued

```
163:            return data[0] & 0x000000FF;
164:        }
165:
166:        // Throws InterruptedIOException if the thread blocked on
167:        // read() is interrupted while waiting for data to arrive.
168:        public int read(byte[] dest)
169:                throws InterruptedIOException, IOException {
170:
171:            return read(dest, 0, dest.length);
172:        }
173:
174:        // Throws InterruptedIOException if the thread blocked on
175:        // read() is interrupted while waiting for data to arrive.
176:        public int read(
177:                byte[] dest,
178:                int offset,
179:                int length
180:            ) throws InterruptedIOException, IOException {
181:
182:            throwExceptionIfClosed();
183:
184:            if ( length < 1 ) {
185:                return 0;
186:            }
187:
188:            if ( ( offset < 0 ) ||
189:                ( ( offset + length ) > dest.length )
190:                ) {
191:
192:                throw new IllegalArgumentException(
193:                    "offset must be at least 0, and " +
194:                    "(offset + length) must be less than or " +
195:                    "equal to dest.length. " +
196:                    "offset=" + offset +
197:                    ", (offset + length )=" + ( offset + length ) +
198:                    ", dest.length=" + dest.length);
199:            }
200:
201:            byte[] data = removeUpTo(length);
202:
203:            if ( data.length > 0 ) {
204:                System.arraycopy(data, 0, dest, offset, data.length);
205:                return data.length;
206:            }
207:
```

```
208:          // no data
209:          if ( eofDetected ) {
210:              return -1;
211:          }
212:
213:          // no data and not end of file, must be exception
214:          stopRequest();
215:
216:          if ( ioxMessage == null ) {
217:              ioxMessage = "stream cannot be read";
218:          }
219:
220:          throw new IOException(ioxMessage);
221:      }
222:
223:      private byte[] removeUpTo(int maxRead) throws IOException {
224:          // Convenience method to assist read(byte[], int, int).
225:          // Waits until at least one byte is ready, EOF is
226:          // detected,  an IOException is thrown, or the
227:          // stream is closed.
228:          try {
229:              synchronized ( buffer ) {
230:                  while ( buffer.isEmpty() &&
231:                          !eofDetected &&
232:                          !ioxDetected &&
233:                          !closeRequested
234:                        ) {
235:
236:                      buffer.wait();
237:                  }
238:
239:                  // If stream was closed while waiting,
240:                  // get out right away.
241:                  throwExceptionIfClosed();
242:
243:                  // Ignore eof and exception flags for now, see
244:                  // if any data remains.
245:                  byte[] data = buffer.removeAll();
246:
247:                  if ( data.length > maxRead ) {
248:                      // Pulled out too many bytes,
249:                      // put excess back.
250:                      byte[] putBackData =
```

continues

LISTING 15.7 Continued

```
251:                            new byte[data.length - maxRead];
252:                    System.arraycopy(data, maxRead,
253:                            putBackData, 0, putBackData.length);
254:                    buffer.add(putBackData);
255:
256:                    byte[] keepData = new byte[maxRead];
257:                    System.arraycopy(data, 0,
258:                            keepData, 0, keepData.length);
259:                    data = keepData;
260:                }
261:
262:                return data;
263:            }
264:        } catch ( InterruptedException ix ) {
265:            // convert to an IOException
266:            throw new InterruptedIOException("interrupted " +
267:                "while waiting for data to arrive for reading");
268:        }
269:    }
270:
271:    public long skip(long n) throws IOException {
272:        throwExceptionIfClosed();
273:
274:        if ( n <= 0 ) {
275:            return 0;
276:        }
277:
278:        int skipLen = (int) Math.min(n, Integer.MAX_VALUE);
279:        int readCount = read(new byte[skipLen]);
280:
281:        if ( readCount < 0 ) {
282:            return 0;
283:        }
284:
285:        return readCount;
286:    }
287:
288:    public int available() throws IOException {
289:        throwExceptionIfClosed();
290:        return buffer.getSize();
291:    }
292:
293:    public boolean markSupported() {
294:        return false;
```

```
295:          }
296:
297:          public synchronized void mark(int readLimit) {
298:              // ignore method calls, mark not supported
299:          }
300:
301:          public synchronized void reset() throws IOException {
302:              throw new IOException(
303:                    "mark-reset not supported on this stream");
304:          }
305: }
```

ThreadedInputStream extends FilterInputStream (line 6) and passes the InputStream handed to the constructor up the constructor for the superclass (line 18). The superclass has a protected member variable called in that holds a reference to the underlying InputStream; this reference is used throughout ThreadedInputStream.

The internal thread basically just reads as much data as it can and loads it into the ByteFIFO buffer (lines 52–61). If the buffer is full, the internal thread blocks waiting for some data to be read out of the buffer (line 104). When the internal thread gets to the end of the file (EOF), it sets a flag (lines 75–80). If the internal thread encounters an IOException while reading into the buffer, it sets a flag (lines 82–87). The ByteFIFO is used for all of the wait-notify signaling.

When an external thread comes in to read some data, it gets the data from the ByteFIFO buffer (lines 201–220, 223–269). The external thread pays attention to the EOF and exception flags only if there is no more data in the buffer. This delays the reporting until the external thread catches up to the internal thread. If the external thread is blocked waiting for some data to arrive (line 236) and is then interrupted, it will jump to the catch block (lines 264–268). There, the InterruptedException is caught, and a new InterruptedIOException is thrown in its place (lines 266–267). This means that a thread blocked on a read() will now respond to interrupts!

The close() method (lines 114–140) is used to shut down the internal thread (notice that in this class, stopRequest() is private). The close() method can be safely invoked more than once because it simply ignores subsequent requests. It starts by signaling that a close has been requested (line 119), which will cause any blocked read() calls on ThreadedInputStream to throw an IOException (line 241). It then uses SureStop to make sure that even if all else fails, the internal thread will be stopped in 10 seconds (line 121). Inside close(), a new thread is created to invoke close() on the underlying stream (lines 125–139). This step is necessary in case the call blocks for quite a while—or even forever if a deadlock scenario occurs. ThreadedInputStream can't control what kind of InputStream it is passed in its constructor, so this extra thread is just added insurance.

Class BufferedThreadedInputStream

The class ThreadedInputStream just focuses on the task of splitting up the transfer of data between two threads. It performs poorly on single-byte reads and does not have any support for the mark-reset mechanism. BufferedThreadedInputStream (see Listing 15.8) makes up for these shortcomings by using a ThreadedInputStream with a BufferedInputStream added on both ends to smooth data flow.

LISTING 15.8   BufferedThreadedInputStream.java—ThreadedInputStream with Buffering

```
 1: import java.io.*;
 2:
 3: // uses ThreadedInputStream
 4:
 5: public class BufferedThreadedInputStream
 6:         extends FilterInputStream {
 7:
 8:     // fixed class that does *not* have a synchronized close()
 9:     private static class BISFix extends BufferedInputStream {
10:         public BISFix(InputStream rawIn, int buffSize) {
11:             super(rawIn, buffSize);
12:         }
13:
14:         public void close() throws IOException {
15:             if ( in != null ) {
16:                 try {
17:                     in.close();
18:                 } finally {
19:                     in = null;
20:                 }
21:             }
22:         }
23:     }
24:
25:     public BufferedThreadedInputStream(
26:                 InputStream rawIn,
27:                 int bufferSize
28:             ) {
29:
30:         super(rawIn); // super-class' "in" is set below
31:
32:         // rawIn -> BufferedIS -> ThreadedIS ->
33:         //       BufferedIS -> read()
34:
35:         BISFix bis = new BISFix(rawIn, bufferSize);
36:         ThreadedInputStream tis =
```

```
37:                    new ThreadedInputStream(bis, bufferSize);
38:
39:          // Change the protected variable 'in' from the
40:          // superclass from rawIn to the correct stream.
41:          in = new BISFix(tis, bufferSize);
42:     }
43:
44:     public BufferedThreadedInputStream(InputStream rawIn) {
45:          this(rawIn, 2048);
46:     }
47:
48:     // Overridden to show that InterruptedIOException might
49:     // be thrown.
50:     public int read()
51:              throws InterruptedIOException, IOException {
52:
53:          return in.read();
54:     }
55:
56:     // Overridden to show that InterruptedIOException might
57:     // be thrown.
58:     public int read(byte[] b)
59:              throws InterruptedIOException, IOException {
60:
61:          return in.read(b);
62:     }
63:
64:     // Overridden to show that InterruptedIOException might
65:     // be thrown.
66:     public int read(byte[] b, int off, int len)
67:              throws InterruptedIOException, IOException {
68:
69:          return in.read(b, off, len);
70:     }
71:
72:     // Overridden to show that InterruptedIOException might
73:     // be thrown.
74:     public long skip(long n)
75:              throws InterruptedIOException, IOException {
76:
77:          return in.skip(n);
78:     }
79:
80:     // The remainder of the methods are directly inherited from
81:     // FilterInputStream and access "in" in the much the same
82:     // way as the methods above do.
83: }
```

`BufferedThreadedInputStream` has a nested class (lines 8–23) called `BISFix` that simply extends `BufferedInputStream` and overrides `close()` so that it is *not* synchronized. This is a critical difference that is needed so that `close()` can be executed while another thread is blocked inside `read()`.

In the constructor (lines 25–42), the raw input stream is wrapped in a `BISFix` (modified `BufferedInputStream`), which is wrapped in a `ThreadedInputStream`, which is wrapped in another `BISFix`. This provides buffering for both the internal thread and any external thread that does some reading.

Using BufferedThreadedInputStream for Interruptible I/O

Now it's time to combine the techniques presented so far. `CalcServerTwo` (see Listing 15.9) has been slightly modified to work with `CalcWorkerTwo`. `CalcWorkerTwo` (see Listing 15.10) now uses a `BufferedThreadedInputStream` as an inline filter so that when it is blocked trying to `read()`, it will respond to an interrupt.

LISTING 15.9   CalcServerTwo.java—Modified to Work with CalcWorkerTwo

```
 1: import java.io.*;
 2: import java.net.*;
 3: import java.util.*;
 4:
 5: public class CalcServerTwo extends Object {
 6:     private ServerSocket ss;
 7:     private List workerList;
 8:
 9:     private Thread internalThread;
10:     private volatile boolean noStopRequested;
11:
12:     public CalcServerTwo(int port) throws IOException {
13:         ss = new ServerSocket(port);
14:         workerList = new LinkedList();
15:
16:         noStopRequested = true;
17:         Runnable r = new Runnable() {
18:                 public void run() {
19:                     try {
20:                         runWork();
21:                     } catch ( Exception x ) {
22:                         // in case ANY exception slips through
23:                         x.printStackTrace();
```

```
24:                         }
25:                     }
26:                 };
27:
28:         internalThread = new Thread(r);
29:         internalThread.start();
30:     }
31:
32:     private void runWork() {
33:         System.out.println(
34:                 "in CalcServer - ready to accept connections");
35:
36:         while ( noStopRequested ) {
37:             try {
38:                 System.out.println(
39:                         "in CalcServer - about to block " +
40:                         "waiting for a new connection");
41:                 Socket sock = ss.accept();
42:                 System.out.println(
43:                     "in CalcServer - received new connection");
44:                 workerList.add(new CalcWorkerTwo(sock));
45:             } catch ( IOException iox ) {
46:                 if ( noStopRequested ) {
47:                     iox.printStackTrace();
48:                 }
49:             }
50:         }
51:
52:         // stop all the workers that were created
53:         System.out.println("in CalcServer - putting in a " +
54:                 "stop request to all the workers");
55:         Iterator iter = workerList.iterator();
56:         while ( iter.hasNext() ) {
57:             CalcWorkerTwo worker = (CalcWorkerTwo) iter.next();
58:             worker.stopRequest();
59:         }
60:
61:         System.out.println("in CalcServer - leaving runWork()");
62:     }
63:
64:     public void stopRequest() {
65:         System.out.println(
66:                 "in CalcServer - entering stopRequest()");
```

continues

LISTING 15.9 Continued

```
67:            noStopRequested = false;
68:            internalThread.interrupt();
69:
70:            if ( ss != null ) {
71:                try {
72:                    ss.close();
73:                } catch ( IOException x ) {
74:                    // ignore
75:                } finally {
76:                    ss = null;
77:                }
78:            }
79:        }
80:
81:    public boolean isAlive() {
82:        return internalThread.isAlive();
83:    }
84:
85:    public static void main(String[] args) {
86:        int port = 2001;
87:
88:        try {
89:            CalcServerTwo server = new CalcServerTwo(port);
90:            Thread.sleep(15000);
91:            server.stopRequest();
92:        } catch ( IOException x ) {
93:            x.printStackTrace();
94:        } catch ( InterruptedException x ) {
95:            // ignore
96:        }
97:    }
98: }
```

LISTING 15.10 CalcWorkerTwo.java—Using BufferedThreadedInputStream

```
1: import java.io.*;
2: import java.net.*;
3:
4: public class CalcWorkerTwo extends Object {
5:     private DataInputStream dataIn;
6:     private DataOutputStream dataOut;
7:
```

```
 8:     private Thread internalThread;
 9:     private volatile boolean noStopRequested;
10:
11:     public CalcWorkerTwo(Socket sock) throws IOException {
12:         dataIn = new DataInputStream(
13:             new BufferedThreadedInputStream(
14:                 sock.getInputStream()));
15:         dataOut = new DataOutputStream(
16:             new BufferedOutputStream(
17:                 sock.getOutputStream()));
18:
19:         noStopRequested = true;
20:         Runnable r = new Runnable() {
21:                 public void run() {
22:                     try {
23:                         runWork();
24:                     } catch ( Exception x ) {
25:                         // in case ANY exception slips through
26:                         x.printStackTrace();
27:                     }
28:                 }
29:             };
30:
31:         internalThread = new Thread(r);
32:         internalThread.start();
33:     }
34:
35:     private void runWork() {
36:         while ( noStopRequested ) {
37:             try {
38:                 System.out.println("in CalcWorker - about to " +
39:                         "block waiting to read a double");
40:                 double val = dataIn.readDouble();
41:                 System.out.println(
42:                         "in CalcWorker - read a double!");
43:                 dataOut.writeDouble(Math.sqrt(val));
44:                 dataOut.flush();
45:             } catch ( InterruptedIOException iiox ) {
46:                 System.out.println("in CalcWorker - blocked " +
47:                         "read was interrupted!!!");
48:             } catch ( IOException x ) {
49:                 if ( noStopRequested ) {
```

continues

LISTING 15.10   Continued

```
50:                        x.printStackTrace();
51:                        stopRequest();
52:                    }
53:                }
54:            }
55:
56:            // In real-world code, be sure to close other streams
57:            // and the socket as part of the clean-up. Omitted here
58:            // for brevity.
59:
60:            System.out.println("in CalcWorker · leaving runWork()");
61:        }
62:
63:        public void stopRequest() {
64:            System.out.println(
65:                    "in CalcWorker - entering stopRequest()");
66:            noStopRequested = false;
67:            internalThread.interrupt();
68:            System.out.println(
69:                    "in CalcWorker · leaving stopRequest()");
70:        }
71:
72:        public boolean isAlive() {
73:            return internalThread.isAlive();
74:        }
75: }
```

CalcWorkerTwo has been modified to take advantage of the interruptible I/O of
BufferedThreadedInputStream (line 13). The InterruptedIOException has been caught in
this code simply to print a message (lines 45–47) but can be ignored. The stopRequest()
method (lines 63–70) has been simplified back down to the self-running object template—only
an interrupt() is necessary to unblock a read().

The same CalcClient code can be used with the new CalcServerTwo and CalcWorkerTwo.
Listing 15.11 shows possible output from CalcServerTwo. Your output should match very
closely with only a message or two swapped.

LISTING 15.11 Possible Output from CalcServerTwo

```
 1: in CalcServer - ready to accept connections
 2: in CalcServer - about to block waiting for a new connection
 3: in CalcServer - received new connection
 4: in CalcServer - about to block waiting for a new connection
 5: in CalcWorker - about to block waiting to read a double
 6: in CalcWorker - read a double!
 7: in CalcWorker - about to block waiting to read a double
 8: in CalcServer - entering stopRequest()
 9: in CalcServer - putting in a stop request to all the workers
10: in CalcWorker - entering stopRequest()
11: in CalcWorker - leaving stopRequest()
12: in CalcWorker - blocked read was interrupted!!!
13: in CalcServer - leaving runWork()
14: in CalcWorker - leaving runWork()
```

The main difference in the output from what was seen before is line 12. Here, a message is printed confirming that an `InterruptedIOException` was thrown when the blocked thread was interrupted.

Summary

Blocked I/O statements can be troublesome to deal with, but this chapter offered a few techniques to avoid this difficulty. A blocked `read()` on an `InputStream` ignores `interrupt()` and `stop()`, but generally will throw an exception if its stream is closed by another thread. A blocked `accept()` on a `ServerSocket` also ignores interrupts, but will throw an exception if the `ServerSocket` is closed by another thread.

`ThreadedInputStream` and `BufferedThreadedInputStream` provide a mechanism that allows a blocked `read()` to be interrupted and throw an `InterruptedIOException`. Although this technique comes with the overhead of another thread, it can be very useful by providing interruptible I/O.

The SureStop Utility

IN THIS CHAPTER

Although the stop() method on the class Thread has been deprecated as of JDK 1.2, there are still times when it can be used as a last resort to get a thread to die. In this chapter, I'll present the SureStop class, which can be used to monitor a thread for a period of time. If the thread is still alive after the specified period of time has elapsed, SureStop will invoke stop() on it to ensure that it finally dies.

Guidelines for Using SureStop

The stop() method on Thread has been deprecated for very good reasons (see Chapter 5, "Gracefully Stopping Threads"). SureStop should only be used in conjunction with other, safer techniques for stopping a thread. If those other techniques happen to fail to get the thread to die, SureStop steps in after a timeout and abruptly stops the defiant thread. Typically, a thread will not die naturally because it is blocked on a statement that ignores interrupts.

For instance, the following statement makes SureStop monitor threadA for 45 seconds and abruptly stop the thread after that timeout if it hasn't died:

```
SureStop.ensureStop(threadA, 45000);
```

The ensureStop() method of SureStop is static so that it can be easily accessed from anywhere. It also very quickly adds the passed Thread reference to the list of monitored threads and returns, allowing the calling thread to continue with other tasks. SureStop has a thread running within it that occasionally checks the list of monitored threads and stops those that have reached their expiration time.

This tool can be very useful in long-running applications like servers that might run for weeks or months at a time. SureStop helps to make sure that the server-side threads of defunct client sessions do not continue to run indefinitely.

As I mentioned earlier, SureStop is a tool that should be added to your arsenal of techniques to get threads to stop running, and should not be used alone. The self-running object model can be extended to add the safety net of SureStop, like this:

```
public void stopRequest() {
    // be sure that it is stopped within 60 secs
    SureStop.ensureStop(internalThread, 60000);
    noStopRequested = false;
    internalThread.interrupt();
    //
    // insert any other techniques used to get the internal
    // thread to die normally...
    //
}
```

The SureStop Class

SureStop (see Listing 16.1) has only one public method, ensureStop(). In addition, this method is static and is used universally to access a single instance of SureStop. When the SureStop class is loaded, a single instance is created using the private constructor. Inside SureStop, a thread is running to check the list of monitored threads and stop them if necessary. This internal thread is a daemon thread, so it continues to run as long as there are other threads running in the VM, and automatically dies when no other non-daemon threads remain (see Chapter 5). When SureStop is compiled, the compiler issues an expected warning because the deprecated stop() method is used.

LISTING 16.1   SureStop.java—The SureStop Utility

```
 1: import java.util.*;
 2:
 3: public class SureStop extends Object {
 4:     // nested internal class for stop request entries
 5:     private static class Entry extends Object {
 6:         private Thread thread;
 7:         private long stopTime;
 8:
 9:         private Entry(Thread t, long stop) {
10:             thread = t;
11:             stopTime = stop;
12:         }
13:     }
14:
15:     // static reference to the singleton instance
16:     private static SureStop ss;
17:
18:     static {
19:         // When class is loaded, create exactly one instance
20:         // using the private constructor.
21:         ss = new SureStop();
22:     }
23:
24:     private List stopList;
25:     private List pendingList;
26:     private Thread internalThread;
27:
```

continues

LISTING 16.1 Continued

```
28:        private SureStop() {
29:            // using a linked list for fast deletions
30:            stopList = new LinkedList();
31:
32:            // Enough initial capacity for 20 pending additions,
33:            // will grow automatically if necessary to keep
34:            // ensureStop() from blocking.
35:            pendingList = new ArrayList(20);
36:
37:            Runnable r = new Runnable() {
38:                    public void run() {
39:                        try {
40:                            runWork();
41:                        } catch ( Exception x ) {
42:                            // in case ANY exception slips through
43:                            x.printStackTrace();
44:                        }
45:                    }
46:                };
47:
48:            internalThread = new Thread(r);
49:            internalThread.setDaemon(true); // no need to run alone
50:            internalThread.setPriority(Thread.MAX_PRIORITY); // high
51:            internalThread.start();
52:        }
53:
54:        private void runWork() {
55:            try {
56:                while ( true ) {
57:                    // Since this is a super-high priority thread,
58:                    // be sure to give other threads a chance to
59:                    // run each time through in case the wait on
60:                    // pendingList is very short.
61:                    Thread.sleep(500);
62:
63:                    // Stop expired threads and determine the
64:                    // amount of time until the next thread is
65:                    // due to expire.
66:                    long sleepTime = checkStopList();
67:
68:                    synchronized ( pendingList ) {
69:                        if ( pendingList.size() < 1 ) {
70:                            pendingList.wait(sleepTime);
71:                        }
72:
```

```
 73:                        if ( pendingList.size() > 0 ) {
 74:                            // Copy into stopList and then remove
 75:                            // from pendingList.
 76:                            stopList.addAll(pendingList);
 77:                            pendingList.clear();
 78:                        }
 79:                    }
 80:                } // while
 81:            } catch ( InterruptedException x ) {
 82:                // ignore
 83:            } catch ( Exception x ) {
 84:                // Never expect this, but print a trace in case
 85:                // it happens.
 86:                x.printStackTrace();
 87:            }
 88:        }
 89:
 90:    private long checkStopList() {
 91:        // called from runWork() by the internal thread
 92:
 93:        long currTime = System.currentTimeMillis();
 94:        long minTime = Long.MAX_VALUE;
 95:
 96:        Iterator iter = stopList.iterator();
 97:        while ( iter.hasNext() ) {
 98:            Entry entry = (Entry) iter.next();
 99:
100:            if ( entry.thread.isAlive() ) {
101:                if ( entry.stopTime < currTime ) {
102:                    // timed out, stop it abruptly right now
103:                    try {
104:                        entry.thread.stop();
105:                    } catch ( SecurityException x ) {
106:                        // Catch this here so that other
107:                        // operations are not disrupted. Warn
108:                        // that thread could not be stopped.
109:                        System.err.println(
110:                            "SureStop was not permitted to " +
111:                            "stop thread=" + entry.thread);
112:                        x.printStackTrace();
113:                    }
114:
115:                    // Since it has stopped, remove it
116:                    // from stopList.
```

continues

LISTING 16.1   Continued

```
117:                        iter.remove();
118:                    } else {
119:                        // Not yet expired, check to see if this
120:                        // is the new minimum.
121:                        minTime = Math.min(entry.stopTime, minTime);
122:                    }
123:                } else {
124:                    // Thread died on its own, remove it from
125:                    // stopList.
126:                    iter.remove();
127:                } // if alive
128:            } // while
129:
130:            long sleepTime = minTime - System.currentTimeMillis();
131:
132:            // ensure that it is a least a little bit of time
133:            sleepTime = Math.max(50, sleepTime);
134:
135:            return sleepTime;
136:        }
137:
138:        private void addEntry(Entry entry) {
139:            // called from ensureStop() by external thread
140:
141:            synchronized ( pendingList ) {
142:                pendingList.add(entry);
143:
144:                // no need for notifyAll(), one waiter
145:                pendingList.notify();
146:            }
147:        }
148:
149:        public static void ensureStop(Thread t, long msGracePeriod) {
150:            if ( !t.isAlive() ) {
151:                // thread is already stopped, return right away
152:                return;
153:            }
154:
155:            long stopTime =
156:                    System.currentTimeMillis() + msGracePeriod;
157:
158:            Entry entry = new Entry(t, stopTime);
159:            ss.addEntry(entry);
160:        }
161: }
```

A `private` nested class called `Entry` (lines 5–13) is used by `SureStop` to encapsulate the data needed to monitor threads. In its constructor (lines 9–12), it is passed a reference to the thread to monitor and the system clock time after which this thread should be stopped.

When the `SureStop` class is brought into memory by the virtual machine's class loader, its `static` block (lines 18–22) is executed. In the `static` block, the `private` constructor is used to create a single instance of `SureStop` that monitors all stop requests. A reference to this singleton is stored in the `private, static` member variable `ss` (line 16).

The `private` constructor for `SureStop` (lines 28–52) initializes its internal lists and starts its internal thread. This class uses the Collections API to manipulate lists. The list of threads currently being monitored is held in `stopList` (lines 24, 30). (Any implementation of `List` would do, but I chose to use `LinkedList` because of its support for efficient deletion of elements from the middle of the list.) A second list is used as a temporary store for recent additions: `pendingList` (lines 25, 35). (Again, any implementation of `List` would do, but I chose to use an `ArrayList` because it would typically hold only a couple of elements until they could be bulk-copied into `stopList`.) Two lists are used so that new entries can be added quickly with minimal blocking. The `ensureStop()` method invokes `addEntry()` where the new entry is added right away to `pendingList`. Because `pendingList` is caching new entries, the internal thread is free to iterate through `stopList` without interference. When the internal thread gets a chance, it moves the entries from `pendingList` into `stopList`.

The remainder of the constructor (lines 37–51) basically follows the self-running object pattern with minor additions. The internal thread is marked as a daemon thread so that it will automatically stop when all the other non-daemon threads in the VM die (line 49). This way, the thread inside `SureStop` will not keep the VM from exiting. Additionally, the internal thread is set to run at the highest available priority (line 50). This is done so that the internal thread will get a chance to run and stop other high-priority threads. If the internal thread was not run at the highest priority, it is possible that it would not get a chance to stop a higher-priority thread. Careful steps are taken in the main loop to be sure that the internal thread blocks for significant amounts of time, giving other threads in the VM a chance to run.

The internal thread spends the bulk of its time inside the `runWork()` method (lines 54–88). The infinite `while` loop (lines 56–80) continues to run until the VM exits. Each time through, `internalThread` sleeps for half a second simply to be sure that other threads are given a chance to run (line 61). It is not critical that a monitored thread be stopped *exactly* on time—it can be stopped a little bit late. Next, `stopList` is checked to see if any monitored threads have died on their own, or if any have timed out and need to be stopped abruptly (line 66). The time interval returned from `stopList` indicates how long the internal thread should wait before checking `stopList` again.

The synchronized block inside runWork() (lines 68–79) controls concurrent access to pendingList. If no items have been added to pendingList since the last time it was checked (line 69), the internal thread waits up to sleepTime milliseconds (line 70) for elements to be added by addEntry(). The internal thread gets to line 73 because of one of the following: pendingList was not empty and no waiting was done, an item was added to pendingList while waiting, or sleepTime milliseconds elapsed while waiting. If there are any elements currently in pendingList (line 73), they are copied into stopList (line 76) and deleted from pendingList (line 77). The while loop is then executed again.

NOTE

There is no need for synchronized access to stopList because internalThread is the one and only thread that ever interacts with the list. On the other hand, synchronized access to pendingList *is* necessary since that list is accessed by internalThread and all the threads that invoke ensureStop().

The checkStopList() method (lines 90–136) scans stopList, removing threads that have stopped on their own and stopping threads that have timed out. It also returns the amount of time remaining until the next monitored thread times out. An Iterator is used to traverse the LinkedList and extract the entries (lines 96–98). If stopList is empty, the while loop (lines 97–128) is bypassed and a very large sleepTime is returned (Long.MAX_VALUE). If stopList has Entry objects in it, each is checked to see if the thread being monitored is still alive (line 100). If it is not alive, it is simply removed from stopList (lines 123–127).

If the thread is still alive, its stopTime is checked against the current time to see if it should be stopped (line 101). If the monitored thread has timed out, it is stopped (line 104). If SureStop is not permitted to stop this thread, a SecurityException is thrown (and caught) and a message is printed (lines 105–113). Whether or not stop() is successful, the entry is removed from stopList (line 117). If it was not time to stop the monitored thread and it is still alive, the entry's stopTime is compared with minTime to determine if it is sooner than the value already held in minTime (line 121).

When all the entries have been checked, a new sleepTime is calculated. The entry that is due to expire sooner than any of the others has its stopTime stored in minTime. The difference between minTime and the current time is used for sleepTime (line 130). If sleepTime is less than 50 milliseconds, it is bumped up to 50 milliseconds (line 133) so that there is some delay.

The addEntry() method (lines 138–147) is used by ensureStop() to add new Entry objects to pendingList. The calling thread blocks until an exclusive lock can be acquired on pendingList (line 141). If this blocks at all, it will be for a very short time while internalThread moves the entries from pendingList to stopList. The Entry reference is added (line 142), and notify() is invoked to signal internalThread if it is waiting (line 145). In this particular case, notifyAll() is not necessary as there is at most one thread waiting.

The only external interface into SureStop is through its only public method: ensureStop() (lines 149–160). It is passed a reference to the thread to be monitored and the number of milliseconds to wait before abruptly stopping it (line 149). If the thread is already dead, ensureStop() returns right away (lines 150–153). If not, a new Entry object is created with a stopTime that is the current time plus the timeout value (lines 155–158). This new Entry instance is added to pendingList by invoking addEntry() on the SureStop singleton (line 159).

Peering Inside Using SureStopVerbose

The class SureStopVerbose (see Listing 16.2) is identical to SureStop except that it provides some detailed output. A new static method print() has been added (lines 198–206) to assist in printing messages. Throughout the code, calls to print() are used to show the internal settings. Other than that, SureStopVerbose works exactly like SureStop. SureStopVerbose is used by the demonstration code in the next section to reveal the class's inner workings. When SureStopVerbose is compiled, the compiler issues an expected warning because the deprecated stop() method is used.

LISTING 16.2   SureStopVerbose.java—Chatty SureStop that Shows Inner Processing

```
 1: import java.util.*;
 2:
 3: public class SureStopVerbose extends Object {
 4:     // nested internal class for stop request entries
 5:     private static class Entry extends Object {
 6:         private Thread thread;
 7:         private long stopTime;
 8:
 9:         private Entry(Thread t, long stop) {
10:             thread = t;
11:             stopTime = stop;
12:         }
13:     }
14:
```

continues

LISTING 16.2   Continued

```
15:        // static reference to the singleton instance
16:        private static SureStopVerbose ss;
17:
18:     static {
19:         // When class is loaded, create exactly one instance
20:         // using the private constructor.
21:         ss = new SureStopVerbose();
22:         print("SureStopVerbose instance created.");
23:     }
24:
25:     private List stopList;
26:     private List pendingList;
27:     private Thread internalThread;
28:
29:     private SureStopVerbose() {
30:         // using a linked list for fast deletions
31:         stopList = new LinkedList();
32:
33:         // Enough initial capacity for 20 pending additions,
34:         // will grow automatically if necessary to keep
35:         // ensureStop() from blocking.
36:         pendingList = new ArrayList(20);
37:
38:         Runnable r = new Runnable() {
39:                 public void run() {
40:                     try {
41:                         runWork();
42:                     } catch ( Exception x ) {
43:                         // in case ANY exception slips through
44:                         x.printStackTrace();
45:                     }
46:                 }
47:             };
48:
49:         internalThread = new Thread(r);
50:         internalThread.setDaemon(true); // no need to run alone
51:         internalThread.setPriority(Thread.MAX_PRIORITY); // high
52:         internalThread.start();
53:     }
54:
55:     private void runWork() {
56:         try {
57:             while ( true ) {
58:                 // Since this is a super-high priority thread,
```

```
59:              // be sure to give other threads a chance to
60:              // run each time through in case the wait on
61:              // pendingList is very short.
62:              print("about to sleep for 0.5 seconds");
63:              Thread.sleep(500);
64:              print("done with sleep for 0.5 seconds");
65:
66:              long sleepTime = checkStopList();
67:              print("back from checkStopList(), sleepTime=" +
68:                      sleepTime);
69:
70:              synchronized ( pendingList ) {
71:                  if ( pendingList.size() < 1 ) {
72:                      print("about to wait on pendingList " +
73:                          "for " + sleepTime + " ms");
74:                      long start = System.currentTimeMillis();
75:                      pendingList.wait(sleepTime);
76:                      long elapsedTime =
77:                          System.currentTimeMillis() - start;
78:                      print("waited on pendingList for " +
79:                          elapsedTime + " ms");
80:                  }
81:
82:
83:                  if ( pendingList.size() > 0 ) {
84:                      // copy into stopList and then remove
85:                      // from pendingList.
86:                      print("copying " + pendingList.size() +
87:                          " elements from pendingList to " +
88:                          "stopList");
89:                      int oldSize = stopList.size();
90:                      stopList.addAll(pendingList);
91:                      pendingList.clear();
92:                      int newSize = stopList.size();
93:                      print("pendingList.size()=" +
94:                          pendingList.size() +
95:                          ", stopList grew by " +
96:                          (newSize - oldSize));
97:                  }
98:              }
99:          } // while
100:      } catch ( InterruptedException x ) {
101:          // ignore
102:      } catch ( Exception x ) {
```

continues

LISTING 16.2 Continued

```
103:                // Never expect this, but print a trace in case
104:                // it happens.
105:                x.printStackTrace();
106:            }
107:        }
108:
109:    private long checkStopList() {
110:        print("entering checkStopList() - stopList.size()=" +
111:                stopList.size());
112:        long currTime = System.currentTimeMillis();
113:        long minTime = Long.MAX_VALUE;
114:
115:        Iterator iter = stopList.iterator();
116:        while ( iter.hasNext() ) {
117:            Entry entry = (Entry) iter.next();
118:
119:            if ( entry.thread.isAlive() ) {
120:                print("thread is alive - " +
121:                        entry.thread.getName());
122:                if ( entry.stopTime < currTime ) {
123:                    // timed out, stop it abruptly right now
124:                    print("timed out, stopping - " +
125:                            entry.thread.getName());
126:                    try {
127:                        entry.thread.stop();
128:                    } catch ( SecurityException x ) {
129:                        // Catch this here so that other
130:                        // operations are not disrupted. Warn
131:                        // that thread could not be stopped.
132:                        System.err.println(
133:                            "SureStop was not permitted to " +
134:                            "stop thread=" + entry.thread);
135:                        x.printStackTrace();
136:                    }
137:
138:                    // Since it's stopped, remove it
139:                    // from stopList.
140:                    iter.remove();
141:                } else {
142:                    // Not yet expired, check to see if this
143:                    // is the new minimum.
144:                    minTime = Math.min(entry.stopTime, minTime);
145:                    print("new minTime=" + minTime);
146:                }
147:            } else {
```

```
148:                    print("thread died on its own - " +
149:                            entry.thread.getName());
150:                    // Thread died on its own, remove it from
151:                    // stopList.
152:                    iter.remove();
153:                } // if alive
154:            } // while
155:
156:            long sleepTime = minTime - System.currentTimeMillis();
157:
158:            // ensure that it is a least a little bit of time
159:            sleepTime = Math.max(50, sleepTime);
160:
161:            print("leaving checkStopList() - stopList.size()=" +
162:                    stopList.size());
163:            return sleepTime;
164:        }
165:
166:        private void addEntry(Entry entry) {
167:            synchronized ( pendingList ) {
168:                pendingList.add(entry);
169:
170:                // no need for notifyAll(), one waiter
171:                pendingList.notify();
172:                print("added entry to pendingList, name=" +
173:                    entry.thread.getName() +
174:                    ", stopTime=" + entry.stopTime + ", in " +
175:                    ( entry.stopTime - System.currentTimeMillis() ) +
176:                    " ms");
177:            }
178:        }
179:
180:        public static void ensureStop(Thread t, long msGracePeriod) {
181:            print("entering ensureStop() - name=" + t.getName() +
182:                ", msGracePeriod=" + msGracePeriod);
183:
184:            if ( !t.isAlive() ) {
185:                // thread is already stopped, return right away
186:                print("already stopped, not added to list - " +
187:                        t.getName());
188:                return;
189:            }
190:
```

continues

LISTING 16.2   Continued

```
191:          long stopTime =
192:                  System.currentTimeMillis() + msGracePeriod;
193:          Entry entry = new Entry(t, stopTime);
194:          ss.addEntry(entry);
195:          print("leaving ensureStop() - name=" + t.getName());
196:      }
197:
198:      private static void print(String msg) {
199:          Thread t = Thread.currentThread();
200:          String name = t.getName();
201:          if ( t == ss.internalThread ) {
202:              name = "SureStopThread";
203:          }
204:
205:          System.out.println(name + ": " + msg);
206:      }
207: }
```

Watching It Work with SureStopDemo

SureStopDemo (see Listing 16.3) starts several threads to demonstrate how SureStop works. But instead of SureStop, SureStopVerbose is used so that more detail about what is going on internally is printed. Although the threads running in SureStopDemo could have been stopped in a more orderly fashion by using interrupt(), they are not so that the functionality of SureStop can be fully exercised. SureStopDemo runs for about 25 seconds before automatically exiting the VM.

LISTING 16.3   SureStopDemo.java—Demonstration Code for SureStopVerbose

```
 1: public class SureStopDemo extends Object {
 2:     private static Thread launch(
 3:                 final String name,
 4:                 long lifeTime
 5:             ) {
 6:
 7:         final int loopCount = (int) ( lifeTime / 1000 );
 8:
 9:         Runnable r = new Runnable() {
10:                 public void run() {
11:                     try {
12:                         for ( int i = 0; i < loopCount; i++ ) {
13:                             Thread.sleep(1000);
```

```
14:                              System.out.println(
15:                                  " -> Running - " + name);
16:                          }
17:                      } catch ( InterruptedException x ) {
18:                          // ignore
19:                      }
20:                  }
21:              };
22:
23:          Thread t = new Thread(r);
24:          t.setName(name);
25:          t.start();
26:
27:          return t;
28:      }
29:
30:      public static void main(String[] args) {
31:          Thread t0 = launch("T0", 1000);
32:          Thread t1 = launch("T1", 5000);
33:          Thread t2 = launch("T2", 15000);
34:
35:          try { Thread.sleep(2000); }
36:          catch ( InterruptedException x ) { }
37:
38:          SureStopVerbose.ensureStop(t0,  9000);
39:          SureStopVerbose.ensureStop(t1, 10000);
40:          SureStopVerbose.ensureStop(t2, 12000);
41:
42:          try { Thread.sleep(20000); }
43:          catch ( InterruptedException x ) { }
44:
45:          Thread t3 = launch("T3", 15000);
46:          SureStopVerbose.ensureStop(t3, 5000);
47:
48:          try { Thread.sleep(1000); }
49:          catch ( InterruptedException x ) { }
50:
51:          Thread t4 = launch("T4", 15000);
52:          SureStopVerbose.ensureStop(t4, 3000);
53:      }
54: }
```

The launch() method (lines 2–28) is used to create a new thread and start it running. A name for the thread is passed in along with the amount of time that the thread should keep running before dying on its own. About once per second, the thread prints a message (lines 12–16). A reference to the Thread created is returned (line 27).

The main() method launches three of these threads (lines 31–33) and then sleeps for 2 seconds (lines 35–36). It then specifies that SureStopVerbose should make certain that the threads are stopped (lines 38–40). The main() method requests that t0 be stopped in 9 seconds, but t0 should have already died on its own about 1 second ago. It requests that t1 be stopped in 10 seconds, but t1 should stop on its own in about 3 more seconds. It requests that t2 be stopped in 12 seconds, and it will need to be stopped because t2 is scheduled to run for about 13 more seconds. The main thread then sleeps for 20 seconds to allow all this to play out (lines 42–43). After this, two more threads are launched and monitored (lines 45–52).

Listing 16.4 shows possible output when SureStopDemo is run. Your output should match closely, but some of the timing might be slightly different.

LISTING 16.4   Possible Output from SureStopDemo

```
 1: -> Running - T0
 2: -> Running - T1
 3: -> Running - T2
 4: -> Running - T1
 5: -> Running - T2
 6: main: SureStopVerbose instance created.
 7: SureStopThread: about to sleep for 0.5 seconds
 8: main: entering ensureStop() - name=T0, msGracePeriod=9000
 9: main: already stopped, not added to list - T0
10: main: entering ensureStop() - name=T1, msGracePeriod=10000
11: main: added entry to pendingList, name=T1,
    ➥stopTime=924307803230, in 9840 ms
12: main: leaving ensureStop() - name=T1
13: main: entering ensureStop() - name=T2, msGracePeriod=12000
14: main: added entry to pendingList, name=T2,
    ➥stopTime=924307805390, in 12000 ms
15: main: leaving ensureStop() - name=T2
16: SureStopThread: done with sleep for 0.5 seconds
17: SureStopThread: entering checkStopList() - stopList.size()=0
18: SureStopThread: leaving checkStopList() - stopList.size()=0
19: SureStopThread: back from checkStopList(),
    ➥sleepTime=9223371112546982037
20: SureStopThread: copying 2 elements from pendingList to stopList
21: SureStopThread: pendingList.size()=0, stopList grew by 2
22: SureStopThread: about to sleep for 0.5 seconds
23: -> Running - T1
24: -> Running - T2
25: SureStopThread: done with sleep for 0.5 seconds
26: SureStopThread: entering checkStopList() - stopList.size()=2
27: SureStopThread: thread is alive - T1
28: SureStopThread: new minTime=924307803230
```

```
29: SureStopThread: thread is alive - T2
30: SureStopThread: new minTime=924307803230
31: SureStopThread: leaving checkStopList() - stopList.size()=2
32: SureStopThread: back from checkStopList(), sleepTime=8960
33: SureStopThread: about to wait on pendingList for 8960 ms
34: -> Running - T1
35: -> Running - T2
36: -> Running - T1
37: -> Running - T2
38: -> Running - T2
39: -> Running - T2
40: -> Running - T2
41: -> Running - T2
42: -> Running - T2
43: -> Running - T2
44: -> Running - T2
45: SureStopThread: waited on pendingList for 8960 ms
46: SureStopThread: about to sleep for 0.5 seconds
47: SureStopThread: done with sleep for 0.5 seconds
48: SureStopThread: entering checkStopList() - stopList.size()=2
49: SureStopThread: thread died on its own - T1
50: SureStopThread: thread is alive - T2
51: SureStopThread: new minTime=924307805390
52: SureStopThread: leaving checkStopList() - stopList.size()=1
53: SureStopThread: back from checkStopList(), sleepTime=1620
54: SureStopThread: about to wait on pendingList for 1620 ms
55: -> Running - T2
56: -> Running - T2
57: SureStopThread: waited on pendingList for 1650 ms
58: SureStopThread: about to sleep for 0.5 seconds
59: SureStopThread: done with sleep for 0.5 seconds
60: SureStopThread: entering checkStopList() - stopList.size()=1
61: SureStopThread: thread is alive - T2
62: SureStopThread: timed out, stopping - T2
63: SureStopThread: leaving checkStopList() - stopList.size()=0
64: SureStopThread: back from checkStopList(),
    ➥sleepTime=9223371112546969897
65: SureStopThread: about to wait on pendingList for
    ➥9223371112546969897 ms
66: main: entering ensureStop() - name=T3, msGracePeriod=5000
67: main: added entry to pendingList, name=T3,
    ➥stopTime=924307818440, in 5000 ms
68: SureStopThread: waited on pendingList for 7530 ms
69: SureStopThread: copying 1 elements from pendingList to stopList
```

continues

LISTING 16.4   Continued

```
 70: SureStopThread: pendingList.size()=0, stopList grew by 1
 71: SureStopThread: about to sleep for 0.5 seconds
 72: main: leaving ensureStop() - name=T3
 73: SureStopThread: done with sleep for 0.5 seconds
 74: SureStopThread: entering checkStopList() - stopList.size()=1
 75: SureStopThread: thread is alive - T3
 76: SureStopThread: new minTime=924307818440
 77: SureStopThread: leaving checkStopList() - stopList.size()=1
 78: SureStopThread: back from checkStopList(), sleepTime=4510
 79: SureStopThread: about to wait on pendingList for 4510 ms
 80: main: entering ensureStop() - name=T4, msGracePeriod=3000
 81: main: added entry to pendingList, name=T4,
     ➥stopTime=924307817430, in 3000 ms
 82: SureStopThread: waited on pendingList for 500 ms
 83: SureStopThread: copying 1 elements from pendingList to stopList
 84: SureStopThread: pendingList.size()=0, stopList grew by 1
 85: SureStopThread: about to sleep for 0.5 seconds
 86: main: leaving ensureStop() - name=T4
 87: -> Running - T3
 88: SureStopThread: done with sleep for 0.5 seconds
 89: SureStopThread: entering checkStopList() - stopList.size()=2
 90: SureStopThread: thread is alive - T3
 91: SureStopThread: new minTime=924307818440
 92: SureStopThread: thread is alive - T4
 93: SureStopThread: new minTime=924307817430
 94: SureStopThread: leaving checkStopList() - stopList.size()=2
 95: SureStopThread: back from checkStopList(), sleepTime=2510
 96: SureStopThread: about to wait on pendingList for 2510 ms
 97: -> Running - T4
 98: -> Running - T3
 99: -> Running - T4
100: -> Running - T3
101: -> Running - T4
102: -> Running - T3
103: SureStopThread: waited on pendingList for 2530 ms
104: SureStopThread: about to sleep for 0.5 seconds
105: SureStopThread: done with sleep for 0.5 seconds
106: SureStopThread: entering checkStopList() - stopList.size()=2
107: SureStopThread: thread is alive - T3
108: SureStopThread: new minTime=924307818440
109: SureStopThread: thread is alive - T4
110: SureStopThread: timed out, stopping - T4
111: SureStopThread: leaving checkStopList() - stopList.size()=1
112: SureStopThread: back from checkStopList(), sleepTime=500
```

```
113: SureStopThread: about to wait on pendingList for 500 ms
114: -> Running - T3
115: SureStopThread: waited on pendingList for 500 ms
116: SureStopThread: about to sleep for 0.5 seconds
117: SureStopThread: done with sleep for 0.5 seconds
118: SureStopThread: entering checkStopList() - stopList.size()=1
119: SureStopThread: thread is alive - T3
120: SureStopThread: timed out, stopping - T3
121: SureStopThread: leaving checkStopList() - stopList.size()=0
122: SureStopThread: back from checkStopList(),
     ➥sleepTime=9223371112546956877
123: SureStopThread: about to wait on pendingList for
     ➥9223371112546956877 ms
```

Notice that as predicted, t0 stopped on its own before being monitored by SureStopVerbose (line 9). Monitoring began on t1 (lines 11, 27), but the thread died on its own before timing out (line 49). Similarly, monitoring began on t2 (lines 14, 29, 50, 61), and the thread timed out and was stopped by SureStopVerbose (line 62).

Summary

SureStop monitors threads for a period of time, and if they fail to die on their own, it steps in and invokes stop(). SureStop should only be used as a last resort and should not be the only method used to try to get a thread to die. Techniques in Chapters 5, 11, and 15 show other ways that threads can be signaled to die in an orderly manner. The SureStop utility is a useful supplement to other thread-stopping techniques.

The BooleanLock Utility

IN THIS CHAPTER

The BooleanLock class, which I present in this chapter, provides a useful encapsulation of a boolean variable that is easily and safely accessed from multiple threads. These threads can test and set the internal value and wait for it to change. The wait/notify mechanism is used internally to support waiting for the value to change, and frees external classes from the error-prone complexity of properly implementing this mechanism.

Background

Using the wait/notify mechanism effectively and correctly requires discipline. It is easy to erroneously code in such a way that a wait() is invoked just *after* a notify() has been issued, resulting in the notification being completely missed. This kind of mistake results in a very subtle race condition that only shows up occasionally and can be painstakingly difficult to track down. Wherever possible, the wait/notify mechanism should be encapsulated within a class to insulate external classes from the signaling complexity.

In this chapter, I present the BooleanLock class. It simply encapsulates a boolean variable and controls access to it through synchronized methods. Multiple threads can safely interact with it. The wait/notify mechanism is hidden within the class and missed notifications are impossible. It also uses the *Waiting for the Full Timeout* technique from Chapter 14, "Waiting for the Full Timeout."

BooleanLock can be used to conveniently signal between two threads. The first thread can block waiting until the value is set to true. When the second thread is ready, it can set the value to true and the first thread will be released from its blocked state.

BooleanLock can also be used to work around the problem of long synchronized blocks. Normally, when a thread is blocked waiting to acquire exclusive access to a lock (through synchronized), it will *not* respond to interrupts. In addition, there is no mechanism for specifying a timeout value that indicates how long a thread should wait to try to get into a synchronized block. The BooleanLock utility can be used to provide an interruptible, timeout-capable, technique for providing exclusive access to a block of code.

BooleanLock Class

The API for BooleanLock consists of the following methods:

```
public BooleanLock(boolean initialValue)
public BooleanLock()
public synchronized void setValue(boolean newValue)
public synchronized boolean waitToSetTrue(long msTimeout)
        throws InterruptedException
public synchronized boolean waitToSetFalse(long msTimeout)
        throws InterruptedException
```

```
public synchronized boolean isTrue()
public synchronized boolean isFalse()
public synchronized boolean waitUntilTrue(long msTimeout)
        throws InterruptedException
public synchronized boolean waitUntilFalse(long msTimeout)
        throws InterruptedException
public synchronized boolean waitUntilStateIs(
        boolean state, long msTimeout) throws InterruptedException
```

Notice that all the methods are synchronized and that many of them might throw an InterruptedException. The no-argument constructor defaults to use an initial value of false. Every time that setValue() is invoked with a new value, any and all threads blocked waiting in the waitXYZ() methods are notified of the change.

All of the waitXYZ() methods take a timeout value indicating how long they should wait for the condition to be met. A timeout of 0 indicates that the method should wait until the condition is met regardless of how long it takes. Otherwise, the timeout value is the maximum number of milliseconds that should elapse before the method returns. These methods return true if the condition was met, and false if the waiting timed out.

The full code for BooleanLock is shown in Listing 17.1.

LISTING 17.1   BooleanLock.java—The BooleanLock Utility

```
 1: public class BooleanLock extends Object {
 2:     private boolean value;
 3:
 4:     public BooleanLock(boolean initialValue) {
 5:         value = initialValue;
 6:     }
 7:
 8:     public BooleanLock() {
 9:         this(false);
10:     }
11:
12:     public synchronized void setValue(boolean newValue) {
13:         if ( newValue != value ) {
14:             value = newValue;
15:             notifyAll();
16:         }
17:     }
18:
19:     public synchronized boolean waitToSetTrue(long msTimeout)
```

continues

LISTING 17.1 Continued

```
20:                throws InterruptedException {
21:
22:         boolean success = waitUntilFalse(msTimeout);
23:         if ( success ) {
24:             setValue(true);
25:         }
26:
27:         return success;
28:     }
29:
30:     public synchronized boolean waitToSetFalse(long msTimeout)
31:             throws InterruptedException {
32:
33:         boolean success = waitUntilTrue(msTimeout);
34:         if ( success ) {
35:             setValue(false);
36:         }
37:
38:         return success;
39:     }
40:
41:     public synchronized boolean isTrue() {
42:         return value;
43:     }
44:
45:     public synchronized boolean isFalse() {
46:         return !value;
47:     }
48:
49:     public synchronized boolean waitUntilTrue(long msTimeout)
50:             throws InterruptedException {
51:
52:         return waitUntilStateIs(true, msTimeout);
53:     }
54:
55:     public synchronized boolean waitUntilFalse(long msTimeout)
56:             throws InterruptedException {
57:
58:         return waitUntilStateIs(false, msTimeout);
59:     }
60:
61:     public synchronized boolean waitUntilStateIs(
62:                 boolean state,
63:                 long msTimeout
64:             ) throws InterruptedException {
```

```
65:
66:            if ( msTimeout == 0L ) {
67:                while ( value != state ) {
68:                    wait();  // wait indefinitely until notified
69:                }
70:
71:                // condition has finally been met
72:                return true;
73:            }
74:
75:            // only wait for the specified amount of time
76:            long endTime = System.currentTimeMillis() + msTimeout;
77:            long msRemaining = msTimeout;
78:
79:            while ( ( value != state ) && ( msRemaining > 0L ) ) {
80:                wait(msRemaining);
81:                msRemaining = endTime - System.currentTimeMillis();
82:            }
83:
84:            // May have timed out, or may have met value,
85:            // calculate return value.
86:            return ( value == state );
87:        }
88: }
```

The member variable value (line 2) holds the most recent setting. The first constructor (lines 4–6) sets value to the specified initial state. The second constructor (lines 8–10) uses a default value of false for the initial state. The setValue() method (lines 12–17) is the primary mechanism used to change value. It is synchronized to coordinate access with other threads. If the value passed in truly represents a change (line 13), value is altered (line 14) and any and all waiting threads are notified of the change (line 15). The methods waitToSetTrue() and waitToSetFalse() both might end up calling setValue().

In waitToSetTrue() (lines 19–28), the calling thread waits until it has exclusive access *and* value is false. If several threads are waiting in this method, only one will get a chance to proceed when value is set to false. Which one of the threads gets to proceed is an arbitrary choice made by the virtual machine's thread scheduler. Internally, waitToSetTrue() invokes waitUntilFalse(), passing along the timeout information. The return value of waitUntilFalse() is stored in the local variable success (line 22). If waitUntilFalse() times out, it returns false; otherwise, it returns true. If true is returned, setValue() is used to alter value (lines 23–35). If the call to waitToSetTrue() succeeded in making a change, true is returned. If it times out while waiting, false is returned. If it is interrupted while waiting, an InterruptedException is thrown. The waitToSetFalse() method (lines 30–39) works in much the same way as waitToSetTrue().

The rest of the methods do not affect `value`, but simply provide information. The `isTrue()` (lines 41–43) and `isFalse()` (lines 45–47) methods provide information about the current setting of `value`.

The `waitUntilTrue()` method (lines 49–53) takes a timeout value (0 indicating never time out) and blocks until `value` is `true`, the specified number of milliseconds elapses, or an `InterruptedException` is triggered. If a timeout occurs, `false` is returned; otherwise, `true` is returned. The `waitUntilFalse()` method (lines 55–59) works in a very similar way. Both methods use the `waitUntilStateIs()` method as a helper.

The `waitUntilStateIs()` method (lines 61–87) is passed a value to match and a timeout. It blocks until the value is matched, the timeout occurs, or an `InterruptedException` is thrown. If it times out waiting for the condition, it returns `false`; otherwise, `true` is returned. A timeout of 0 indicates that it should block until the condition is met—regardless of how long that takes. This method uses the full-wait technique shown in Chapter 14.

Inter-Thread Signaling Using BooleanLock

`BooleanLock` can be a useful tool for signaling between two or more threads. For example, if one thread needs to wait for another thread to complete a task before proceeding, it can invoke the `waitUntilTrue()` method. When the other thread completes the task, that thread would invoke `setValue(true)`. Using `BooleanLock` allows the wait/notify mechanism to remain hidden from the two threads. The class `Signaling` (see Listing 17.2) demonstrates this pattern.

LISTING 17.2   Signaling.java—Inter-thread Signaling with BooleanLock

```
 1: public class Signaling extends Object {
 2:     private BooleanLock readyLock;
 3:
 4:     public Signaling(BooleanLock readyLock) {
 5:         this.readyLock = readyLock;
 6:
 7:         Runnable r = new Runnable() {
 8:                 public void run() {
 9:                     try {
10:                         runWork();
11:                     } catch ( Exception x ) {
12:                         // in case ANY exception slips through
13:                         x.printStackTrace();
14:                     }
15:                 }
16:             };
```

```
17:
18:            Thread internalThread = new Thread(r, "internal");
19:            internalThread.start();
20:        }
21:
22:        private void runWork() {
23:            try {
24:                print("about to wait for readyLock to be true");
25:                readyLock.waitUntilTrue(0);  // 0 - wait forever
26:                print("readyLock is now true");
27:            } catch ( InterruptedException x ) {
28:                print("interrupted while waiting for readyLock " +
29:                        "to become true");
30:            }
31:        }
32:
33:        private static void print(String msg) {
34:            String name = Thread.currentThread().getName();
35:            System.err.println(name + ": " + msg);
36:        }
37:
38:        public static void main(String[] args) {
39:            try {
40:                print("creating BooleanLock instance");
41:                BooleanLock ready = new BooleanLock(false);
42:
43:                print("creating Signaling instance");
44:                new Signaling(ready);
45:
46:                print("about to sleep for 3 seconds");
47:                Thread.sleep(3000);
48:
49:                print("about to setValue to true");
50:                ready.setValue(true);
51:                print("ready.isTrue()=" + ready.isTrue());
52:            } catch ( InterruptedException x ) {
53:                x.printStackTrace();
54:            }
55:        }
56: }
```

The Signaling class has two parts: the instance-specific code (lines 2–31) and the static methods used for the demonstration (lines 33–55). The static method print() (lines 33–36) is used by both parts to print detailed messages.

In the `main()` method (lines 38–55), an instance of `BooleanLock` is created (line 41). Next an instance of `Signaling` is created with a reference to the `BooleanLock` passed to its constructor (line 44). The `main` thread then sleeps for three seconds to allow the thread within the `Signaling` instance to start running (line 47). Finally, the `main` thread signals the internal thread by invoking `setValue()` with `true` (line 50) and verifies the change in state (line 51).

The constructor for `Signaling` (lines 4–20) uses the self-running object pattern and also stores the reference to the `BooleanLock` in `readyLock` (line 5).

In the `runWork()` method (lines 22–30), the internal thread prints a message and then waits for the signal to proceed (line 25). When the `BooleanLock` is finally set to `true`, the internal thread moves on and prints another message (line 26) before returning from `runWork()` to die.

Listing 17.3 shows the likely output from `Signaling`. Your output should match closely. The only possible differences are that lines 3 and 4 might be swapped with each other and lines 6 and 7 might be swapped with each other.

LISTING 17.3   Likely Output from Signaling

```
1: main: creating BooleanLock instance
2: main: creating Signaling instance
3: main: about to sleep for 3 seconds
4: internal: about to wait for readyLock to be true
5: main: about to setValue to true
6: main: ready.isTrue()=true
7: internal: readyLock is now true
```

Avoiding Blocking on synchronized

The `synchronized` keyword can be used for methods and statement blocks to ensure that only one thread is allowed access at a time. When threads are blocked waiting to acquire the `synchronized` lock, they do not respond to interrupts. In addition, there is no way to limit the amount of time that a thread will wait to enter a `synchronized` section. This can become a problem when the work done inside a `synchronized` section takes a relatively long time to complete. The examples in this section demonstrate how to work around this situation.

SyncBlock

`SyncBlock` (see Listing 17.4) demonstrates how threads blocked on a `synchronized` statement ignore interrupt requests.

LISTING 17.4   SyncBlock.java—Threads Blocked on synchronized Ignore Interrupts

```
 1: public class SyncBlock extends Object {
 2:     private Object longLock;
 3:
 4:     public SyncBlock() {
 5:         longLock = new Object();
 6:     }
 7:
 8:     public void doStuff() {
 9:         print("about to try to get exclusive access " +
10:                 "to longLock");
11:
12:         synchronized ( longLock ) {
13:             print("got exclusive access to longLock");
14:             try { Thread.sleep(10000); }
15:             catch ( InterruptedException x ) { }
16:             print("about to relinquish exclusive access to " +
17:                     "longLock");
18:         }
19:     }
20:
21:     private static void print(String msg) {
22:         String name = Thread.currentThread().getName();
23:         System.err.println(name + ": " + msg);
24:     }
25:
26:     private static Thread launch(
27:                     final SyncBlock sb,
28:                     String name
29:                 ) {
30:
31:         Runnable r = new Runnable() {
32:                 public void run() {
33:                     print("in run()");
34:                     sb.doStuff();
35:                 }
36:             };
37:
38:         Thread t = new Thread(r, name);
39:         t.start();
40:
```

continues

LISTING 17.4   Continued

```
41:            return t;
42:        }
43:
44:        public static void main(String[] args) {
45:            try {
46:                SyncBlock sb = new SyncBlock();
47:
48:                Thread t1 = launch(sb, "T1");
49:                Thread.sleep(500);
50:
51:                Thread t2 = launch(sb, "T2");
52:                Thread t3 = launch(sb, "T3");
53:
54:                Thread.sleep(1000);
55:
56:                print("about to interrupt T2");
57:                t2.interrupt();
58:                print("just interrupted T2");
59:
60:            } catch ( InterruptedException x ) {
61:                x.printStackTrace();
62:            }
63:        }
64: }
```

The SyncBlock class has two parts: the instance-specific code (lines 2–19) and the static methods used for the demonstration (lines 21–63). The static method print() (lines 21–24) is used by both parts to print detailed messages.

In main() (lines 44–63), an instance of SyncBlock is constructed to be shared by three threads (line 46). The launch() method (lines 26–42) takes a reference to this shared instance, creates a new Runnable (and Thread to run it), and uses this thread to simply invoke the doStuff() method of SyncBlock (line 34). A reference to this Thread is returned by launch().

The doStuff() method (lines 8–19) prints a message (lines 9–10) and then tries to acquire an exclusive lock on longLock (line 12). Once a thread gets exclusive access, it prints a message, sleeps for 10 seconds, and prints another message (lines 13–17). While one thread is inside sleeping for 10 seconds, other threads line up and block waiting to get exclusive access.

Back in main(), thread T1 is launched (line 48). It gets right into the synchronized block of doStuff() because no other threads are competing with it. After a half-second sleep, T2 is launched, immediately followed by T3 (lines 49–52). These two threads block on the synchronized statement (line 12) waiting for T1 to finish up and release the lock.

Meanwhile, the main thread sleeps for one second to be sure that T2 and T3 get a chance to block (line 54). Next, the main thread interrupts T2 (line 57) hoping to free it from its blocked state. As Listing 17.5 shows, this interrupt does *not* free T2.

LISTING 17.5   Possible Output from SyncBlock

```
 1: T1: in run()
 2: T1: about to try to get exclusive access to longLock
 3: T1: got exclusive access to longLock
 4: T3: in run()
 5: T3: about to try to get exclusive access to longLock
 6: T2: in run()
 7: T2: about to try to get exclusive access to longLock
 8: main: about to interrupt T2
 9: main: just interrupted T2
10: T1: about to relinquish exclusive access to longLock
11: T3: got exclusive access to longLock
12: T3: about to relinquish exclusive access to longLock
13: T2: got exclusive access to longLock
14: T2: about to relinquish exclusive access to longLock
```

Lines 8 and 9 are printed just before and just after T2 is interrupted. As you can see, this does not have the desired effect; T2 continues to wait and ultimately gains access (lines 13–14).

InterruptibleSyncBlock

InterruptibleSyncBlock (see Listing 17.6) uses the functionality of BooleanLock to have threads blocked on an interruptible wait() statement instead of a non-interruptible synchronized statement.

LISTING 17.6   InterruptibleSyncBlock.java—An Alternative Waiting List

```
 1: public class InterruptibleSyncBlock extends Object {
 2:     private Object longLock;
 3:     private BooleanLock busyLock;
 4:
 5:     public InterruptibleSyncBlock() {
 6:         longLock = new Object();
 7:         busyLock = new BooleanLock(false);
 8:     }
 9:
10:     public void doStuff() throws InterruptedException {
```

continues

LISTING 17.6   Continued

```
11:          print("about to try to get exclusive access " +
12:                  "to busyLock");
13:          busyLock.waitToSetTrue(0);
14:
15:          try {
16:              print("about to try to get exclusive access " +
17:                      "to longLock");
18:              synchronized ( longLock ) {
19:                  print("got exclusive access to longLock");
20:                  try {
21:                      Thread.sleep(10000);
22:                  } catch ( InterruptedException x ) {
23:                      // ignore
24:                  }
25:                  print("about to relinquish exclusive access " +
26:                          "to longLock");
27:              }
28:          } finally {
29:              print("about to free up busyLock");
30:              busyLock.setValue(false);
31:          }
32:      }
33:
34:      private static void print(String msg) {
35:          String name = Thread.currentThread().getName();
36:          System.err.println(name + ": " + msg);
37:      }
38:
39:      private static Thread launch(
40:                  final InterruptibleSyncBlock sb,
41:                  String name
42:              ) {
43:
44:          Runnable r = new Runnable() {
45:                  public void run() {
46:                      print("in run()");
47:                      try {
48:                          sb.doStuff();
49:                      } catch ( InterruptedException x ) {
50:                          print("InterruptedException thrown " +
51:                                  "from doStuff()");
52:                      }
53:                  }
54:              };
```

```
55:
56:          Thread t = new Thread(r, name);
57:          t.start();
58:
59:          return t;
60:      }
61:
62:      public static void main(String[] args) {
63:          try {
64:              InterruptibleSyncBlock sb =
65:                      new InterruptibleSyncBlock();
66:
67:              Thread t1 = launch(sb, "T1");
68:              Thread.sleep(500);
69:
70:              Thread t2 = launch(sb, "T2");
71:              Thread t3 = launch(sb, "T3");
72:
73:              Thread.sleep(1000);
74:
75:              print("about to interrupt T2");
76:              t2.interrupt();
77:              print("just interrupted T2");
78:
79:          } catch ( InterruptedException x ) {
80:              x.printStackTrace();
81:          }
82:      }
83: }
```

InterruptibleSyncBlock is very similar to SyncBlock, except for a few enhancements inside the doStuff() method (lines 10–32). A new member variable busyLock has been added (line 3), and it is an instance of BooleanLock (line 7). It is used inside doStuff() to control concurrent access. The waitToSetTrue() method is invoked by each thread as it enters doStuff() (line 13). Because a timeout of 0 is passed, threads will wait forever to get their turn—or at least until they are interrupted. When one of the threads gets notified that it can set the state to true, it does so and returns from waitToSetTrue(). All the other threads will get notified, but will see that some other thread has beat them and will go back to waiting inside waitToSetTrue(). The thread that gets to set busyLock to true then proceeds into the try block (lines 15–27). No matter how this thread leaves the try block (even by throwing an Exception or Error), it will enter the finally block (lines 28–31) and set busyLock back to false (line 30) to allow another thread to get into the exclusive section.

Because busyLock is now protecting the synchronized block, there might not be any need to synchronize on longLock. If there are other areas where longLock was being used to control concurrent access (which is not the case in the example), you have two options. One option is to protect concurrent access by using busyLock everywhere that longLock was previously used. The other option is to continue to have longLock protect all sections (as in this example) and to have busyLock provide a preliminary, interruptible barrier for long-running sections of code.

Listing 17.7 shows possible output when InterruptibleSyncBlock is run.

LISTING 17.7   Possible Output from InterruptibleSyncBlock

```
 1: T1: in run()
 2: T1: about to try to get exclusive access to busyLock
 3: T1: about to try to get exclusive access to longLock
 4: T1: got exclusive access to longLock
 5: T2: in run()
 6: T2: about to try to get exclusive access to busyLock
 7: T3: in run()
 8: T3: about to try to get exclusive access to busyLock
 9: main: about to interrupt T2
10: main: just interrupted T2
11: T2: InterruptedException thrown from doStuff()
12: T1: about to relinquish exclusive access to longLock
13: T1: about to free up busyLock
14: T3: about to try to get exclusive access to longLock
15: T3: got exclusive access to longLock
16: T3: about to relinquish exclusive access to longLock
17: T3: about to free up busyLock
```

This time, when T2 is interrupted (lines 9–10), it throws an InterruptedException (line 11) and is broken out of the blocked state.

This use of BooleanLock is great when a synchronized section of code might run for a long time. Also consider passing a non-zero timeout so that threads will not block forever waiting for exclusive access.

Noticing Brief Changes in Value Using TransitionDetector

The BooleanLock class is very useful when you need to know that the value inside has been changed *and remains changed*. As an example, consider this situation where there is an instance of BooleanLock

```
BooleanLock bl = new BooleanLock(false);
```

and you have two threads, threadA and threadB, each simultaneously running this code:

```
synchronized ( bl ) {
    bl.waitUntilTrue();
    bl.setValue(false);
}
```

Both threadA and threadB are blocked waiting inside the waitUntilTrue() method of BooleanLock. If a third thread, threadC, comes along and sets the value to true, both threadA and threadB are notified and compete to reacquire the lock before returning from wait() inside waitUntilTrue(). In this case, let's say that threadA reacquires the lock first, returns from wait(), returns from waitUntilTrue, and then invokes setValue() right away, passing in false. This all occurs before threadB returns from wait() because the synchronized statement block ensures that the object-level lock on bl is held until setValue() completes.

After threadA has set the value of bl back to false and left the synchronized block, threadB is able to reacquire the lock. threadB reacquires the lock, returns from the wait() inside waitUntilTrue(), and sees that the value is not true. Because the value is not true, threadB invokes wait() again and does not return from waitUntilTrue().

In many cases, this is the type of behavior that you need. However, there are times when you'll want your code to detect that the value changed from false to true *even if the value is no longer true*. BooleanLock does not provide this kind of information. You can used a class like TransitionDetector (see Listing 17.8) when you need to know that a change occurred—no matter how briefly the value remained in the new state.

LISTING 17.8   TransitionDetector.java—Sensing All the Changes in Value

```
 1: public class TransitionDetector extends Object {
 2:       private boolean value;
 3:       private Object valueLock;
 4:       private Object falseToTrueLock;
 5:       private Object trueToFalseLock;
 6:
 7:       public TransitionDetector(boolean initialValue) {
 8:           value = initialValue;
 9:           valueLock = new Object();
10:           falseToTrueLock = new Object();
11:           trueToFalseLock = new Object();
12:       }
13:
14:       public void setValue(boolean newValue) {
```

continues

LISTING 17.8   Continued

```
15:            synchronized ( valueLock ) {
16:                if ( newValue != value ) {
17:                    value = newValue;
18:
19:                    if ( value ) {
20:                        notifyFalseToTrueWaiters();
21:                    } else {
22:                        notifyTrueToFalseWaiters();
23:                    }
24:                }
25:            }
26:    }
27:
28:    public void pulseValue() {
29:        // Sync on valueLock to be sure that no other threads
30:        // get into setValue() between these two setValue()
31:        // calls.
32:        synchronized ( valueLock ) {
33:            setValue(!value);
34:            setValue(!value);
35:        }
36:    }
37:
38:    public boolean isTrue() {
39:        synchronized ( valueLock ) {
40:            return value;
41:        }
42:    }
43:
44:    public void waitForFalseToTrueTransition()
45:            throws InterruptedException {
46:
47:        synchronized ( falseToTrueLock ) {
48:            falseToTrueLock.wait();
49:        }
50:    }
51:
52:    private void notifyFalseToTrueWaiters() {
53:        synchronized ( falseToTrueLock ) {
54:            falseToTrueLock.notifyAll();
55:        }
56:    }
57:
58:    public void waitForTrueToFalseTransition()
```

The BooleanLock Utility

CHAPTER 17

423

17

THE
BOOLEANLOCK
UTILITY

```
59:                 throws InterruptedException {
60:
61:            synchronized ( trueToFalseLock ) {
62:                trueToFalseLock.wait();
63:            }
64:        }
65:
66:        private void notifyTrueToFalseWaiters() {
67:            synchronized ( trueToFalseLock ) {
68:                trueToFalseLock.notifyAll();
69:            }
70:        }
71:
72:        public String toString() {
73:            return String.valueOf(isTrue());
74:        }
75: }
```

`TransitionDetector` maintains three locks to control access and communication about the `boolean` value it encapsulates. In the constructor (lines 7–12), an initial value for `value` is passed in and stored. The three objects used for locking and inter-thread communication are created (lines 9–11). The `valueLock` object is used to control simultaneous access to `value`. The `falseToTrueLock` facilitates the use of the wait/notify mechanism to notify threads waiting for `value` to transition from `false` to `true`. The `trueToFalseLock` object is used to notify threads waiting for `value` to change from `true` to `false`.

Threads that want to know when `value` changes from `false` to `true` invoke the `waitForFalseToTrueTransition()` method (lines 44–50). Inside, the invoking thread simply waits on the `falseToTrueLock` for notification (line 48). On the other hand, threads that want to know when `value` changes from `true` to `false` invoke the `waitForTrueToFalseTransition()` method (lines 58–64). The threads that invoke this method simply wait on the `trueToFalseLock` for notification (line 62).

Inside `setValue()` (lines 14–26), exclusive access to `value` is controlled by synchronizing on `valueLock` (line 15). If the new value is indeed different than the current value (line 16), `value` is changed (line 17). Depending on which transition occurred, one of the two methods `notifyFalseToTrueWaiters()` or `notifyTrueToFalseWaiters()` is invoked to signal any threads waiting for that particular change (lines 19–23).

The `private` method `notifyFalseToTrueWaiters()` (lines 52–56) is only called from within `setValue()` while the lock is still held on `valueLock`. Inside, any and all threads waiting on `falseToTrueLock` are notified (line 54). The `notifyTrueToFalseWaiters()` method (lines 66–70) works similarly, but instead notifies threads waiting on the `trueToFalseLock` (line 68).

The pulseValue() method (lines 28–36) is used to momentarily change value. If value is false, it is changed to true and then changed right back to false. Likewise, if value is true, it is changed to false and immediately back to true. Both calls to setValue() occur inside a synchronized block to ensure that no other thread can get a lock on valueLock while between the calls (lines 32–35). Calling pulseValue() has the effect of notifying both the threads waiting inside waitForTrueToFalseTransition() and the threads waiting inside waitForFalseToTrueTransition().

TransitionDetectorMain (Listing 17.9) demonstrates how TransitionDetector can be used.

LISTING 17.9   TransitionDetectorMain.java—Demonstrating the Use of TransitionDetector

```
 1: public class TransitionDetectorMain extends Object {
 2:     private static Thread startTrueWaiter(
 3:             final TransitionDetector td,
 4:             String name
 5:         ) {
 6:
 7:         Runnable r = new Runnable() {
 8:             public void run() {
 9:                 try {
10:                     while ( true ) {
11:                         print("about to wait for false-to-" +
12:                             "true transition, td=" + td);
13:
14:                         td.waitForFalseToTrueTransition();
15:
16:                         print("just noticed for false-to-" +
17:                             "true transition, td=" + td);
18:                     }
19:                 } catch ( InterruptedException ix ) {
20:                     return;
21:                 }
22:             }
23:         };
24:
25:         Thread t = new Thread(r, name);
26:         t.start();
27:
28:         return t;
29:     }
30:
31:     private static Thread startFalseWaiter(
```

```
32:                final TransitionDetector td,
33:                String name
34:            ) {
35:
36:        Runnable r = new Runnable() {
37:                public void run() {
38:                    try {
39:                        while ( true ) {
40:                            print("about to wait for true-to-" +
41:                                "false transition, td=" + td);
42:
43:                            td.waitForTrueToFalseTransition();
44:
45:                            print("just noticed for true-to-" +
46:                                "false transition, td=" + td);
47:                        }
48:                    } catch ( InterruptedException ix ) {
49:                        return;
50:                    }
51:                }
52:            };
53:
54:        Thread t = new Thread(r, name);
55:        t.start();
56:
57:        return t;
58:    }
59:
60:    private static void print(String msg) {
61:        String name = Thread.currentThread().getName();
62:        System.err.println(name + ": " + msg);
63:    }
64:
65:    public static void main(String[] args) {
66:        try {
67:            TransitionDetector td =
68:                    new TransitionDetector(false);
69:
70:            Thread threadA = startTrueWaiter(td, "threadA");
71:            Thread threadB = startFalseWaiter(td, "threadB");
72:
73:            Thread.sleep(200);
74:            print("td=" + td + ", about to set to 'false'");
```

continues

LISTING 17.9   Continued

```
75:                    td.setValue(false);
76:
77:                    Thread.sleep(200);
78:                    print("td=" + td + ", about to set to 'true'");
79:                    td.setValue(true);
80:
81:                    Thread.sleep(200);
82:                    print("td=" + td + ", about to pulse value");
83:                    td.pulseValue();
84:
85:                    Thread.sleep(200);
86:                    threadA.interrupt();
87:                    threadB.interrupt();
88:              } catch ( InterruptedException x ) {
89:                    x.printStackTrace();
90:              }
91:       }
92: }
```

Inside main() (lines 65–91), an instance of TransitionDetector is constructed (line 68) and two threads are started to wait for transitions. After sleeping for a short period, the main thread invokes setValue(), passing in false (lines 73–75). 200 milliseconds later, main again invokes setValue(), this time passing in true (lines 77–79). After another 200 milliseconds pass, the main thread calls pulseValue() to notify both kinds of transition waiters (lines 81–83). Finally, main interrupts both of the threads that were started to get them to die (lines 86–87).

The startTrueWaiter() method (lines 2–29) creates a new thread that continually waits on waitForFalseToTrueTransition() (line 14). This new thread is called threadA. Each time through the infinite while loop, threadA prints information about the state of the instance of TransitionDetector (lines 11–17).

The startFalseWaiter() method (lines 31–58) works much like startTrueWaiter() but instead waits on waitForTrueToFalseTransition() (line 43).

Listing 17.10 shows the output produced when TransitionDetectorMain is run. Due to the indeterminate nature of the thread scheduler, your output might vary slightly.

LISTING 17.10   Possible Output from TransitionDetectorMain

```
 1: threadA: about to wait for false-to-true transition, td=false
 2: threadB: about to wait for true-to-false transition, td=false
 3: main: td=false, about to set to 'false'
 4: main: td=false, about to set to 'true'
 5: threadA: just noticed for false-to-true transition, td=true
 6: threadA: about to wait for false-to-true transition, td=true
 7: main: td=true, about to pulse value
 8: threadB: just noticed for true-to-false transition, td=true
 9: threadB: about to wait for true-to-false transition, td=true
10: threadA: just noticed for false-to-true transition, td=true
11: threadA: about to wait for false-to-true transition, td=true
```

Both `threadA` and `threadB` start up and wait for their desired transitions (lines 1–2). Note that it does not matter what the current setting of `value` is—both threads are waiting for `value` to *change*. The `main` thread sets `value` to `false`, but this has no effect because `value` was already `false` (line 3). Next, `main` sets `value` to `true` (line 4), which causes `threadA` to return from `waitForFalseToTrueTransition()` (line 5) and to loop again (line 6). After another 200-millisecond delay, `main` invokes `pulseValue()` (line 7). This causes both `threadA` and `threadB` to return and report that they noticed the transitions that they were waiting for (lines 8–11). Notice that `value` is `true` before *and after* `pulseValue()` is invoked.

Summary

`BooleanLock` can be used to simplify inter-thread communication. It nicely encapsulates the error-prone complexity of the wait/notify mechanism. Another useful application of `BooleanLock` is to provide an interruptible alternative to control access to `synchronized` blocks of code. `TransitionDetector` can be used when the fact that the internal value has changed is important, regardless of whether it has been changed back to its original value.

428

First-In-First-Out (FIFO) Queue

IN THIS CHAPTER

The First-In-First-Out (FIFO) queue is a data structure that has many applications in systems development. In this chapter, I'll show you a version of a FIFO queue that supports simultaneous access by multiple threads. In particular, I'll present two versions that are usable in the real world, as they are, and extendable:

- ObjectFIFO, which holds references to objects
- ByteFIFO, which holds byte values directly

How a FIFO Queue Works

As elements are added to a FIFO queue, they are stored in order. When elements are removed from a FIFO queue, they come out in exactly the same order as they were added. The first element put into the queue will be the first element taken out of the queue, the second element added to the queue will be the second element removed from the queue, and so on.

Figure 18.1 shows an example of how elements are added to a FIFO queue. In the first step, item A is added to an *empty* FIFO queue. In the second step, you can see that item A is at the bottom (where it will eventually be removed) and that item B is being added. In the third step, items A and B are in the queue, and item C is being added. The result is that items A, B, and C are inside the queue and are stacked in the order they were added.

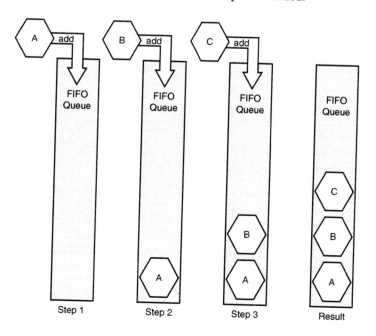

FIGURE 18.1

Adding items to a FIFO queue.

Figure 18.2 continues this example. In the first step, you can see that items A, B, and C are in the queue and that item A is about to be removed. In the second step, item A is gone, and items B and C have shifted down. When item D is added, it ends up behind item C. In the third step, items B, C, and D are in the FIFO queue, and item B is being removed. The fourth step shows only items C and D remaining; item C is about to be removed. The result is that only item D remains inside the queue, and items A, B, and C were removed in the same order as they were added. If another element were to be removed, it would be item D, after which the queue would be empty again.

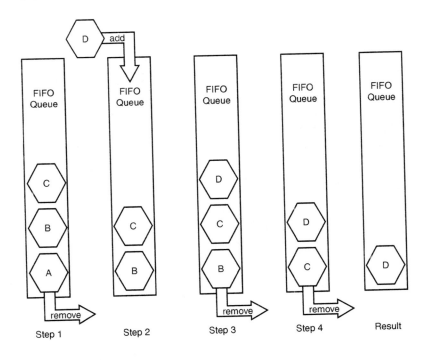

FIGURE 18.2
Removing items from and adding items to a FIFO queue.

Implementing a FIFO with an Array

You can implement a FIFO queue in many ways, including using a `Vector`, a linked list, an array, or any number of other options. In this chapter, I use an array of a fixed size to hold the elements. Because the array is fixed in size, the `capacity` of the FIFO is the length of the array. The `capacity` is the maximum number of elements that can be inside the queue at any one time. When all the array positions are filled, the FIFO is considered to be *full*. In addition, when the FIFO is full, calls to the `add()` method should block until space is available. Space becomes available when another thread invokes the `remove()` method. The slots are reused when items have been removed so that the array can be thought of as *circular*—after getting to the end, it wraps around to the beginning.

Figure 18.3 shows a FIFO implemented with an array that has a length of 5. The cells are numbered from 0 to 4. The `capacity` is the maximum number of elements the FIFO can hold. In this case, `capacity` is 5. The `size` is the number of elements currently being held inside the FIFO queue. In all FIFO queues, `size` is initially 0 and can grow to a maximum value that equals `capacity`.

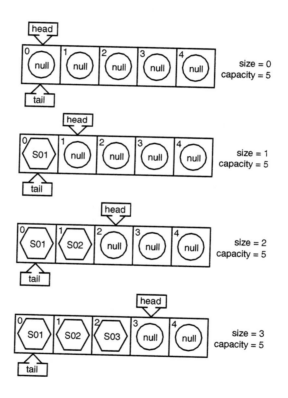

FIGURE 18.3

A FIFO implementation that uses an array to hold the items.

Two indexes into the array are held: the `head` and the `tail`. The `head` points to the cell where the next element added will be put. An element may be added to the cell pointed to by `head` only when the FIFO queue is not full. The `tail` points to the cell that holds the next element to be removed. An element may be removed from the cell pointed to by `tail` only when the FIFO is not empty. Initially, both `head` and `tail` point to cell 0.

The first snapshot of the FIFO in Figure 18.3 shows an empty queue. The next snapshot shows how it looks after item S01 is added. You can see that `size` has increased to 1, and that `head` now points to cell 1 (`capacity` and `tail` remain unchanged). The third snapshot shows how the FIFO looks after item S02 is added. Notice that `size` has increased to 2, and that `head` now points to cell 2. The last snapshot of this figure shows how the FIFO looks after item S03 has been added.

Figure 18.4 continues this example. The first snapshot shows how the FIFO queue looks after one item has been removed. The item removed used to be in cell 0 and was S01. As a result of this removal, `size` decreased to 2, and `tail` now points to cell 1. The second snapshot shows how the FIFO looks after item S04 has been added. The third snapshot shows the result of adding S05. The `size` has increased to 4, and the `head` pointer wrapped around and now points to cell 0. When S06 is added, it goes into cell 0, and `head` moves over to point to cell 1. At this time, both `head` and `tail` are pointing to the same cell. When the FIFO queue is empty or full, `head` and `tail` will point to the same cell.

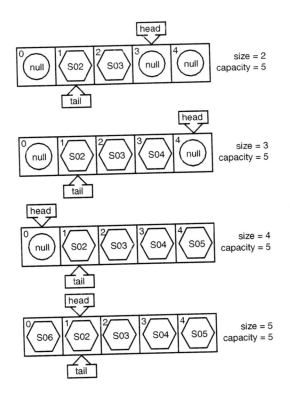

FIGURE 18.4

Adding and removing items with an array-based FIFO Queue.

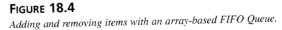

Table 18.1 summarizes how a FIFO queue is implemented with a fixed-size array.

TABLE 18.1   An Array Implementation of a FIFO Queue: A Summary of Terms

Term	Explanation
capacity	The maximum number of items that can be held (the length of the array)
size	The current number of items in the queue
head	The index into the array where the next item will be added
tail	The index into the array where the next item will be removed
empty	When size is equal to 0
full	When size is equal to capacity

Simple Implementation in Java: SimpleObjectFIFO

The class SimpleObjectFIFO shows how this model can be implemented in Java. This version holds references to objects as its item type. Synchronization is used to ensure that two or more threads can safely interact with the FIFO queue (see Chapter 7, "Concurrent Access to Objects and Variables"). The wait-notify mechanism is used to signal between threads when the state of the FIFO queue changes (see Chapter 8, "Inter-thread Communication"). Whenever an item is added or removed, notifyAll() is used to signal any and all waiting threads that the state of the FIFO queue has changed.

When one thread tries to add an item to a full queue, it blocks until the queue is no longer full. It does this by entering a wait state (which implicitly releases the lock) to allow another thread to come along and remove an item. When the other thread removes an item, it signals the waiting thread by invoking notifyAll(). The waiting thread then wakes up, reacquires the lock, returns from wait(), and completes the request to add the item.

Similarly, when one thread tries to remove an item from an empty queue, it blocks until the queue is no longer empty. It enters a wait state to allow another thread to come along and add an item. Listing 18.1 shows the code for SimpleObjectFIFO.

LISTING 18.1   SimpleObjectFIFO.java—A Simple FIFO Queue That Uses an Array Internally

```
1: public class SimpleObjectFIFO extends Object {
2:     private Object[] queue;
3:     private int capacity;
4:     private int size;
5:     private int head;
```

```
 6:      private int tail;
 7:
 8:      public SimpleObjectFIFO(int cap) {
 9:          capacity = ( cap > 0 ) ? cap : 1; // at least 1
10:          queue = new Object[capacity];
11:          head = 0;
12:          tail = 0;
13:          size = 0;
14:      }
15:
16:      public synchronized int getSize() {
17:          return size;
18:      }
19:
20:      public synchronized boolean isFull() {
21:          return ( size == capacity );
22:      }
23:
24:      public synchronized void add(Object obj)
                              � throws InterruptedException {
25:          while ( isFull() ) {
26:              wait();
27:          }
28:
29:          queue[head] = obj;
30:          head = ( head + 1 ) % capacity;
31:          size++;
32: c
33:          notifyAll(); // let any waiting threads know about change
34:      }
35:
36:      public synchronized Object remove()
                              � throws InterruptedException {
37:          while ( size == 0 ) {
38:              wait();
39:          }
40:
41:          Object obj = queue[tail];
42:          queue[tail] = null; // don't block GC by keeping reference
43:          tail = ( tail + 1 ) % capacity;
44:          size--;
45:
46:          notifyAll(); // let any waiting threads know about change
```

continues

LISTING 18.1   Continued

```
47:
48:            return obj;
49:        }
50:
51:        public synchronized void printState() {
52:            StringBuffer sb = new StringBuffer();
53:
54:            sb.append("SimpleObjectFIFO:\n");
55:            sb.append("          capacity=" + capacity + "\n");
56:
57:            sb.append("              size=" + size);
58:            if ( isFull() ) {
59:                sb.append(" - FULL");
60:            } else if ( size == 0 ) {
61:                sb.append(" - EMPTY");
62:            }
63:            sb.append("\n");
64:
65:            sb.append("              head=" + head + "\n");
66:            sb.append("              tail=" + tail + "\n");
67:
68:            for ( int i = 0; i < queue.length; i++ ) {
69:                sb.append("          queue[" + i + "]=" +
                        ➥ queue[i] + "\n");
70:            }
71: c
72:            System.out.print(sb);
73:        }
74: }
```

SimpleObjectFIFO has several member variables. None of them are marked as volatile
because all accesses and modifications to them occur within synchronized methods. The
private member variable queue is an array of Objects used to hold the references to objects
added (line 2). The length of this array is held in capacity (line 3). The current number of
items in the FIFO queue is held in size (line 4). The index into queue for the next addition is
held in head (line 5). The index into queue for the next item to be removed is held in tail
(line 6).

The constructor (lines 8–14) takes as its only argument the capacity of the new FIFO queue.
If the indicated capacity is less than 1, a minimum of 1 is silently used (line 9). An array is
allocated (line 10), and the head and tail pointers and size are all set to 0 (lines 10–13).

The getSize() method is synchronized to ensure that the most recent value for size is returned (lines 16–18). The isFull() method is synchronized to ensure that nothing changes while the full determination is being made (lines 20–22). The queue is considered to be full if the current size is equal to the capacity.

The add() method c (lines 24–34) also must be synchronized for multithread safety. Because add() could potentially have to wait if the FIFO queue is currently full, it declares that it might throw an InterruptedException (line 24). This exception is thrown if the thread is interrupted before it has a chance to add the item to the queue. The while loop (lines 25–27) is used to keep the thread from proceeding if the FIFO queue is currently full. It must be a while loop because if more than one thread is trying to simultaneously add items, the following statements would *not* always work:

```
if ( isFull() ) { // dangerous to use 'if' instead of 'while'
    wait();
}
```

If two threads are trying to add an item, and a third thread removes one item, only one of the two trying to add may proceed. The notifyAll() method is used instead of notify() so that *all* waiting threads return from wait() to check out the changed conditions (this is a deliberate choice to support the notification of threads that don't want to add or remove items, but simply want to know about the changes to the FIFO queue). If only one slot is available, only one of the threads waiting to add an item should proceed. This is why a while loop is necessary to ensure that—although the thread was notified and returned from wait()—it won't proceed unless the condition it was waiting on is *still* being met.

When the thread trying to add an item gets to line 29, at least one space is available in the FIFO queue for its item. The reference to the item is assigned to the slot where head is currently pointing (line 29). Next, head is incremented to point to the next cell. If head is already pointing to the last array position, it will be wrapped around to point to the first array position (line 30). Because an item has been added, size is incremented to reflect this change (line 31). Just before returning from add(), any and all waiting threads are notified of the change (line 33).

The remove() method (lines 36–49) also must be synchronized for multithread safety. Because remove() could potentially have to wait if the FIFO queue is currently empty, it declares that it might throw an InterruptedException (line 36). This exception is thrown if the thread is interrupted before it has a chance to remove an item from the queue. The while loop (lines 37–39) is used to keep the thread from proceeding if the FIFO queue is currently empty. The FIFO queue is considered empty as long as its size is 0. A while loop is also necessary here (for generally the same reasons that it was necessary inside add()), in case two threads are simultaneously blocked waiting to remove an item.

When the thread trying to remove an item gets to line 41, at least one item is available for removal in the FIFO queue. The reference to this item is stored in obj (line 41) so that it can be returned at the end of the method. Next, the slot in the FIFO queue has its value set to null (line 42) to ensure that the queue doesn't keep any unnecessary references to items that have been removed. If this were not done, it's possible that an item would not be available for garbage collection solely because of an outdated reference held in the FIFO queue. After this, tail is incremented to point to the next cell. If tail is already pointing to the last array position, it will be wrapped around to point to the first array position (line 43). Because an item has been removed, size is reduced to reflect this change (line 44). Just before returning from remove(), any and all waiting threads are notified of the change (line 46). Finally, the reference to the item just removed is returned to the caller (line 48).

The printState() method (lines 51–73) cis used to print out the values of all the member variables and the current contents of the queue. It is synchronized to ensure that nothing changes during printing. This method isn't really part of a FIFO queue implementation, but I include it here to show you the internal values of the FIFO queue at various points in time.

The class SimpleObjectFIFOTest, in Listing 18.2, isc used to show how SimpleObjectFIFO works.

LISTING 18.2   SimpleObjectFIFOTest.java—Code to Demonstrate SimpleObjectFIFO

```
 1: public class SimpleObjectFIFOTest extends Object {
 2:     public static void main(String[] args) {
 3:         try {
 4:             SimpleObjectFIFO fifo = new SimpleObjectFIFO(5);
 5:             fifo.printState();
 6:
 7:             fifo.add("S01");
 8:             fifo.printState();
 9:
10:             fifo.add("S02");
11:             fifo.printState();
12:
13:             fifo.add("S03");
14:             fifo.printState();
15:
16:             Object obj = fifo.remove();
17:             System.out.println("just removed obj=" + obj);
18:             fifo.printState();
19:
20:             fifo.add("S04");
21:             fifo.printState();
22:
```

```
23:                fifo.add("S05");
24:                fifo.printState();
25:
26:                fifo.add("S06");
27:                fifo.printState();
28:            } catch ( InterruptedException x ) {
29:                x.printStackTrace();
30:            }
31:        }
32: }
```

`SimpleObjectFIFOTest` simply performs the steps shown in Figures 18.3 and 18.4 and invokes `printState()` after each change. When cit is run, it produces the output shown in Listing 18.3.

LISTING 18.3 Output from SimpleObjectFIFOTest

```
 1: SimpleObjectFIFO:
 2:         capacity=5
 3:             size=0 - EMPTY
 4:             head=0
 5:             tail=0
 6:         queue[0]=null
 7:         queue[1]=null
 8:         queue[2]=null
 9:         queue[3]=null
10:         queue[4]=null
11: SimpleObjectFIFO:
12:         capacity=5
13:             size=1
14:             head=1
15:             tail=0
16:         queue[0]=S01
17:         queue[1]=null
18:         queue[2]=null
19:         queue[3]=null
20:         queue[4]=null
21: SimpleObjectFIFO:
22:         capacity=5
23:             size=2
24:             head=2
25:             tail=0
26:         queue[0]=S01
27:         queue[1]=S02
```

18

continues

LISTING 18.3   Continued

```
28:         queue[2]=null
29:         queue[3]=null
30:         queue[4]=null
31: SimpleObjectFIFO:
32:         capacity=5
33:            size=3
34:            head=3c
35:            tail=0
36:         queue[0]=S01
37:         queue[1]=S02
38:         queue[2]=S03
39:         queue[3]=null
40:         queue[4]=null
41: just removed obj=S01
42: SimpleObjectFIFO:
43:         capacity=5
44:            size=2
45:            head=3
46:            tail=1
47:         queue[0]=null
48:         queue[1]=S02
49:         queue[2]=S03
50:         queue[3]=null
51:         queue[4]=null
52: SimpleObjectFIFO:
53:         capacity=5
54:            size=3
55:            head=4
56:            tail=1
57:         queue[0]=null
58:         queue[1]=S02
59:         queue[2]=S03
60:         queue[3]=S04
61:         queue[4]=null
62: SimpleObjectFIFO:
63:         capacity=5
64:            size=4
65:            head=0
66:            tail=1
67:         queue[0]=null
68:         queue[1]=S02
69:         queue[2]=S03
70:         queue[3]=S04
71:         queue[4]=S05
```

```
72: SimpleObjectFIFO:
73:         capacity=5
74:            size=5 - FULL
75:            head=1
76:            tail=1
77:        queue[0]=S06
78:        queue[1]=S02
79:        queue[2]=S03
80:        queue[3]=S04
81:        queue[4]=S05
```

You will cnotice that capacity remains constant throughout but that size moves up and down as items are added and removed from the FIFO queue. In particular, take note of what happens when S01 is removed (line 41). The FIFO queue's size decreases from 3 to 2, and the tail pointer moves from cell 0 to cell 1. Also, take special note that the reference that was held to S01 is set to null (line 47). You should compare the output here with Figures 18.3 and 18.4 and notice that they correspond closely with one another.

An Expanded FIFO Queue for Object References: ObjectFIFO

The class ObjectFIFO removes the printState() method from SimpleObjectFIFO and expands on its foundation to create a more feature-rich FIFO queue for holding object references. The public API for ObjectFIFO consists of the following:

```
public ObjectFIFO(int cap)
public int getCapacity()
public synchronized int getSize()
public synchronized boolean isEmpty()
public synchronized boolean isFull()
public synchronized void add(Object obj) throws InterruptedException
public synchronized void addEach(Object[] list)
            ➥ throws InterruptedException
public synchronized Object remove() throws InterruptedException
public synchronized Object[] removeAll() throws InterruptedException
public synchronized Object[] removeAtLeastOne()
            ➥ throws InterruptedException
public synchronized boolean waitUntilEmpty(long msTimeout)
            ➥ throws InterruptedException
public synchronized void waitUntilEmpty() throws InterruptedException
public synchronized void waitWhileEmpty() throws InterruptedException
public synchronized void waitUntilFull() throws InterruptedException
public synchronized void waitWhileFull() throws InterruptedException
```

All the methods (except getCapacity()) are synchronized to ensure that multiple threads can safely and simultaneously interact with ObjectFIFO. The getCapacity() method does not have to be synchronized because the capacity never changes. The methods that might block waiting for something to change declare that they will throw an InterruptedException if interrupted while waiting. Listing 18.4 shows the code for ObjectFIFO. You should feel free to expand on this functionality by adding more methods—especially consider adding timeout options to all the methods that can block!

LISTING 18.4 ObjectFIFO.java—Fuller Implementation of a FIFO for Objects

```
 1: public class ObjectFIFO extends Object {
 2:      private Object[] queue;
 3:      private int capacity;
 4:      private int size;
 5:      private int head;
 6:      private int tail;
 7:
 8:      public ObjectFIFO(int cap) {
 9:          capacity = ( cap > 0 ) ? cap : 1; // at least 1
10:          queue = new Object[capacity];
11:          head = 0;
12:          tail = 0;
13:          size = 0;
14:      }
15:
16:      public int getCapacity() {
17:          return capacity;
18:      }
19:
20:      public synchronized int getSize() {
21:          return size;
22:      }
23:
24:      public synchronized boolean isEmpty() {
25:          return ( size == 0 );
26:      }
27:
28:      public synchronized boolean isFull() {
29:          return ( size == capacity );
30:      }
31:
32:      public synchronized void add(Object obj)
33:                  throws InterruptedException {
34:
```

```
35:            waitWhileFull();
36:
37:            queue[head] = obj;
38:            head = ( head + 1 ) % capacity;
39:            size++;
40:
41:            notifyAll(); // let any waiting threads know about change
42:        }
43:
44:    public synchronized void addEach(Object[] list)
45:            throws InterruptedException {
46:
47:            //
48:            // You might want to code a more efficient
49:            // implementation here ... (see ByteFIFO.java)
50:            //
51:
52:            for ( int i = 0; i < list.length; i++ ) {
53:                add(list[i]);
54:            }
55:        }
56:
57:    public synchronized Object remove()
58:            throws InterruptedException {
59:
60:            waitWhileEmpty();
61:
62:            Object obj = queue[tail];
63:
64:            // don't block GC by keeping unnecessary reference
65:            queue[tail] = null;
66:
67:            tail = ( tail + 1 ) % capacity;
68:            size--;
69:
70:            notifyAll(); // let any waiting threads know about change
71:
72:            return obj;
73:        }
74:
75:    public synchronized Object[] removeAll()
76:            throws InterruptedException {
77:
```

continues

LISTING 18.4   Continued

```
78:        //
79:        // You might want to code a more efficient
80:        // implementation here ... (see ByteFIFO.java)
81:        //
82:
83:        Object[] list = new Object[size]; // use the current size
84:
85:        for ( int i = 0; i < list.length; i++ ) {
86:            list[i] = remove();
87:        }
88:
89:        // if FIFO was empty, a zero-length array is returned
90:        return list;
91:    }
92:
93:    public synchronized Object[] removeAtLeastOne()
94:            throws InterruptedException {
95:
96:        waitWhileEmpty(); // wait for at least one to be in FIFO
97:        return removeAll();
98:    }
99:
100:   public synchronized boolean waitUntilEmpty(long msTimeout)
101:           throws InterruptedException {
102:
103:       if ( msTimeout == 0L ) {
104:           waitUntilEmpty();   // use other method
105:           return true;
106:       }
107:
108:       // wait only for the specified amount of time
109:       long endTime = System.currentTimeMillis() + msTimeout;
110:       long msRemaining = msTimeout;
111:
112:       while ( !isEmpty() && ( msRemaining > 0L ) ) {
113:           wait(msRemaining);
114:           msRemaining = endTime - System.currentTimeMillis();
115:       }
116:
117:       // May have timed out, or may have met condition,
118:       // calc return value.
119:       return isEmpty();
120:   }
121:
```

```
122:        public synchronized void waitUntilEmpty()
123:                throws InterruptedException {
124:
125:            while ( !isEmpty() ) {
126:                wait();
127:            }
128:        }
129:
130:        public synchronized void waitWhileEmpty()
131:                throws InterruptedException {
132:
133:            while ( isEmpty() ) {
134:                wait();
135:            }
136:        }
137:
138:        public synchronized void waitUntilFull()
139:                throws InterruptedException {
140:
141:            while ( !isFull() ) {
142:                wait();
143:            }
144:        }
145:
146:        public synchronized void waitWhileFull()
147:                throws InterruptedException {
148:
149:            while ( isFull() ) {
150:                wait();
151:            }
152:        }
153: }
```

In ObjectFIFO, the member variables, the constructor, and the getSize() and isFull() methods work the same as in SimpleObjectFIFO (described earlier in this chapter).

The getCapacity() method (lines 16–18) has been added for convenience to determine the maximum number of object references that can be held in the FIFO queue. The isEmpty() method (lines 24–26) returns true if the size is currently 0.

The add() method (lines 32–42) has been changed slightly to call waitWhileFull(), rather than handle the wait() call directly. Otherwise, the add() in ObjectFIFO is the same as in SimpleObjectFIFO.

The addEach() method (lines 44–55) supports adding each element in an Object[] as its own item. If an Object[] should be added as one item, add() should be called instead. Inside addEach(), the array is simply stepped through, and each element is individually put into the FIFO queue by invoking add() (lines 52–54). This could be done in a more efficient manner that directly works with queue, head, tail, and size (see ByteFIFO for one technique).

The remove() method (lines 57–73) has been changed slightly to call waitWhileEmpty(), rather than handle the wait() call directly. Otherwise, the remove() in ObjectFIFO is the same as in SimpleObjectFIFO.

The removeAll() method (lines 75–91) supports removing all the items currently in the FIFO queue and returning them in an Object[]. This method does not block—even if the current size is 0. If the queue is empty, a zero-length array will be returned. Inside removeAll(), an Object[] is created based on the current value of size (line 83). Then for each item, remove() is called, and the value returned is stored in this new array (line 86). Finally, the Object[] is returned (line 90). This could be done in a more efficient manner that directly works with queue, head, tail, and size (see ByteFIFO for one technique).

The removeAtLeastOne() method (lines 93–98) is used to wait until at least one item is in the FIFO queue and then to remove and return all the items in the queue. This method will block as long as the queue is empty (line 96). As soon as it is not empty (or if it wasn't empty to start with), removeAll() is invoked, and the Object[] it generates is returned (line 97).

The rest of the methods (waitUntil*X* and waitWhile*X*) kindly encapsulate the wait-notify mechanism so that users of ObjectFIFO don't have to burden themselves with synchronized and wait(). One of them, waitUntilEmpty(long msTimeout), takes a timeout value so that the waiting is not indefinite. You should consider extending this functionality to the others.

The waitUntilEmpty(long msTimeout) method (lines 100–120) is used to block until either no more items are in the FIFO queue or until the specified number of milliseconds elapses. If the queue is empty, true is returned; otherwise, false is returned. If the timeout is 0, the indefinite waitUntilEmpty() is called, and after that returns, true is returned (lines 103–106). Otherwise, the "waiting for the full timeout" technique from Chapter 14 is used (lines 109–119).

The ObjectFIFOTest class, in Listing 18.5, is used to demonstrate the ObjectFIFO class.

LISTING 18.5 ObjectFIFOTest.java—Demonstration Code for ObjectFIFO

```
1: public class ObjectFIFOTest extends Object {
2:
3:     private static void fullCheck(ObjectFIFO fifo) {
4:         try {
5:             // Sync'd to allow messages to print while
```

```
 6:                    // condition is still true.
 7:                    synchronized ( fifo ) {
 8:                        while ( true ) {
 9:                            fifo.waitUntilFull();
10:                            print("FULL");
11:                            fifo.waitWhileFull();
12:                            print("NO LONGER FULL");
13:                        }
14:                    }
15:                } catch ( InterruptedException ix ) {
16:                    return;
17:                }
18:            }
19:
20:            private static void emptyCheck(ObjectFIFO fifo) {
21:                try {
22:                    // Sync'd to allow messages to print while
23:                    // condition is still true.
24:                    synchronized ( fifo ) {
25:                        while ( true ) {
26:                            fifo.waitUntilEmpty();
27:                            print("EMPTY");
28:                            fifo.waitWhileEmpty();
29:                            print("NO LONGER EMPTY");
30:                        }
31:                    }
32:                } catch ( InterruptedException ix ) {
33:                    return;
34:                }
35:            }
36:
37:            private static void consumer(ObjectFIFO fifo) {
38:                try {
39:                    print("just entered consumer()");
40:
41:                    for ( int i = 0; i < 3; i++ ) {
42:                        synchronized ( fifo ) {
43:                            Object obj = fifo.remove();
44:                            print("DATA-OUT - did remove(), obj=" + obj);
45:                        }
46:                        Thread.sleep(3000);
47:                    }
```

continues

LISTING 18.5 Continued

```
48:
49:                synchronized ( fifo ) {
50:                    boolean resultOfWait = fifo.waitUntilEmpty(500);
51:                    print("did waitUntilEmpty(500), resultOfWait=" +
52:                            resultOfWait + ", getSize()=" +
53:                            fifo.getSize());
54:                }
55:
56:                for ( int i = 0; i < 3; i++ ) {
57:                    synchronized ( fifo ) {
58:                        Object[] list = fifo.removeAll();
59:                        print("did removeAll(), list.length=" +
60:                                list.length);
61:
62:                        for ( int j = 0; j < list.length; j++ ) {
63:                            print("DATA-OUT - list[" + j + "]=" +
64:                                    list[j]);
65:                        }
66:                    }
67:                    Thread.sleep(100);
68:                }
69:
70:                for ( int i = 0; i < 3; i++ ) {
71:                    synchronized ( fifo ) {
72:                        Object[] list = fifo.removeAtLeastOne();
73:                        print(
74:                            "did removeAtLeastOne(), list.length=" +
75:                            list.length);
76:
77:                        for ( int j = 0; j < list.length; j++ ) {
78:                            print("DATA-OUT - list[" + j + "]=" +
79:                                    list[j]);
80:                        }
81:                    }
82:                    Thread.sleep(1000);
83:                }
84:
85:                while ( !fifo.isEmpty() ) {
86:                    synchronized ( fifo ) {
87:                        Object obj = fifo.remove();
88:                        print("DATA-OUT - did remove(), obj=" + obj);
89:                    }
90:                    Thread.sleep(1000);
91:                }
92:
```

```
93:                    print("leaving consumer()");
94:            } catch ( InterruptedException ix ) {
95:                return;
96:            }
97:        }
98:
99:        private static void producer(ObjectFIFO fifo) {
100:            try {
101:                print("just entered producer()");
102:                int count = 0;
103:
104:                Object obj0 = new Integer(count);
105:                count++;
106:                synchronized ( fifo ) {
107:                    fifo.add(obj0);
108:                    print("DATA-IN - did add(), obj0=" + obj0);
109:
110:                    boolean resultOfWait = fifo.waitUntilEmpty(500);
111:                    print("did waitUntilEmpty(500), resultOfWait=" +
112:                            resultOfWait + ", getSize()=" +
113:                            fifo.getSize());
114:                }
115:
116:                for ( int i = 0; i < 10; i++ ) {
117:                    Object obj = new Integer(count);
118:                    count++;
119:                    synchronized ( fifo ) {
120:                        fifo.add(obj);
121:                        print("DATA-IN - did add(), obj=" + obj);
122:                    }
123:                    Thread.sleep(1000);
124:                }
125:
126:                Thread.sleep(2000);
127:
128:                Object obj = new Integer(count);
129:                count++;
130:                synchronized ( fifo ) {
131:                    fifo.add(obj);
132:                    print("DATA-IN - did add(), obj=" + obj);
133:                }
134:                Thread.sleep(500);
135:
```

continues

LISTING 18.5 Continued

```
136:                Integer[] list1 = new Integer[3];
137:                for ( int i = 0; i < list1.length; i++ ) {
138:                    list1[i] = new Integer(count);
139:                    count++;
140:                }
141:
142:                synchronized ( fifo ) {
143:                    fifo.addEach(list1);
144:                    print("did addEach(), list1.length=" +
145:                            list1.length);
146:                }
147:
148:                Integer[] list2 = new Integer[8];
149:                for ( int i = 0; i < list2.length; i++ ) {
150:                    list2[i] = new Integer(count);
151:                    count++;
152:                }
153:
154:                synchronized ( fifo ) {
155:                    fifo.addEach(list2);
156:                    print("did addEach(), list2.length=" +
157:                            list2.length);
158:                }
159:
160:                synchronized ( fifo ) {
161:                    fifo.waitUntilEmpty();
162:                    print("fifo.isEmpty()=" + fifo.isEmpty());
163:                }
164:
165:                print("leaving producer()");
166:            } catch ( InterruptedException ix ) {
167:                return;
168:            }
169:        }
170:
171:        private static synchronized void print(String msg) {
172:            System.out.println(
173:                Thread.currentThread().getName() + ": " + msg);
174:        }
175:
176:        public static void main(String[] args) {
177:            final ObjectFIFO fifo = new ObjectFIFO(5);
178:
179:            Runnable fullCheckRunnable = new Runnable() {
```

```
180:                public void run() {
181:                    fullCheck(fifo);
182:                }
183:            };
184:
185:        Thread fullCheckThread =
186:                new Thread(fullCheckRunnable, "fchk");
187:        fullCheckThread.setPriority(9);
188:        fullCheckThread.setDaemon(true); // die automatically
189:        fullCheckThread.start();
190:
191:        Runnable emptyCheckRunnable = new Runnable() {
192:                public void run() {
193:                    emptyCheck(fifo);
194:                }
195:            };
196:
197:        Thread emptyCheckThread =
198:                new Thread(emptyCheckRunnable, "echk");
199:        emptyCheckThread.setPriority(8);
200:        emptyCheckThread.setDaemon(true); // die automatically
201:        emptyCheckThread.start();
202:
203:        Runnable consumerRunnable = new Runnable() {
204:                public void run() {
205:                    consumer(fifo);
206:                }
207:            };
208:
209:        Thread consumerThread =
210:                new Thread(consumerRunnable, "cons");
211:        consumerThread.setPriority(7);
212:        consumerThread.start();
213:
214:        Runnable producerRunnable = new Runnable() {
215:                public void run() {
216:                    producer(fifo);
217:                }
218:            };
219:
220:        Thread producerThread =
221:                new Thread(producerRunnable, "prod");
222:        producerThread.setPriority(6);
223:        producerThread.start();
224:    }
225: }
```

ObjectFIFOTest starts four threads to simultaneously access an ObjectFIFO created with a capacity of 5 items (line 177). The fullCheckThread (lines 179–189) is used to run the fullCheck() method (lines 3–18). The fullCheck() method first waits until the FIFO queue is full (line 9) and then prints a message (line 10). It then waits until the FIFO queue is no longer full (line 11) and then prints a message (line 12). It continues to loop through these two checks indefinitely (line 8).

Next, the "main" thread creates the emptyCheckThread (lines 191–201) to run emptyCheck() (lines 20–35). This method works just like fullCheck() but instead prints messages when the FIFO queue transitions to and from the empty state.

The consumerThread is then created (lines 203–212) to run consumer() (lines 37–97). Inside the consumer() method, the thread exercises all the removeX methods.

Finally the producerThread is created (lines 214–223) to run producer() (lines 99–169). Inside the producer() method, several of the addX methods are used to sporadically add items to the queue.

The print() method (lines 171–174) is used to produce all the console output. It prefixes each message with the name of the thread that sent the message.

Listing 18.6 shows the output from a particular run of ObjectFIFOTest. Your output is likely to differ slightly because the four threads running will be scheduled somewhat randomly. The main thing to notice is that all the items added are eventually removed in the proper order.

LISTING 18.6   Possible Output from ObjectFIFOTest

```
 1: echk: EMPTY
 2: cons: just entered consumer()
 3: prod: just entered producer()
 4: prod: DATA-IN - did add(), obj0=0
 5: echk: NO LONGER EMPTY
 6: cons: DATA-OUT - did remove(), obj=0
 7: echk: EMPTY
 8: prod: did waitUntilEmpty(500), resultOfWait=true, getSize()=0
 9: prod: DATA-IN - did add(), obj=1
10: echk: NO LONGER EMPTY
11: prod: DATA-IN - did add(), obj=2
12: prod: DATA-IN - did add(), obj=3
13: cons: DATA-OUT - did remove(), obj=1
14: prod: DATA-IN - did add(), obj=4
15: prod: DATA-IN - did add(), obj=5
16: prod: DATA-IN - did add(), obj=6
17: fchk: FULL
18: cons: DATA-OUT - did remove(), obj=2
```

```
19: fchk: NO LONGER FULL
20: prod: DATA-IN - did add(), obj=7
21: fchk: FULL
22: cons: did waitUntilEmpty(500), resultOfWait=false, getSize()=5
23: cons: did removeAll(), list.length=5
24: cons: DATA-OUT - list[0]=3
25: cons: DATA-OUT - list[1]=4
26: cons: DATA-OUT - list[2]=5
27: cons: DATA-OUT - list[3]=6
28: cons: DATA-OUT - list[4]=7
29: fchk: NO LONGER FULL
30: echk: EMPTY
31: prod: DATA-IN - did add(), obj=8
32: echk: NO LONGER EMPTY
33: cons: did removeAll(), list.length=1
34: cons: DATA-OUT - list[0]=8
35: echk: EMPTY
36: cons: did removeAll(), list.length=0
37: prod: DATA-IN - did add(), obj=9
38: echk: NO LONGER EMPTY
39: cons: did removeAtLeastOne(), list.length=1
40: cons: DATA-OUT - list[0]=9
41: echk: EMPTY
42: prod: DATA-IN - did add(), obj=10
43: echk: NO LONGER EMPTY
44: cons: did removeAtLeastOne(), list.length=1
45: cons: DATA-OUT - list[0]=10
46: echk: EMPTY
47: prod: DATA-IN - did add(), obj=11
48: echk: NO LONGER EMPTY
49: cons: did removeAtLeastOne(), list.length=1
50: cons: DATA-OUT - list[0]=11
51: echk: EMPTY
52: prod: did addEach(), list1.length=3
53: echk: NO LONGER EMPTY
54: fchk: FULL
55: cons: DATA-OUT - did remove(), obj=12
56: fchk: NO LONGER FULL
57: fchk: FULL
58: cons: DATA-OUT - did remove(), obj=13
59: fchk: NO LONGER FULL
60: fchk: FULL
61: cons: DATA-OUT - did remove(), obj=14
62: fchk: NO LONGER FULL
```

18

FIRST-IN-FIRST-OUT
(FIFO) QUEUE

continues

LISTING 18.6 Continued

```
63: fchk: FULL
64: cons: DATA-OUT - did remove(), obj=15
65: fchk: NO LONGER FULL
66: fchk: FULL
67: cons: DATA-OUT - did remove(), obj=16
68: fchk: NO LONGER FULL
69: fchk: FULL
70: cons: DATA-OUT - did remove(), obj=17
71: fchk: NO LONGER FULL
72: prod: did addEach(), list2.length=8
73: fchk: FULL
74: cons: DATA-OUT - did remove(), obj=18
75: fchk: NO LONGER FULL
76: cons: DATA-OUT - did remove(), obj=19
77: cons: DATA-OUT - did remove(), obj=20
78: cons: DATA-OUT - did remove(), obj=21
79: cons: DATA-OUT - did remove(), obj=22
80: echk: EMPTY
81: prod: fifo.isEmpty()=true
82: prod: leaving producer()
83: cons: leaving consumer()
```

A FIFO Queue for Bytes: ByteFIFO

The class ByteFIFO is very similar to ObjectFIFO, except that it holds byte values instead of object references. It is much more efficient to store bytes directly, rather than wrap them in Byte instances and store them as references. The public API for ByteFIFO consists of the following:

```
public ByteFIFO(int cap)
public int getCapacity()
public synchronized int getSize()
public synchronized boolean isEmpty()
public synchronized boolean isFull()
public synchronized void add(byte b) throws InterruptedException
public synchronized void add(byte[] list) throws InterruptedException
public synchronized byte remove() throws InterruptedException
public synchronized byte[] removeAll()
public synchronized byte[] removeAtLeastOne()
            ➡ throws InterruptedException
public synchronized boolean waitUntilEmpty(long msTimeout)
            ➡ throws InterruptedException
```

```
public synchronized void waitUntilEmpty() throws InterruptedException
public synchronized void waitWhileEmpty() throws InterruptedException
public synchronized void waitUntilFull() throws InterruptedException
public synchronized void waitWhileFull() throws InterruptedException
```

This is pretty much the same API as ObjectFIFO, except that byte and byte[] are passed and returned instead of Object and Object[]. In addition, the addEach() method is gone; it is replaced with an overloaded add() method that takes a byte[] as the parameter.

All the methods (except getCapacity()) are synchronized to ensure that multiple threads can safely and simultaneously interact with ByteFIFO. The getCapacity() method does not have to be synchronized because the capacity never changes. The methods that might block, waiting for something to change, declare that they will throw an InterruptedException if interrupted while waiting. Listing 18.7 shows the code for ByteFIFO.

LISTING 18.7 ByteFIFO.java—A FIFO Queue That Holds Bytes

```
 1: public class ByteFIFO extends Object {
 2:        private byte[] queue;
 3:        private int capacity;
 4:        private int size;
 5:        private int head;
 6:        private int tail;
 7:
 8:        public ByteFIFO(int cap) {
 9:            capacity = ( cap > 0 ) ? cap : 1; // at least 1
10:            queue = new byte[capacity];
11:            head = 0;
12:            tail = 0;
13:            size = 0;
14:        }
15:
16:        public int getCapacity() {
17:            return capacity;
18:        }
19:
20:        public synchronized int getSize() {
21:            return size;
22:        }
23:
24:        public synchronized boolean isEmpty() {
25:            return ( size == 0 );
```

continues

LISTING 18.7   Continued

```
26:      }
27:
28:      public synchronized boolean isFull() {
29:          return ( size == capacity );
30:      }
31:
32:      public synchronized void add(byte b)
33:              throws InterruptedException {
34:
35:          waitWhileFull();
36:
37:          queue[head] = b;
38:          head = ( head + 1 ) % capacity;
39:          size++;
40:
41:          notifyAll(); // let any waiting threads know about change
42:      }
43:
44:      public synchronized void add(byte[] list)
45:              throws InterruptedException {
46:
47:          // For efficiency, the bytes are copied in blocks
48:          // instead of one at a time. As space becomes available,
49:          // more bytes are copied until all of them have been
50:          // added.
51:
52:          int ptr = 0;
53:
54:          while ( ptr < list.length ) {
55:              // If full, the lock will be released to allow
56:              // another thread to come in and remove bytes.
57:              waitWhileFull();
58:
59:              int space = capacity - size;
60:              int distToEnd = capacity - head;
61:              int blockLen = Math.min(space, distToEnd);
62:
63:              int bytesRemaining = list.length - ptr;
64:              int copyLen = Math.min(blockLen, bytesRemaining);
65:
66:              System.arraycopy(list, ptr, queue, head, copyLen);
67:              head = ( head + copyLen ) % capacity;
68:              size += copyLen;
69:              ptr += copyLen;
70:
```

```
71:                    // Keep the lock, but let any waiting threads
72:                    // know that something has changed.
73:                    notifyAll();
74:                }
75:        }
76:
77:        public synchronized byte remove()
78:                   throws InterruptedException {
79:
80:            waitWhileEmpty();
81:
82:            byte b = queue[tail];
83:            tail = ( tail + 1 ) % capacity;
84:            size - ;
85:
86:            notifyAll(); // let any waiting threads know about change
87:
88:            return b;
89:        }
90:
91:        public synchronized byte[] removeAll() {
92:            // For efficiency, the bytes are copied in blocks
93:            // instead of one at a time.
94:
95:            if ( isEmpty() ) {
96:                    // Nothing to remove, return a zero-length
97:                    // array and do not bother with notification
98:                    // since nothing was removed.
99:                    return new byte[0];
100:           }
101:
102:           // based on the current size
103:           byte[] list = new byte[size];
104:
105:           // copy in the block from tail to the end
106:           int distToEnd = capacity - tail;
107:           int copyLen = Math.min(size, distToEnd);
108:           System.arraycopy(queue, tail, list, 0, copyLen);
109:
110:           // If data wraps around, copy the remaining data
111:           // from the front of the array.
112:           if ( size > copyLen ) {
113:               System.arraycopy(
```

continues

LISTING 18.7   Continued

```
114:                        queue, 0, list, copyLen, size - copyLen);
115:         }
116:
117:         tail = ( tail + size ) % capacity;
118:         size = 0; // everything has been removed
119:
120:         // Signal any and all waiting threads that
121:         // something has changed.
122:         notifyAll();
123:
124:         return list;
125:     }
126:
127:     public synchronized byte[] removeAtLeastOne()
128:             throws InterruptedException {
129:
130:         waitWhileEmpty(); // wait for at least one to be in FIFO
131:         return removeAll();
132:     }
133:
134:     public synchronized boolean waitUntilEmpty(long msTimeout)
135:             throws InterruptedException {
136:
137:         if ( msTimeout == 0L ) {
138:             waitUntilEmpty();  // use other method
139:             return true;
140:         }
141:
142:         // wait only for the specified amount of time
143:         long endTime = System.currentTimeMillis() + msTimeout;
144:         long msRemaining = msTimeout;
145:
146:         while ( !isEmpty() && ( msRemaining > 0L ) ) {
147:             wait(msRemaining);
148:             msRemaining = endTime - System.currentTimeMillis();
149:         }
150:
151:         // May have timed out, or may have met condition,
152:         // calc return value.
153:         return isEmpty();
154:     }
155:
156:     public synchronized void waitUntilEmpty()
157:             throws InterruptedException {
158:
```

```
159:            while ( !isEmpty() ) {
160:                wait();
161:            }
162:        }
163:
164:        public synchronized void waitWhileEmpty()
165:                throws InterruptedException {
166:
167:            while ( isEmpty() ) {
168:                wait();
169:            }
170:        }
171:
172:        public synchronized void waitUntilFull()
173:                throws InterruptedException {
174:
175:            while ( !isFull() ) {
176:                wait();
177:            }
178:        }
179:
180:        public synchronized void waitWhileFull()
181:                throws InterruptedException {
182:
183:            while ( isFull() ) {
184:                wait();
185:            }
186:        }
187: }
```

The getCapacity(), getSize(), isEmpty(), isFull(), waitUntilEmpty(long msTimeout), waitUntilEmpty(), waitWhileEmpty(), waitUntilFull(), and waitWhileFull() methods work exactly the same as in ObjectFIFO (see the descriptions earlier in this chapter). The removeAtLeastOne() method (lines 127–132) differs only in that it returns a byte[]. The add(byte b) method (lines 32–42) differs only in that it is passed a byte (line 32) and stores a byte (line 37).

The remove() method (lines 77–89) is much the same as before but instead handles bytes. In addition, it no longer has to set the vacated cell to null (or any other value) because the values in a byte[] don't interfere with garbage collection.

The add(byte[] list) method (lines 44–75) efficiently stores the values directly into the queue, rather than repeatedly invoking add(byte b). If list has a length greater than 0, the while loop is entered. Inside the while, waitWhileFull() is invoked (line 57) to block and wait, if necessary, for more space to become available. The number of open cells (space) is calculated (line 59). The number of cells (distToEnd) between the current position of head and the end of the array is calculated (line 60). The lesser of space and distToEnd is used to calculate blockLen, which is the largest block that can be copied in one operation (line 61).

Next, the number of bytes that still have to be copied (bytesRemaining) from list into queue is calculated (line 63). The number of bytes that will be copied this time through the loop (copyLen) is the lesser of blockLen and bytesRemaining (line 64). The actual copying from list into queue is performed for copyLen bytes (line 66). The values for head, size, and ptr are all adjusted based on copyLen (lines 67–69). Any and all waiting threads are notified that the state of the FIFO queue has changed (line 73). The while loop continues until all the bytes in list have been copied into queue. Each time through the while loop, the thread may block in waitWhileFull() to allow another thread to come in and remove some bytes to make more space.

The removeAll() method (lines 91–125) efficiently copies bytes from queue into a new byte array. Note that it has no need to throw an InterruptedException because it never blocks. This byte array has a length equal to the current number of bytes in the FIFO queue—possibly a length of 0 if the FIFO queue is currently empty (lines 95–100). If the queue is not empty, a byte[] is created, with a length equal to the current number of items in the queue (line 103). The number of cells from the tail pointer to the end of the array is calculated and stored in distToEnd (line 106). The number of bytes to copy (copyLen) is the minimum of distToEnd and size (line 107). These bytes are copied into list, which will be returned (line 108). If more bytes have to be copied from the beginning of the queue because the data wrapped around, they are copied based on the difference between size and copyLen (lines 112–115). The tail pointer is adjusted by size to reflect the removal of the bytes (line 117). The size is set to 0 because the FIFO queue is now empty (line 118). Any and all waiting threads are notified of the changes to the FIFO queue (line 122). Finally, the array containing the copied bytes is returned (line 124).

ByteFIFOTest, in Listing 18.8, is used to demonstrate some of the functionality of ByteFIFO. Basically, a set of strings is serialized and passed by one thread through a ByteFIFO to another thread. This other thread gathers up the bytes as they come through the FIFO queue and reconstructs the strings.

LISTING 18.8 ByteFIFOTest.java—Code to Demonstrate ByteFIFO

```
1: import java.io.*;
2:
3: public class ByteFIFOTest extends Object {
4:     private ByteFIFO fifo;
5:     private byte[] srcData;
6:
```

```
 7:        public ByteFIFOTest() throws IOException {
 8:            fifo = new ByteFIFO(20);
 9:
10:            makeSrcData();
11:            System.out.println("srcData.length=" + srcData.length);
12:
13:            Runnable srcRunnable = new Runnable() {
14:                    public void run() {
15:                        src();
16:                    }
17:                };
18:            Thread srcThread = new Thread(srcRunnable);
19:            srcThread.start();
20:
21:            Runnable dstRunnable = new Runnable() {
22:                    public void run() {
23:                        dst();
24:                    }
25:                };
26:            Thread dstThread = new Thread(dstRunnable);
27:            dstThread.start();
28:        }
29:
30:        private void makeSrcData() throws IOException {
31:            String[] list = {
32:                    "The first string is right here",
33:              "The second string is a bit longer and also right here",
34:                    "The third string",
35:                    "ABCDEFGHIJKLMNOPQRSTUVWXYZ",
36:                    "0123456789",
37:                    "The last string in the list"
38:                };
39:
40:            ByteArrayOutputStream baos = new ByteArrayOutputStream();
41:            ObjectOutputStream oos = new ObjectOutputStream(baos);
42:            oos.writeObject(list);
43:            oos.flush();
44:            oos.close();
45:
46:            srcData = baos.toByteArray();
47:        }
48:
49:        private void src() {
50:            try {
51:                boolean justAddOne = true;
52:                int count = 0;
```

LISTING 18.8   Continued

```
53:
54:                    while ( count < srcData.length ) {
55:                        if ( !justAddOne ) {
56:                            int writeSize =
                                    ➥ (int) ( 40.0 * Math.random() );
57:                            writeSize = Math.min(writeSize,
                                    ➥ srcData.length - count);
58:
59:                            byte[] buf = new byte[writeSize];
60:                            System.arraycopy(
                                        ➥ srcData, count, buf, 0, writeSize);
61:                            fifo.add(buf);
62:                            count += writeSize;
63:
64:                            System.out.println(
                                        ➥ "just added " + writeSize + " bytes");
65:                        } else {
66:                            fifo.add(srcData[count]);
67:                            count++;
68:
69:                            System.out.println(
                                        ➥ "just added exactly 1 byte");
70:                        }
71:
72:                        justAddOne = !justAddOne;
73:                    }
74:            } catch ( InterruptedException x ) {
75:                x.printStackTrace();
76:            }
77:        }
78:
79:    private void dst() {
80:        try {
81:            boolean justAddOne = true;
82:            int count = 0;
83:            byte[] dstData = new byte[srcData.length];
84:
85:            while ( count < dstData.length ) {
86:                if ( !justAddOne ) {
87:                    byte[] buf = fifo.removeAll();
88:                    if ( buf.length > 0 ) {
89:                        System.arraycopy(buf, 0,
                                    ➥ dstData, count, buf.length);
```

```
90:                              count += buf.length;
91:                          }
92:
93:                          System.out.println(
94:                              "just removed " + buf.length + " bytes");
95:                      } else {
96:                          byte b = fifo.remove();
97:                          dstData[count] = b;
98:                          count++;
99:
100:                         System.out.println(
101:                             "just removed exactly 1 byte");
102:                     }
103:
104:                     justAddOne = !justAddOne;
105:                 }
106:
107:                 System.out.println(
                         ➥ "received all data, count=" + count);
108:
109:                 ObjectInputStream ois = new ObjectInputStream(
110:                         new ByteArrayInputStream(dstData));
111:
112:                 String[] line = (String[]) ois.readObject();
113:
114:                 for ( int i = 0; i < line.length; i++ ) {
115:                     System.out.println("line[" + i + "]=" + line[i]);
116:                 }
117:         } catch ( ClassNotFoundException x1 ) {
118:             x1.printStackTrace();
119:         } catch ( IOException iox ) {
120:             iox.printStackTrace();
121:         } catch ( InterruptedException x ) {
122:             x.printStackTrace();
123:         }
124:     }
125:
126:     public static void main(String[] args) {
127:         try {
128:             new ByteFIFOTest();
129:         } catch ( IOException iox ) {
130:             iox.printStackTrace();
131:         }
132:     }
133: }
```

The constructor for ByteFIFOTest creates a relatively small ByteFIFO with a capacity of 20 (line 8) for transferring data from one thread to another. The makeSrcData() method is called (line 10) to load srcData (line 5) with the bytes that will be pushed through the ByteFIFO. Next, a thread is created to run the src() method, and another thread is created to run the dst() method.

Inside makeSrcData() (lines 30–47), an array of strings (lines 31–38) is created and written to an ObjectOutputStream (lines 41–44). The ObjectOutputStream() passes the serialized data on to a ByteArrayOutputStream() (line 40). The bytes collected are turned into a byte[] and stored in srcData (line 46).

The src() method (lines 49–77) takes the bytes from srcData and pushes them into the FIFO queue. It alternates between adding a single byte and adding a byte array each time through the while loop by toggling the justAddOne variable (lines 51, 55, and 72). The size of the byte[] to be added is randomly determined (line 56) to keep things interesting. As data is added to the ByteFIFO, messages are printed (lines 64 and 69). This method completes when all the bytes in srcData have been added to the FIFO queue.

The dst() method (lines 79–124) removes the bytes from the ByteFIFO, stores them in a local array, and then de-serializes the object to confirm its successful transmission. The dst() method alternates between remove() and removeAll() each time through the while loop. The looping continues until the specified number of bytes has been removed (lines 83–85). As data is removed from the ByteFIFO, messages are printed (lines 93–94, 100, and 101). When all the bytes have been retrieved, they are used to create a ByteArrayInputStream that is, in turn, used to create an ObjectInputStream (lines 109–110). The one object that is serialized is a String[], and an attempt to read it back and cast it into its proper type is made (line 112). The String[] is then iterated through, and each string is printed to confirm uncorrupted delivery (lines 114–116).

Listing 18.9 shows possible output when ByteFIFOTest is run. Your output is likely to differ a bit, but ultimately, the list of strings printed at the end should match exactly.

Listing 18.9   Possible Output from Running ByteFIFOTest

```
 1: srcData.length=224
 2: just added exactly 1 byte
 3: just removed exactly 1 byte
 4: just removed 19 bytes
 5: just added 26 bytes
 6: just added exactly 1 byte
 7: just added 7 bytes
 8: just added exactly 1 byte
 9: just removed exactly 1 byte
```

```
10: just removed 20 bytes
11: just added 20 bytes
12: just removed exactly 1 byte
13: just added exactly 1 byte
14: just removed 15 bytes
15: just added 18 bytes
16: just removed exactly 1 byte
17: just added exactly 1 byte
18: just removed 18 bytes
19: just removed exactly 1 byte
20: just added 21 bytes
21: just removed 20 bytes
22: just added exactly 1 byte
23: just removed exactly 1 byte
24: just added 0 bytes
25: just removed 0 bytes
26: just added exactly 1 byte
27: just removed exactly 1 byte
28: just removed 20 bytes
29: just added 33 bytes
30: just removed exactly 1 byte
31: just added exactly 1 byte
32: just removed 13 bytes
33: just removed exactly 1 byte
34: just removed 20 bytes
35: just added 23 bytes
36: just added exactly 1 byte
37: just removed exactly 1 byte
38: just removed 19 bytes
39: just added 24 bytes
40: just added exactly 1 byte
41: just added 5 bytes
42: just added exactly 1 byte
43: just removed exactly 1 byte
44: just added 6 bytes
45: just removed 19 bytes
46: just added exactly 1 byte
47: just removed exactly 1 byte
48: just added 20 bytes
49: just removed 20 bytes
50: just added exactly 1 byte
51: just removed exactly 1 byte
52: just added 8 bytes
53: just removed 8 bytes
```

continues

LISTING 18.9   Continued

```
54: received all data, count=224
55: line[0]=The first string is right here
56: line[1]=The second string is a bit longer and also right here
57: line[2]=The third string
58: line[3]=ABCDEFGHIJKLMNOPQRSTUVWXYZ
59: line[4]=0123456789
60: line[5]=The last string in the list
```

Summary

First-In-First-Out queues that can be simultaneously and safely accessed by multiple threads play a useful role in system development. In this chapter, I showed you two types of FIFO queues: one that holds object references (ObjectFIFO) and one that holds byte values (ByteFIFO). These implementations conveniently encapsulate the complexity of the wait-notify mechanism to simplify the use of the classes.

Appendixes

PART

III

IN THIS PART

The Thread API

IN THIS APPENDIX

This appendix summarizes the `public` and `protected` members of the `Thread` class. It is based on Sun Microsystems' Java Development Kit 1.2. Information has been combined from Sun's API documentation, source code, reflection on the distributed classes, and the *Java Language Specification*.

Many of the methods and some of the constructors can throw a `SecurityException`. `SecurityException` is a subclass of `RuntimeException`, so try/catch blocks are not *required* for any of the methods of `Thread` that might throw it. By default, an application does not have a `SecurityManager` defined (using JDK 1.0, 1.1, or 1.2 from Sun Microsystems). An applet, on the other hand, *might* have a `SecurityManager` present. In general, this exception is thrown when the calling thread is not permitted to perform the requested action. Many times, the security check is done by invoking the `checkAccess()` method on `Thread`, which in turn checks to see if a `SecurityManager` has been installed, and if so, invokes its `checkAccess(Thread)` method. For most of your application programming, you can safely ignore the possibility of a `SecurityException` being thrown.

Throughout this appendix, the terms "this thread" and "current thread" are used. The "current thread" term refers to the thread that invoked the method. The "this thread" term refers to the `Thread` instance that the method will affect. For example, suppose `threadA` executes the following statement:

```
threadB.checkAccess();
```

`threadA` would be considered the "current thread," and `threadB` would be considered "this thread." The API documentation for `checkAccess()` would read something like: throws a `SecurityException` if the *current thread* is not permitted to access *this thread*. This translates to: throws a `SecurityException` if `threadA` is not permitted to access `threadB`. It's a subtle difference worth noticing.

Member Variables

The only publicly accessible member variables are used to specify the range of priority values that can be passed to `setPriority()`.

Thread.MAX_PRIORITY

```
public static final int MAX_PRIORITY
```

The highest thread-scheduling priority that can be passed to `setPriority()` for a particular VM. Generally, it is `10` for an application and `6` for an applet. Threads running at this level might hog the processor and should be designed to block frequently to give other threads a chance to run. See Chapter 6, "Thread Prioritization," for more information.

Thread.MIN_PRIORITY

`public static final int MIN_PRIORITY`

The lowest thread-scheduling priority that can be passed to `setPriority()` for a particular VM. Generally, it is 1. Threads running at this priority might not get much processor time and might not get any if there are other higher-priority threads running. See Chapter 6 for more information.

Thread.NORM_PRIORITY

`public static final int NORM_PRIORITY`

A not-too-high, not-too-low thread-scheduling priority for `setPriority()`. Generally, it is 5. Threads running at this priority usually get a chance to run without hogging the processor. See Chapter 6 for more information.

Constructors

Several constructors are available for creating new `Thread` instances. Most of them are variations on the main constructor with certain values defaulted.

Thread(ThreadGroup, Runnable, String)

```
public Thread(ThreadGroup group, Runnable target, String name)
        throws SecurityException
```

Creates a new thread that belongs to group, executes the `run()` method of target, and is named name. This is the main constructor for `Thread` that is invoked indirectly by the other constructors.

The new `Thread` will belong to the `ThreadGroup` referenced by group. If group is null, the new `Thread` will belong to the same `ThreadGroup` as the thread that constructed it (`Thread.currentThread().getThreadGroup()`). A `SecurityException` is thrown if the thread that invoked the constructor is not permitted by the `SecurityManager` to add a thread to the specified `ThreadGroup`.

When the thread is started, the `run()` method of the `Runnable` referenced by target will be invoked. When `run()` returns, the thread dies. If target is null, the `run()` method of the `Thread` itself will be invoked (typically this will have been overridden in a subclass to do something useful).

The thread will be named using name. If name is null, a `NullPointerException` will be thrown. To automatically generate a name for the thread, use a different constructor.

The new `Thread` will have the same priority, daemon status, and context class loader as the `Thread` that creates it. These settings can be changed with `setPriority()`, `setDaemon()`, and `setContextClassLoader()`. See Chapter 3, "Creating and Starting a Thread," for more information.

Thread(ThreadGroup, Runnable)

```
public Thread(ThreadGroup group, Runnable target)
        throws SecurityException
```

Equivalent to using the main constructor like this: `Thread(group, target, genName)`, where `genName` is an automatically generated name of the form `Thread-16`.

Thread(ThreadGroup, String)

```
public Thread(ThreadGroup group, String name) throws SecurityException
```

Equivalent to using the main constructor like this: `Thread(group, null, name)`.

Thread(Runnable, String)

```
public Thread(Runnable target, String name)
```

Equivalent to using the main constructor like this: `Thread(null, target, name)`.

Thread(Runnable)

```
public Thread(Runnable target)
```

Equivalent to using the main constructor like this: `Thread(null, target, genName)`, where `genName` is an automatically generated name of the form `Thread-2`.

Thread(String)

```
public Thread(String name)
```

Equivalent to using the main constructor like this: `Thread(null, null, name)`.

Thread()

```
public Thread()
```

Equivalent to using the main constructor like this: `Thread(null, null, genName)`, where `genName` is an automatically generated name of the form `Thread-25`.

static methods

Thread has several `static` methods that are used without reference to a specific thread. Generally, they implicitly refer to the current thread.

Thread.activeCount()

```
public static int activeCount()
```

Returns the number of active threads in the invoking thread's `ThreadGroup`. Convenience method for:

```
Thread.currentThread().getThreadGroup().activeCount()
```

See Chapter 10, "Thread Groups," for more information.

Thread.currentThread()

```
public static native Thread currentThread()
```

Returns a reference to the `Thread` object associated with the thread that invoked the method. Used in code to determine which thread is currently executing the section of code. See Chapter 3 for more information.

Thread.dumpStack()

```
public static void dumpStack()
```

Used only during debugging to print a stack trace for the current thread. Convenience method for:

```
(new Exception("Trace")).printStackTrace()
```

Thread.enumerate()

```
public static int enumerate(Thread[] dest) throws SecurityException
```

Collects a reference to all the threads in the current thread's thread group (and recursively in all its subgroups) and copies these `Thread` references into `dest`. A `SecurityException` might be thrown if the operation is not allowed (by the `checkAccess()` method of `ThreadGroup`). The number of references copied into `dest` is returned. If `dest` is too small, the extra `Thread` references are quietly thrown away. The `activeCount()` method can be used to estimate the size needed for the `dest` array. In general, `dest` should be about twice the size you think you'll need to be sure that all the threads get copied into it. This is a convenience method for:

```
Thread.currentThread().getThreadGroup().enumerate(dest)
```

See Chapter 10 for more information.

Thread.interrupted()

```
public static boolean interrupted()
```

Returns the interrupted status of the current thread and sets the status `false`. If this method is called twice in a row, the second call will always return `false` (provided that the current thread is not re-interrupted between calls!). Related methods: `interrupt()` and `isInterrupted()`. See Chapter 5, "Gracefully Stopping Threads," for more information.

Thread.sleep(long)

```
public static native void sleep(long ms) throws InterruptedException
```

Causes the current thread to stop execution for the specified number of milliseconds (approximately). If the thread is interrupted while sleeping, it wakes up early and throws an `InterruptedException`. Unlike the `wait()` method on `Object`, `sleep()` does not release any locks while resting. Related method: `interrupt()`. See Chapter 3 for more information.

Thread.sleep(long, int)

```
public static void sleep(long ms, int nanoseconds)
        throws InterruptedException
```

Causes the current thread to stop execution for the specified number of milliseconds *plus* the specified number of nanoseconds (approximately). If the thread is interrupted while sleeping, it wakes up early and throws an `InterruptedException`. Unlike the `wait()` method on `Object`, `sleep()` does not release any locks while resting. Related method: `interrupt()`. See Chapter 3 for more information.

Thread.yield()

```
public static native void yield()
```

Causes the current thread to yield the processor to other threads. Generally only threads of equal priority that were waiting to run get a chance. Depending on the VM implementation, lower-priority threads might or might not get a chance to run. This method can be used to better share the processor resources. Related method: `Thread.sleep()`. See Chapter 6 for more information.

Instance Methods

The instance methods refer to a specific thread, unlike the `static` methods that refer to the current thread.

checkAccess()

`public final void checkAccess() throws SecurityException`

Checks to see if there is a `SecurityManager` and if it will allow the current thread to access this `Thread`. It throws a `SecurityException` if the current thread is denied access. Many other methods of `Thread` invoke `checkAccess()` internally.

destroy()

`public void destroy()`

Destroys the thread without any cleanup. Still not implemented as of JDK 1.2—it will throw a `NoSuchMethodError` if called.

getContextClassLoader()

`public ClassLoader getContextClassLoader() throws SecurityException`

Returns the context `ClassLoader` for this thread. `SecurityException` might be thrown if the current thread is not allowed to access the class loader. Related method: `setContextClassLoader()`.

getName()

`public final String getName()`

Returns the name of the thread. Related method: `setName()`. See Chapter 3 for more information.

getPriority()

`public final int getPriority()`

Returns the priority of the thread. Related method: `setPriority()`. Related variables: `Thread.MAX_PRIORITY`, `Thread.MIN_PRIORITY`, and `Thread.NORM_PRIORITY`. See Chapter 6 for more information.

getThreadGroup()

`public final ThreadGroup getThreadGroup()`

Returns the `ThreadGroup` to which the thread belongs if the thread is still alive, or `null` if it has died.

interrupt()

```
public void interrupt() throws SecurityException
```

Interrupt this thread by setting its interrupted status to `true`. This will cause some blocking methods like the `wait()` method on `Object` and the `sleep` method on `Thread` to throw an `InterruptedException`. It can throw a `SecurityException` if the current thread is not permitted to access this thread. Related methods: `isInterrupted()`, `Thread.interrupted()`, and `Thread.sleep()`. See Chapter 5 for more information.

isAlive()

```
public final native boolean isAlive()
```

Returns `true` if this thread is still alive, `false` otherwise. A thread is considered to be alive from just after it has been started until just after the `run()` method returns. Related methods: `start()`, `run()`, `stop()`. See Chapter 5 for more information.

isDaemon()

```
public final boolean isDaemon()
```

Returns `true` if this thread is a daemon thread, or `false` otherwise. A daemon thread continues to run only as long as there is at least one non-daemon thread still running in the VM. Related method: `setDaemon()`. See Chapter 5 for more information.

isInterrupted()

```
public boolean isInterrupted()
```

Returns the interrupted status of this thread and (unlike `interrupted()`)does *not* change the status. Related methods: `interrupt()`, `Thread.interrupted()`. See Chapter 5 for more information.

join()

```
public final void join() throws InterruptedException
```

Causes the current thread to block and wait an unlimited amount of time for this thread to die. It will throw an `InterruptedException` if interrupted while waiting for this thread to die. Related methods: `join(long)`, `join(long, int)`, `interrupt()`, and `isAlive()`. See Chapter 8, "Inter-thread Communication," for more information.

join(long)

```
public final synchronized void join(long ms)
        throws InterruptedException
```

Causes the current thread to block and wait `ms` milliseconds for this thread to die. It will throw an `InterruptedException` if interrupted while waiting for this thread to die. Related methods: `join()`, `join(long, int)`, `interrupt()`, and `isAlive()`. See Chapter 8 for more information.

join(long, int)

```
public final synchronized void join(long ms, int ns)
        throws InterruptedException
```

Causes the current thread to block and wait `ms` milliseconds *plus* `ns` nanoseconds for this thread to die. It will throw an `InterruptedException` if interrupted while waiting for this thread to die. Related methods: `join()`, `join(long)`, `interrupt()`, and `isAlive()`. See Chapter 8 for more information.

run()

```
public void run()
```

If this method was not overridden in a subclass, it does nothing but call the `run()` method of the `Runnable` passed to the constructor. If no `Runnable` was specified, this method returns right away. When this method returns, the thread dies. Related method: `start()`. See Chapter 4, "Implementing Runnable Versus Extending Thread," for more information.

setContextClassLoader(ClassLoader)

```
public void setContextClassLoader(ClassLoader newLoader)
        throws SecurityException
```

Specifies a new class loader for this thread. Throws a `SecurityException` if the current thread is not permitted to modify this thread. Related method: `getContextClassLoader()`.

setDaemon(boolean)

```
public final void setDaemon(boolean newStatus)
        throws SecurityException
```

If `newStatus` is `true`, this thread will be a daemon thread and will automatically die when no non-daemon threads are left running in the VM. If `newStatus` is `false`, this thread is a normal thread. This method *must* be called before this thread is started. It throws a `SecurityException` if the current thread is not permitted to modify this thread. Related method: `isDaemon()`. See Chapter 5 for more information.

setName(String)

```
public final void setName(String newName) throws SecurityException
```

Changes the name of this thread to `newName`. Throws a `SecurityException` if the current thread is not permitted to modify this thread. Related method: `getName()`. See Chapter 3 for more information.

setPriority(int)

```
public final void setPriority(int newPriority)
        throws SecurityException, IllegalArgumentException
```

Changes the thread-scheduling priority of this thread to `newPriority`. If this thread's `ThreadGroup` has a maximum priority set for the group and `newPriority` exceeds that maximum, `newPriority` is silently reduced to the group's maximum allowable value. Throws an `IllegalArgumentException` if `newPriority` is not at least `Thread.MIN_PRIORITY` or if greater than `Thread.MAX_PRIORITY`. Throws a `SecurityException` if the current thread is not permitted to modify this thread. Related method: `getPriority()`. Related methods on `ThreadGroup` are `setMaxPriority()` and `getMaxPriority()`. See Chapter 6 for more information.

start()

```
public native synchronized void start()
        throws IllegalThreadStateException
```

Causes the VM to spawn a new thread that begins execution by calling `run()`; `start()` immediately returns. Throws `IllegalThreadStateException` (subclass of `RuntimeException`) if the thread has already been started. Related methods: `run()`, `isAlive()`, and `stop()`. See Chapter 3 for more information.

toString()

```
public String toString()
```

Returns a string representation of the current state of this thread including its name, priority, and thread group.

Deprecated Methods

The methods in this section have been deprecated and should only be used if absolutely necessary. Alternatives for `stop()`, `suspend()`, and `resume()` are presented in Chapter 5.

countStackFrames()

```
public native int countStackFrames()
```

Deprecated! Counts the number of stack frames for a suspended thread.

resume()

```
public final void resume() throws SecurityException
```

Deprecated! Allows this thread to resume execution after being suspended. Throws a SecurityException if the current thread is not permitted to access this thread. Related method: suspend(). See Chapter 5 for more information.

stop()

```
public final void stop() throws SecurityException
```

Deprecated! Causes this thread to stop what it is doing and throw a ThreadDeath (subclass of Error). Throws a SecurityException if the current thread is not permitted to modify this thread. Related methods: start(), suspend(), resume(). See Chapter 5 for more information.

stop(Throwable)

```
public final synchronized void stop(Throwable except)
        throws SecurityException
```

Deprecated! Causes this thread to stop what it is doing and throw the Throwable object except. Throws a SecurityException if the current thread is not permitted to modify this thread. Related methods: stop(), start(), suspend(), resume(). See Chapter 5 for more information.

suspend()

```
public final void suspend() throws SecurityException
```

Deprecated! Causes this thread to temporarily stop execution until the resume() method is invoked. Throws a SecurityException if the current thread is not permitted to modify this thread. Related methods: resume(), stop(). See Chapter 5 for more information.

The ThreadGroup API

IN THIS APPENDIX

This appendix summarizes the `public` and `protected` members of the `ThreadGroup` class. It is based on Sun Microsystems' Java Development Kit 1.2. Information has been combined from Sun's API documentation, source code, reflection on the distributed classes, and the *Java Language Specification*.

Many of the methods and both of the constructors can throw a `SecurityException`. `SecurityException` is a subclass of `RuntimeException`, so try/catch blocks are not *required* for any of the methods of `ThreadGroup` that might throw it. By default, an application does not have a `SecurityManager` defined (using JDK 1.0, 1.1, or 1.2 from Sun Microsystems). An applet, on the other hand, *might* have a `SecurityManager` present. In general, this exception is thrown when the calling thread is not permitted to perform the requested action. Many times, the security check is done by invoking the `checkAccess()` method on `ThreadGroup`, which in turn checks to see if a `SecurityManager` has been installed, and if so, invokes its `checkAccess(ThreadGroup)` method. For most of your application programming, you can safely ignore the possibility of a `SecurityException` being thrown.

Throughout this appendix, the terms "this thread" and "current thread" are used. The "current thread" term refers to the thread that invoked the method. The "this thread" term refers to the `Thread` instance that the method will affect. For example, suppose `threadA` executes the following statement:

```
threadB.checkAccess();
```

`threadA` would be considered the "current thread," and `threadB` would be considered "this thread." The API documentation for `checkAccess()` would read something like, "throws a `SecurityException` if the *current thread* is not permitted to access *this thread*." This translates to "throws a `SecurityException` if `threadA` is not permitted to access `threadB`." It's a subtle difference worth noticing.

Constructors

Two constructors exist for creating new thread groups.

ThreadGroup(ThreadGroup, String)

```
public ThreadGroup(ThreadGroup parentGroup, String groupName)
        throws SecurityException
```

Creates a new `ThreadGroup` that is a child group of `parentGroup` and has the name `groupName`. The parent group's `checkAccess()` method is invoked to see if the current thread is allowed to create a new `ThreadGroup` in `parentGroup`, which can result in a `SecurityException` being thrown. If `parentGroup` is `null`, a `NullPointerException` will be thrown.

The new `ThreadGroup` will have the same maximum thread priority and daemon status as its parent. These can be changed with `setMaxPriority()` and `setDaemon()`. See Chapter 10 for more information.

ThreadGroup(String)

```
public ThreadGroup(String groupName) throws SecurityException
```

Equivalent to using the main constructor like this:
```
ThreadGroup(Thread.currentThread().getThreadGroup(), groupName).
```

Instance Methods

There are no `static` methods on `ThreadGroup`; all the methods are instance methods.

activeCount()

```
public int activeCount()
```

Returns the number of active threads in this thread group and all its subgroups. Related method: `enumerate()`. See Chapter 10 for more information.

activeGroupCount()

```
public int activeGroupCount()
```

Returns the number of active thread groups in this thread group and all its subgroups.

checkAccess()

```
public final void checkAccess() throws SecurityException
```

Checks to see if there is a `SecurityManager` and if it will allow the current thread to access this `ThreadGroup`. Throws a `SecurityException` if the current thread is denied access. Many other methods of `ThreadGroup` invoke `checkAccess()` internally.

destroy()

```
public final void destroy()
        throws SecurityException, IllegalThreadStateException
```

Destroys this thread group and all its subgroups. If any of the groups is not empty (meaning that all the threads within have not died), an `IllegalThreadStateException` will be thrown. It throws a `SecurityException` if the current thread is denied access to this thread group.

enumerate(Thread[], boolean)

```
public int enumerate(Thread[] dest, boolean includeSubgroups)
        throws SecurityException
```

Collects a reference to all the threads in this thread group (and recursively all its subgroups if includeSubgroups is true) and copies these Thread references into dest. A SecurityException can be thrown if the operation is not allowed by checkAccess(). The number of references copied into dest is returned. If dest is too small, the extra Thread references are quietly thrown away. The activeCount() method can be used to estimate the size needed for the dest array. In general, dest should be about twice the size you think you'll need to be sure that all the threads get copied into it. Related methods: activeCount(), enumerate(Thread[]). See Chapter 10 for more information.

enumerate(Thread[])

```
public int enumerate(Thread[] dest) throws SecurityException
```

Equivalent to: enumerate(dest, true).

enumerate(ThreadGroup[], boolean)

```
public int enumerate(ThreadGroup[] dest, boolean includeSubgroups)
        throws SecurityException
```

Collects a reference to all the thread groups in this thread group (and recursively all its subgroups if includeSubgroups is true) and copies these ThreadGroup references into dest. A SecurityException can be thrown if the operation is not allowed by checkAccess(). The number of references copied into dest is returned. If dest is too small, the extra ThreadGroup references are quietly thrown away. The activeGroupCount() method can be used to estimate the size needed for the dest array. In general, dest should be about twice the size you think you'll need to be sure that all the thread groups get copied into it. Related methods: activeGroupCount(), enumerate(ThreadGroup[]).

enumerate(ThreadGroup[])

```
public int enumerate(ThreadGroup[] dest) throws SecurityException
```

Equivalent to: enumerate(dest, true).

getMaxPriority()

```
public final int getMaxPriority()
```

Returns the maximum priority that any thread in this group or one of its subgroups can have. Related method: setMaxPriority(). See Chapters 6 and 10 for more information.

getName()

`public final String getName()`

Returns the name of this thread group. See Chapter 10 for more information.

getParent()

`public final ThreadGroup getParent() throws SecurityException`

Returns the parent thread group of this thread group, or `null` if this thread group does not have a parent (top thread group). A `SecurityException` can be thrown if the parent is not `null` and its `checkAccess()` method disapproves. See Chapter 10 for more information.

interrupt()

`public final void interrupt() throws SecurityException`

Interrupts all the threads in this thread group and all its subgroups. A `SecurityException` can be thrown if any of the threads or thread groups disapprove. See Chapter 5 for more information.

isDaemon()

`public final boolean isDaemon()`

Returns `true` if this thread group is a daemon thread group, `false` otherwise. A daemon thread group is automatically destroyed when the last of its threads dies. Related method: `setDaemon()`.

isDestroyed()

`public synchronized boolean isDestroyed()`

Returns `true` if this thread group has been destroyed, `false` otherwise. Related method: `destroy()`.

list()

`public void list()`

Dumps information about all the threads in this thread group and all its subgroups to `System.out` by invoking `toString()` on each `Thread`. Really only useful for debugging.

parentOf(ThreadGroup)

```
public final boolean parentOf(ThreadGroup group)
```

Returns `true` if this thread group is an ancestor of `group`, `false` otherwise. Related method: `getParent()`.

setDaemon(boolean)

```
public final void setDaemon(boolean newStatus)
        throws SecurityException
```

If `newStatus` is `true`, this thread group will be automatically destroyed when all its threads have died. Otherwise, if `newStatus` is `false`, it will be a normal thread group. A `SecurityException` will be thrown if the current thread does not have permission to modify this thread group. Related method: `isDaemon()`.

setMaxPriority(int)

```
public final void setMaxPriority(int newMax) throws SecurityException
```

Sets the maximum priority that a thread in this thread group (and all its subgroups) can have. Threads already running at a priority higher than this are not affected. A `SecurityException` will be thrown if the current thread does not have permission to modify this thread group. Related method: `getMaxPriority()`.

toString()

```
public String toString()
```

Returns a string representation of this thread group including its name and maximum thread priority.

uncaughtException(Thread, Throwable)

```
public void uncaughtException(Thread deadThread, Throwable exception)
```

The Java VM calls this method when a thread in this thread group throws an `Exception` or `Error` that is not caught inside `run()`. The thread that did not catch the exception is `deadThread`, and the `Throwable` that it did not catch is `exception`. This method can be overridden in a subclass of `ThreadGroup` to intercept this information. If it is not overridden, the default behavior is for it to invoke the `uncaughtException()` method of this group's parent group. If this group does not have a parent and the `Throwable` is anything other than an instance of `ThreadDeath`, a stack trace is printed to `System.err`.

Deprecated Methods

The methods in this section have been deprecated and should only be used if absolutely necessary.

allowThreadSuspension(boolean)

```
public boolean allowThreadSuspension(boolean newState)
```

Deprecated! Behavior has never been fully specified.

resume()

```
public final void resume() throws SecurityException
```

Deprecated! Resumes all the threads in this thread group (and its subgroups). A `SecurityException` will be thrown if the current thread does not have access permission. Related method: `suspend()`. See Chapter 10 for more information.

stop()

```
public final void stop() throws SecurityException
```

Deprecated! Stops all the threads in this thread group (and its subgroups). A `SecurityException` will be thrown if the current thread does not have access permission. Related methods: `suspend()` and `resume()`. See Chapter 10 for more information.

suspend()

```
public final void suspend() throws SecurityException
```

Deprecated! Suspends all the threads in this thread group (and its subgroups). A `SecurityException` will be thrown if the current thread does not have access permission. Related method: `resume()`. See Chapter 10 for more information.

INDEX

J-K

Other Related Titles

Java 2 for Professional Developers
Mike Morgan
0-672-31697-8
$34.99 USA
$52.95 CAN

Java Distributed Objects
Bill McCarty and Luke Cassady-Dorion
0-672-31537-8
$49.99 USA
$71.95 CAN

Java GUI Development
Vartan Piroumian
0-672-31546-7
$34.99 USA
$52.95 CAN

The Official VisiBroker for Java Handbook
Michael McCaffery and Bill Scott
0-672-31451-7
$39.99 USA
$59.95 CAN

Pure JFC Swing
Satyaraj Pantham
0-672-31423-1
$19.99 USA
$28.95 CAN

Developing Java Servlets
James Goodwill
0-672-31600-5
$29.99 USA
$44.95 CAN

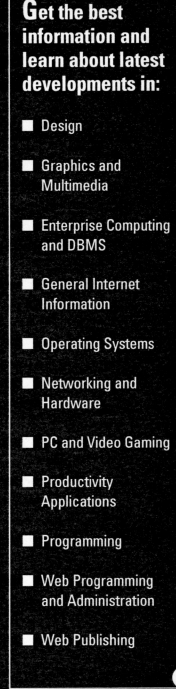

Get FREE books and more...when you register this book online for our Personal Bookshelf Program

http://register.samspublishing.com/